Understanding Cognitive Development

This volume examines the state of the art in key areas of developmental cognitive neuroscience, focusing on theoretically-driven research on cognition and its development. The past decade has seen an increasing number of empirical papers on the relationship between brain and cognitive development. But despite the clearly burgeoning interest in this topic, there is a relative paucity of work motivated by deep theoretical questions about the nature of cognition and its development. Many papers are still in the mode of reporting brain-cognition correlations with a focus on regional activations during brain imaging – a useful approach, but one that is limited with respect to its contributions to understanding the structure of cognition and its development. The papers in this volume consider a number of domains and mechanisms in cognition, including language, number, space, faces, reading, memory, and attention, and represent the wealth of approaches and techniques that can be used to shed light on the nature of cognitive development in brain and mind. These include cross-species comparisons, studies of development under experiential deprivation or genetic differences, classical developmental experimentation, and imaging techniques such as NIRS and fMRI which have recently been applied to developmental questions. The combination of solid theorizing together with a broad range of approaches allows a critical but constructive look at the latest findings in the field relevant to answering enduring questions about cognition, its development, and its realization in the developing brain.

This book was originally published as a special issue of *Cognitive Neuropsychology.*

Barbara Landau is the Dick and Lydia Todd Professor of Cognitive Science at the Johns Hopkins University, USA, where she was Chair of the Cognitive Science Department from 2006–2011. She received her Ph.D. from the University of Pennsylvania in 1982. She is a Fellow of the American Academy of Arts and Sciences, the American Association for the Advancement of Science, the Cognitive Science Society, the Association for Psychological Science, and the American Psychological Association. Dr. Landau's scientific research addresses the nature of human spatial understanding, the nature of language, and the relationship between these two systems of knowledge in development and adulthood. Her most recent book is *Spatial representation: From gene to mind* (2012).

Understanding Cognitive Development
Approaches from Mind and Brain

A Special Issue of *Cognitive Neuropsychology*

Edited by
Barbara Landau

Routledge
Taylor & Francis Group
LONDON AND NEW YORK

First published in paperback 2024

First published 2013 by Psychology Press

Published 2018
by Routledge
4 Park Square, Milton Park, Abingdon, Oxon OX14 4RN

and by Routledge
605 Third Avenue, New York, NY 10158

Routledge is an imprint of the Taylor & Francis Group, an informa business

This book is a reproduction of *Cognitive Neuropsychology*, volume 29, issues 1-2. The Publisher requests to those authors who may be citing this book to state, also, the bibliographical details of the special issue on which the book was based.

Publisher's Note
The publisher would like to make readers aware that the chapters in this book may be referred to as articles as they are identical to the articles published in the special issue. The publisher accepts responsibility for any inconsistencies that may have arisen in the course of preparing this volume for print.

British Library Cataloguing in Publication Data
A catalogue record for this book is available from the British Library

ISBN: 978-1-84872-776-2 (hbk)
ISBN: 978-1-03-292530-1 (pbk)
ISBN: 978-1-315-53980-5 (ebk)

DOI: 10.4324/9781315539805

Typeset in Times New Roman and Georgia
by Taylor & Francis Books

Contents

Part III: Integrative approaches to specific cognitive domains

Citation Information

The chapters in this book were originally published in the journal *Cognitive Neuropsychology*, volume 29, issues 1-2 (February & March 2012). When citing this material, please use the original page numbering for each article, as follows:

Chapter 1

Introduction: Understanding cognitive development: Approaches from mind and brain
Barbara Landau
Cognitive Neuropsychology, volume 29, issues 1-2 (February & March 2012) pp. 1-6

Chapter 2

Questioning the questions that have been asked about the infant brain using near-infrared spectroscopy
Richard N. Aslin
Cognitive Neuropsychology, volume 29, issues 1-2 (February & March 2012) pp. 7-33

Chapter 3

The maps problem and the mapping problem: Two challenges for a cognitive neuroscience of speech and language
David Poeppel
Cognitive Neuropsychology, volume 29, issues 1-2 (February & March 2012) pp. 34-55

Chapter 4

Insights into the origins of knowledge from the cognitive neuroscience of blindness
Marina Bedny and Rebecca Saxe
Cognitive Neuropsychology, volume 29, issues 1-2 (February & March 2012) pp. 56-84

Chapter 5

Routes to short-term memory indexing: Lessons from deaf native users of American Sign Language
Elizabeth A. Hirshorn, Nina M. Fernandez, and Daphne Bavelier
Cognitive Neuropsychology, volume 29, issues 1-2 (February & March 2012) pp. 85-103

Chapter 6

Developmental dyslexia: The difficulties of interpreting poor performance, and the importance of normal performance
Franck Ramus and Merav Ahissar
Cognitive Neuropsychology, volume 29, issues 1-2 (February & March 2012) pp. 104-122

Chapter 7

Genes, language, and the nature of scientific explanations: The case of Williams syndrome
Julien Musolino and Barbara Landau
Cognitive Neuropsychology, volume 29, issues 1-2 (February & March 2012) pp. 123-148

Chapter 8

The origins and structure of quantitative concepts
Cory D. Bonn and Jessica F. Cantlon
Cognitive Neuropsychology, volume 29, issues 1-2 (February & March 2012) pp. 149-173

Chapter 9

A critical review of the development of face recognition: Experience is less important than previously believed
Elinor McKone, Kate Crookes, Linda Jeffery, and Daniel D. Dilks
Cognitive Neuropsychology, volume 29, issues 1-2 (February & March 2012) pp. 174-212

Chapter 10

Core knowledge of object, number, and geometry: A comparative and neural approach
Giorgio Vallortigara
Cognitive Neuropsychology, volume 29, issues 1-2 (February & March 2012) pp. 213-236

INTRODUCTION
Understanding cognitive development: Approaches from mind and brain

Barbara Landau

Department of Cognitive Science, Johns Hopkins University, Baltimore, MD, USA

The concept for this special issue emerged in the summer of 2010, when a small group of cognitive scientists—including some authors of papers in this volume—assembled for an informal thought session regarding the status of research on cognitive development in the context of the explosive growth in the field of cognitive neuroscience. As is well known, the past few decades have seen enormous growth in the brain sciences, and intense attention to questions of how we understand characteristics of the mind as embodied in a physical system, the brain. Moreover, the past decade has witnessed particular growth in the field of developmental cognitive neuroscience, with increasing numbers of empirical papers and specialized volumes published, driven not only by improvements and availability of new methods appropriate to infants and children, but also by the recognition that if we are to understand cognitive function and how it is carried out by the brain, we will have to understand how both mind and brain develop—how they change over the lifetime.

Given the recent explosive growth in the new field of developmental cognitive neuroscience and concomitant increase in empirical papers, edited volumes, and new journals, why assemble another set of articles?

The reason is the strong sense from at least some of us that *development of mind* has been left out of the mind–brain equation. Although we have increasing knowledge of brain structure and its change from infancy through adulthood, accumulating data on the regional activations typical for different tasks and domains, and evidence on the nature of changes in connectivity over development, we have made little progress in understanding how *cognition* is embodied in the brain. Part of the reason for this is that relatively little progress has been made in connecting levels of explanation; e.g., discovering computational schemes that can help us understand how neural tissue accomplishes cognitive functions. Another reason is that rapid improvements in brain imaging techniques have made it more and more straightforward to carry out studies in which we can see the brain in action, as we carry out cognitive tasks; and this has invited ever more research examining the "brain" end of the equation. The question remains, however, as to how cognitive function—instantiated either by an entire task or its subparts—maps onto the action of individual neurons, groups of neurons, and networks of neurons across different regions of the brain. In short, although the past decade has seen an increasing number of empirical

Correspondence should be addressed to Barbara Landau, Department of Cognitive Science, Johns Hopkins University, 241 Krieger Hall, Baltimore, MD 21218 USA. (E-mail: landau@jhu.edu).

http://www.psypress.com/cogneuropsychology http://dx.doi.org/10.1080/02643294.2012.716635

papers on the relationship between brain and cognitive development, there is a relative paucity of work motivated by deep theoretical questions about the nature of cognition and its development. Many papers are still in the mode of reporting brain–cognition correlations with a focus on regional activations during brain imaging—a useful approach, but one that is limited with respect to its contributions to understanding the structure of *cognition* and its development.

The special issue of *Cognitive Neuropsychology* was conceptualized as a response to this problem, and accordingly, the authors of papers in the issue were invited to submit a paper using the following guidelines. Authors were advised that their papers would principally and most crucially be required to focus on theoretical questions important to the study of cognition and its development—that is, the *mind* end of the equation. In particular, authors were invited to contribute a "position paper" in which they would explore a theoretically important question or set of questions about cognitive development in mind and brain, using any approaches and methods they saw fit. These approaches and methods turned out to be quite varied, including experimental studies of human behavior, brain imaging using near-infrared spectroscopy (NIRS) and functional magnetic resonance imaging (fMRI), cross-species comparisons that include neurophysiology, behavior, and outcomes under conditions of controlled rearing, linguistic theory and the broad methods of psycholinguistics, and studies of cognitive structure comparing normally developing individuals with those who have learning differences, genetic differences, or substantial differences in sensory experience due to deafness or blindness.

The result is a collection of nine papers that embrace a range of theoretical and empirical approaches, and address important questions about cognition in a range of empirical domains, including basic visual and auditory perception, face recognition, number, space, working memory, and language (spoken, signed, written). The wide range of approaches reminds us that we now have within our scientific repertoire a marvellously broad range of tools that can be used to understand the development of cognition in mind and brain.

The broad reach of the papers spans a number of themes that are threaded throughout the volume. The first is the theoretical imperative: All authors motivate their papers by posing key theoretical questions about cognition. The second is methodological scrutiny. The authors offer both cautionary tales about methodology and design and refreshing perspectives that remind us of how sometimes small differences in method can result in quite different experimental outcomes (see, e.g., Aslin, 2012 this issue; Ramus & Ahissar, 2012 this issue; Hirshorn, Fernandez, & Bavelier, 2012 this issue; McKone, Crookes, Jeffrey, & Dilks, 2012 this issue). The third theme is the breadth of approaches relevant to questions of human cognition and its development in mind and brain. As noted above, the approaches offered in the volume range from cross-species comparisons (e.g., Bonn & Cantlon, 2012 this issue; Vallortigara, 2012 this issue) and controlled rearing studies in nonhuman species (Vallortigara, 2012 this issue) to brain imaging (Aslin, 2012 this issue; Poeppel, 2012 this issue; Bedny & Saxe, 2012 this issue; McKone et al., 2012 this issue) and work with deficit populations such as the congenitally blind (Bedny & Saxe, 2012 this issue) or deaf (Hirshorn, Fernandez, & Bavelier, 2012 this issue), people who are dyslexic (Ramus & Ahissar, 2012 this issue) and people with Williams syndrome (Musolino & Landau, 2012 this issue). The fourth theme is the importance of development in understanding both how the brain works and how it realizes cognitive function. Studies of deficit populations inform us about the plasticity of the brain (Bedny & Saxe, 2012 this issue), which cognitive functions are most robust and likely to be privileged, "core", or innate (Bedny & Saxe, 2012 this issue; Bonn & Cantlon, 2012 this issue; McKone et al., 2012 this issue Musolino & Landau, 2012 this issue), and which functions are susceptible to differences in experience (Hirshorn et al., 2012 this issue). Indeed, a number of authors point out that the most fundamental properties of human cognitive systems—

the innate "parts list" in Poeppel's terms—can be best discovered by studying the organism as it develops, placing developmental studies at the forefront of inquiry in terms of importance.

The papers are organized into three sections. The first section is *Issues of Theory and Method*, containing papers by Aslin and Poeppel. These opening papers help us to situate studies of mind–brain relationships over development in the context of both the excitement of new methodologies and the challenges inherent in connecting these methods and their results to theories of cognition. Aslin (2012 this issue) focuses on the new tool of NIRS to study infant cognition, broadly reviewing the literature and raising important issues about potential pitfalls of experimental designs that have been used, the need for hypothesis-driven work, and questions about the kinds of inferences we have made and that we *can* make from NIRS results, given inherent limitations in the method. In the end, Aslin suggests that we may have so far attempted to ask questions about infant cognition that are simply too complex for our current understanding of what NIRS can tell us; and he encourages the field to first map out some of the most basic perceptual functions in order to provide a strong foundation for attacking more complex cognitive functions. Poeppel (2012 this issue), too, challenges us to think hard about what we can learn about cognition from existing methods about properties of the brain and mind. He discusses two problems. One is the "practical" *maps problem*, for which he emphasizes that although localization and spatial activation are by far the most common kind of empirical result in the field, still, "uncontroversially, localization and spatial mapping are not explanation". The question, then, is whether—given ever-increasing technical sophistication—the approach of regional mapping will ever satisfy the explanatory needs for understanding how the functions of perception and cognition are carried out. The second problem he discusses is the "principled" *mapping problem*—how to formulate the correspondences and, ultimately, the causal links between the "parts list" for cognition (e.g., syllable, morpheme, noun phrase) and the parts list of neurobiology (e.g., neurons, synapses, long-term potentiation). Ultimately, Poeppel challenges all of us—across the cognitive sciences and neurosciences—to reformulate our thinking, by making a powerful but undoubtedly controversial argument that the cognitive sciences (dealing as they do with the functional units of cognition) provide the elements (representations) and computations that neuroscientists should then seek to identify at the neural (implementational) level.

Section 2, *Atypical Experience and Genetic Differences*, focuses on how unusual cases of human development can shed light on the nature of cognitive structure. Bedny and Saxe (2012 this issue) lead the section, presenting compelling studies of cognition in the congenitally blind, using data from behavioural and brain-imaging studies to explore how lifelong absence of visual experience affects cognitive structure and function. They begin by discussing now extensive evidence showing that primary visual cortex in congenitally blind people can take on other sensory/perceptual functions (e.g., spatial functions underlying the perception of Braille) as well as high-level functions involved in language. Given this significant evidence for the plasticity of the human brain in its basic organization, and its dependence on particular types of sensory experience (i.e., vision), the authors then ask whether the same plasticity effects extend to higher-level functions such as concepts. They argue that, contrary to classical empiricist hypotheses about the role of sensory experience in the development of cognition, blind and sighted individuals possess much the same conceptual structure for lexical concepts; moreover, these structures are housed in virtually identical areas of the brain for the blind and sighted. This, together with the compelling evidence for plasticity in sensory and perceptual representations, makes a beautiful case for understanding both what aspects of brain and mind remain the same under changes in sensory and perceptual input, and what aspects are subject to change.

Hirshorn, Fernandez, and Bavelier (2012 this issue) make an equally compelling point in their paper, illustrating that the way that one theoretically conceptualizes a cognitive difference between populations can have profound effects on how these differences are tested, and the conclusions that one draws. They start with a well-known and persistent finding showing consistent differences between deaf signers and hearing speakers in short-term memory (STM) tasks, with deaf signers regularly underperforming hearing speakers. This has most often been interpreted as a deficit in temporal order processing that stems from differences in experience. Hirshorn and colleagues show that deaf signers' performance in such tasks depends not on differences in the ability to process temporal order, but rather on the different biases that hearing/deaf speakers develop regarding the kinds of cues they use to carry out the task. In showing this, they provide evidence for a very different kind of theoretical explanation underlying the difference shown between groups, emphasizing the role that different language modalities afford (rather than available perceptual systems *per se*), with speech and sign experience leading to different biases in the kinds of coding that are most likely in many STM tasks. Their studies also illustrate how conclusions about the effects of different kinds of experience must undergo rigorous examination with respect to alternative hypotheses.

Ramus and Ahissar (2012 this issue) address theoretical problems in understanding the root causes of dyslexia. They note that this disorder has invited a proliferation of theories and that conflicting patterns of data abound, despite decades of systematic work and more than a century of clinical observation. Most crucially, however, they argue that the field has tended to focus too much on poor performance by dyslexics, and not enough on strong performance by dyslexics, leading to theories that explain only half of the overall profile—which results in no explanation at all. Ramus and Ahissar argue that the key to understanding dyslexia (as well as other disorders, such as autism and amusia) is to carry out careful and systematic task analyses of both tasks that elicit poor performance and those that elicit strong performance. For example, they note that tasks involving phonology typically elicit poor performance among dyslexics; however, tasks that are used often engage a wide range of cognitive processes such as mental manipulations of speech sounds, strong working memory, rapid responses, or metalinguistic judgements. The same complexities hold for tasks examining the visual system's potential contribution to dyslexia. Ramus and Ahissar end by encouraging the field to focus on much deeper and more systematic task analyses—understanding the basic cognitive representations and processes that are required in order to carry out a task. They also encourage scientists to round out the task battery in order to document both strengths and weaknesses, and to consider examining quite basic perceptual functions before moving on to cognitive functions that are undeniably complex. Little of this has been done, in the authors' view, but much more will be needed in order to construct accurate theories of the underlying deficit or deficits.

Musolino and Landau (2012 this issue) then take up the case of Williams syndrome, a genetic syndrome in which roughly 25 genes are missing, giving rise to an unusual cognitive profile in which people show strong linguistic abilities but severe spatial impairment. The authors use this syndrome to explore how one could address one of cognitive science's holy grails—the possibility of unravelling the causal chains between genes and cognition—and focus their attention on thinking about the kind of theory that might be able to account for the language profile. They argue that to do this, we need to have a theory at the appropriate level of complexity and power to explain what is to be acquired—this turns out to be available in the form of linguistic theory. This theory offers the opportunity to develop test cases to ask whether people with Williams syndrome possess knowledge of complex aspects of linguistic structure. Musolino and Landau present positive evidence on this question. They then contrast this linguistic theory-driven approach with the neuroconstructivist approach to language learning, which has been offered to support the idea that language in people with Williams syndrome is not structurally intact, but rather is qualitatively different from normal individuals. By comparing the two approaches' power to explain the data, Musolino and Landau show that the two are in fact not commensurate in what they can explain, and therefore simply do not compete equally in advancing our understanding of what is learned and how this is accomplished. By emphasizing the role of theory in understanding cognition and its development, Musolino and Landau challenge us to become more precise in the theories we use to explain both normal and unusual development.

The third section, *Integrative Approaches to Specific Cognitive Domains* includes papers that focus on number (Bonn & Cantlon), face processing (McKone et al.), and "core" knowledge including objects and space (Vallortigara), all of which are foundational to cognition in humans as well as other species. Bonn and Cantlon (2012 this issue) lead the section by reviewing data from human behaviour in infancy, childhood, and adulthood, as well as brain imaging in humans and behaviour and neurophysiology in other species. They examine the fundamental neural and cognitive relations among different quantitative dimensions (e.g., number, size, pitch, loudness, brightness), exploring how these relationships could have evolved over time, and how they might be realized over human development. They argue that the fundamental conceptual domain of *number* unifies many different phenomena, using theory and evidence from a wide range of sources—empirical studies of humans (of different ages, patients and intact individuals) and other species, both brain-based and behavioural. Bonn and Cantlon show us the power of drawing on such wide-ranging sources of evidence, enriching our understanding of the most fundamental aspects of human cognition and their development.

McKone et al. (2012 this issue) then provide a quite comprehensive review of the literature on face representation in development, focusing on the evaluation of the classical hypothesis for face identification that has proposed an extremely protracted developmental timetable, with maturity arriving only in adolescence. Contrary to this idea, McKone et al. present compelling evidence that all *qualitative* indicators of key phenomena can be observed quite early in development (including, for example, encoding of novel faces, holistic processing, face-selective responding during brain imaging tasks, face individuation); and *quantitative* maturity in behavioural studies by early childhood, once critical methodological issues are resolved. Making this argument, the authors draw on a wide variety of approaches, including behavioural and imaging studies in infants and children, deficits of face recognition (prosopagnosia), human/monkey comparative studies, and studies of the genetics of face recognition (twin studies). Importantly, they explore in detail the methodological nuances of comparing performance across tasks and populations, especially noting the critical role that is played by the restriction of range (i.e., floor and ceiling effects). Finally, they also advance the field by showing the importance of technical issues such as the size of the head coil that is used in studies of children. Results change dramatically when head coil size is adjusted, with appropriate coils revealing measurements that suggest mature patterns of activation quite early in life.

In the final paper of the special issue, Vallortigara (2012 this issue) shows us the power of using cross-species comparisons to determine the phylogenetic and ontogenetic origins of systems of "core knowledge"—the often evolutionarily ancient systems that appear across many species (including human infants and toddlers) and that are likely to serve as foundations for later human cognitive acquisitions. Vallortigara cleverly uses the disarmingly simple method of filial imprinting in newborn chicks, showing that chicks show preferences that follow the principles of core knowledge. He also uses controlled rearing experiments to cleanly test the role of the environment in the emergence of core knowledge, and uncovers evidence for innate sensitivity to the basic mechanical properties of animate and inanimate objects (e.g., solidity for the latter; self-propulsion for the former), cardinality, and geometry. These results contribute to Vallortigara's conclusions, which are justifiably nativist.

In sum, the papers represent a combination of solid theorizing together with a broad range of approaches to problems in a wide set of cognitive domains. They represent a critical but constructive look at the latest findings in the field relevant to answering enduring questions about cognition, its development, and its realization in the developing brain. As a whole, the papers show that there is much to celebrate in our current state of understanding of the relationship between mind and brain over the course of development. They show the importance of theories of cognition in understanding what develops and how. And they tell us that continuing progress will be made not only by refining our technologies and measurement, but by constructing powerful and testable theories about the nature of human cognition itself.

REFERENCES

Aslin, R. (2012 this issue). Questioning the questions that have been asked about the infant brain using near-infrared spectroscopy. *Cognitive Neuropsychology*, *29*, 7–33.

Bedny, M., & Saxe, R. (2012 this issue). Insights into the origins of knowledge from the cognitive neuroscience of blindness. *Cognitive Neuropsychology*, *29*, 56–84.

Bonn, C., & Cantlon, J. (2012 this issue). The origins and structure of quantitative concepts. *Cognitive Neuropsychology*, *29*, 149–173.

Hirshorn, E., Fernandez, N., & Bavelier, D. (2012 this issue). Routes to short term memory indexing: Lessons from deaf native users of American Sign Language. *Cognitive Neuropsychology*, *29*, 85–103.

McKone, E., Crookes, K., Jeffery, L., & Dilks, D. D. (2012 this issue). A critical review of the development of face recognition: Experience is less important than previously believed. *Cognitive Neuropsychology*, *29*, 174–212.

Musolino, J., & Landau, B. (2012 this issue). Genes, language, and the nature of scientific explanations: The case of Williams syndrome. *Cognitive Neuropsychology*, *29*, 123–148.

Poeppel, D. (2012 this issue). The maps problem and the mapping problem: Two challenges for a cognitive neuroscience of speech and language. *Cognitive Neuropsychology*, *29*, 34–55.

Ramus, F., & Ahissar, M. (2012 this issue). Developmental dyslexia: The difficulties of interpreting poor performance, and the importance of normal performance. *Cognitive Neuropsychology*, *29*, 104–122.

Vallortigara, G. (2012 this issue). Core knowledge of object, number and geometry: A comparative and neural approach. *Cognitive Neuropsychology*, *29*, 213–236.

Questioning the questions that have been asked about the infant brain using near-infrared spectroscopy

Richard N. Aslin

Department of Brain and Cognitive Sciences and Rochester Center for Brain Imaging, University of Rochester, Rochester, NY, USA

Near-infrared spectroscopy (NIRS) is a noninvasive diffuse optical-imaging technique that can measure local metabolic demand in the surface of the cortex due to differential absorption of light by oxygenated and deoxygenated blood. Over the past decade, NIRS has become increasingly used as a complement to other neuroimaging techniques, such as electroencephalography (EEG), magnetoencephalography (MEG), and functional magnetic resonance imaging (fMRI), particularly in paediatric populations who cannot easily be tested using fMRI and MEG. In this review of empirical findings from human infants, ranging in age from birth to 12 months of age, a number of interpretive concerns are raised about what can be concluded from NIRS data. In addition, inconsistencies across studies are highlighted, and strategies are proposed for enhancing the reliability of NIRS data gathered from infants. Finally, a variety of new and promising advances in NIRS techniques are highlighted.

Keywords: Infancy; Brain imaging; Near-infrared spectroscopy.

"Shedding light" on a scientific question took on new meaning when it was discovered (Jobsis, 1977) that near-infrared light could (literally) be pumped through the skull, and a small fraction of that light that returned through the skull was modulated by the underlying brain haemodynamics. Thus, just like functional magnetic resonance imaging (fMRI), near-infrared spectroscopy (NIRS) provides an indirect measure of neural activity because of the correlation between blood oxygenation and local metabolic demand.

Over 20 years after this discovery, and 10 years after fMRI entered the mainstream in the field of cognitive neuroscience, developmental psychologists became excited about the potential of NIRS to complement fMRI in studies of the infant brain.[1] Seeking a complement to fMRI was a natural response to the enormous technical problems

Correspondence should be addressed to Richard N. Aslin, Department of Brain and Cognitive Sciences, Meliora Hall, River Campus, University of Rochester, Rochester, NY 14627, USA. (E-mail: aslin@cvs.rochester.edu).

Preparation of this article was supported in part by grants from NIH (HD-37082) and the McDonnell Foundation (220020096) to the author, and from NSF (CBET-0931687) to Andrew Berger. Helpful comments on an earlier draft were provided by Andrew Berger, Mohinish Shukla, and two anonymous reviewers.

[1]Direct measures of neural activity from surface electrodes on the scalp have been used with infants since the 1960s, but that voluminous literature is beyond the scope of the present review.

http://www.psypress.com/cogneuropsychology http://dx.doi.org/10.1080/02643294.2012.654773

associated with gathering fMRI data from infants. Despite a small number of heroic efforts to use fMRI with infants (Anderson et al., 2001; Blasi et al., 2011; Dehaene-Lambertz, Dehaene, & Hertz-Pannier, 2002), it is now clear that the requirements of fMRI (unless the infant is asleep) are exceptionally limiting. The most daunting hurdle is the need for rigid head stabilization, although both safety concerns (radio frequency, RF, gradients and acoustic noise) and the cost of a scanner (even at typical hourly rates) render fMRI with infants a method suitable for only a handful of research centres.

In contrast, NIRS does not demand rigid head stabilization, as the optical fibres are embedded in a "cap" attached to the infant's head (see Figure 1, left), and there are no safety concerns beyond limiting the laser powers to readily acceptable levels. In addition, the cost of a NIRS system is about one tenth of a 3-T magnetic resonance (MR) system. NIRS is not without its own limitations, however. Spatial resolution is approximately 1 cm^2, and the primary target of sampling from the brain is the surface of the cortex (see Figure 1, right). Deeper brain structures are not accessible because the detection of photons that travel further distances from the optical emitters would require laser-light intensities that damage brain tissue. Finally, in contrast to an fMRI voxel, which is typically a 3–4-mm cube, NIRS gathers data from a less precisely defined 3D volume that is captured by a 2D array of emitter–detector pairs. That is, several layers of tissue, including skin, skull, surface vasculature, and grey matter, are collapsed into the 2D samples.

Given this very brief background about what NIRS is and generally how it works with infants (see extensive reviews by Gervain et al., 2011; Hespos, Ferry, Cannistraci, Gore, & Park, 2009; Lloyd-Fox, Blasi, & Elwell, 2010), we now consider how NIRS has been used to address questions in the field of developmental cognitive neuroscience. Our focus here is on what kinds of conclusions about brain function and cognitive development *have* been reached by investigators using NIRS, as well as what kinds of conclusions *could* be drawn from NIRS data even under ideal circumstances. The overall goal is to push the field to go beyond rudimentary (largely confirmatory) demonstrations of neural activity to test specific hypotheses about neural organization during development.

Questions typically asked

The most basic question one could ask about a new method, especially a method applied to human infants, is whether it provides a reliable measure of neural activity. Consider the example of electroencephalography (EEG) activity and the averaging of evoked responses to a particular stimulus over repeated trials. This event-related potential (ERP) can be sampled from one electrode location

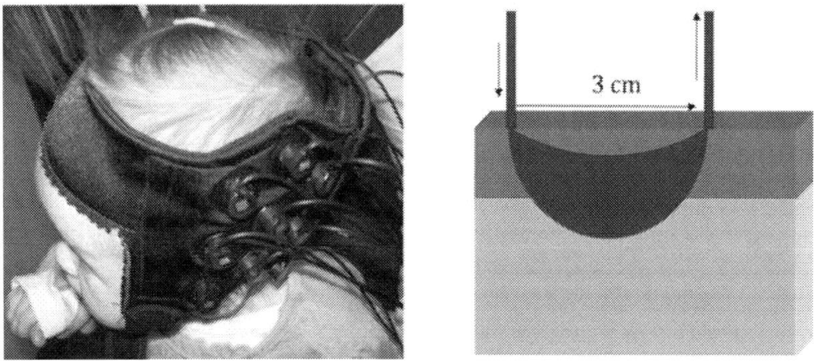

Figure 1. *Left: Infant wearing a cap holding an array of 9 optical fibres to gather data from 12 near-infrared spectroscopy (NIRS) channels over the left temporal cortex. Right: Schematic of a NIRS channel, showing the input and output optical fibres and the banana-shaped pathway of photons that dip into the grey matter of the brain after passing through superficial layers of skin, skull, and surface vasculature. To view a colour version of this figure, please see the online issue of the Journal.*

on the scalp or from over 100 such electrode locations. Given uncertainty about where in the brain these ERPs originate, it would not be terribly informative to record from a single channel. Such an ERP would reveal only that some aspect of the sensory information contained in the stimulus, or some aspect of the processing of that information by one or more brain regions, was sufficient to generate an ERP that differed from a no-stimulus baseline.

The situation with NIRS is a bit less ambiguous because the origin of the haemodynamic signal must reside in brain regions proximal to the emitter–detector pair that defines a channel. However, just like a single-channel ERP response that is above a no-stimulus baseline, a reliable activation in a single NIRS channel is not very informative, particularly because the number of stimulus events typically presented to infants in a NIRS study is an order of magnitude fewer than the number presented in an ERP study. This is the natural outcome of the fact that blocked and event-related NIRS designs are sampling a sluggish haemodynamic response over many seconds, whereas ERP events can be repeated at rates up to 10 Hz. Moreover, because the NIRS signal contains both deep (brain-level) and surface (non-brain-level) activations, it is quite possible to obtain a NIRS activation that is no more specific than a change in heart rate or systemic blood oxygenation correlated with respiration. This is particularly likely in NIRS because of the relatively large magnitude of haemodynamic signals in the surface vasculature, an artefact not present in fMRI.[2] Thus, unless some NIRS channels show a response above a no-stimulus baseline, and other channels do not (or show less of a response), it is not clear that a response from a single NIRS channel provides any brain-specific information.

Here is what I mean by *brain-specific*. We know from behavioural methods that infants respond differently to stimuli that vary along a variety of dimensions—some well defined such as intensity, and others less well defined such as "face-like". If a single NIRS channel shows reliable activation (i.e., above a no-stimulus baseline) to a face stimulus and no reliable (or less) activation to a nonface stimulus, it is seductive to conclude that this NIRS channel is sampling a region of the brain that processes faces. The problem with this conclusion is that face stimuli elicit increases in a variety of other psychological processes that are not face-specific, such as attention and arousal. Because these nonspecific responses are the *outcome* of processing a face stimulus, and because we have no measure of attention or arousal independent of the face and nonface stimuli presented to the infant, it is unclear whether activation in a single NIRS channel is face-specific or a general index of attention or arousal.

Given the need to demonstrate at least some degree of channel-specific (i.e., regional) selectivity to conclude that a given NIRS channel is stimulus-specific and not merely reflective of attention or arousal, multiple NIRS channels provide an obvious way forward. To that end, NIRS studies have been conducted using 2 to over 100 channels, although the depth of the resultant NIRS signals is reduced if tightly packed channels have smaller emitter–detector separations on the infant's head. There are two rather obvious benefits, then, to the use of multiple NIRS channels: (a) to assess stimulus specificity, and (b) to assess regional selectivity. Studies focusing on this second benefit typically assess the presence and degree of lateralization, particularly in the language domain (see reviews by Minagawa-Kawai, Cristia, & Dupoux, 2011; Obrig, Rossi, Telkemeyer, & Wartenburger, 2010), because of substantial lateralization of function in the adult brain. However, regional selectivity can be examined at a more fine-grained level than the two hemispheres, including any pair of NIRS channels. As we will see, conclusions about regional selectivity, in the limit, are not immune from interpretive difficulties.

[2]Systemic vascular responses can be measured directly using a pulse oximeter, but recent evidence from adults suggests that regressing out these global responses only marginally improves the signal/noise of fMRI (Cooper, Gagnon, Goldenholz, Boas, & Greve, 2012).

Presence versus absence of a stimulus

In the early days of infant NIRS, it was exciting to see *any* evidence that the method worked. Meek et al. (1998) were the first to show a NIRS response over occipital cortex in awake 1- to 3-month-olds as they viewed the presence/absence of a flickering chequerboard in 10-s blocks. A separate group of infants tested with the same single NIRS channel over frontal cortex revealed no significant activations. Given this evidence of regional selectivity to visual stimulation, albeit in separate groups of infants, it is surprising that similar demonstrations are still being reported a decade later. Karen et al. (2008) presented a flickering LED stimulus versus darkness in 20-s blocks to neonates (1-week-olds) and reported significant activations in one or more of the 10 NIRS channels over occipital cortex, but no other cortical region was assessed to guard against nonselective regional activations.

One clear advantage of using visual stimuli is the presence of highly constrained anatomical pathways from the eye to the cortex, which, as we see in a later section, leads to a very specific prediction about the pattern of regional cortical activation. The auditory system is not so constrained anatomically, with substantial precortical overlap in the mapping of signals from the ears to the cortex. As a result, there is tremendous spread of activations elicited by auditory stimuli across diverse cortical regions. It is perhaps not surprising, therefore, that early infant NIRS studies reported activations that were highly variable. For example, Sakatani, Chen, Lichty, Zuo, and Wuang (1999) presented newborns with piano music versus silence while recording from a single NIRS channel over frontal cortex, and Zaramella et al. (2001) presented newborns with tone frequency-sweeps while recording from a single NIRS channel over right or left temporal cortex. Although reliable differences in activation between sound and silence were obtained, the absence of other (control) NIRS channels prevented an assessment of regional selectivity.

Moreover, in contrast to studies of visual stimuli, where at a minimum the infant's eyelids must be open (i.e., quiet wakefulness), many auditory NIRS studies are conducted while the infant is asleep. There is some evidence to suggest that NIRS activations are less robust in newborns during periods of quiet sleep than during periods of quiet awake (Kotilahti et al., 2005). If so, then level of arousal could complicate interpretations of infant NIRS data in two ways. First, if arousal is low, then any regional differences may appear to be binary, with activation in one region and no activation in the other. However, as arousal increases, the gain of the "weaker" region may rise faster than the gain of the "stronger" region. As a result, what appears to be robust regional selectivity during periods of sleep may disappear during periods of wakefulness. Second, if infants at different ages are compared to ask whether activations change over postnatal development, then any age differences in arousal could contaminate what appear to be regional differences in stimulus specificity.

Assessments of stimulus specificity

It should be apparent from the previous section that simply recording from multiple NIRS channels is not a powerful way to assess stimulus specificity at a given channel location. The presence of a stimulus probably leads to changes in attention or arousal that could elicit different activations in some NIRS channels, and these activations could be nonspecific (i.e., systemic) but modulated by differences in the gain of the haemodynamic response at different channel locations. A more powerful design is to ask whether the same NIRS channel shows different levels of activation to variations along some stimulus dimension. If these stimulus variations can be assumed to avoid changes in arousal, then the differences in the gain of the haemodynamic response across channels is mitigated.

A canonical NIRS design consists of two blocks of stimuli (A and B) as well as a no-stimulus baseline. In a later section, we discuss the limitations of two-stimulus designs, but for the moment we focus on the power of such designs and how results should be (cautiously) interpreted. There are two general strategies employed in infant NIRS studies that utilize two-stimulus designs: (a) a hypothesis-driven prediction based on adult data, or (b) an exploratory search for stimulus specificity and/or regional selectivity. Both of these strategies have their limitations. For example, the hypothesis-driven strategy makes it seductive to conclude, when there is a correspondence between infants and adults in how certain classes of stimuli activate the two hemispheres, that there is similarity of processing by these lateralized brain regions across development. That is a risky inference because, as noted earlier, evidence of differential activation across NIRS channels can only be interpreted as support for specialization if the gain of every NIRS channel's haemodynamic response function (HRF) is the same. This assumption is made in fMRI studies to deal with a whole brain consisting of over 100,000 voxels, each of which is presumed to be minimally contaminated by systemic vascular responses and surface (nonbrain) vasculature. In NIRS studies with only two dozen or so channels, all of which are contaminated by surface vasculature, this uniform-gain assumption is extremely unlikely. Moreover, in fMRI, the HRF can be measured empirically by presenting adults with a very brief stimulus and recording the resultant response in a low-level sensory area of the cortex (see Boynton, Engel, Glover, & Heeger, 1996). Although in principle this same technique could be used to measure the HRF in single NIRS channels, this has only been estimated in one infant study using the Finite Impulse Response (FIR) method of Friston et al. (1995). Minagawa-Kawai, van der Lely, et al. (2011) concluded that the HRF of 4-month-olds, at least in temporal cortex, has the same shape as the adult HRF, but is delayed 2.8 s (see Figure 2).[3] Because HRFs are likely to be different across brain regions, the mere presence of a lateralized response to the same stimulus is rather weak evidence of functional brain lateralization, unless it is accompanied by variations in stimulus specificity. Despite these limitations, the hypothesis-driven strategy is preferable because of the multiple-comparison problem. As we see later, when many NIRS activations are compared to chance, it is essential to rule out false positives, and statistical corrections for multiple comparisons have not always been conducted appropriately.

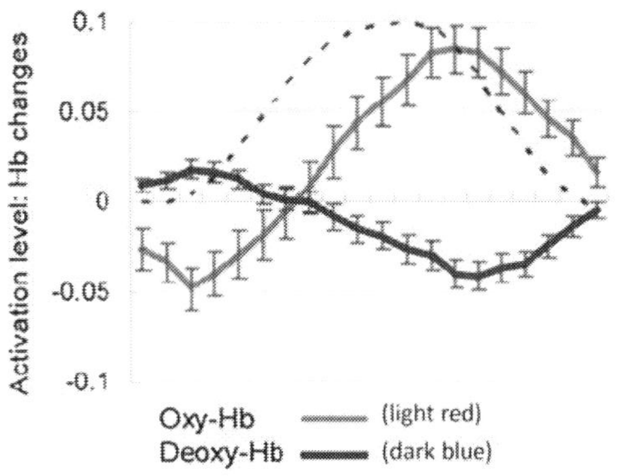

Figure 2. *Estimates of the haemodynamic response functions (HRFs) from the newborn temporal cortex (dashed line = adult HRF from functional magnetic resonance imaging, fMRI). Hb = haemoglobin. From "Optical Brain Imaging Reveals General Auditory and Language-Specific Processing in Early Infant Development", by Y. Minagawa-Kawai, H. van der Lely, et al., 2011,* Cerebral Cortex, 21, *pp. 254–261. Copyright 2011 by permission of Oxford University Press. To view a colour version of this figure, please see the online issue of the Journal.*

The exploratory-search strategy is much more common in the infant NIRS literature. This is the natural outcome of knowing less about what to predict, especially since the infant brain may not be organized in the same way, or with the same specificity, as the adult brain. As a result, most of the infant NIRS literature consists of studies that conform to the following logic. First, activations are gathered simultaneously from many NIRS channels (e.g., 24) located over two or more regions of the cortex. Second, each

[3]Note that this delayed HRF in infants could be the result, at least in part, of the contaminating effects of surface vascular signals. Minagawa-Kawai, van der Lely, et al. (2011) did not measure the adult HRF with NIRS to make a direct comparison with infants.

infant is presented with two stimulus conditions (and a no-stimulus baseline). Third, activations in each channel are compared across stimulus conditions, and often clusters of channels are averaged to create regions of interest (ROIs). Fourth, significant differences present in individual channels or ROIs are interpreted as evidence of stimulus specificity and/or regional selectivity, often with reference to (a) prior behavioural or ERP studies of infants, (b) behavioural, ERP, and fMRI studies of adults, or (c) studies of animals (outside the language domain). This fourth and final step is the most problematic because the "explanation" of the obtained differences in NIRS activations is made post hoc.

Exploratory-search NIRS studies: Audition

The vast majority of infant NIRS studies have investigated activations elicited by auditory stimuli, largely because these studies have been conducted with sleeping newborns, thereby reducing movement artefacts. However, there have been several studies of activations to visual stimuli, including simple chequerboards like those used by Meek et al. (1998), complex objects varying along various dimensions, and "social" events such as facial expressions. There is even a recent study of newborns' differential response to the olfactory stimulus of their mother's breast milk compared to artificial (formula) milk (Aoyama et al., 2010). They reported greater activation over orbitofrontal cortex (implicated in odour perception by adults) to mother's milk than to formula milk. This study is illustrative of several limitations discussed earlier. For example, there were only two NIRS channels (right and left orbitofrontal locations), with no comparison channels to assess regional selectivity. Thus, the differential activation to the two odour stimuli could be an arousal effect and not a brain-specific effect (as previously defined).

The first study to deal effectively with the stimulus specificity and regional-selectivity issues for auditory stimuli was reported by Pena et al. (2003). They presented newborns with two types of speech stimuli (forward and backward sentences) as well as a no-stimulus control (baseline). An array of 12 NIRS channels was positioned over the left temporal cortex and 12 channels over the right temporal cortex. Activations were greater to forward than to backward speech, but only over the left hemisphere. A more detailed analysis (see Figure 3), which defined two 6-channel ROIs above and below the Silvian fissure in each hemisphere, revealed that the left-hemisphere effect for forward versus backward speech was carried by the posterior ROI (i.e., below the Silvian fissure). Moreover, channel-by-channel comparisons between the two hemispheres showed that one channel in the left ventral-anterior temporal cortex was differentially activated to forward versus backward speech.

These are important findings for two reasons. First, forward and backward speech have the same average spectrum and are matched in intensity. Thus, the activation difference between stimulus conditions cannot be a low-level effect of arousal. Second, the activation difference between stimulus conditions was regionally selective (i.e., posterior channels in the left hemisphere), arguing against a more complicated "outcome of arousal" effect. There are, however, some interpretative limitations. Although speech is preferentially processed in the left hemisphere of the adult brain (in both frontal and temporal areas), similar activations in newborns does not confirm that same underlying processing. It could be that pathways from primary auditory cortex (A1 is too small to measure in isolation using NIRS) radiate to higher level processing areas in the left temporal cortex for acoustic features that are "language relevant" and to the right temporal cortex for more general properties that are shared with language stimuli. And in fact two recent studies of newborns (Telkemeyer et al., 2009) and 3- and 6-month-olds (Telkemeyer et al., 2011) provide evidence of greater NIRS activations over right-hemisphere temporal cortex for slowly modulated acoustic events than for rapid events, which show bilateral activations (see also Minagawa-Kawai, Cristia, Vendelin, Cabrol, & Dupoux, 2011). Thus, cortical areas in infants that will develop language specializations in adults could be viewed as

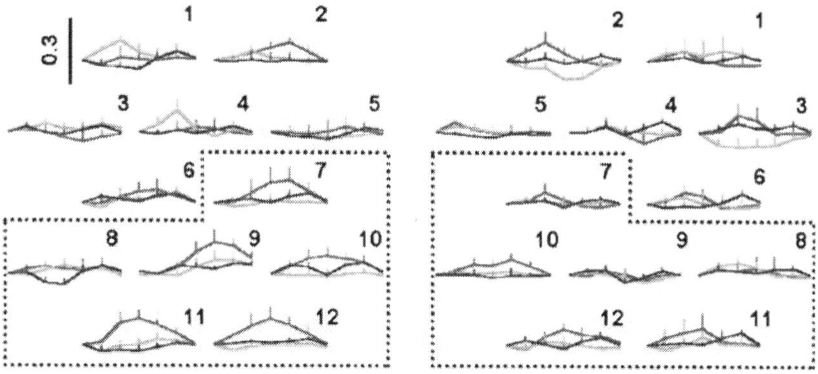

Figure 3. *Data from Pena et al. (2003), showing 12 NIRS channels from the left and right temporal cortices. Each channel provided a measure of oxyhaemoglobin (red), deoxy (blue), and total (green) to forward versus backward speech. Dashed area in each hemisphere indicates targeted region of interest (ROI; posterior temporal). From "Sounds and Silence: An Optical Topography Study of Language Recognition at Birth", by M. Pena et al., 2003, by* Proceedings of the National Academy of Sciences of the USA, 100, *pp. 11702–11705. Copyright 2003 by permission of National Academy of Sciences, USA. To view a colour version of this figure, please see the online issue of the Journal.*

proto-areas rather than as fully homologous to the adult brain.

Another concern with Pena et al. (2003) is that alternative ROIs were not tested. It is certainly acceptable to collapse NIRS channels based on an anatomical landmark (like the Silvian fissure), but there are a large number of alternative landmarks and other ROIs that were not examined. The proper way to test the significance of any ROI is to conduct a Monte Carlo procedure in which all possible ROIs of size *N* are examined, including channels that are not spatially adjacent. Nevertheless, the Pena et al. (2003) study is a landmark in providing convincing evidence of both stimulus specificity and regional selectivity, unconfounded by low-level arousal effects.

A follow-up to the Pena et al. (2003) study asked whether newborns would respond differently to native versus non-native language stimuli when they were presented in forward versus backward conditions. In contrast to the infants in Italy who were presented with forward and backward Italian sentences, May, Byers-Heinlein, Gervain, and Werker (2011) presented infants in Canada with forward and backward sentences in English (their native language) and Tagalog (a foreign language). The same ROIs as those used by Pena et al. (above/below the Silvian fissure) revealed no differences between activations for forward and backward speech in English, and no hemisphere differences, thereby failing to replicate the findings from Pena et al. for the infants' native language. However, May et al. low-pass filtered their sentences, whereas Pena et al. did not. Thus, the segmental information was masked but the prosodic information was not, perhaps rendering the acoustic differences between forward and backward speech less salient. The results from Tagalog showed greater activation to backward than to forward speech, a pattern opposite to what Pena et al. reported for the infants' native language. But again, with low-pass filtered speech, the very different prosody of Tagalog compared to English may have resulted in primary attention to the different prosody and not the different directions of the speech signals. Sato et al. (in press) did not use filtered speech and replicated Pena et al. in Japanese infants presented with Japanese forward and backward speech, but not when Japanese infants were presented with English forward and backward speech. Thus, familiarity with native-language speech may be a requirement for the differential findings using forward and backward speech in newborns.

Several studies extended the work of Pena et al. (2003) by contrasting two types of forward speech:

normally intonated and monotone. Unfortunately, these studies have failed to clarify our understanding of how the infant brain processes speech stimuli because the pattern of results does not conform to a simple role for the two hemispheres. Saito et al. (2007) reported that newborns have a greater activation over frontal cortex to intonated than to monotone speech. However, the use of only a single NIRS channel renders these results subject to an arousal interpretation rather than a specific role for the frontal cortex in the processing of prosody.

Homae, Watanabe, Nakano, Asakawa, and Taga (2006) presented intonated and monotone speech to 3-month-olds and recorded 48 NIRS channels, 24 over the left-hemisphere temporal-parietal areas and 24 over the right-hemisphere areas. Consistent with data from adults, which suggest that segmental (typically rapid) speech cues preferentially activate the left hemisphere, and prosodic (slow) speech cues preferentially activate the right hemisphere, they reported greater NIRS activation over the right hemisphere for intonated than for monotone speech.[4] An identical follow-up experiment with 10-month-olds (Homae, Watanabe, Nakano, & Taga, 2007) revealed exactly the opposite effect to that of the 3-month-olds: Right-hemisphere channels showed greater activation to monotone speech than to intonated speech. The problem here is not that these studies failed to demonstrate stimulus specificity or regional selectivity, but rather that the pattern of results across development does not conform to any simple prediction about what these NIRS activations mean.

Homae et al. (2007) went to great pains to offer a variety of plausible explanations for the flip in activations between 3 and 10 months of age. Perhaps the 10-month-olds have a greater expectation (via listening experience) to hear infant-directed speech, thereby sending a violation of expectation signal (from frontal cortex) to the right temporal cortex. Perhaps 10-month-olds find it more difficult to process monotone speech and activate right-hemisphere temporal areas that are involved in processing intonation. Perhaps the right hemisphere is involved in processing the emotional content of speech signals, and the monotone stimulus triggers a negative emotional response. All of these hypotheses are plausible, but they are also unverifiable in these two experiments. And they highlight a problem that is not unique to these two particular NIRS studies. The problem is the linking hypothesis between the level of NIRS activation and the underlying (inferred) psychological process that the activation is presumed to measure. If a study can report statistically significant effects without a priori constraints on what interpretation will be given to those results, then researchers are simply making a post hoc story about what they think the results *could* mean. In later sections, I argue that we must move beyond these "just so" stories about our data and into a new regime where specific predictions, and their required linking hypotheses, are stated clearly before the data are collected. It is not clear what we learn from studies that compare two stimuli (speech and music) that differ on so many dimensions, making it nearly impossible to know what specific difference led to greater left-hemisphere activation for speech (e.g., Kotilahti et al., 2010). To be clear, this criticism is not unique to NIRS studies, to neuroimaging methods, or to studies of infants. Every dependent measure, whether behavioural, neural, or haemodynamic, provides the researcher with data that must be interpreted relative to some underlying assumptions about unobserved psychological processes (e.g., attention, learning, discrimination). The clearer the linking hypothesis between the data and the unobserved process, the more confidence we have in the interpretation. Behavioural and ERP studies of infants are not immune from these interpretative issues, nor are ERP or fMRI studies of adults.

[4]The statistical tests of hemisphere differences for the two stimulus conditions do not appear to have been corrected for multiple comparisons. However, even a conservative Bonferroni correction would render the most significant p-value of $<.0005$ equal to $<.025$.

Exploratory-search NIRS studies: Vision

The first follow-up to the Meek et al. (1998) study, using a large number of NIRS channels and the simultaneous recording of activations over targeted and control regions of cortex, was published by Taga, Asakawa, Maki, Konishi, and Koizumi (2003). Using 12 NIRS channels over occipital cortex and 12 (control) channels over frontal cortex, Taga et al. presented 2- to 4-month-olds with a flickering chequerboard. The design also moved from the lengthy stimulus blocks (10–20 s) used with auditory stimuli to 3-s stimuli and jittered interstimulus intervals as in event-related fMRI designs. The predicted pattern of results was that occipital but not frontal channels would show significant activations. Those expectations were confirmed, thereby replicating Meek et al. within individual infants. The Taga et al. study also highlighted an important methodological issue that must be dealt with when using visual stimuli rather than auditory stimuli. Because the infants were awake rather than asleep, there was a greater incidence of movement artefacts. These movements were exacerbated during the no-stimulus (control) condition if no visual stimulus was available to maintain the infant's attention. Thus, a nontarget (i.e., minimally interesting) visual stimulus was presented during the control periods. This means that NIRS studies using visual stimuli are minimally comparing two conditions (target stimulus vs. control stimulus) and referencing both activations to a short prestimulus baseline.

The Taga et al. (2003) study provided compelling evidence for regional selectivity, but minimal evidence for stimulus specificity. A subsequent study by Watanabe, Homae, Nakano, and Taga (2008) recorded 48 NIRS channels over expanded occipital-parietal and fronto-prefrontal regions as 3-month-olds viewed a flickering chequerboard, a complex motion (mobile) stimulus, and a nontarget (dim fireworks) control. Consistent with expectations, a central region over occipital cortex showed reliable activations to both of the visual stimuli (chequerboard and mobile). However, the mobile stimulus showed a much more extensive pattern of activation across many channels over lateral occipital, prefrontal, and frontal areas than did the chequerboard stimulus. And the chequerboard stimulus also activated a few channels in the prefrontal areas. There were no significant lateralization effects. Watanabe et al. controlled for multiple comparisons by using the false discovery rate (FDR) method that is also used in fMRI studies (Benjamini & Hochberg, 1995; see excellent review in Ashby, 2011).

Although Watanabe et al. (2008) provided evidence of stimulus specificity (chequerboard vs. mobile), in addition to replicating and extending the regional selectivity of Taga et al. (2003), the pattern of regional selectivity was complex and subject to a variety of post hoc interpretations. Perhaps the lateral-occipital cortex (LOC) activations to the mobile but not the chequerboard are reflective of similar "object" responses in adult fMRI studies. Perhaps the greater temporal activation in the mobile condition results from the pairing of sounds with all of the visual events, but with infants having a greater expectation that mobiles and sounds will be paired than chequerboards and sounds (due to experience with mobiles in their homes). But why would both the chequerboard and the mobile elicit activations in prefrontal cortex? Is this a region that is involved with stimulus comparison, temporal expectation, or some other psychological process? Again, there are many plausible but untested post hoc explanations of these effects that can only be resolved by future hypothesis-driven experiments.

There are two additional lines of NIRS research with infants that employ visual stimuli, and both of them ask questions about the neural correlates of high-level cognitive and social-cognitive events. The first line of research presents 6-month-olds with a variety of object-occlusion events. Consider a red ball that moves behind an occluding surface and reemerges on the opposite side of the box as an object with a different colour (green ball), a different shape (red cube), or a change in both colour and shape (green cube). Behavioural studies have shown that infants at this age are more attentive (surprised) by a change in the object during occlusion than by the absence of a change. However, this preference to attend longer to the change is more pronounced when the occluding surface is narrow than when it is wide. The explanation for this occluder-size effect is that a wide occluder could hide a second object that was hidden while the first object moved behind the occluder, whereas the narrow occluder could not accommodate both objects. Thus, the wide occluder event is "possible" whereas the narrow occluder event is "impossible".

Wilcox and colleagues have conducted a series of four experiments to assess NIRS activations during these occlusion events. In all studies, two NIRS channels are located over the occipital cortex and reveal activations that do not differ by stimulus condition. These results suggest that the events are equally complex at the level of early visual cortex. Two additional NIRS channels over left temporal cortex reveal no difference in activations to the possible and impossible events (Wilcox, Bortfeld, Woods, Wruck, & Boas, 2005), but significant differences if the object undergoes a shape or shape + colour change during occlusion (the colour change was marginally significant; Wilcox, Bortfeld, Woods, Wruck, & Boas, 2008). In addition, if the wide occluder (possible event) depicted the sudden jump of the object from one side to the other (rendering the event impossible), then this spatiotemporally impossible event elicited a temporal activation different from the control (possible) condition. Interestingly, possible events involving a change in shape + colour elicited activations in more anterior temporal regions than impossible events involving spatiotemporal discontinuities (Wilcox, Bortfeld, Woods, Wruck, Armstrong, & Boas, 2009). Finally, additional NIRS channels over parietal cortex revealed a complex pattern of temporal and parietal activations to changes in shape, colour, spatiotemporal discontinuity, and invisible spatial displacement events (occipital activations remained invariant across all stimulus conditions; Wilcox, Haslup, & Boas, 2010).

These four studies by Wilcox and colleagues involve many different levels of stimulus processing that could reflect a variety of underlying cognitive mechanisms. Low-level visual stimulation associated with each visual display, such as changes in local luminance and contrast, is reflected in the occipital activations. However, the temporal and parietal activations could reflect object tracking, motion perception, change detection, violation of expectation, visual working memory, or other components of cognition. As with Homae et al. (2006, 2007) in the speech domain, and Watanabe et al. (2008) in the visual object domain, teasing apart these alternative hypotheses awaits future experiments that control (or manipulate) all but one alternative explanation.

The second line of research that examines NIRS responses to high-level visual events involves the presentation of stimuli that contain a social or social–cognitive component. Grossmann et al. (2008) presented 4-month-olds with dynamic facial events depicting either mutual gaze or averted gaze. Sixteen NIRS channels were recorded over prefrontal and temporal locations on each hemisphere. Two channels (one frontal and one posterior temporal), both in the right hemisphere, showed differential activations to the two gaze conditions.

Minagawa-Kawai et al. (2009) asked whether the infant's own mother is responded to differently than another infant's mother. Four NIRS channels were recorded over the frontal cortex of 12-month-olds, and results revealed greater activation to the infant's own mother's face, but only when the mother was smiling. The region showing the greatest mother–stranger effect was over the orbital-frontal cortex, which has been implicated in studies of positive emotional responses to social stimuli in adult fMRI studies.

Lloyd-Fox et al. (2009) presented 5-month-olds with two dynamic visual events—a face with occluding hands playing the peek-a-boo game, and a rotating three-dimensional multipart object—as well as a low-salience visual baseline condition. Ten NIRS channels were collected from prefrontal-temporal-parietal locations on each hemisphere (20 channels total). Results showed greater activation to the dynamic face than to the dynamic nonface object in a subset of temporal and prefrontal channels. Because one of these temporal channels corresponds to the superior temporal sulcus (STS), which is known to be activated by biological motion and dynamic social stimuli in adult fMRI studies, it is seductive to conclude that the infant brain is organized in a similar stimulus-specific manner. However, there are many differences between the dynamic face and nonface stimuli, including their patterns of motion. Thus, it is not possible to know for certain that the social nature of the face event is driving this effect in 5-month-olds. A follow-up experiment by Lloyd-Fox, Blasi, Everdell, Elwell, and Johnson (2011) contrasted three different dynamic face events (moving gaze, moving mouth, moving hand) with the same dynamic nonface comparison event. Again, 5-month-olds were tested with 10 NIRS channels over prefrontal-temporal-parietal locations in each hemisphere. Results indicated a gradient of activations bilaterally, with prefrontal regions dominated by the moving hand stimulus, prefrontal-temporal regions by the moving gaze stimulus, and middle temporal regions by the moving mouth stimulus. Thus, the face–nonface comparison in Lloyd-Fox et al. (2009) cannot be the simple result of the presence/absence of facial features, as all three conditions in Lloyd-Fox et al. (2011) contained facial features but elicited regionally specific responses.

Exploratory-search NIRS studies: Visual–auditory interactions

Another approach to the question of regional selectivity is to ask how NIRS activations are distributed over cortical areas known to be involved in particular sensory modalities. For example, the traditional view of primary sensory pathways is that they carry modality-specific information from the sensory receptors (e.g., retina for vision and cochlea for hearing) to the respective primary cortical areas (e.g., V1 for vision and A1 for hearing). If this separation of sensory information were present in the infant brain, then one would predict little or no cross-talk between modality-specific activations.

Bortfeld, Wruck, and Boas (2007) located two NIRS channels over occipital cortex and two channels over left temporal cortex, while 5-month-olds were presented with visual stimuli on half the blocks and a combination of visual and auditory stimuli on the other blocks. The first prediction was that occipital channels would be activated in both conditions because a visual stimulus was present in each, and this prediction was confirmed. The second prediction was that temporal channels would only be activated in the visual + auditory condition and not in the visual-only condition. This prediction was partially supported—temporal channels were activated in the visual + auditory condition, but these same channels were *negatively* activated in the visual-only condition. This unexpected finding could be the result of "stealing" oxygenated blood from temporal areas when the visual-only stimulus was presented, or it could be the result of sluggish attentional switching from the multimodal to the unimodal conditions. In the absence of an auditory-only condition, these two possibilities remain unresolved.

Bortfeld, Fava, and Boas (2009) conducted a follow-up experiment with 6- to 9-month-olds who were presented with visual-only stimuli and visual + auditory stimuli, just as in Bortfeld et al. (2007). However, now NIRS channels were positioned over each hemisphere's temporal cortex, rather than over occipital and left-temporal cortices. Activations were reliable only over the left temporal channels in the visual + auditory condition. In contrast to Bortfeld et al. (2007), there was no significant negative activation over left temporal cortex in the visual-only condition. These results suggest that the left temporal cortex is specialized for speech processing and that there is minimal cross-talk between modalities.

Taga and Asakawa (2007) recorded 12 NIRS channels over each hemisphere's temporal cortex in 2- to 4-month-olds. Stimuli consisted of auditory (speech) and visual (flashing chequerboards), each of which was presented for 3 s, but out of phase with each other (interstimulus interval, ISI, 12 s for auditory, 15 s for visual). The auditory stimulus activated several temporal channels bilaterally, but the visual stimulus activated none of the temporal channels (the FDR correction method was used to control for multiple comparisons). These results are somewhat different from Bortfeld et al. (2007) in that visual-only stimuli did not lead to a decrease in temporal activations. However, Taga and Asakawa used shorter stimulus durations (3 s vs. 20 s), tested younger infants (2–4 months vs. 5 months), and did not present the auditory and visual stimuli synchronously.

One other study bears on the question of multimodal interaction, although it was not designed specifically for that purpose. As summarized earlier, Watanabe et al. (2008) presented 3-month-olds with two different visual stimuli (flickering chequerboard and dynamic mobile) and recorded NIRS activations over 48 channels in occipital-parietal and prefrontal-frontal areas. They presented a uniform auditory stimulus in synchrony with the onset of each visual stimulus (5-s duration; 10-s ISI). In a follow-up experiment, they increased the number of NIRS channels from 48 to 60 and focused their coverage on temporal and occipital cortex. Results indicated that both the occipital and temporal cortices, bilaterally, were activated by the combined visual + auditory stimuli, and that the two visual stimuli (chequerboard + sound and mobile + sound) elicited equivalent activations in both left and right hemispheres.

Hypothesis-driven NIRS studies

The majority of infant NIRS studies employ an exploratory strategy of gathering activations from multiple channels elicited by the presentation of two or more stimuli. The goal is to determine whether there are *differential* activations to specific stimuli and to selective regions of the brain. The interpretation of these findings is largely post hoc, with a variety of plausible accounts consistent with the pattern of results. We turn now to the second major strategy: hypothesis-driven predictions about NIRS activations in infants. One limitation of exploratory studies is that they rely on properties of the infant brain that have been established prior to entering the experiment. Thus, unless the experimenter has clear evidence of early experiences attained by some infants and not by others, the only way to gain experimental control over the predicted NIRS activations is to have a strong hypothesis on which to base that prediction. These strong hypotheses have so far been limited to studies of discrimination, learning, and focal activation.

Studies of discrimination

There is a long tradition of behavioural research with infants that relies on measures of preference, typically using looking time as the dependent variable (see review by Aslin, 2007). When infants show longer looking times to stimulus X over stimulus Y, that constitutes clear evidence of discrimination as well as preference. However, when stimulus X and stimulus Y are equally preferred, it is not clear whether that negative effect is the result of a failure to discriminate X from Y. It is quite possible for infants to discriminate two stimuli but not to prefer one over the other. The same interpretive limitation is present for NIRS activations. The absence of differential activation to stimulus X over stimulus Y does not of necessity imply that a given NIRS channel, and the brain region it samples, is incapable of processing the difference between X and Y. Looking-time studies progressed beyond simple preference paradigms to "entice" infants to exhibit a latent preference by repeating stimulus X and then asking whether they prefer stimulus Y over stimulus X. This is the habituation paradigm, and in many cases it reveals the ability to discriminate X and Y when a preference test fails to do so.

It is surprising, in light of the extensive behavioural literature on infants' discrimination abilities using the habituation paradigm, that it has been used in only a few NIRS studies (see Turk-Browne, Scholl, & Chun, 2008, for a discussion of the parallels between behavioural habituation and fMRI adaptation). Minagawa-Kawai, Mori, Naoi, and Kojima (2007) asked whether infants could discriminate a speech contrast (vowel duration) that is used phonemically in their native Japanese language and compared their performance to a nonphonemic contrast. They tested a broad age range (3- to 28-month-olds) using four NIRS channels over each hemisphere's temporal cortex. Each infant was presented with alternating 20-s blocks of two types: a single repeating stimulus versus a random mixture of two stimuli. Each infant was tested in two sessions: with the phonemic contrast (discriminable by Japanese adults), and with the nonphonemic contrast (within-category and therefore not discriminable by Japanese adults). The prediction of this modified habituation paradigm is that infants who can discriminate the speech contrast should show greater activation to the mixed block than to the uniform block. That prediction was supported by a main effect of block type (mixed > uniform), and it did not interact with whether the speech contrast was phonemic or not. In addition, the language-relevance effect (phonemic vs. nonphonemic) was present only in activations from the left hemisphere, and only in three of the five age groups (6–7 months, 11–14 months, and 25–28 month, but not 3–4 months or 10–11 months). The absence of the language-relevance effect in the youngest age group could be attributed to the subtle nature of the phonemic contrast, and the absence of the effect in the 10- to 11-month-old group was due to exceptionally high between-subject variance. These results, therefore, provide convincing evidence for the utility of the mixed versus uniform stimulus-block paradigm as a measure of discrimination, as well as for the development of sensitivity to language-relevant phonemic information.

A subsequent study by Sato, Sogabe, and Mazuka (2009) examined a different speech contrast in Japanese infants. Both 4- and 10-month-olds were tested with a pitch-accent contrast (high–low versus low–high) in a set of 14 words as NIRS activations were gathered from 12 channels over each temporal cortex. As in Minagawa-Kawai et al. (2007), each infant was presented with two types of blocks: uniform in which all 14 words had the same pitch accent, and mixed in which half of the 14 words were high–low and the other half low–high, in random order. The uniform blocks were 20–25 s long, and the mixed blocks were 10 s long. The prediction was that infants should show greater activation to the mixed than to the uniform blocks. The results from the 10-month-olds were consistent with this prediction: There was significantly greater activation to the mixed than to the uniform blocks. In addition, this discrimination effect was greater in the left hemisphere than in the right hemisphere. For the 4-month-olds there was also significantly greater activation to the mixed than to the uniform blocks, but there was no hemisphere difference. Sato et al. also presented the same high–low pitch contrast in a nonword context (pure tones). Interestingly, the 10-month-olds did not show the same pattern of left-hemisphere enhancement of the mixed versus uniform block-effect as they did for the word stimuli. The 4-month-olds showed no hemisphere effect, consistent with their performance with the word stimuli.

Nakano, Watanabe, Homae, and Taga (2009) extended these results from the domain of vowel duration and pitch contrasts to that of consonants by asking whether 3- to 4-month-old Japanese infants could discriminate a /ba/–/pa/ contrast. The experimental design was virtually identical to what has traditionally been used with behavioural measures. Each infant was presented with 15 trials during a habituation phase, with each 5-s trial consisting of 10 repetitions of either /ba/ or /pa/ followed by 15 s of silence. Infants were then presented with 5 posthabituation test trials, each consisting of 5-s trials with a different repeating syllable (e.g., a shift from /ba/ to /pa/) or the very same syllable presented during the habituation phase (i.e., a no-shift control). Separate infants were assigned either to the experimental (shift) or to the control (no-shift) groups. During the habituation phase, infants in both groups showed widespread activations across most of the 48 NIRS channels, which were positioned over temporal and prefrontal cortices. Both groups also showed highly significant decreases over the 15 habituation trials (see Figure 4), consistent with behavioural measures such as looking time and sucking. The key question was whether infants in the experimental (shift) group showed increases in activation from the final set of habituation trials to the test trials,

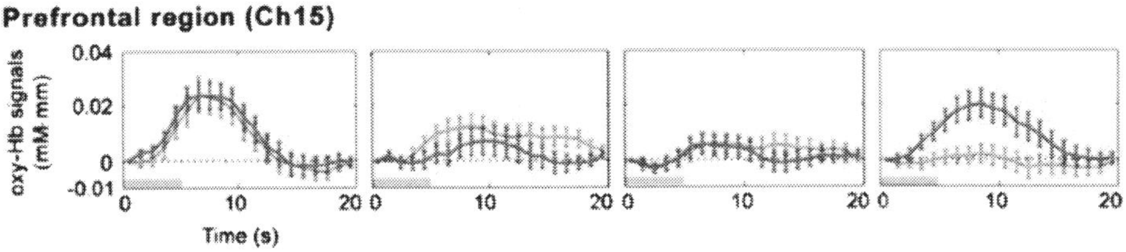

Figure 4. *A single near-infrared spectroscopy (NIRS) channel over prefrontal cortex from Nakano et al. (2009) showing decreasing activations in 3 blocks of 5 trials to a speech category, following by recovery to a novel speech category (orange) in the 4th block but not to a no-change control group (green). Hb = haemoglobin. From "Prefrontal Cortical Involvement in Young Infants' Analysis of Novelty", by T. Nakano, H. Watanabe, F. Homae, and G. Taga, 2009,* Cerebral Cortex, 19, *pp. 455–463. Copyright 2009 by permission of Oxford University Press. To view a colour version of this figure, please see the online issue of the Journal.*

and whether these increases were absent (or less reliable) in the control (no-shift) group. Again, there was clear evidence of recovery of activation in a small set of NIRS channels (bilateral prefrontal) that was greater in the experimental group than in the control group.

The Nakano et al. (2009) study is an excellent example of hypothesis-driven research. The pattern of NIRS activations was not determined by preexisting differences in the responsiveness of the infant brain, but rather to the repeated presentation of a particular speech stimulus (counterbalanced across infants) during the habituation phase of the experiment. Thus, the differences in NIRS activations cannot be due to acoustic differences per se, but must be due to the *change* in sensitivity to these acoustic differences induced by the habituation phase that preceded the test phase. It is interesting to note that all of the infants in this study were asleep, thereby providing clear evidence that a state of wakefulness is not required for infants up to 4 months of age to exhibit speech discrimination.

A final NIRS study of speech discrimination was reported by Arimitsu et al. (2011). They presented sleeping newborns with two Japanese speech contrasts, one that was phonemic (vowel duration) and one that was prosodic (pitch rise/fall). Again, the uniform versus mixed design was used with 15-s blocks. Twelve NIRS channels over each temporal cortex revealed significant activations to both the phonemic and prosodic contrasts. Although there was evidence of a right-hemisphere bias for the prosodic contrast (see Telkemeyer et al., 2009), there was no significant evidence of a left-hemisphere bias for the phonemic contrast, perhaps because this contrast did not involve rapid acoustic cues. The Arimitsu et al. study reported on individual NIRS channels as well as several ROIs. However, the rationale for choosing a particular ROI was based more on a visual inspection of the data than on an objective criterion. As noted earlier, ROIs should never be selected post hoc, but should be defined by using either anatomical or statistical (i.e., Monte Carlo) criteria.

Studies of learning

Another potential outcome of exposure to stimuli in the laboratory, which contrasts with habituation and recovery to a novel stimulus, is learning from the stimuli and showing an increase in activation across blocks. Gervain, Macagno, Cogoi, Pena, and Mehler (2008) asked whether newborns could discriminate between three-syllable sequences that conformed to an ABB or an ABC pattern. Twelve NIRS channels were positioned over each temporal cortex, and alternating 18-s blocks of ABB and ABC patterns, each involving a new set of syllables, were presented with 25–35 s of silence between blocks. Results showed greater activation to ABB blocks than to ABC blocks from most channels, with a greater activation difference for these two patterns in the left hemisphere (see Figure 5). Most relevant to the question of learning, Gervain et al. also found that this activation difference between ABB and ABC was not significant in Block 1,

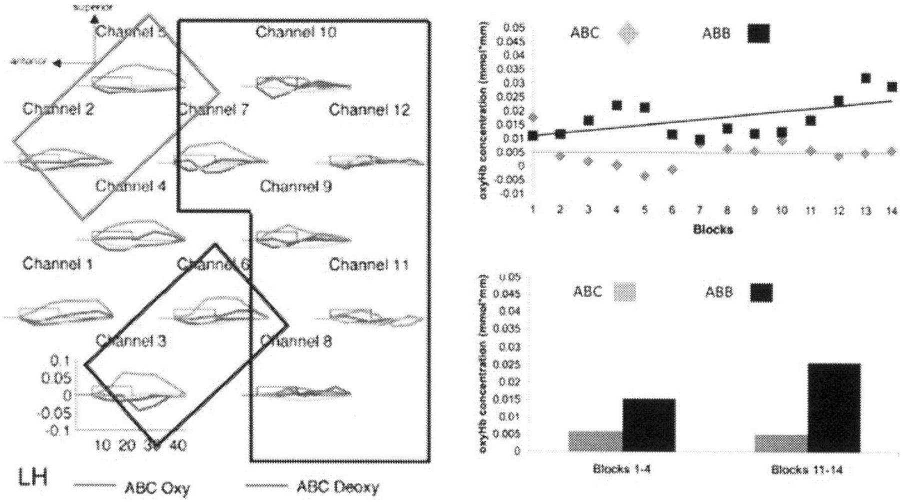

Figure 5. *Data from Gervain et al. (2008) showing left anterior responses and a learning effect. Hb = haemoglobin. From "The Neonate Brain Detects Speech Structure", by J. Gervain, F. Macagno, S. Cogoi, M. Pena, and J. Mehler, 2008,* Proceedings of the National Academy of Sciences of the USA, 105, *pp. 14222–14227. Copyright 2008 by permission of National Academy of Sciences, USA. To view a colour version of this figure, please see the online issue of the Journal.*

but became significant and increased over the 14 alternating blocks. Interestingly, this learning effect for the ABB pattern was present in the left frontal ROI, but not in the right frontal or either of the two temporal ROIs.

Gervain et al. (2008) conducted a follow-up experiment that compared ABA patterns to ABC patterns to determine whether the immediate repetition of the B element in ABB patterns was easier for newborns to extract than the nonadjacent repetition of the A element in the ABA patterns. They found no evidence of differential activation to ABA and ABC patterns and no learning effect across alternating blocks. Gervain, Berent, and Werker (2012) then asked whether the immediate repetition could be equally as effective for learning in the initial syllables (AAB) as for learning in the final syllables (ABB). Their results replicated the ABB versus ABC comparison in Gervain et al. (2008), with greater activation to AAB than to ABC and a bias for this differential effect to be stronger in the left hemisphere. Gervain et al. (2012) then asked whether newborns could discriminate early AAB from late ABB repetitions. Instead of alternating blocks of AAB and ABB, they used the mixture versus uniform design of Minagawa-Kawai et al. (2007). That is, half of the blocks consisted of *either* AAB or ABB patterns, and the other half of the blocks consisted of *both* AAB and ABB patterns. Newborns showed reliable evidence of discrimination, but the direction of the effect was unexpected, with greater activation elicited by the *uniform* blocks (i.e., AAB or ABB) than the *mixture* blocks (i.e., AAB and ABB). In a final experiment, they reverted to the alternating uniform-block design and contrasted AAB with ABB to determine whether early versus late repetition provided any advantage. However, there was no significant differential activation to the initial and final repetition patterns.

Unfortunately, in none of the follow-up experiments to Gervain et al. (2008) was there a learning effect over blocks. Thus, it is not clear whether the initial report of this effect was spurious or whether such learning effects are less robust when the patterns being contrasted are more difficult to discriminate. The comparison of ABB and ABC patterns was examined in 7- and 9-month-olds by Wagner, Fox, Tager-Flusberg, and Nelson (2011) to determine whether older infants would more robustly show the learning effects. They used the same stimuli and 12-channel arrays over left and right temporal cortex, but found no significant effects of pattern, hemisphere, or cortical ROI using the same oxyhaemoglobin measure as Gervain et al. (2008, 2012). However, there were effects of pattern and hemisphere in the deoxyhaemoglobin measure (which is typically small in magnitude and often unreported in infant studies; see Telkemeyer et al., 2009, 2011 for exceptions). The direction of deoxyhaemoglobin responses is opposite to that of oxy-haemoglobin responses, and therefore the significant effect reported by Wagner et al. in the 7-month-olds was consistent with the newborns in the original Gervain et al. (2008) study—activations to ABB patterns were greater (negative deoxy) than those to ABC patterns. However, this pattern was evident only in the right hemisphere, not the left hemisphere as in newborns (although it was present in frontal and not temporal ROIs, as in newborns). Moreover, this pattern reversed in the 9-month-olds—activations to ABC patterns were greater (negative deoxy) than those to ABB patterns. Finally, there was a hint of a learning effect, with a significant reduction in the activations to the ABC pattern over blocks in both ages. These diverse results across age cannot be attributed to state of arousal (sleeping newborns vs. awake 7- and 9-month-olds) because the 7- to 9-month shift was present despite similar states of wakefulness.

Studies of focal activation

The foregoing studies of pattern learning have the distinct flavour of "the more we study X, the less we know about X". Results that appear to be consistent within a given experiment do not replicate, or do not make a coherent story as more data are collected under similar conditions. Certainly one expects differences across age, but within an age one would hope that proposed explanations for effects are supported when the next experiment is conducted to examine that explanation. At present, it is very difficult to make specific predictions as one embarks on a new line of research, perhaps because we are trying to study complex cognitive phenomena before we fully understand what NIRS activations mean. That is, the field suffers from placing little emphasis on the specific linking hypothesis for how changes in oxy- or deoxyhaemoglobin indicate an underlying perceptual, cognitive, or language process. In general, the history of infant NIRS studies is peculiar in that it began by tackling high-level cognition rather than focusing first on low-level (i.e., less interesting to some researchers) sensory and motor phenomena. The reason such a bottom-up strategy might have been more fruitful is that sensory and motor systems are well studied in adults and animals, and they have considerable uniformity across age and species. Thus, the predictions one can make about these systems are quite constrained, thereby limiting the predicted outcomes if NIRS activations are valid measures of these low-level processes.

There are three domains within which specific predictions based on clear anatomical constraints have been made for infant NIRS studies: somatosensory cortex, visual cortex, and the intraparietal sulcus. Not only does the somatosensory cortex have a well-defined spatial organization, but pathways from the sensory periphery send information contralaterally to termination sites in somatosensory cortex. For example, tactile stimulation of the palm of the right hand activates the primary somatosensory cortex in the left hemisphere. The same contralateral organization holds for the motor cortex, leading many NIRS labs to use a finger tapping or tactile stimulus on the palm as a "sanity check" on the recording equipment. Surprisingly, there is only one such study of infants (Kusaka et al., 2011). They stimulated sleeping newborns by passively moving the elbow or the knee while 12 NIRS channels were recorded over the right and left somatosensory cortex, and they reported stronger contralateral than ipsilateral activations (although the statistics were poorly specified). These results are consistent with an earlier fMRI study of sleeping newborns using similar stimulation (Erberich, Panigrahy, Friedlich, Seri, Nelson, & Gilles, 2006).

The second domain in which NIRS signals are constrained by sensory anatomy is the visual system. There is a longstanding subfield of fMRI research that uses flickering chequerboards that are limited to portions of the visual field. Because any visual stimulus on the right half of the visual field (i.e., the two left hemiretinas) projects only to the left primary visual cortex, and any visual stimulus on the left half of the visual field projects only to the right visual cortex, activations must conform to the timing of these visual stimuli. Many investigators have used this method to elicit fMRI activations in visual cortex while an adult fixates the centre of a display. In the simplest case, a chequerboard fills either the right or the left half of the visual field. The expected pattern of activation is for the right-half stimulus to activate the left visual cortex, and the left-half stimulus to activate the right visual cortex. A more complex case is when the chequerboard fills only one quadrant of the visual field and rotates slowly (i.e., upper right, lower right, lower left, upper left). In this case, the expected pattern of activation is a 180-deg phase-shift (i.e., inferior-left cortex, superior-left cortex, superior-right cortex, inferior-right cortex). These are precisely the patterns of activation that have been obtained from many fMRI studies (see Wandell, Dumoulin, & Brewer, 2007).

Two reports using NIRS in adults (Plichta, Heinzel, Ehlis, Pauli, & Fallgatter, 2007; Zeff, White, Dehghani, Schlaggar, & Culver, 2007) demonstrated that flickering chequerboards in subsets of the visual field activate NIRS channels over the occipital cortex in the same way as they activate fMRI voxels in the visual cortex. Moreover, adult NIRS activations show the characteristic 180-deg phase shift to a rotating chequerboard wedge (see Figure 6) or expanding chequerboard ring that have been obtained with fMRI (see review by White & Culver, 2010).

A key requirement of these visual-field stimulation studies is for the subject to maintain central fixation while the flickering chequerboard is presented in the retinal periphery. Infants are likely to direct their gaze to this flickering chequerboard rather than attending consistently to a small central fixation target. However, pilot data from my lab suggest that this problem can be overcome. Custom software enables an eye-tracker (Tobii T60XL) to monitor the infant's gaze online and to move the central fixation target to compensate for gaze shifts into the periphery where the chequerboard is located. This is not a perfect image stabilization technique because there is a 100–200-ms lag in detecting gaze deviations from the central fixation target and moving the display accordingly to recentre it at the infant's current (eccentric) gaze position. If the infant's gaze moves off screen, then the display automatically recentres itself on the screen before the chequerboard is reintroduced. We have gathered eye-tracking data from several 6-month-olds whose gaze was directed to the central fixation target for more than 50% of the 2-minute display. Thus, we are encouraged that retinotopic mapping of the visual cortex will be possible, at least for some infants, using this online gaze-centring paradigm and an array of NIRS channels over occipital cortex.

A third domain in which NIRS activations are constrained by prior knowledge of cortical anatomy is a region of parietal cortex specialized for numerosity judgements—the intraparietal sulcus (IPS). Based on extensive fMRI studies in children and adults, as well as single unit recording in animals, the IPS is uniquely activated when processing differences in number, even when there are correlated variations in element size, area, perimeter, and density (Cantlon, Brannon, Carter, & Pelphrey, 2006). Hyde, Boas, Blair, and Carey (2010) used a focal array of four NIRS channels, two centred on bilateral IPS and two centred on occipital cortex (control). Six-month-old infants were presented with visual arrays consisting of 16 elements that were flashed for 500 ms, with an ISI of 500–1000 ms. Every 5–11 flashes, a novel number of elements (either 8 or 32) was presented for a single flash, thereby serving as an oddball event with respect to the more predictable base rate of 16-element events. A separate control group was presented with the same set of displays, except that the oddball events consisted of the same number of elements but of a different shape (squares rather than circles). Greater activations to the oddball events, either number or shape, were only significant in the right

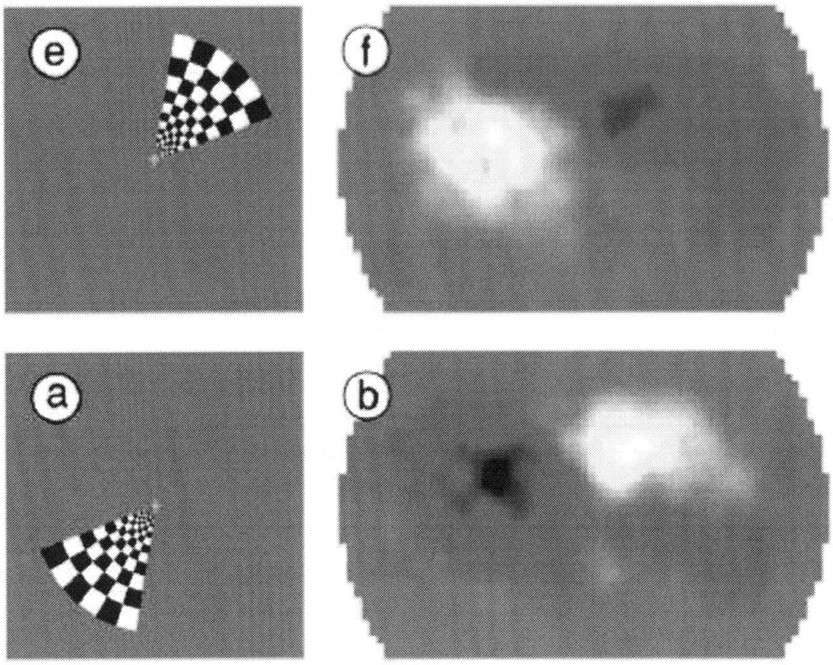

Figure 6. *Data from White and Culver (2010) gathered over occipital near-infrared spectroscopy (NIRS) channels as a flickered chequerboard wedge rotates around the visual field. NIRS activations (right panels) are 180 deg out of phase with the location of the wedge stimulus. From "Phase-Encoded Retinotopy as an Evaluation of Diffuse Optical Neuroimaging", by B. R. White and J. P. Culver, 2010,* NeuroImage, 49, *pp. 568–577. Copyright 2010 with permission from Elsevier. To view a colour version of this figure, please see the online issue of the Journal.*

hemisphere. Although both lateral-occipital areas are known to be responsive to shape changes, only the right IPS is responsive to number changes. This pattern of results was present in the infant NIRS data: Right parietal activations were greater than right occipital activations for a change in number (see Figure 7), but there was no significant difference in left parietal and left occipital activations for a change in number. Moreover, right occipital activations differed from baseline for a change in shape (it is not clear why left occipital activations were not above baseline for a change in shape). These results from 6-month-olds closely mirror those obtained with fMRI from children and adults, suggesting that the right IPS is specialized for numerosity processing from a very early age. However, further control studies are needed, especially with a larger number of NIRS channels, to verify that right parietal channels located near the IPS are the only ones that show this effect.

Questions that should be asked in the future

So far we have reviewed nearly 50 infant NIRS studies, many of which fall short of answering the questions that motivated their authors. Findings across studies are remarkably consistent and inconsistent at the same time. They are consistent in finding *some* channels that are activated by suprathreshold stimuli, but this is hardly surprising – surely there is some region of cortex that responds to just about any stimulus. The most important question one can ask about NIRS findings from infants is: What have we learned that we didn't know already from other measures? That is, what is the "value-added" of NIRS for studies of infant perception, cognition,

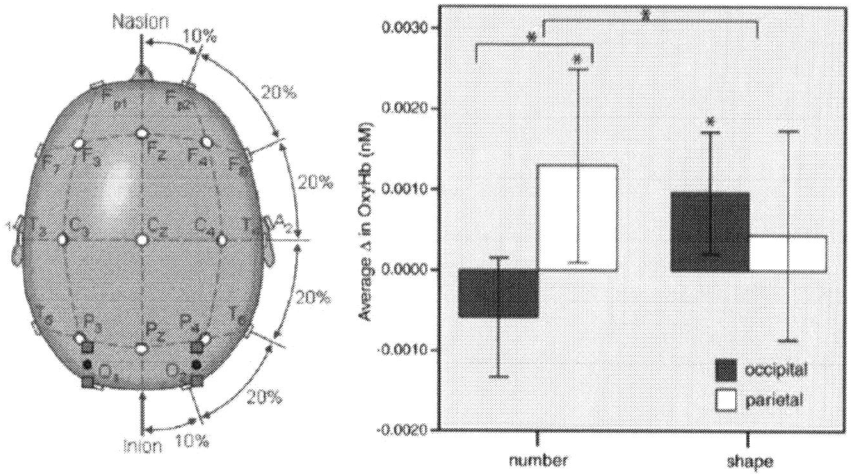

Figure 7. *Placement of the near-infrared spectroscopy (NIRS) channels in Hyde et al. (2010) and the resultant activations to changes in number or shape over right hemisphere occipital and parietal locations in 6-month-olds. Hb = haemoglobin. From "Near-Infrared Spectroscopy Shows Right Parietal Specialization for Number in Pre-Verbal Infants", by D. C. Hyde, D. A. Boas, C. Blair, and S. Carey, 2010,* NeuroImage, 53, *pp. 647–652. Copyright 2010 with permission from Elsevier. To view a colour version of this figure, please see the online issue of the Journal.*

and language? The answer, unfortunately, is rather modest. Almost all infant NIRS studies are largely confirmatory and fail to clarify the underlying neural mechanism, beyond specifying its regional selectivity.

Consider evidence that NIRS activations show hemisphere lateralization. If brain area X is activated by stimulus Y, and this regional selectivity mirrors what is present in adults, does this imply a similar functional role for area X? The problem with such an interpretation—that there is developmental continuity of regional brain function—is that haemodynamic responses are slow. Thus, they could reflect feed-forward activation (processing the stimulus), feedback activation (sending information from somewhere else), or some combination of the two (comparing inputs and stored representations). One clear way of overcoming this interpretive limitation is to present a stimulus that can *only* activate certain NIRS channels because of known anatomical constraints, but this research strategy, as noted earlier, is extremely rare in the literature (see Minagawa-Kawai, Cristia, & Dupoux, 2011, for a developmental theory of lateralization).

A similar concern can be raised about stimulus specificity in a given brain region. Typically conclusions about stimulus specificity are weak—brain area X is activated by stimulus Y but not (or less so) by stimulus Z. But how specific is this pattern of activation—what stimuli other than Y activate area X, and what stimuli other than Z fail to activate area X? Clearly, there is a need to move away from two-stimulus designs and focus on multiple levels along a particular stimulus dimension to get a better handle on the linking hypothesis between NIRS activation and underlying psychological processes. As noted by Aslin and Fiser (2005), when only two levels along a stimulus dimension are used, and one observes an increase (or decrease) in a dependent measure (e.g., NIRS activation), it is often concluded that the relevant NIRS activation indicates a brain region that represents that stimulus dimension. But if so, one would expect a third level along that stimulus dimension to show a further increase (or decrease) in activation. If that does not happen, then it calls into question the validity of the conclusion about what the NIRS activation means. In other words, it may be less important to know whether a given brain area is activated by a stimulus than to know that a change in a stimulus is correlated with a change in NIRS activation. This is because the assumption that brain areas are independent is very unlikely, leading to substantial "cross talk" across areas. The challenge here is to understand how these interactions among brain areas are organized and to differentiate such interactions from measurement errors stemming from systemic haemodynamic responses.

Finally, developmental questions are rarely asked in infant NIRS studies or in any neuroimaging modality (see Karmiloff-Smith, 2010). Rather, a single age is often the target of a given study, which makes comparisons across studies difficult because of variations in stimuli, testing designs, probe placements, criteria for data rejection, signal processing, and statistical analysis. The best studies begin with robust behavioural evidence that ability X is absent at age 1 and present at age 2. Then one can ask whether NIRS activation emerges between age 1 and age 2. If so, then it is seductive to conclude that the emerging NIRS activation mediates that behavioural change. But of course this correlation does not confirm causality. Moreover, if there is no change in neural activation between ages 1 and 2, then it suggests either an insensitive neural measure or a nonlocalist mechanism responsible for the developmental change.

There is a caveat to the foregoing picture of NIRS as a technique that has so far underachieved on its promise of revealing brain mechanisms of infant development. One can view neural signals—ERP, magnetoencephalography (MEG), fMRI, NIRS—as merely dependent measures and not as brain-specific per se. If one's goal is to find *some* measure of detection, discrimination, or learning, and NIRS provides such a reliable signal, then it has potential utility in answering questions about when during development an underlying process is present. Of course, the presence of a neural response does not necessarily imply that it is functional in supporting perception or influencing behaviour. A reliable neural signal may be necessary but not sufficient to enable a neural network to rise above some critical threshold required to support behaviour. If NIRS signals were more reliably present at a given age than any other dependent measure, and/or NIRS signals were easier to record from infants than these other measures, then it would be a clear win to use NIRS even with weak linking hypotheses between neural signals and behaviour.

Prospects for technical advances

At least some of the foregoing problems can be reduced or eliminated by technical improvements in the reliability of NIRS signals. One such promising technique has been described by Saager and Berger (2005). They reasoned that because optical signals must pass through the surface vasculature to provide estimates of brain-based haemodynamic responses, it would improve the signal-to-noise ratio of the brain-based responses if the surface "noise" could be estimated. They placed a detector at a near distance from the emitter to measure this surface vascular noise (see Figure 8) and used regression techniques to examine the residual signals after this surface noise was "subtracted off". In simulations, subsequently verified by NIRS measurements from adults (Saager & Berger, 2008, 2011), they showed that this near-channel regression technique improved signal/noise by a factor of 3. Liao et al. (2010) capitalized on this technique in a study of sleeping newborns who received visual stimulation (flashes) through their closed eyelids. Their results confirmed a three-fold improvement in signal/noise, which also means that the same statistical power could be achieved in fewer than half the stimulus events.

A natural outcome of improved signal/noise in NIRS activations is greater use of event-related than blocked designs. This same trend occurred in the fMRI literature as pulse sequences and gradient strengths were improved, and 3-T magnets replaced 1.5-T magnets. Surprisingly few infant NIRS studies have employed event-related designs (see Hyde et al., 2010; Taga et al., 2003; and Watanabe et al., 2008, for exceptions).

Analysis techniques in the NIRS literature are surprisingly primitive compared to the fMRI

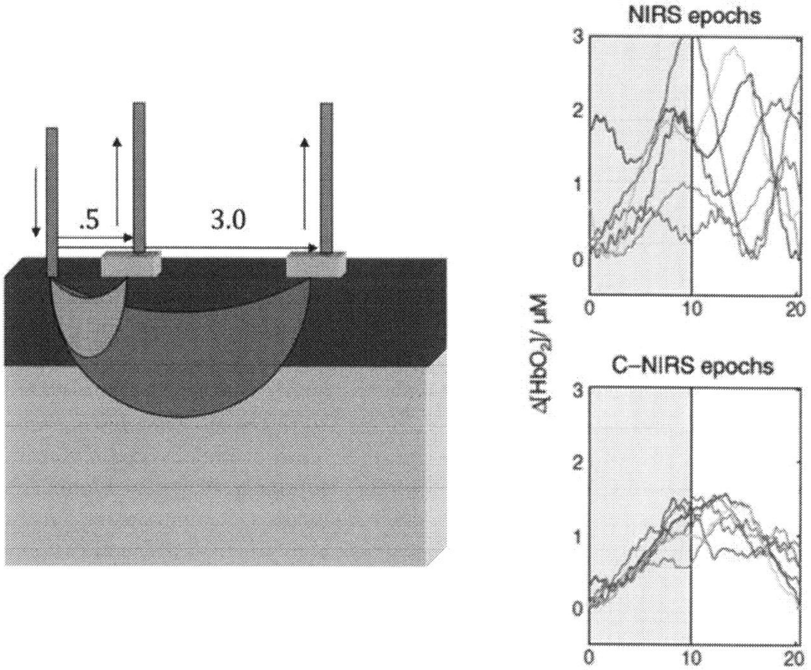

Figure 8. *Configuration of near and far channel separations from Saager, Telleri, and Berger (2011) and the resultant reduction in variance for individual subjects in far-only versus near-corrected corrected near infrared spectroscopy (C-NIRS) activations.* HbO_2 *= oxyhaemoglobin. From "Two-Detector Corrected Near Infrared Spectroscopy (C-NIRS) Detects Hemodynamic Activation Responses More Robustly Than Single-Detector NIRS", by R. B. Saager, N. L. Telleri, and A. J. Berger, 2011,* NeuroImage, *55, pp. 1679–1685. Copyright 2011 with permission from Elsevier. To view a colour version of this figure, please see the online issue of the Journal.*

literature. Only a few NIRS studies have used the standard generalized linear model (GLM) tools from fMRI (Minagawa-Kawai, van der Lely, et al., 2011; Obrig et al., 2010; Telkemeyer et al., 2011), despite modifications to widely used fMRI analysis packages such as SPM (Koh et al., 2007).

Another potentially fruitful approach to studying brain development is to gather estimates of what in the fMRI literature is called functional connectivity. The basic idea is that voxels whose blood-oxygen-level-dependent (BOLD) activations are highly correlated are somehow functionally related, even if the anatomical pathways that connect these voxels are quite indirect (i.e., multiple synapses away). There is evidence in adults that, in the absence of any task, clusters of voxels are correlated with other clusters of voxels, forming a so-called resting-state network of functionally connected modules (Raichle & Snyder, 2007). Two recent infant studies have demonstrated the feasibility of estimating functional connectivity using 94 NIRS channels, thereby providing coverage of most of the cortex. Homae et al. (2010) measured pairwise correlations among all 94 NIRS channels while newborns, 3-month-olds, and 6-month-olds were asleep. As in adults, correlations were clustered *within* hemispheres (e.g., occipital, temporal, prefrontal, etc.). More interesting, correlations were also clustered *between* hemispheres (e.g., left and right temporal), and there was a progressive increase in the consistency of these between-hemisphere correlations across age (see Figure 9).

The second infant study examined how functional connectivity changed between states of sleep and wakefulness. Studies of adults using fMRI have shown that resting-state functional

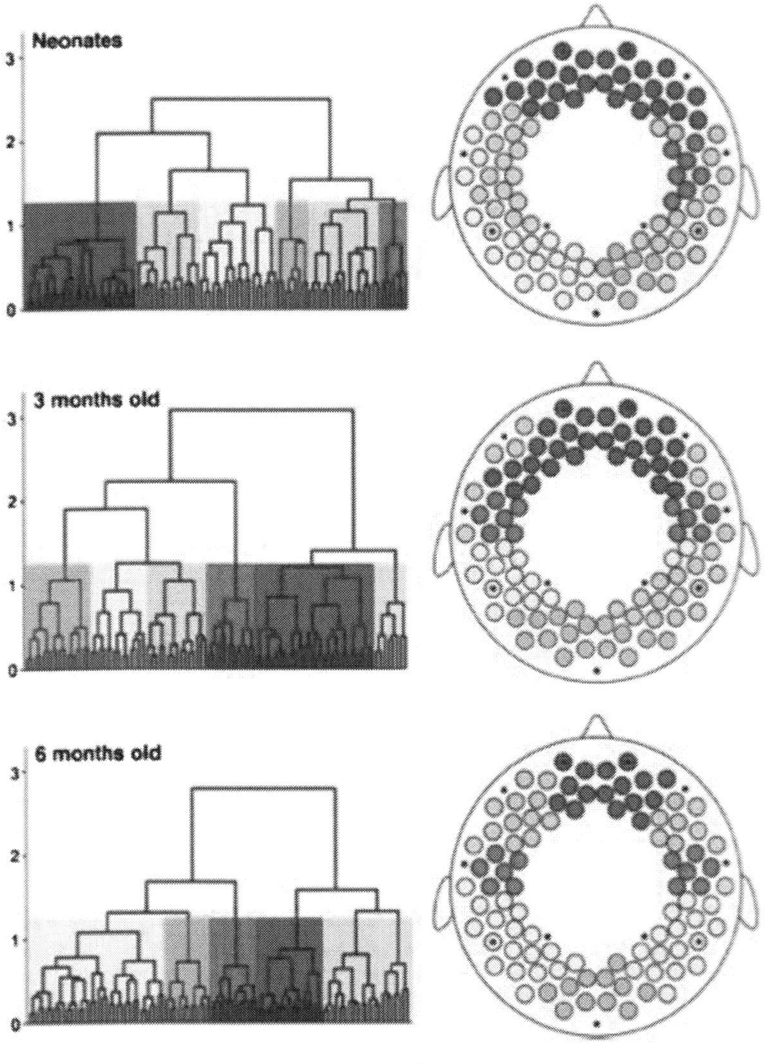

Figure 9. *Functional connectivity among 94 near-infrared spectroscopy (NIRS) channels during sleep gathered from newborns, 3-month-olds, and 6-month-olds by Homae et al. (2010). From "Development of Global Cortical Networks in Early Infancy", by F. Homae et al., 2010,* Journal of Neuroscience, 30, *pp. 4877–4882. Copyright 2010 by permission from the Society for Neuroscience. To view a colour version of this figure, please see the online issue of the Journal.*

connectivity is modulated when the state of wakefulness varies in adults (Larson-Prior et al., 2009), perhaps indicating that the network properties undergo reorganization to differentially recruit specialized neural computations (e.g., to process information that is task relevant and to prepare and execute a motor response). Homae, Watanabe, Nakano, and Taga (2011) recorded 94 NIRS channels from 3-month-olds across three periods consisting of: no-stimulus, speech stimulation, and no-stimulus. Not only did they find similar resting-state connectivity in the initial no-stimulus period as in Homae et al. (2010), but during the speech stimulation period they found a substantial reorganization of functional connectivity, with greater ipsilateral connectivity between temporal and frontal areas (as well as some connectivity with occipital areas). Finally, in the third period when no stimulus was presented, there continued to be significant ipsilateral connectivity, suggesting that further processing of the stimulus-elicited activations during the second period continued to occur after the stimulus had ended. Taga, Watanabe, and Homae (2011) replicated all of these patterns of functional connectivity in 3- to 4-month-olds with pure-tone stimuli, suggesting that these effects are not specific to language. Although functional connectivity during sleep has been assessed using fMRI in 21-month-olds (Redcay, Haist, & Courchesne, 2008), it has proven virtually impossible to gather fMRI data from awake children at this young age. The importance of the Homae et al. (2011) study is that it shows that NIRS can be used to measure both resting-state and stimulus-elicited functional connectivity in awake infants.

A final set of improvements in the reliability of NIRS will come from conducting test–retest studies in which the optodes are removed and repositioned on the infant's head. This has never been done in a systematic way and provides a crucial measure of the replicability of NIRS signals from particular channels in the same infant.[5] Because the precision of repositioning the NIRS probes will be subject to some error, it will be essential to measure this error with an objective alignment system that is referenced to external landmarks on the infant's skull. In addition, there are systems that can provide a detailed measure of where the NIRS probes are located with respect to the infant's *brain* rather than relying on skull landmarks. A structural MRI of a sleeping infant provides a 3D image of the skull and the brain that can be mapped, in a subsequent testing session, with a stylus that documents the skull landmarks and the location of the NIRS probes on the skull (see https://www.rogue-research.com/TMS/Brainsight2.html).

Concluding remarks

The present article has provided a summary of findings obtained from infants using NIRS. It is both exciting and sobering to review these findings. The excitement comes from the potential of a new noninvasive neuroimaging technique that does not require rigid head stabilization, has no acoustic noise, and can be purchased for a fraction of the cost of an MRI system. The sobering nature of this review is that the application of NIRS to address fundamental questions in perceptual, cognitive, and language development is still in the very early stages. Not only have very few studies assessed the reliability of NIRS activations to highly constrained (predictable) stimulus events, but the "value added" of NIRS data for understanding the organization of the infant brain or the mechanisms that lead to changes in behaviour has so far been minimal. There are, however, improvements on the horizon that raise the prospect of solving many of the current limitations of NIRS research with infants, including the advances summarized in the previous section of this review.

It is with these encouraging prospects in mind that we conclude by describing a particularly compelling application of NIRS that addressed a fundamental question of functional brain organization. The parents of deaf children, over 90% of whom are hearing and therefore do not use a sign language, seek to restore auditory function in their child. It is now quite common for deaf children to receive a surgically implanted device that converts sound into electrical signals and transduces those signals onto the auditory nerve. These children who receive a cochlear implant often gain the ability to sense sound, but less reliably gain the full appreciation of speech, with highly variable language outcomes even after years of postimplant training (Peterson, Pisoni, & Miyamoto, 2010). A key question is whether the implant, even if it stimulates the auditory nerve, transmits those peripheral neural signals to

[5]Tsuzuki et al. (2007) provided evidence, in adults, that external skull landmarks provide a reasonable alternative to structural MRI data for transforming NIRS probe locations to MNI space.

the auditory cortex. The implant precludes the use of fMRI to answer this question because the implant poses a safety hazard in the high magnetic field. Thus, NIRS provides an alternative neuroimaging method to address this question. Sevy et al. (2010) provided compelling evidence that young cochlear implant patients, even in the first few hours after the implant has been activated, receive inputs to auditory cortex. Moreover, by using bilateral NIRS probes, they discovered that the dominant cortical activation was in the ipsilateral temporal cortex. This finding runs counter to the expectation that the primary auditory pathway is contralateral, and it may change the accepted strategy of implanting the right ear because it is contralateral to the left hemisphere, which is language dominant. This study illustrates the power of using NIRS to address a fundamental question, and we can hope that such clear hypothesis-driven studies serve as a model for future NIRS studies of infants and children.

REFERENCES

Anderson, A. W., Marois, R., Colson, E. R., Peterson, B. S., Duncan, C. C., Ehrenkranz, R. A., et al. (2001). Neonatal auditory activation detected by functional magnetic resonance imaging. *Magnetic Resonance Imaging, 19,* 1–5.

Aoyama, S., Toshima, T., Saito, Y., Konishi, N., Motoshige, K., Ishikawa, N., et al. (2010). Maternal breast milk odour induces frontal lobe activation in neonates: A NIRS study. *Early Human Development, 86,* 541–545.

Arimitsu, T., Uchida-Ota, M., Yagihashi, T., Kojima, S., Watanabe, S., Hokuto, I., et al. (2011). Functional hemisphere specialization in processing phonemic and prosodic auditory changes in neonates. *Frontiers in Psychology, 2*(202). doi:10.3389/fpsyg.2011.00202

Ashby, F. G. (2011). *Statistical analysis of fMRI data.* Cambridge, MA: MIT Press.

Aslin, R. N. (2007). What's in a look? *Developmental Science, 10,* 48–53.

Aslin, R. N., & Fiser, J. (2005). Methodological challenges for understanding cognitive development in infants. *Trends in Cognitive Sciences, 9,* 92–98.

Benjamini, Y., & Hochberg, Y. (1995). Controlling the false discovery rate: A practical and powerful approach to multiple testing. *Journal of the Royal Statistical Society, Series B, 57,* 289–300.

Blasi, A., Mercune, E., Lloyd-Fox, S., Thomson, A., Brammer, M., Sauter, D., et al. (2011). Early specialization for voice and emotion processing in the infant brain. *Current Biology, 21,* 1220–1224.

Bortfeld, H., Fava, E., & Boas, D. A. (2009). Identifying cortical lateralization of speech processing in infants using near-infrared spectroscopy. *Developmental Neuropsychology, 34,* 52–65.

Bortfeld, H., Wruck, E., & Boas, D. A. (2007). Assessing infants' cortical response to speech using near-infrared spectroscopy. *NeuroImage, 34,* 407–415.

Boynton, G. M., Engel, S. A., Glover, G. H., & Heeger, D. J. (1996). Linear systems analysis of functional magnetic resonance imaging in human V1. *Journal of Neuroscience, 16,* 4207–4221.

Brainsight 2 [Apparatus and software]. (2012). Montreal, Quebec, Canada: Rogue Research.

Cantlon, J. F., Brannon, E. M., Carter, E. J., & Pelphrey, K. A. (2006). Functional imaging of numerical processing in adults and four-year-old children. *PLoS Biology, 4*(5), e125.

Cooper, R. J., Gagnon, L., Goldenholz, D., Boas, D. A., & Greve, D. N. (2012). The utility of near-infrared spectroscopy in the regression of low-frequency physiological noise from functional magnetic resonance imaging data. *NeuroImage, 59,* 3128–3138.

Dehaene-Lambertz, G., Dehaene, S., & Hertz-Pannier, L. (2002). Functional neuroimaging of speech perception in infants. *Science, 298,* 2013–2015.

Erberich, S. G., Panigrahy, A., Friedlich, P., Seri, I., Nelson, M. D., & Gilles, F. (2006). Somatosensory lateralization in the newborn brain. *NeuroImage, 29,* 155–161.

Friston, K. J., Holmes, A. P., Worsley, K. J., Poline, J. B., Frith, C. D., & Frackowiak, R. S. J. (1995). Statistical parametric maps in functional imaging: A general linear approach. *Human Brain Mapping, 2,* 189–210.

Gervain, J., Berent, I., & Werker, J. F. (2012). Binding at birth: The newborn brain detects identity relations and sequential position in speech. *Journal of Cognitive Neuroscience, 24,* 564–574.

Gervain, J., Macagno, F., Cogoi, S., Pena, M., & Mehler, J. (2008). The neonate brain detects speech structure. *Proceedings of the National Academy of Sciences of the USA, 105,* 14222–14227.

Gervain, J., Mehler, J., Werker, J. F., Nelson, C. A., Csibra, G., Lloyd-Fox, S., et al. (2011). Near-infrared spectroscopy: A report from the McDonnell Infant Methodology Consortium. *Developmental Cognitive Neuroscience, 1,* 22–46.

Grossmann, T., Johnson, M. H., Lloyd-Fox, S., Blasi, A., Deligianni, F., Elwell, C., et al. (2008). *Proceedings of the Royal Society B, Biological Sciences* (Vol. 275, pp. 2803–2811).

Hespos, S. J., Ferry, A. L., Cannistraci, C., Gore, J., & Park, S. (2009). Optical imaging on human infants. In A. W. Roe (Ed.), *Imaging the brain with optical methods* (pp. 159–176). New York, NY: Springer.

Homae, F., Watanabe, H., Nakano, T., Asakawa, K., & Taga, G. (2006). The right hemisphere of sleeping infant perceives sentential prosody. *Neuroscience Research, 54,* 276–280.

Homae, F., Watanabe, H., Nakano, T., & Taga, G. (2007). Prosodic processing in the developing brain. *Neuroscience Research, 59,* 29–39.

Homae, F., Watanabe, H., Nakano, T., & Taga, G. (2011). Large-scale brain networks underlying language acquisition in early infancy. *Frontiers in Psychology, 2*(93). doi:10.3389/fpsyg.2011.00093

Homae, F., Watanabe, H., Otobe, T., Nakano, T., Go, T., Konishi, Y., et al. (2010). Development of global cortical networks in early infancy. *Journal of Neuroscience, 30,* 4877–4882.

Hyde, D. C., Boas, D. A., Blair, C., & Carey, S. (2010). Near-infrared spectroscopy shows right parietal specialization for number in pre-verbal infants. *NeuroImage, 53,* 647–652.

Jobsis, F. F. (1977). Noninvasive infrared monitoring of cerebral and myocardial oxygen sufficiency and circulatory parameters. *Science, 198,* 1264–1267.

Karen, T., Morren, G., Haensse, D., Bauschatz, A. S., Bucher, H. U., & Wolf, M. (2008). Hemodynamic response to visual stimulation in newborn infants using functional near-infrared spectroscopy. *Human Brain Mapping, 29,* 453–460.

Karmiloff-Smith, A. (2010). Neuroimaging of the developing brain: Taking "developing" seriously. *Human Brain Mapping, 31,* 934–941.

Koh, P. H., Glaser, D. E., Flandin, G., Kiebel, S., Butterworth, B., Maki, A., et al. (2007). Functional optical signal analysis: A software tool for near-infrared spectroscopy data processing incorporating statistical parametric mapping. *Journal of Biomedical Optics, 12,* 064010.

Kotilahti, K., Nissila, I., Huotilainen, M., Makela, R., Gavrielides, N., Noponen, T., et al. (2005). Bilateral hemodynamic responses to auditory stimulation in newborn infants. *Neuroreport, 16,* 1373–1377.

Kotilahti, K., Nissila, I., Nasi, T., Lipiainen, L., Naponen, T., Merilainen, P., et al. (2010). Hemodynamic responses to speech and music in newborn infants. *Human Brain Mapping, 31,* 595–603.

Kusaka, T., Isobe, K., Miki, T., Ueno, M., Koyano, K., Nakamura, S., et al. (2011). Functional lateralization of sensorimotor cortex in infants measured using multichannel near-infrared spectroscopy. *Pediatric Research, 69,* 430–435.

Larson-Prior, L. J., Zempel, J. M., Nolan, T. S., Prior, F. W., Snyder, A. Z., & Raichle, M. E. (2009). Cortical network functional connectivity in the descent to sleep. *Proceedings of the National Academy of Sciences, USA, 106,* 4489–4494.

Liao, S. M., Gregg, N. M., White, B. R., Zeff, B. W., Bjerkaas, K. A., Inder, T. E., et al. (2010). Neonatal hemodynamic response to visual cortex activity: High-density near-infrared spectroscopy study. *Journal of Biomedical Optics, 15,* 026101.

Lloyd-Fox, S., Blasi, A., & Elwell, C. E. (2010). Illuminating the developing brain: The past, present and future of functional near infrared spectroscopy. *Neuroscience and Biobehavioral Reviews, 34,* 269–284.

Lloyd-Fox, S., Blasi, A., Everdell, N., Elwell, C. E., & Johnson, M. H. (2011). Selective cortical mapping of biological motion processing in young infants. *Journal of Cognitive Neuroscience, 23,* 2521–2532.

Lloyd-Fox, S., Blasi, A., Volein, A., Everdell, N., Elwell, C. E., & Johnson, M. H. (2009). Social perception in infancy: A near-infrared spectroscopy study. *Child Development, 80,* 986–999.

May, L., Byers-Heinlein, K., Gervain, J., & Werker, J. F. (2011). Language and the newborn brain: Does prenatal language experience shape the neonate neural response to speech? *Frontiers in Psychology, 2*(222). doi:10.3389/fpsyg.2011.00222

Meek, J. H., Firbank, M., Elwell, C. E., Atkinson, J., Braddick, O., & Wyatt, J. S. (1998). Regional hemodynamic responses to visual stimulation in awake infants. *Pediatric Research, 43,* 840–843.

Minagawa-Kawai, Y., Cristia, A., & Dupoux, E. (2011). Cerebral lateralization and early speech acquisition: A developmental scenario. *Developmental Cognitive Neuroscience, 1,* 217–232.

Minagawa-Kawai, Y., Cristia, A., Vendelin, I., Cabrol, D., & Dupoux, E. (2011). Assessing signal-driven

mechanisms in neonates: Brain responses to temporally and spectrally different sounds. *Frontiers in Psychology*, *2*(135). doi:10.3389/fpsyg.2011.00135
Minagawa-Kawai, Y., Matsuoka, S., Dan, I., Naoi, N., Nakamura, K., & Kojima, S. (2009). Prefrontal activation associated with social attachment: Facial-emotion recognition in mothers and infants. *Cerebral Cortex*, *19*, 284–292.
Minagawa-Kawai, Y., Mori, K., Naoi, N., & Kojima, S. (2007). Neural attunement processes in infants during the acquisition of a language-specific phonemic contrast. *Journal of Neuroscience*, *27*, 315–321.
Minagawa-Kawai, Y., van der Lely, H., Ramus, F., Sato, Y., Mazuka, R., & Dupoux, E. (2011). Optical brain imaging reveals general auditory and language-specific processing in early infant development. *Cerebral Cortex*, *21*, 254–261.
Nakano, T., Watanabe, H., Homae, F., & Taga, G. (2009). Prefrontal cortical involvement in young infants' analysis of novelty. *Cerebral Cortex*, *19*, 455–463.
Obrig, H., Rossi, S., Telkemeyer, S., & Wartenburger, I. (2010). From acoustic segmentation to language processing: Evidence from optical imaging. *Frontiers in Neuroenergetics*, *2*(13). doi:10.3389/fnene.2010.00013
Pena, M., Maki, A., Kovacic, D., Dehaene-Lambertz, G., Koizumi, H., Bouquet, F., et al. (2003). Sounds and silence: An optical topography study of language recognition at birth. *Proceedings of the National Academy of Sciences of the USA*, *100*, 11702–11705.
Peterson, N. R., Pisoni, D. B., & Miyamoto, R. T. (2010). Cochlear implants and spoken language processing abilities: Review and assessment of the literature. *Restorative Neurology and Neuroscience*, *28*, 237–250.
Plichta, M. M., Heinzel, S., Ehlis, A.-C., Pauli, P., & Fallgatter, A. J. (2007). Model-based analysis of rapid event-related functional near-infrared spectroscopy (NIRS) data: A parametric validation study. *NeuroImage*, *35*, 625–634.
Raichle, M. E., & Snyder, A. Z. (2007). A default mode of brain function: A brief history of an evolving idea. *NeuroImage*, *37*, 1083–1090.
Redcay, E., Haist, F., & Courchesne, E. (2008). Functional neuroimaging of speech perception during a pivotal period in language acquisition. *Developmental Science*, *11*, 237–252.
Saager, R. B., & Berger, A. J. (2005). Direct characterization and removal of interfering absorption trends in two-layer turbid media. *Journal of the Optical Society of America, A*, *22*, 1874–1882.
Saager, R. B., & Berger, A. J. (2008). Measurement of layer-like hemodynamic trends in scalp and cortex: Implications for physiological baseline suppression in functional near-infrared spectroscopy. *Journal of Biomedical Optics*, *13*, 034017.
Saager, R. B., Telleri, N. L., & Berger, A. J. (2011). Two-detector corrected near infrared spectroscopy (C-NIRS) detects hemodynamic activation responses more robustly than single-detector NIRS. *NeuroImage*, *55*, 1679–1685.
Saito, Y., Kondo, T., Aoyama, S., Fukumoto, R., Konishi, N., Kakamura, K., et al. (2007). The function of the frontal lobe in neonates for response to a prosodic voice. *Early Human Development*, *83*, 225–230.
Sakatani, K., Chen, S., Lichty, W., Zuo, H., & Wuang, Y. (1999). Cerebral blood oxygenation changes induced by auditory stimulation in newborn infants measured by near-infrared spectroscopy. *Early Human Development*, *55*, 229–236.
Sato, H., Hirabayashi, Y., Tsubokura, H., Kanai, M., Ashida, T., Konishi, I., et al. (in press). Cerebral hemodynamics in newborn infants exposed to speech sounds: A whole-head optical topography study. *Human Brain Mapping*, Advance online publication. doi:10.1002/hbm.21350.
Sato, Y., Sogabe, Y., & Mazuka, R. (2009). Development of hemispheric specialization for lexical pitch-accent in Japanese infants. *Journal of Cognitive Neuroscience*, *22*, 2503–2513.
Sevy, A., Bortfeld, H., Huppert, T., Beauchamp, M., Tonini, R., & Oghalai, J. (2010). Neuroimaging with near-infrared spectroscopy demonstrates speech-evoked activity in the auditory cortex of deaf children following cochlear implantation. *Hearing Research*, *270*, 39–47.
Taga, G., & Asakawa, K. (2007). Selectivity and localization of cortical response to auditory and visual stimulation in awake infants aged 2 to 4 months. *NeuroImage*, *36*, 1246–1252.
Taga, G., Asakawa, K., Maki, A., Konishi, Y., & Koizumi, H. (2003). Brain imaging in awake infants by near-infrared optical topography. *Proceedings of the National Academy of Sciences of the USA*, *100*, 10722–10727.
Taga, G., Watanabe, H., & Homae, F. (2011). Spatiotemporal properties of cortical haemodynamic response to auditory stimuli in sleeping infants revealed by multi-channel near-infrared

spectroscopy. *Philosophical Transactions of the Royal Society A: Mathematical, Physical & Engineering Sciences, 369,* 4495–4511.

Telkemeyer, S., Rossi, S., Koch, S. P., Nierhaus, T., Steinbrink, J., Poeppel, D., et al. (2009). Sensitivity of newborn auditory cortex to the temporal structure of sounds. *Journal of Neuroscience, 29,* 14726–14733.

Telkemeyer, S., Rossi, S., Nierhaus, T., Steinbrink, J., Obrig, H., & Wartenburger, I. (2011). Acoustic processing of temporally modulated sounds in infants: Evidence from a combined near-infrared spectroscopy and EEG study. *Frontiers in Psychology, 2*(62). doi:10.3389/fpsyg.2011.00062

Tsuzuki, D., Jurcak, V., Singh, A. K., Okamoto, M., Watanabe, E., & Dan, I. (2007). Virtual spatial registration of stand-alone functional NIRS data to MNI space. *NeuroImage, 34,* 1506–1518.

Turk-Browne, N. B., Scholl, B. J., & Chun, M. M. (2008). Babies and brains: Habituation in infant cognition and functional neuroimaging. *Frontiers in Human Neuroscience, 2,* 16. doi:10.3389/neuro.09.016.2008

Wagner, J. B., Fox, S. E., Tager-Flusberg, H., & Nelson, C. A. (2011). Neural processing of repetition and non-repetition grammars in 7- and 9-month-old infants. *Frontiers in Psychology, 2*(168). doi:10.3389/fpsyg.2011.00168

Wandell, B. A., Dumoulin, S. O., & Brewer, A. A. (2007). Visual field maps in visual cortex. *Neuron, 56,* 366–383.

Watanabe, H., Homae, F., Nakano, T., & Taga, G. (2008). Functional activation in diverse regions of the developing brain of human infants. *NeuroImage, 43,* 346–357.

White, B. R., & Culver, J. P. (2010). Phase-encoded retinotopy as an evaluation of diffuse optical neuroimaging. *NeuroImage, 49,* 568–577.

Wilcox, T., Bortfeld, H., Woods, R., Wruck, E., Armstrong, J., & Boas, D. A. (2009). Hemodynamic changes in the infant cortex during the processing of featural and spatiotemporal information. *Neuropsychologia, 47,* 657–662.

Wilcox, T., Bortfeld, H., Woods, R., Wruck, E., & Boas, D. A. (2005). Using near-infrared spectroscopy to assess neural activation during object processing in infants. *Journal of Biomedical Optics, 10,* 011010.

Wilcox, T., Bortfeld, H., Woods, R., Wruck, E., & Boas, D. A. (2008). Hemodynamic response to featural changes in the occipital and inferior temporal cortex in infants: A preliminary methodological exploration. *Developmental Science, 11,* 361–370.

Wilcox, T., Haslup, J. A., & Boas, D. A. (2010). Dissociation of processing of featural and spatiotemporal information in the infant cortex. *NeuroImage, 53,* 1256–1263.

Zaramella, P., Freato, F., Amigoni, A., Salvadori, S., Marangoni, P., Suppjei, A., et al. (2001). Brain auditory activation measured by near-infrared spectroscopy (NIRS) in neonates. *Pediatric Research, 49,* 213–219.

Zeff, B. W., White, B. R., Dehghani, H., Schlaggar, B. L., & Culver, J. P. (2007). Retinotopic mapping of adult human visual cortex with high-density diffuse optical tomography. *Proceedings of the National Academy of Sciences of the USA, 104,* 12169–12174.

The maps problem and the mapping problem: Two challenges for a cognitive neuroscience of speech and language

David Poeppel

Department of Psychology, New York University, New York, NY, USA

Research on the brain basis of speech and language faces theoretical and empirical challenges. Most current research, dominated by imaging, deficit-lesion, and electrophysiological techniques, seeks to identify regions that underpin aspects of language processing such as phonology, syntax, or semantics. The emphasis lies on localization and spatial characterization of function. The first part of the paper deals with a practical challenge that arises in the context of such a research programme. This *maps problem* concerns the extent to which spatial information and localization can satisfy the explanatory needs for perception and cognition. Several areas of investigation exemplify how the neural basis of speech and language is discussed in those terms (regions, streams, hemispheres, networks). The second part of the paper turns to a more troublesome challenge, namely how to formulate the formal links between neurobiology and cognition. This principled problem thus addresses the relation between the primitives of cognition (here speech, language) and neurobiology. Dealing with this *mapping problem* invites the development of linking hypotheses between the domains. The cognitive sciences provide granular, theoretically motivated claims about the structure of various domains (the "cognome"); neurobiology, similarly, provides a list of the available neural structures. However, *explanatory* connections will require crafting of computationally explicit linking hypotheses at the right level of abstraction. For both the practical *maps problem* and the principled *mapping problem*, developmental approaches and evidence can play a central role in the resolution.

Keywords: Localization; Computation; Cognitive neuroscience; Linking hypothesis.

Research on the neurobiological foundations of cognition, in general, and speech and language processing, in particular, faces a variety of interesting empirical and theoretical challenges. Two problems are discussed here, a practical one and a principled one. The practical problem has to do with how we should conceive of (one of) the main forms of data that lie at the basis of cognitive neuroscience: maps of the brain and maps of brain activation. This *maps problem* concerns the extent to which spatial information about brain activity provides satisfactory descriptions of the neural basis of perception and cognition. The techniques that currently dominate the field (whether spatially specialized, such as fMRI, or temporally specialized, such as MEG) predominantly characterize

Correspondence should be addressed to David Poeppel, Department of Psychology, NYU, 6 Washington Place, New York, NY 10003, USA. (E-mail: david.poeppel@nyu.edu).

http://www.psypress.com/cogneuropsychology http://dx.doi.org/10.1080/02643294.2012.710600

data in terms of spatial attributes (such as local topographic organization like retinotopy or somatotopy, processing streams like dorsal versus ventral pathways, or networks of interconnected brain regions). Thinking and talking about brain activity in spatial terms is very intuitive (spot A "does"/houses/executes function X, spot B does Y, etc.), is often more or less correct (at some level of description), and has captured both the professional the popular imaginations. Visually compelling publications such as *Images of Mind* (Posner & Raichle, 1997), *Mapping the Mind* (Carter & Frith, 2000), or *Portraits of the Mind* (Schoonover, 2010) elegantly summarize the successes of the research programme. They also clearly reflect (in their titles as well as their substantive content) the deeply held, implicit presupposition that making a visual, spatial map of mental faculties is a critical step in a proper explanatory account of the brain basis of psychological function. This stance is likely to be correct *in part*, but at best will reflect an incomplete understanding; uncontroversially, localization and spatial mapping are not explanation (e.g. Poeppel, 2008). In a typical cognitive neuroscience study of speech, lexical, or sentence-level processing, participants will engage in some naturalistic or artificial task while their brain activity is monitored. The analyses show that some area or areas are selectively modulated, and it is then argued that activation of a given area underpins, say, phonological processing or lexical access or syntax. Although this superficial characterization underestimates the state of the field, it is fair to say that the canonical results—very much at the center of current research—are correlational; that is to say, systematic relations consistently occur between brain areas and some functions that reappear across studies, but we have no *explanation*, no sense in which properties of neuronal circuits that we understand account for the execution of function. How to proceed? I suggest that even high-resolution data from (existing or to be developed) new techniques will remain inadequate unless we decompose the cognitive tasks under investigation into computational primitives that can be related to local brain structure and function, in a sense instrumentalizing the computational theory of mind (e.g., Pinker, 1997) more aggressively. We will need to seek theoretically well-motivated, computationally explicit, and biologically realistic characterizations of function to take the work to the next level. Some of the issues that arise in this central part of cognitive neuroscience, making maps, are discussed in the next section, with a view towards how maps implicate functions, and how a developmental perspective can sharpen the issues and help construct productive links between structural description and functional analysis.

The principled problem deals with the "alignment" between the putative primitives of cognition and neurobiology and constitutes a more abstract challenge. Addressing this *mapping problem*—what is the relationship between the "parts list" of cognition and the "parts list" of neurobiology?—is considerably more difficult than it might seem at first, ultimately requiring the development of appropriate linking hypotheses between the different domains of study. I use the expression *mapping* here not to refer to the assignment of putative linguistic or psychological function to brain areas, be they distributed or localized, microscopic or macroscopic. Rather, I mean by mapping the investigation of the (ultimately necessary) *formal relations* between two sets of hypothesized inventories, the inventory constructed by the language sciences and that constructed by the neurosciences: How do the primitive units of analysis of the cognitive sciences map on to the primitive units of analysis of the neurosciences? The cognitive sciences, including linguistics and psychology, provide detailed analyses of the ontological structure of various domains (call this the "human cognome," i.e. the comprehensive list of elementary mental representations and operations), and neurobiology provides a growing list of the available neural structures. To exemplify, the infrastructure of linguistics—building on formally specified concepts such as *syllable* or *noun phrase* or *discourse representation*—provides a structured body of concepts that permit linguists and psychologists to make a wide range of precise generalizations about knowledge of language that speakers bring to bear, about language acquisition, online language processing, historical change, and so on. Similarly, the infrastructure of the neurosciences—drawing on units of analysis such as *dendrite* or *cortical column* or *long-term potentiation*—captures a variety of structural and functional features of the brain, with profound consequences for the neural basis of cognition and perception. However, how do the hypothesized units of analysis relate? Simple reductionist assumptions cannot even be stated in any sensible way (e.g., "neuron = syllable"). Such alignments may seem potentially pleasing at first glance, but that pleasure subsides quickly if one actually has to develop such a view and do the work of representation and computation. The fact of the matter is that we have very little to no idea as to how the stuff of thought relates to the stuff of brains, in the case of speech and language—and virtually all other cases (Gallistel & King, 2011; Mausfeld, 2012). In the third section, I argue that to link cognition and neurobiology in an explanatory fashion will require the formulation of computationally explicit linking hypotheses at the right level of abstraction. With respect to this principled issue, too, developmental data provide critical insights, for example in specifying the parts lists attributed to the infant from the start (innate, precompiled toolbox) versus the representations and operations argued to be acquired and constructed.

The guiding perspective throughout is that of a Marr-style approach (Marr, 1982). Separating computational, algorithmic, and computational levels of analysis, rather than being anachronistic, will be helpful in better defining the nature of the challenges and pointing to some tentative answers, or at least plausible approaches to possible answers. Cognitive neuroscience has made immense progress in the past 20 years, and the grounds for optimism are justified. However, what constitutes an explanation is rarely addressed. Adapting the position articulated by Marr (and others) on the distinct but tightly yoked levels of description, I suggest that a focus on the algorithmic and representational level can provide a potentially productive perspective in seeking hypotheses that bridge between high-level computational and low-level implementational characterizations.

In the next section, on maps, I outline four types of spatial organization that form the basis for much of contemporary research on the brain basis of speech and language: local regional organization of a given brain region (e.g. "Broca's region"), the notion of processing streams (e.g. "dorsal" versus "ventral" streams), hemispheric asymmetries, and putative networks of connected brain areas. This "brain mapping" programme of research, emphasizing different "functional anatomic units of analysis" ranging from the microscopic to the network level, has been productive and successful and remarkably popular in the public understanding of cognitive neuroscience—but it needs to be considered what the next steps could be to flesh out the promise of specifying such spatial maps. After discussing the issues surrounding the maps problem and suggesting some questions for which developmental evidence can and should play a critical role for progress, I turn to the mapping (or alignment) problem in the third section, developing the argument as to why it is so difficult to establish the principled relations between linguistic or psychological primitives and neurobiological primitives. The paper closes with some tentative suggestions about how one might proceed in a way that could bridge the *maps* and *mapping* problems, endorsing a computational approach that attempts to identify a level of analysis that might facilitate at least the formulation of linking hypotheses.

THE STANDARD RESEARCH STRATEGY IN COGNITIVE NEUROSCIENCE: MAKING MAPS

Defining the spatial layout of brain organization has a long and successful history. In fact, perhaps the first large-scale model of brain organization in systems neuroscience was the so-called "connectionist model" for language based on the seminal insights by Broca (1861) and Wernicke (1874), arguing that there are two localized centers that underpin language production and comprehension

(Geschwind, 1970). (Though this model has been extremely influential to this day, especially in clinical contexts, it is widely accepted that it remains woefully underspecified, from both the linguistic and neurobiological points of view. For discussion, see, e.g., Poeppel & Hickok, 2004; Grodzinsky & Amunts, 2006.) Spatial organization of one form or another has been investigated profitably at many levels of description, from determining (i) at a microscopic level the features that specify local neural analysis within a brain region (e.g., retinotopic mapping in the visual system) to (ii) information processing streams (e.g., the *what* versus *where* systems in vision) to (iii) sophisticated network analyses (Sporns, 2010) that model how distributed regions are connected in support of function and (iv) attempts to understand the human connectome (Seung, 2012); that is, the comprehensive mapping of how all areas are connected, cell by cell: the total wiring diagram of the human brain.

Why does the search for finding a map with local topographic organization induce such yearning in the field? What underlies the seductive appeal of map-making? Maps of one form or another are, of course, on target for sensory and motor systems, revealing fundamental organizational principles that have helped model aspects of perception and motor control. Searching for topographies has been extremely successful in the case of vision (e.g., retinotopic organization of numerous visual areas), in the case of the somatosensory system (the sensory homunculus), widely attested in auditory processing (tonotopic mapping), and so on. So, in a strategic sense, aiming to understand the spatial organization of *cognitive* functions builds on well-established neuroscientific observations.

The study of the visual system has formed the conceptual basis for many aspects of the standard paradigm in cognitive neuroscience. Much of the original work is elegantly summarized in a monograph by David Hubel, one of the chief architects of visual neuroscience: *Eye, Brain, and Vision* (Hubel, 1995). In that domain, it was assumed that the external visual world is represented by decomposition into elementary features (or basis functions) and subsequent composition into higher-order, complex visual representations. (The model of vision espoused is ultimately underspecified and no longer the dominant view; however, it has been a remarkably productive empiricist paradigm.) Local features (e.g., retinal position, edges, luminance) are aggregated along feedforward pathways, leading to the construction of more complex visual representations (e.g., faces, as an obvious example). Three generalizations emerged from this work. First, decades of visual neurophysiology confirm that there is *localization of function*: Neurons and ensembles of neurons perform operations that are regionally specific. Cells in an early visual area such as primary visual cortex (V1) have firing properties that reflect strikingly different receptive field size and response selectivity than cells in a higher order area, say in the infero-temporal cortex. The operations underlying visual decomposition (and composition) are localized and specific. Second, the feedforward pathways along which the visual information is aggregated suggest *hierarchical processing*. Neurons along a processing stream reflect ever more integrated (in space, time) and abstract properties of the external world. Third, there exist *concurrent pathways* for information processing that underlie different larger-scale functions. Originally, these were conceived as "what versus where" streams (Mishkin, Ungerleider, & Macko, 1983); subsequently the discussion has focused on object identification versus action, sensorimotor transformation, and other visual tasks (Goodale & Milner, 1992). Cumulatively, this research on the neurobiological foundations of vision has profoundly influenced the way of asking questions about the neural basis of perception and cognition.

But it is not at all clear how such spatial thinking plausibly extends to cognition, and especially language. Research on the brain basis of language has (implicitly) adopted the approach of vision, going as it were "from the outside in," assuming that sounds (or signs) are analysed in one region, aggregated into morphemes in another, followed by some sequential syntactic processing in yet another region, and so on. In fact, an enormous part of the neuroscience of language literature is dedicated to functional localization at a very high level, seeking to identify segregated regions for speech perception, phonology, morphology, syntax, semantics, etc. But it is an empirical question whether *any* spatial mapping principles as they appear in sensory systems extend to cognition or language. (Verbs here, nouns there? Phonemeotopy? Spatial distribution of syntactic categories? It is not even clear if such questions can be properly formulated in a theoretically motivated context—although precisely these examples have been discussed in the cognitive neuroscience literature; Pulvermueller, Lutzenberger, & Preissl, 1999; Obleser, Elbert, Lahiri, & Eulitz, 2003; Hillis & Caramazza, 1995.) We have, of course, learned a great deal about the likely functional contribution of certain brain regions (e.g., the superior temporal gyrus), processing streams (e.g., dorsal and ventral streams in speech), hemispherically organized brain structures, and so on. The examples of spatial organization raised in the next sections are intended to be forward looking, hoping to extend what spatial maps of the future might tell us. The point to bear in mind throughout is that the spatial organization of information-processing systems can be a useful, and even necessary, intermediate step in explaining a system, but even fantastic localization of function, incorporating the newest techniques (e.g., multivoxel pattern classification of imaging data or various new approaches to electrophysiology), does not constitute an explanation (Poeppel, 2008). The cartographic imperative does not suffice. It is the mechanistic understanding of the *function* that we seek, and that is not going to be tractable by localization of function and spatial topographic mapping alone.

In what follows, I discuss four examples that describe progress in speech and language research in the context of spatial mapping studies and that exemplify the challenge of relating brain maps to language processing. One lesson from the perspective developed here is that a traditional, quasimodular view (assigning phonology here, syntax there, etc.) cannot succeed, in part because the spatial studies suggest that much more fine-grained computational decomposition of linguistic domains into elementary representations and computations will be required.

Maps of regions

Two examples of brain regions are discussed. First, the canonical language region, Broca's area, is examined. Second, we consider the contribution to language processing of visual areas located early in the processing hierarchy.

Subsequent to the original definition by Broca (the third frontal convolution of the inferior frontal gyrus), the first detailed anatomic analysis of the inferior frontal gyrus was provided by Brodmann (1909). He argued for a division of that region into two or three subregions; typically, the cytoarchitectonically distinct Brodmann areas 44 and 45 are included (some authors also count area 47). Roughly until 2000, generalizations about Broca's area—whether deriving from imaging data or from neuropsychological deficit–lesion correlation data—were made at best at that level of analysis (see Grodzinsky & Amunts, 2006, for an extensive review). That is to say, researchers made claims about "Broca's area"—or on occasion about areas 44 versus 45—in the interpretation of their experimental data. The resolution of the analysis was very rarely higher than that. There exist some interesting connectivity studies (e.g., Anwander, Tittgemeyer, von Cramon, Friederici, & Knösche, 2007), but the functional anatomic characterization has been coarse.

New anatomic techniques (imaging as well as immunocytochemistry) have been applied more recently, and data in an influential paper by Amunts et al. (2010) show that the organization of this one cortical region is much more complex, incorporating, depending how one counts, 5–10 local areas that are distinguished by their cellular properties. Figure 1, taken from from Amunts et al., illustrates the currently hypothesized organization of Broca's region, highlighting anterior and posterior as well as dorsal and ventral subdivisions of known fields and also pointing to the additional opercular and sulcal tissue that has been implicated.

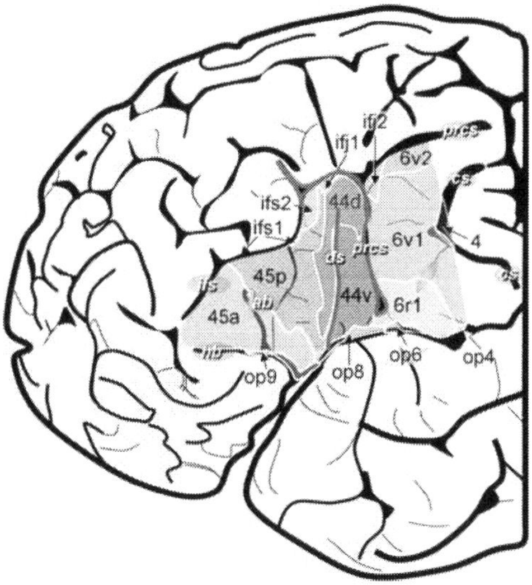

Figure 1. *The organization of Broca's region (Amunts et al., 2010). Reproduced with permission. To view a colour version of this figure, please see the online issue of the Journal.*

Now, it is extremely likely that each subregion performs at least *one* different local computation—after all, they are anatomically distinct. And it is worth remembering that we have not even scratched the surface of possible laminar differences within and across these cortical fields. (Recall that cortex is a sheet of layers, each of which is distinct in terms of cell types, receptor distribution, inputs and outputs, etc. We know from the study of other regions, using animal models, that there are intricate feedforward and feedback projection schemes, canonical cortical circuits (Douglas & Martin, 1991), and a rich infrastructure mediating locally distinct organization.) Suppose then, for the sake of argument, that there are merely five anatomic subdomains in Broca's region, and suppose that each anatomic subdomain supports two types of operation. These are rather conservative numbers, but we must then still identify 10 types of computation. (This is likely to underestimate vastly the actual complexity.) Some of the computations will be applicable to any input data structure (structured linguistic representation, speech signal, or other), since it is well established that Broca's region is engaged by numerous cognitive tasks (Embick & Poeppel, 2006). Other computations may be dedicated to data structures native to the linguistic cognitive system. We know next to nothing about precisely what kind of conditions need to be met to be processed by Broca's region, and in particular by one of the many areas that constitute this part of the inferior frontal cortex.

So how to proceed? If other examples from the central nervous system can serve as a guide (say the retina with its many cell types and associated functions, or primary visual cortex with its ocular dominance columns and orientation pinwheels), Broca's region is likely either (i) to support a number of different types of operations/computations, or (ii) to support similar operations on very different input data structures to yield different outputs. In either case, it is our job to acquire and describe data at a much higher resolution than has been customary to do justice to the known organizational complexity, at least at the level of known anatomic distinctions as shown by Amunts et al. (2010). (Imagine, for comparison, studying visual perception without acknowledging the role primary visual cortex plays in eye-specific and orientation-selective processing; it would be bizarre.) How can this be achieved? In the next decades, we will presumably have access to new techniques with higher spatial resolving power.

And existing but relatively new analytic techniques (say multivoxel pattern classification in the context of fMRI) also will provide a way to make necessary anatomic distinctions. In the meantime, we will rely on invasive approaches (e.g. Sahin, Pinker, Cash, Schomer, & Halgren, 2009), animal studies (which are, of course, limited in their value with respect to questions of speech and language), and the coarser techniques that we currently use in cognitive neuroscience. But notwithstanding any technical progress, it is quite clear that generalizations of the type "Broca's region supports syntax" or "Broca's region supports hierarchical processing" or "Broca's region underpins verbal working memory" are idealizations or simplifications that are not just insufficient but possibly misleading. What appears to be required is a much finer decomposition, and the question is what the most appropriate level of decomposition might be. This is an issue discussed in the context of the *mapping problem* below, but the challenges of the *maps problem* already point to the nature of the matter.

In acknowledging the architectural complexity of Broca's region as depicted in Figure 1, it becomes clear that the classical model of brain and language—Wernicke's region (e.g., for comprehension), Broca's region (e.g., for production), and the arcuate fasciculus connecting them—must be abandoned (see Poeppel & Hickok, 2004 for discussion). Virtually any angle from which one examines the classical model (linguistic, psycholinguistic, neurobiological, computational) undermines its utility.

Next, let us turn to another brain region, occipital cortex, and a different type of "local region" issue. The early visual areas are not typically associated with language processing, but recent research reveals how processing linguistic materials implicates very early visual regions and how language experience shapes early visual processing. Contrary to intuition, the data from neurophysiology suggest that even unquestionably domain-general regions such as early visual cortex participate in rather abstract aspects of processing, not just the superficial, feedforward perceptual analysis of input signals. To be clear: It is not surprising that visual areas play a role in processing visually presented language. There exist, of course, relations between linguistic representations and sensory representations in vision (text), but also in hearing (speech), and touch (Braille). At stake is, rather, whether the visual activations observed in some recent studies can help illuminate the computational subroutines and constitutive representations that are invoked during language processing. The relevant concept that connects the studies is predictive processing.

How does language processing generate neural activity in early visual areas? Unlike Broca's region, early visual areas are decidedly not counted among the typical language areas. Yet recent MEG studies by Dikker, Pylkkanen, and colleagues show that syntactic and lexical–semantic cues in the input affect neural activity in occipital cortex between 100 and 130 ms—that is to say, in very early visual areas (Dikker & Pylkkänen, 2011; Dikker, Rabagliati, Farmer, & Pylkkänen, 2010; Dikker, Rabagliati, & Pylkkänen, 2009). These authors experimented with expected versus unexpected word *categories* (syntactic predictions) in sentential contexts and showed enhanced activity in visual cortex by 120 ms. Similarly, lexical–semantic predictions affected early visual processing, again by 100 ms. The authors interpret these findings, plausibly, in the context of predictive models of language processing: The brain generates (syntactic, semantic) predictions about upcoming input whenever any prediction is possible; some of these predictions might be actualized as form-based estimates available to sensory areas (say, like an orthographic or even more basic code). In other words, these regions are not language areas but do reflect consequences of the predictive nature of online language processing.

A different type of predictive effect, one driven by linguistic experience and reflecting rather profound developmental plasticity, is demonstrated in electrophysiological results by Almeida, Poeppel, & Corina (2012). They studied the MEG responses in visual cortex elicited by possible and impossible gestures in signers and non-signers. Both subject populations showed completely canonical responses to faces and inverted faces. However, when viewing signs and gestures, although both groups were able to detect carefully crafted biological anomalies in the gestures, the congenitally deaf signers showed marked changes and facilitation (in terms of sensitivity, reaction time, and neural activation). That work provides new evidence that high-level visual–perceptual properties related to human form processing can be detected within the first 100 ms of visual processing—and that this early processing has functional significance. The data show modulatory effects within the vicinity of primary visual cortex (V1), a neural region that historically has been considered to be reactive to only low-level visual properties. The altered response properties are driven by linguistic experience. The findings derive from comparing the visual processing capabilities of normal hearing listeners with profoundly deaf individuals, whose necessary reliance on visual information makes them plausible candidates for significant cortical reorganization of the visual system. Profoundly deaf signers show exquisite sensitivity to the detection of these gestural manipulations, unlike normally hearing subjects. These data suggest that sophisticated, rather abstract visual constraints may be realized remarkably early in sensory processing streams. It is argued that these constraints may be a reflection of the encoding of *linguistic* properties of signed languages, reflecting a visually driven internal forward model for human gestures that recruits even primary visual areas. As in the other examples of visual cortex activation, the interpretation centres on the predictive nature of the language system, whether it is studied in written English or in signed ASL.

In addition to accounts that are motivated by predictive operations in language processing and their consequences for perceptuo-motor activations, as above, there is intriguing imaging evidence for language processing proper being executed in early visual areas, in congenitally blind adults (Bedny, Pascual-Leone, Dodell-Feder, Fedorenko, Saxe, 2011; Bedny & Saxe, this issue). They show that phonological, semantic, and syntactic information is differentially processed in visual cortex in these participants, suggesting that these areas can be recruited in addition to classical areas of the language network. Whatever the properties of the local visual neural circuits are, they can operate over linguistic representations in a way that distinguishes language processing from other tasks, suggesting that the computations that comprise language processing are sufficiently generic to interface with those types of circuit.

What are we to conclude from such examples? Both classical language areas (Broca's region) and putatively domain-general areas (early visual cortex) are implicated in different forms of language task. Critically, it is not just the visual form of the materials that drive the low-level activation. In the cases mentioned here, early visual cortex is (re)organized to reflect sensitivity to high-order properties of high-level category information in one case and human-form-based analysis in the other. In neither case do feedforward analyses account for the patterns; rather, predictive aspects of processing, based on knowledge of language, appear to condition the neural response properties. Similarly, (the subregions of) Broca's region are not just driven by high-level language constructs; relatively low-level discriminations implicate Broca's region as well. Presumably it follows from this discussion of maps of regions that we must decompose linguistic computation into constituent elements that are much finer (and perhaps of a different kind) than we are used to doing. For instance, arguing that a brain region forms the basis for "syntax" or "phonology" fails to capture the computational structure that actually comprises something as richly structured as syntax (which is obviously not monolithic). Surely we will not want to argue that, say, visual cortex "hosts" syntax. But we are then required (as linguists, psychologists, cognitive neuroscientists) to provide an analysis that captures which component of syntactic computation in fact is compatible with what is executed in visual cortex. In the cases sketched out above, aspects of predictive coding that lead to sensorimotor predictions are the likely suspects.

Maps of streams

In vision, the concept of processing streams has been immensely influential in shaping research since the 1980s. The existence of concurrent *what*, *where*, and *how* streams showed how certain large-scale computational challenges (localization, identification, sensorimotor transformation/action–perception linking) could be supported in parallel by streams consisting of hierarchically organized cortical regions. This architecture provided a functional anatomic blueprint for supporting parallel processes as well as the hierarchical elaboration of visual representations within a stream (Goodale & Milner, 1992; Mishkin et al., 1983).

This key idea from systems neuroscience was adopted and adapted for speech and language processing in the past 10 years (Hickok & Poeppel, 2004, 2007; Friederici, 2012; Rauschecker & Scott, 2009). Figure 2 illustrates one such model, constructed to account for a range of phenomena in speech processing. A ventral stream can be considered responsible for supporting the transformation from auditory input to lexical representations. A dorsal stream is primarily critical for sensorimotor transformations. One noteworthy feature, and a clear departure from previous models, is that current data suggest much more bilateral support for speech and language processing than was previously suggested. The ventral stream structures, in particular, are robustly bilateral.

As is true for vision, identifying objects is one fundamental computational challenge in speech perception. The other computational role (in speech), in the sense of Marr, is to provide the infrastructure for production. That is to say, the words we know must be able to make contact with both articulatory representations and auditory representations. The dorsal stream regions appear to host the operations that permit the seamless translation from auditory type (e.g., spectrogram) to articulatory type (e.g., motor code) representations.

Note how both of these computational challenges link to some foundational questions of speech acquisition. If the characterization of such processing streams is on the right track, developmental data will illuminate the role of these structures. For example, consider that the identification of speech sounds and early lexical processing far precedes their articulation. In fact, performance in relatively complex language tasks—such as mapping novel word forms to visual referents, exploiting some remarkably high-level intonational cues—can be documented by six months of age (Shukla, White, & Aslin, 2011). Does that mean that the ventral stream is mature prior to the dorsal stream? More provocatively, does this mean that articulatory information is not causally necessary for the establishment of phonological and lexical representations? Is dorsal stream information merely modulatory? That speech motor information plays an important modulatory role in perception is not under debate; however, data on the development of these processing streams will sharpen the questions about what information is necessary and sufficient for establishing the speech system, in the learner.

Maps of hemispheres: Lateralization of function

Zooming even further out (than regions and streams), arguably the coarsest level of brain mapping is at the level of cerebral lateralization. However, coarse or not, hemispheric asymmetry has been an issue at the very foundation of cognitive neuroscience, and particularly in the context of language processing. Since the very first insights by Broca, Wernicke, Lichtheim, and others, the strong lateralization of "language" processing to the dominant hemisphere has been one of the hallmarks of brain organization.

If the analysis proceeds at the level of "language," as if it were an unanalysed whole, an equivalently coarse biological analysis is commensurate—and well deserved. As soon as one begins to decompose language into its constituent domains and operations, the question of cerebral asymmetry becomes more complicated and nuanced. For example, there is now emerging

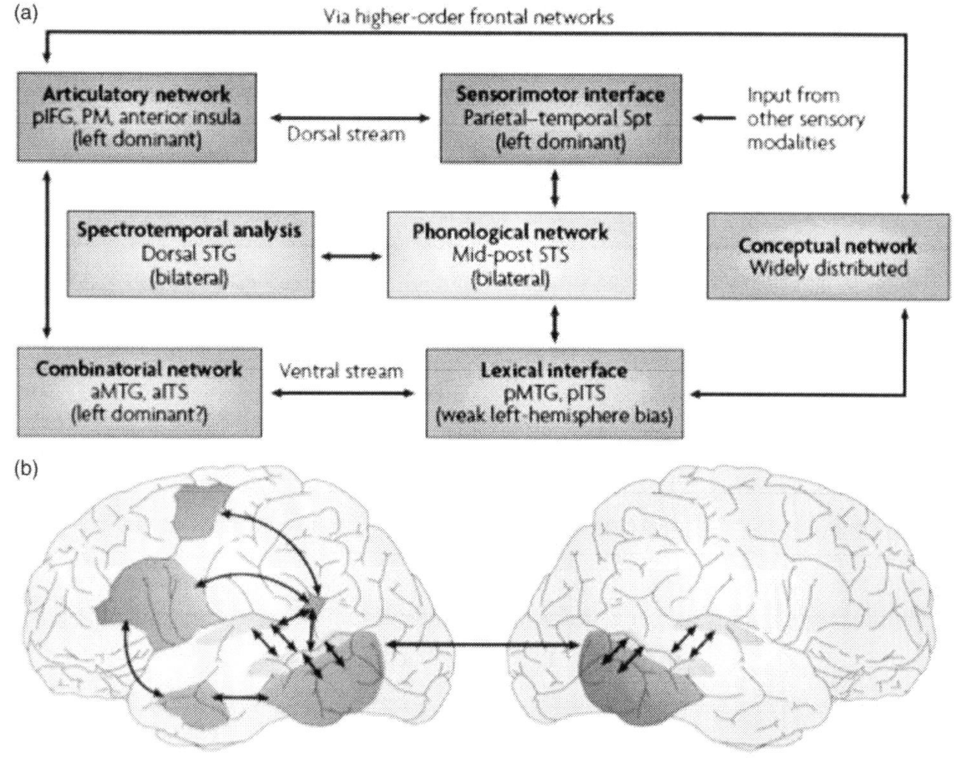

Figure 2. *Dorsal and ventral streams (Hickok & Poeppel, 2007). Reproduced with permission. To view a colour version of this figure, please see the online issue of the Journal.*

consensus that speech perception—roughly the mapping from acoustic waveform to lexical representation—is a bilaterally mediated subroutine of language comprehension (cf. Figure 2). There is also a growing body of evidence to suggest that some aspects of lexical level processing (especially lexical semantics) are executed in both hemispheres (Federmeier, Wlotko, & Meyer, 2008). In contrast, syntactic processing and production appear to be rather lateralized to the dominant hemisphere. To caricature the pattern, the linguistic operations that appear to be robustly associated with left hemisphere mechanisms are "COM–COM–PRE–PRO": combinatorics, composition, prediction, and production. Notice that these terms refer to operations or computations, not to representational primitives. To date there exists no compelling evidence that, say, distinctive features, or morphemes, or roots, or phrasal types are selectively lateralized. Stored linguistic information may be encoded in various cortical regions in the left and right hemispheres, but the computations that operate over the putative representations appear to reflect lateralized specializations.

One area of investigation in which there has been vigorous debate concerns the relative contributions of left and right hemispheres to speech perception proper. Given that speech perception appears to be bilaterally mediated, what are the two sides doing? Are they fully redundant? Completely different? Are there relative specializations?

To get a flavor for some of the recent hypotheses, it is helpful to recall what the perceptual system must ultimately achieve, with speech or other auditory inputs. On one hand, the system must extract sequential items at a time resolution that permits identifying the correct order of parts. Words, in particular, comprise a sequence of relatively short segments, and correctly identifying their order is a prerequisite for recognition (the *pest* versus *pets* issue). The high time resolution necessary to succeed demands neural circuits optimized to integrate information over short time scales (on the order of tens of milliseconds). On the other hand, listeners must be able to analyse and use small frequency deviations, for example in the context of suprasegmental prosody (the *lunch!* versus *lunch?* issue). Such changes demand a high frequency resolution and are often associated with longer time constants. Again, neural circuitry must be responsive to slower time constants and high spectral sensitivity. The output of both types of perceptual analysis must be in a form that can interface with the language system—let us say for the sake of argument, lexical representations.

It has been suggested, in the context of two slightly different but closely related theories (Poeppel, 2003; Zatorre, Belin, & Penhune, 2002), that right hemisphere auditory mechanisms show a higher sensitivity to spectral change and are optimized for longer time constants, whereas left lateralized mechanisms may reflect better temporal resolving power. The spectral versus temporal theory by Zatorre and colleagues and the asymmetric sampling in time (AST) theory by Poeppel appeal to slightly different attributes of cortical neurons, but the models by and large agree that some type of split must be performed (Zatorre & Gandour, 2008). It is fair to say that there is emerging consensus about right hemisphere properties. Whether the left hemisphere is optimized for rapid temporal integration or short temporal sampling remains quite controversial (e.g., McGettigan & Scott, 2012). To test whether such asymmetries were *intrinsic* properties of the auditory system (and not just associated with processing overt stimuli), Giraud and colleagues (2007) recorded concurrent EEG and fMRI data while subjects were resting (no stimulus input). They filtered the EEG data into bands commensurate with the time scales of interest (~theta, ~gamma) and used that electrophysiological pattern (convolved with the hemodynamic response function) to query the fMRI data. In two separate studies, the same lateral asymmetry was observed: The higher modulation rate gamma band responses correlated with left-hemisphere auditory structures, the lower rate theta responses with the right auditory cortex (Figure 3). These data demonstrate that *there exists some intrinsic asymmetry such that auditory neuronal ensembles "hear" the world at different time scales simultaneously*. This (implementational) asymmetry provides the basis for the (algorithmic) multitime resolution approach that solves the (computational) integration–resolution tension for auditory signals.

Maps of the whole network

Recently, the neurosciences have witnessed substantial enthusiasm for trying to map across local as well as distant areas, or even the entire brain, using increasingly sophisticated network analyses (e.g. Sporns, 2010), and building on the new techniques and their improved ability to reveal connections at both fine and coarse scales. The appetite for this type of work culminates in connectomics (Seung, 2011), the presupposition of which is that understanding all the connections will lead to understanding of how the mind works.

Attempting to map the connections of the brain is, surely, a laudable goal. What lies behind this surge in research effort? There are at least two strands of work that fuel the desire to map everything—and connect everything. One motivating factor presumably derives from the remarkable insights gleaned from the cutting-edge techniques in neuroscience. *Two-photon microscopy* (Homma et al., 2009) and *optogenetics* (Yizhar, Fenno, Davidson, Mogri, & Deisseroth, 2011) are generating stunning new data on local circuitry and connectivity. These are, it should go without saying, not techniques easily applied to undergraduates or babies ... They are, however, unveiling in animal preparations obscenely high-resolution views on the structure and function of small local regions of central nervous system. If it is possible to map local circuits with such clarity—and, indeed, such aesthetic beauty—then it stands to reason that it would be exciting to scale up such

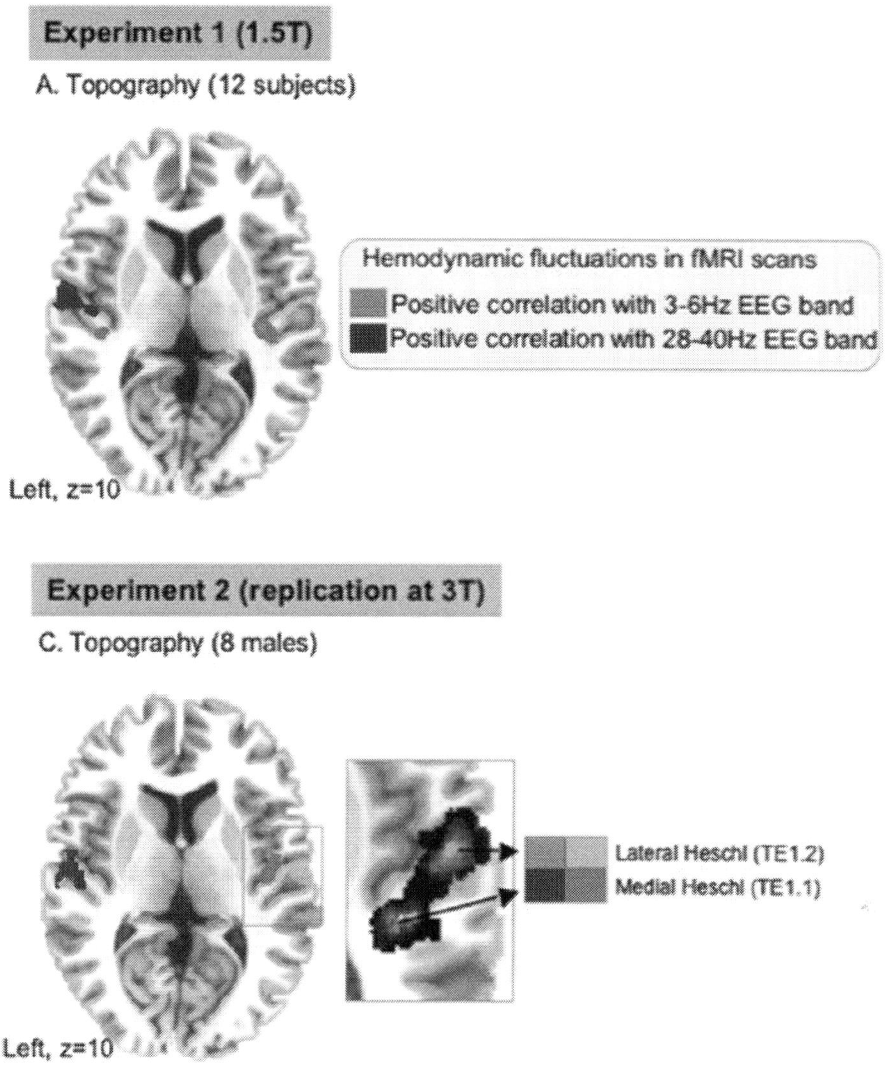

Figure 3. *FMRI experiments (Giraud et al. 2007). Reprinted from* Neuron, 56*(6), Anne-Lise Giraud, Andreas Kleinschmidt, David Poeppel, Torben E. Lund, Richard S. J. Frackowiak & Helmut Laufs, Endogenous cortical rhythms determine cerebral specialization for speech perpception and prodcution, pp. 1127–1134, Copyright 2007, with permission from Elsevier. To view a colour version of this figure, please see the online issue of the Journal.*

approaches to whole brains. A second motivating factor appears to lie in the belief that acquiring enormous amounts of data and mining them statistically will yield new types of insight. There is an unending thirst for more and more data (the same cannot be said for more and more theory) (for an engaging perspective on the problem of data collecting versus theory constructing, in physics and in linguistics, see Weinberg, 2009 and Chomsky, 2000, respectively). But beyond being numerically awesome, will a comprehensive map, the connectome of the human brain, form the basis for the explanation of the human mind? Will the wiring diagram suffice? It seems unlikely. For example, the worm *C. elegans* has a nervous system that is completely known and described, yet our understanding of the function is embarrassingly inadequate (Bargmann, 1993).

It is therefore possible that that even something as sophisticated and data-driven as the connectome will be at best an intermediate step—unless we also make serious, theory-driven progress on the cognome (the specification of the representational and computational parts list of human cognition) and function. Genomics has been a triumph of computational biology in terms of capturing something truly numerically awesome, but its real utility won't be revealed until we understand the *coding* at a much more comprehensive level (including, say, the proteome).

In conclusion, can making maps or defining topography ever meet the criterion of explanatory adequacy? Spatial maps are not explanations, so there is an important ingredient missing, a detailed functional analysis. We need to begin to address the difficult link between maps and computation. This presumably requires computational theories of a certain granularity; that is to say, what is localized is computations for which a certain circuit is specialized (perhaps "canonical computations," as recently discussed by Carandini, 2012). The maps we make will therefore be maps of computations.

The maps problem and developmental data

A variety of developmental questions intersect with the map perspective outlined above (admittedly, from the naïve point of view of a nondevelopmentalist). I describe just three in brief below, focusing on data that speak to three of the four map types. However, it is worth emphasizing that data collection in a developmental context will also not suffice without theory building. In particular, computational theories will provide the most useful framework for addressing the development of the cognitive and neural foundations of perception and cognition (Aslin & Fiser, 2005).

Figure 1 depicts the organization of the adult Broca's region subsequent to normal language acquisition. An obvious question is whether the infant brain is similarly structured. More specifically, are such cytoarchitectural subdivisions consequences of the acquisition of speech and language (and other aspects of cognition)—or causes? Are different subregions more or less susceptible to modification by experience? Can we use data from developmental cognitive neuroscience to begin to unpack the potential contribution of distinct regions? Given the enormous appetite for data from the infant brain—including for speech and language processing (e.g. Dehaene-Lambertz, Hertz-Pannier, & Dubois, 2006; Telkemeyer et al., 2009; Perani et al., 2011)—one viable research strategy is to use knowledge of development to understand features of the brain (rather than the other way around).

Turning from Broca's region to the dual pathways, there is now a growing body of fibre tracking evidence (largely from diffusion tensor imaging) that suggests that in two-day-old infants, many ventral pathway structures are in place in an adult-like configuration, while the dorsal stream is anatomically underspecified (Friederici, 2012b; Perani et al., 2011). Figure 4 illustrates some relevant data. This pattern is certainly consistent with an interpretation that dorsal stream regions have a critical role for production, or the linking of representations from temporal to frontal regions by sensorimotor transformation. Note that more than one dorsal stream projection is depicted in Figure 2. It has been argued that the projection targeting Broca's region is not in place, whereas the more dorsal structures are available earlier in ontogeny. If this finding is correct, it reinforces the issue raised in the section above on Broca's region: Does the fine-grained spatial structure visible there arise in development with the "arrival" of the fibre tracts from temporal lobe origins—and can we document concomitant performance changes—or is it in place and merely modified as the fiber tracts mature? Many more normative data sets on the developing brain will be necessary to sort out such issues.

Finally, consider hemispheric asymmetries. There now exists a growing body of evidence that right-hemisphere mechanisms are developmentally slightly advanced. This developmental asymmetry appears to be the case both for the auditory and visual systems. Given that, by hypothesis, the local circuitry in the right

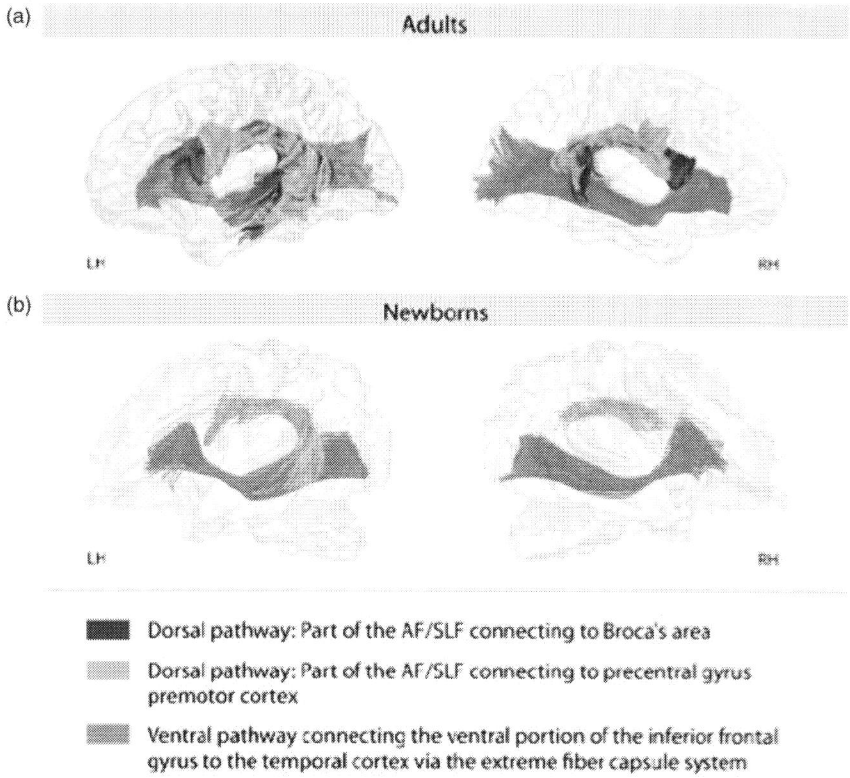

Figure 4. *PNAS, dorsal stream developmen (Perani et al. 2011). Reproduced with permission. To view a colour version of this figure, please see the online issue of the Journal.*

hemisphere is different with respect to its processing preferences (not necessarily different in kind, just in allocation of amount of neural ensembles with certain properties, say slow temporal integration), this implementational difference provides a way to address a few perceptual phenomena that require explanation. For example, in the auditory domain, it would be plausible for infants to show enhanced sensitivity to syllabically mediated information as well as other, suprasegmental prosodic phenomena, even *in utero*. The "universal" listener may start out with a syllable-based segmentation strategy. In general, larger units, preferentially processed by right hemisphere mechanisms, would be favored in early development. Similarly, configural perceptual information should be preferred to locally detailed, high-resolution cues.

Given some of the properties that have been discussed concerning hemispheric asymmetry, the dorsal and ventral streams, and the anatomic specification of Broca's region, one can advance a (simplified) developmental hypothesis arising from these cognitive neuroscience descriptions.

1. The right-hemisphere mechanisms, especially in the superior temporal lobe portions of the ventral stream, are available slightly (weeks to a few months) earlier in ontogenesis, perhaps even *in utero*. Given the hypothesized specialization of right temporal lobe mechanisms for longer integration time constants, the perceptual information attended to preferentially by the learner occurs on these longer timescales. Units of approximately syllabic size/duration—which corresponds closely to the

envelope of spoken language—have epistemological priority at this stage; perceptual analysis at this temporal granularity is especially effective at helping the learner segment the input into units that correspond well to certain linguistic grouping principles (stress, consonant–vowel alternation, possibly even rhythm class) (cf. Bertoncini & Mehler, 1981).

2. Convergence by the learner on the phonetic repertoire of her language over the first year of life (see, e.g., Kuhl, 2004 for review) coincides with the increasing specification of the structures underlying segmental phonology. Since left-hemisphere mechanisms have been argued to reflect some degree of specialization for short timescale processing, and dorsal stream structures are implicated in processing segmental phonology, this accords well with the requirement to analyse segmental and subsegmental phonetic information. On balance, it is plausible to assume that the ventral stream structures are in place by approximately one year. The learner is now optimally positioned to analyse input at both syllabic and segmental timescales, concurrently. This combination constitutes critical ingredients for successful decoding of words—the second big milestone the learner has to achieve (i.e., the incremental construction of the mental lexicon). That is not to say that younger infants cannot discriminate segmental information or fail to map auditory word forms to visual referents (see, e.g., Shukla et al., 2011). These tasks, though, could be achieved by the learner based on representations that are underspecified with respect to the linguistic inventory that is ultimately specified for their native language; that is to say, more acoustically driven, episodic representations could form the basis for executing such tasks in the first few months of development.

3. The structures of the dorsal stream—or at least one of the dorsal streams—are argued to develop later than those of the ventral stream. The dorsal stream projection from the temporal lobe to premotor areas has been suggested to be present at birth. In contrast, the dorsal projections to the inferior frontal gyrus, including Broca's region, show a delayed developmental trajectory (Perani et al., 2011, Friederici, 2012). The structures of the dorsal stream play a critical role in sensorimotor transformation for speech. The seamless interaction of the perception and production systems is arguably coordinated by dorsal stream structures, and it is therefore plausible that there is a tight association between the neural development of the dorsal stream and the developments of speech production. Uncontroversially, perception precedes production, and it is reasonable to hypothesize that this delay in part reflects the constraints imposed by a developing sensorimotor dorsal stream.

4. If inferior frontal gyrus regions, and in particular Broca's region, receive a changing innervation pattern over development because the dorsal stream projecting there is not fully developed, it is reasonable to conjecture that the functional specification of some of these regions changes (perhaps sharpens) over time. It is not possible to conclude whether or not the many cytoarchitectural subregions of the IFG (Figure 1) are available at birth, or whether this region becomes increasingly specified over development. One can, however, conclude that the computational infrastructure is still changing over time, as the inputs to this rich and complex structure change quite dramatically. A thoughtful analysis of the development of speech and its cerebral lateralization is provided by Minagawa-Kawai, Cristià, & Dupoux (2011). They discuss the interaction between signal-driven lateralization versus lateralization as a function of learning biases and derive a model of the acquisition of speech that covers many of the phenomena raised here. It is worth noting that several of the subregions of the IFG play critical functional role in the processing of complex sentential representations, as well as in other domains of language and nonlanguage processing. (Similarly, the thorny issues of semantics

remain untouched in this conjectured scenario.) The sequence outlined here is narrowly focused on the possible development of speech processing.

THE FUTURE OF COGNITIVE NEUROSCIENCE: MAKING MAPPINGS

We now turn from making maps, which lies at the very foundation of cognitive neuroscience, to the problem of *mappings*. This latter problem refers to a very different way of thinking about the challenges that the field faces. What is at stake is whether we are able to identify the possible formal *relations* (mappings) between the putative primitives of cognitive science, and in particular language research, and the putative primitives of neurobiology. Whereas the maps problem raises a number of practical questions—for example, what might be the right techniques to generate topographic maps at the right level of analysis—the mapping problem raises principled questions about the nature of the relation between psychology and neuroscience. This issue has been addressed in some detail by Poeppel and Embick (2005) for language and is, of course, raised by many investigators who grapple with the challenges at the interface of mind and matter (Smolensky & Legendre, 2006).

Granularity mismatch and the ontological incommensurability: Misaligned parts lists

One way to develop an intuition for the problem is to think about it in the context of specifying the "parts lists" of the mind and brain. More formally speaking, this refers to the goal of specifying the *set of primitives*, or the ontological structure, of the two domains in question. As cognitive scientists, we aim to determine an exhaustive list of the components of the human mind—call it *the human cognome*. We use the inventory of components to explain fundamental features of perception and cognition; this is done by appealing to the hypothesized primitives and the rules that govern their interaction to yield the phenomena that we are investigating. This is no different in kind from physics, where the field aims, for example, to specify the elementary particles as well as the forces that condition their interaction—and these two features of a theory provided an explanation of the phenomena. Similarly, as neuroscientists we seek to determine the infrastructure of the nervous system, from subcellular components to large-scale systems.

Let us make the problem a bit more concrete, building on the notion of the parts list. Suppose we write to a large (even exhaustive) list of speech and language researchers, asking what they consider to be the primitive elements of their domain without which they could not account for the elementary phenomena of their fields. In other words, what are the set of primitives that are absolutely required to provide an explanatory account of the canonical phenomena in speech perception, language comprehension, and production? An answer to such a query will yield a *parts list of representational elements* as well as a *list of elementary functions, or computations*. Figure 5 (left column) illustrates a hypothetical answer. An enumeration of primitives might include concepts such as distinctive feature, syllable, morpheme, small clause, and variable. The elementary functions might include concatenation, recursion, variable binding, etc. Note that such a list will be theory-dependent. A particular theory might dispute the fundamental nature of distinctive features or the relevance of recursion. However, specific commitments of a given theory are beside the point; *any* theory (of linguistics, psycholinguistics, neurolinguistics) must be able to provide an inventory of its constituent representations and computations. Obviously, it is of particular interest to develop a consensus position on what the "linguistic cognome" must necessarily contain to begin to get a grip on what is the ontological infrastructure of language research.

Now, this very same exercise can be performed with neuroscientists. The right column in Figure 5 illustrates the type of responses one might expect. The goal there, too, is to identify an emerging consensus about the neurobiological units that form the basis of central nervous system structure and

Linguistics	Neuroscience
Fundamental elements of representation (at a given analytic level)	
distinctive feature	dendrites, spines
syllable	neuron
morpheme	cell-assembly/ensemble
noun phrase	population
clause	cortical column
Fundamental operations on primitives (at a given analytic level)	
concatenation	long-term potentiation (LTP)
linearization	receptive field
phrase-structure generation	oscillation
semantic composition	synchronization

Figure 5. *Sets of primitives for linguistics and neuroscience. First published in Poeppel, D., & Embick, D. (2005). Defining the relation between linguistics and neuroscience. In A. Cutler (ed.),* Twenty-first century psycholinguistics: Four cornerstones *(pp. 103–118). Mahwah, NJ: Lawrence Erlbaum Associates. (Figure 1, p. 105.)*

function. For the sake of argument, Figure 5 now provides a *parts lists for the language sciences* and a *parts list for the neurosciences.* The evidence for the primitives is extensive. That is to say, there is a rich body of empirically based as well as theoretical argumentation to support every given member of these two "alphabets."

The mapping problem is now quite obvious: What is the relation between the ontological structure of the language sciences and the neurosciences? More colloquially, what are the lines/arrows that one can draw from one side to the other in Figure 5 that can capture the systematic mapping from one set of elementary units to another? The answer, too, is obvious: *there is absolutely no mapping to date that we understand in even the most vague sense.* There are no equivalence relations, no isomorphisms, no easy mappings from the theoretical infrastructure of the cognitive sciences to that of neurobiology. On the assumption that one is adopting a nondualist research strategy, it is entirely unclear how to link the two approaches (beyond stating some relatively gross correlations). In what follows, a brief diagnosis for this state of affairs is provided. Then a suggestion is made, in the spirit of Marr (1982) and Gallistel & King (2011) about how to move forward, adopting an optimistic stance about computational cognitive science and computational neuroscience. The central question will be: What are plausible linking hypotheses between the two domains; what form can they (or must they) take? Can cognitive neuroscience of speech and language processing move beyond a purely correlational state of affairs?

There are (at least) two reasons why the formulation of linking hypotheses has been slow—beyond the fact that it is rarely if ever acknowledged that there is a problem to begin with. One reason that it has proven difficult derives from the level of analysis that is typical of the different fields. Linguistic research comes at the questions of interest with a toolbox that permits a very high "resolution." An area of research as conceptually straightforward as *word recognition* approaches the issue by incorporating subtle features of phonology, the statistical adjacency relations between sounds, the role of morphological structure, the role syntactic categories may play for lexical access, nuanced theories about the semantics of words, theories exploiting the predictive nature of language processing, etc. to understand aspects of facilitated or impeded lexical processing, and so on. That is to say, even a process as *allegedly* straightforward as recognizing a spoken word interfaces in a variety of ways with phonology, morphology, syntax, lexical semantics, compositional semantics, and aspects of discourse. In contrast, neurobiological research on language attempts to address much broader questions. Typical issues that are investigated in imaging studies, for example, include whether syntax is localized or where the mental lexicon is localized. This is, to be sure, not a problem that cannot be overcome. It is a practical challenge and simply reflects what has been called the *granularity mismatch problem* (Poeppel & Embick, 2005), to highlight the fact that the granularity of analysis is too different to permit links that are more than correlational. The techniques available to the brain sciences investigate the issues in a manner commensurate with what can be measured and analysed; the techniques available to the cognitive sciences attempt to capture generalizations about speech and language processing at the highest possible "conceptual resolution." The practical consequence of such a granularity mismatch is that issues at very different levels of representation end up being addressed. This is not intrinsically bad, but it is limiting in that it fails to move the field forward in developing mechanistic linking hypotheses between brain structure and function and the organization of this particular cognitive system. In recent years, this has been changing in a positive direction in the context of the ever closer relations between theoreticians, cognitive scientists, and neurobiologists applying state-of-the-art techniques.

In contrast to the granularity mismatch problem, which can be overcome by forging closer links between language researchers and brain researchers to better coordinate the nature of the questions that can be profitably addressed, there is another consideration that is a bit more insidious, and for which a solution is more elusive. We seek to account for the phenomena of cognition by appealing to the neurobiological infrastructure that lies at its basis. However, as is illustrated in Figure 5 and intimated above, there is no comprehensible way in which we can *link* the two sides beyond correlation—and this may reflect more than just a mismatch in the granularity of analysis. It may reflect a principled incommensurability. The *ontological incommensurability problem* (Poeppel & Embick, 2005) suggests that the primitive elements of the two domains cannot be mapped onto each other at all given the current formulation of the parts lists. On such a view, the concepts that form the basis of cognition and neurobiology are impossible to align in principle. If that is the case, then there is no opportunity for identifying plausible isomorphisms and certainly no opportunity for reduction (if that were a goal). Given—plausibly—that there is no hope to reduce perception and cognition to neurobiology at present (and in the most primitive sense of reductionism), an alternative goal is to aim for unification (Chomsky, 2000) or consilience (Wilson, 1999). The larger question thus becomes: What steps need to be taken in terms of how we talk about a given domain in order for it to be unified with a different domain? A historical example that illustrates such a case comes from the relation between chemistry and physics at the beginning of the twentieth century. Chemistry was, contrary to intuition, not reduced to the principles of physics. Rather, the conceptual structure (ontology) of physics had to change to adjust to the new insights coming from the (putatively higher order) area of chemistry. Provocatively, a similar situation might present itself in the relationship between the brain and cognitive sciences (Chomksy, 2000; Gallistel & King, 2009). Perhaps what are considered elementary functional units in the neurosciences will change through closer consideration of what the demands of perception and cognition are. Conceivably, a representational primitive such as "neuron" may not end up playing as foundational a role as some other functional units yet to be determined, even if it is presumably constructed out of the existing parts (say, for example, a canonical cortical microcircuit; Douglas & Martin, 1991).

To summarize, the *granularity mismatch problem* is a practical problem, a pragmatic approach to which will play a productive role in dealing with the maps problems addressed in the first section. The *ontological incommensurability problem* reflects a principled problem, and to make progress on this challenge, practitioners may need to consider how to reformulate the nature of interdisciplinary research in this area—

and question the commitments we make to the primitives of representation and computation.

A tentative strategy for progress

One approach to explore can be called the "radical decomposition" strategy. Adopting such a strategy means questioning whether the primitives we hold to be foundational are possibly decomposable into finer-grained elements (that may themselves not seem like natural units at first glance). For example, from the perspective of the cognitive sciences, consider a concept such as the "phoneme." Many decades of research show that the phoneme is a bundle of more elementary units (features) and that generalizations about knowledge of phonology are not made at the level of phonemes but at the level of features. Similarly, consider the tension between a theoretically poorly motivated concept such as "word" compared to a theoretically richly supported concept such as "morpheme." Whereas morphemes play an essential role in accounting for a range of properties of lexical structure and lexical access, an informal notion such as "word" has been largely unsuccessful. By analysing traditional concepts at a higher resolution, the field has successfully identified smaller (or different) units that appear to do a better job at capturing the phenomena under investigation.

What kind of smaller—or different—units might be plausible? One strategy is to identify representations and operations that can be linked to the types of operation that simple electrical circuits can execute. One might begin, for example, with theoretically well-motivated units of representation or processing deriving from cognitive science research (here, say linguistics); then one attempts to decompose these into elementary constituent operations that are formally generic (something like "concatenation," for example). Now, in a role reversal, linguists should challenge neurobiologists to define and characterize the neural circuitry that can underpin something as elementary as concatenation. Instead of seeking validation of the hypothesized units from cognition by putative reduction to neuroscience, assume that the cognitive evidence is *as foundational* and motivate research to seek a neural circuit can execute the type of operation known to be necessary for a variety of cognitive tasks that are beyond debate. Why might such a (more muscular) stance of cognition be helpful? The field has taken for granted that the elementary units of neurobiology constitute the fact of the matter, the ground truth, from a functional point of view. Neurons, dendrites, dendritic spines, cortical columns, long-term potentiation ... The extremely impressive parts list of the neurosciences is not under debate. What one might question, though, is whether the arrangement of units as they are currently discussed reflects the functionally appropriate arrangements to account for the phenomena we know to require explanation. The interaction between the evidence coming from cognitive science theory and experimentation, on one hand, and the practice and interpretation of neurobiology, on the other, needs to be significantly more synergistic to go beyond correlation and develop genuinely explanatory models.

At this point it is worth considering once more the research strategy outlined by Marr and others. The computational level of analysis, provided by linguistics, psychology, and aspects of computer science, must be linked to the implementational level of analysis, neurobiology. What was suggested by Marr is that an intermediate (algorithmic) level of description specifies the representations and computations that are executed by the implementational circuitry to form the basis of the computational level of characterization. If this strategy is on the right track, current research should in part focus on the operations and algorithms that underpin language processing. The commitment to an algorithm or computation in this domain commits one to representations of one form or another with increasing specificity and also provides clear constraints for what the neural circuitry must accomplish. The kinds of operation that might provide the basis for investigation include concatenation, segmentation, combination, labelling, and other elementary (and generic) operations that could be implemented quite straightforwardly in neural circuits.

A developmental wedge

On the view sketched here, a prerequisite to develop principled linking hypotheses between (linguistic) cognition and neurobiology is the definition of the parts list, or the cognome. Developmental research has a central role to play in this research endeavor. No area of psychological investigation deals more explicitly with the question of what the elementary constituents of the mind are. An essential perspective on the question of the ontological primitives comes from the developmental literature, and specifically the question "what is the parts list at the start?" It would be of tremendous value to the enterprise of mapping from cognition to neurobiology if developmental approaches could integrate questions about the computational constituents. For example, instead of framing a developmental linguistic question in terms of the domain (e.g., speech, phonology) or the tasks employed (e.g., is phonetic categorization evident in the neonate?), if such questions could be characterized in terms of their elementary constituents it would license a claim about the elementary computational infrastructure. Much as in adult cognitive neuroscience research, describing the nature of the perceptual and cognitive tasks not as tasks but as a set of primitive operations and representations will allow the formulation of linking hypotheses that translate more seamlessly to computational neuroscience.

There are, to be sure, good examples of the direction that can be taken. A lot of excellent work in vision research demonstrates how tightly one can link theoretically motivated and computationally explicit theories of visual perception to detailed neural models that link these domains. My own favorite example comes from the auditory research area of sound localization. The avian (e.g., barn owl) versus mammalian (e.g., hamster) brain solve the same sound localization problem (computational level of analysis) using different algorithms (delay line model versus phase) using specialized circuits that implement only one kind of computation and not another—that is to say, the circuits explain the computation (Grothe, 2003). The overall goal, presumably, remains to provide *explanations* of how the properties of the brain account for perception and cognition—not just *descriptions*. The state of the art is impressive, and perhaps even descriptively adequate, but our accounts of the relation between brain and cognition remain in large part correlational. Cognitive neuroscience ought to be more ambitious than that, striving for explanations. A big issue in this context is whether we are investigating cognition at the right granularity, if our goal is to develop linking hypotheses to neurobiology. If we stick to cognition *per se*, and we achieve adequate explanations, then perhaps the analyses are on the right track. However, a more radical decomposition approach might be necessary to develop successful linking hypotheses.

Many of the issues that lie at the centre of current research are extremely relevant, and only a slight shift in perspective can provide a different view on how they help address the linking challenge. For example, making maps, or localization of function, continues to be extremely influential; but localization of function might better be spelled out as localization of local computation—where computation is now construed to be the midlevel, generic set of operations that underlie cognitive representation of computation. Similarly, the relentless enthusiasm for prediction in perception and cognition, now largely subsumed under Bayesian approaches, exemplifies the types of elementary computation that might hold in different parts of perception and cognition, linguistic or otherwise.

REFERENCES

Almeida, D., Poeppel, D., & Corina, D. (2012). *The brain tuning to the body: Cortical plasticity and the perceptual encoding of gestures*. Manuscript submitted for publication.

Amunts, K., Lenzen, M., Friederici, A. D., Schleicher, A., Morosan, P., Palomero-Gallagher, N., & Zilles, K. (2010). Broca's region: Novel organizational principles and multiple receptor mapping. *PLoS Biology, 8,* e1000489.

Anwander, A., Tittgemeyer, M., von Cramon, D. Y., Friederici, A. D., & Knösche, T. R. (2007). Connectivity-based parcellation of Broca's area. *Cerebral Cortex, 17,* 816–825.

Aslin, R. N., & Fiser, J. (2005). Methodological challenges for understanding cognitive development in infants. *Trends in Cognitive Sciences, 9,* 92–98.

Bargmann, C. I. (1993). Genetic and cellular analysis of behavior in *C. elegans*. *Annual Review of Neuroscience, 16,* 47–71.

Bedny, M., Pascual-Leone, A., Dodell-Feder, D., Fedorenko, E., & Saxe, R. (2011). Language processing in the occipital cortices of congenitally blind adults. *Proceedings of the National Academy of Sciences of the United States of America, 108,* 4429–4434.

Bertoncini, J., & Mehler, J. (1981). Syllables as units in infant speech perception. *Infant Behavior and Development, 4,* 247–260.

Broca, P. (1861). Perte de la parole, ramollissement chronique et destruction partielle du lobe antérieur gauche du cerveau. *Bulletin de la Société d'Anthropologie de Paris, 2,* 235–238.

Brodmann, K. (1909). *Vergleichende Lokalisationslehre der Grosshirnrinde in ihren Prinzipien dargestellt auf Grund des Zellenbaues.* Leipzig: Johann Ambrosius Barth Verlag.

Carandini, M. (2012). From circuits to behavior: A bridge too far? *Nature Neuroscience, 15,* 507–509.

Carter, R., & Frith, C. D. (2000). *Mapping the mind.* Berkeley, CA: University of California Press.

Chomsky, N. (2000). *New horizons in the study of language and mind.* Cambridge, UK: Cambridge University Press.

Dehaene-Lambertz, G., Hertz-Pannier, L., & Dubois, J. (2006). Nature and nurture in language acquisition: Anatomical and functional brain-imaging studies in infants. *Trends in Neurosciences, 29,* 367–373.

Dikker, S., & Pylkkanen, L. (2011). Before the N400: Effects of lexical–semantic violations in visual cortex. *Brain and Language, 118,* 23–28.

Dikker, S., Rabagliati, H., Farmer, T. A., & Pylkkänen, L. (2010). Early occipital sensitivity to syntactic category is based on form typicality. *Psychological Science, 21,* 629–634.

Dikker, S., Rabagliati, H., & Pylkkänen, L. (2009). Sensitivity to syntax in visual cortex. *Cognition, 110,* 293–321.

Douglas, R. J., & Martin, K. A. (1991). A functional microcircuit for cat visual cortex. *Journal of Physiology, 440,* 735–769.

Embick, D., & Poeppel, D. (2006). Mapping syntax using imaging: Problems and prospects for the study of neurolinguistic computation. In K. Brown (ed.), *Encyclopedia of language and linguistics* (2nd ed.). New York, NY: Elsevier.

Federmeier, K. D., Wlotko, E. W., & Meyer, A. M. (2008). What's "right" in language comprehension: ERPs reveal right hemisphere language capabilities. *Language and Linguistics Compass, 2,* 1–17.

Friederici, A. D. (2012a). The cortical language circuit: From auditory perception to sentence comprehension. *Trends in Cognitive Sciences, 16,* 262–268.

Friederici, A. D. (2012b). Language development and the ontogeny of the dorsal pathway. *Frontiers in Evolutionary Neuroscience, 4.* Advance online publication. Retrieved May 31, 2012. doi:10.3389/fnevo.2012.00003

Gallistel, C. R., & King, A. P. (2011). *Memory and the computational brain: Why cognitive science will transform neuroscience.* Hoboken, NJ: Wiley.

Geschwind, N. (1970). The organization of language and the brain. *Science, 170,* 940.

Giraud, A. L., Kleinschmidt, A., Poeppel, D., Lund, T. E., Frackowiak, R. S., & Laufs, H. (2007). Endogenous cortical rhythms determine cerebral specialization for speech perception and production. *Neuron, 56,* 1127–34.

Goodale, M. A., & Milner, A. D. (1992). Separate visual pathways for perception and action. *Trends in Neurosciences, 15,* 20–25.

Grodzinsky, Y., & Amunts, K. (2006). *Broca's region* (illustrated ed.). Oxford, UK: Oxford University Press.

Grothe, B. (2003). New roles for synaptic inhibition in sound localization. *Nature Reviews Neuroscience, 4,* 540–550.

Hickok, G., & Poeppel, D. (2004). Dorsal and ventral streams: A framework for understanding aspects of the functional anatomy of language. *Cognition, 92,* 67–99.

Hickok, G., & Poeppel, D. (2007). The cortical organization of speech processing. *Nature Reviews Neuroscience, 8,* 393–402.

Hillis, A. E., & Caramazza, A. (1995). Representation of grammatical categories of words in the brain. *Journal of Cognitive Neuroscience, 7,* 396–407.

Homma, R., Baker, B. J., Jin, L., Garaschuk, O., Konnerth, A., Cohen, L. B., et al. (2009). Wide-field and two-photon imaging of brain activity with voltage- and calcium-sensitive dyes. *Philosophical Transactions of the Royal Society B: Biological Sciences, 364,* 2453–2467.

Hubel, D. (1995). *Eye, brain, and vision.* New York, NY: Scientific American Library.

Kuhl, P. K. (2004). Early language acquisition: Cracking the speech code. *Nature Reviews Neuroscience, 5,* 831–843.

Marr, D. (1982). *Vision: A computational approach.* San Francisco, CA: Freeman.

Mausfeld, R. (2012). On some unwarranted tacit assumptions in cognitive neuroscience. *Frontiers in Psychology, 3,* 67.

McGettigan, C., & Scott, S. K. (2012). Cortical asymmetries in speech perception: What's wrong, what's right and what's left? *Trends in Cognitive Sciences, 16,* 269–276.

Minagawa-Kawai, Y., Cristià, A., & Dupoux, E. (2011). Cerebral lateralization and early speech acquisition: A developmental scenario. *Developmental Cognitive Neuroscience, 1,* 217–232.

Mishkin, M., Ungerleider, L. G., & Macko, K. A. (1983). Object vision and spatial vision: Two cortical pathways. *Trends in Neurosciences, 6,* 414–417.

Obleser, J., Elbert, T., Lahiri, A., & Eulitz, C. (2003). Cortical representation of vowels reflects acoustic dissimilarity determined by formant frequencies. *Cognitive Brain Research, 15,* 207–213.

Perani, D., Saccuman, M. C., Scifo, P., Anwander, A., Awander, A., Spada, D., et al. (2011). Neural language networks at birth. *Proceedings of the National Academy of Sciences of the United States of America, 108,* 16056–16061.

Pinker, S. (1997). *How the mind works.* New York, NY: Norton.

Poeppel, D. (2003). The analysis of speech in different temporal integration windows: Cerebral lateralization as 'asymmetric sampling in time'. *Speech Communication, 41,* 245–255.

Poeppel, D. (2008). The cartographic imperative: Confusing localization and explanation in human brain mapping. *In Bildwelten des Wissens: Vol. 6.1. Bildwelten des wissens* (p. 13). Berlin, Germany: Akademie Verlag.

Poeppel, D., & Embick, D. (2005). Defining the relation between linguistics and neuroscience. In A. Cutler (ed.), *Twenty-first century psycholinguistics: Four cornerstones* (pp. 103–118). Mahwah, NJ: Lawrence Erlbaum Associates.

Poeppel, D., & Hickok, G. (2004). Towards a new functional anatomy of language. *Cognition, 92,* 1–12.

Posner, M. I., & Raichle, M. E. (1997). *Images of mind.* New York, NY: Scientific American Library.

Pulvermüller, F., Lutzenberger, W., & Preissl, H. (1999). Nouns and verbs in the intact brain: Evidence from event-related potentials and high-frequency cortical responses. *Cerebral Cortex, 9,* 497–506.

Rauschecker, J. P., & Scott, S. K. (2009). Maps and streams in the auditory cortex: Nonhuman primates illuminate human speech processing. *Nature Neuroscience, 12,* 718–724.

Sahin, N. T., Pinker, S., Cash, S. S., Schomer, D., & Halgren, E. (2009). Sequential processing of lexical, grammatical, and phonological information within Broca's area. *Science, 326,* 445–449.

Schoonover, C. E. (2010). *Portraits of the mind: Visualizing the brain from antiquity to the 21st century.* New York, NY: Abrams.

Seung, S. (2011). *Connectome: How the brain's wiring makes us who we are.* Boston, MA: Houghton Mifflin Harcourt.

Shukla, M., White, K. S., & Aslin, R. N. (2011). Prosody guides the rapid mapping of auditory word forms onto visual objects in 6-mo-old infants. *Proceedings of the National Academy of Sciences of the United States of America, 108,* 6038.

Smolensky, P., & Legendre, G. (2006). *The harmonic mind: From neural computation to optimality-theoretic grammar.* Cambridge, MA: MIT Press.

Sporns, O. (2010). *Networks of the brain.* Cambridge, MA: MIT Press.

Telkemeyer, S., Rossi, S., Koch, S. P., Nierhaus, T., Steinbrink, J., Poeppel, D., et al. (2009). Sensitivity of newborn auditory cortex to the temporal structure of sounds. *Journal of Neuroscience, 29,* 14726–14733.

Weinberg, S. (2009). *Lake views: This world and the universe.* Cambridge, MA: Harvard University Press.

Wernicke, C. (1874). *Der aphasische Symptomencomplex: Eine psychologische Studie auf anatomischer Basis.* Breslau, Poland: Cohn & Weigert.

Wilson, E. O. (1999). *Consilience: The unity of knowledge.* New York, NY: Random House Digital.

Yizhar, O., Fenno, L. E., Davidson, T. J., Mogri, M., & Deisseroth, K. (2011). Optogenetics in neural systems. *Neuron, 71,* 9–34.

Zatorre, R. J., & Gandour, J. T. (2008). Neural specializations for speech and pitch: Moving beyond the dichotomies. *Philosophical Transactions of the Royal Society of London B: Biological Sciences, 363,* 1087–1104.

Zatorre, R. J., Belin, P., & Penhune, V. B. (2002). Structure and function of auditory cortex: Music and speech. *Trends in Cognitive Sciences, 6,* 37–46.

Insights into the origins of knowledge from the cognitive neuroscience of blindness

Marina Bedny and Rebecca Saxe

Department of Brain and Cognitive Sciences, Massachusetts Institute of Technology, Cambridge, MA, USA

Children learn about the world through senses such as touch, smell, vision, and audition, but they conceive of the world in terms of objects, events, agents, and their mental states. A fundamental question in cognitive science is how nature and nurture contribute to the development of such conceptual categories. What innate mechanisms do children bring to the learning problem? How does experience contribute to development? In this article we discuss insights into these longstanding questions from cognitive neuroscience studies of blindness. Despite drastically different sensory experiences, behavioural and neuroscientific work suggests that blind children acquire typical concepts of objects, actions, and mental states. Blind people think and talk about these categories in ways that are similar to sighted people. Neuroimaging reveals that blind people make such judgements relying on the same neural mechanisms as sighted people. One way to interpret these findings is that neurocognitive development is largely hardwired, and so differences in experience have little consequence. Contrary to this interpretation, neuroimaging studies also show that blindness profoundly reorganizes the visual system. Most strikingly, developmental blindness enables "visual" circuits to participate in high-level cognitive functions, including language processing. Thus, blindness qualitatively changes sensory representations, but leaves conceptual representations largely unchanged. The effect of sensory experience on concepts is modest, despite the brain's potential for neuroplasticity.

Keywords: Conceptual development; Innateness; Experience; Blindness; Concepts.

... imagine a child, growing up in a certain city, born blind, but otherwise intelligent and well endowed, with a sound memory and an apt mind. Through his remaining channels of perception he will get to know the people as well as all sorts of animals and objects, and the streets and alleys, houses and markets—eventually well enough to walk through the city without a guide, recognizing at once everyone he meets. But colours, and colours alone, he will know only by descriptive explanation and ostensive definition. Suppose after he had come this far, his eyesight were restored and he could see. He would walk all through the town finding nothing in contradiction to what he had believed, nor would anything look wrong to him. The colours he encountered would conform to the guidelines that had been sketched out for him. Still there would be two great changes, the second dependent on the first: first the daybreak on a new visual world, and second, his great joy.
(from *Hayy Ibn Yaqzan*, by Ibn Tufayl, 12th century Andalusian Islamic scholar)

Correspondence should be addressed to Marina Bedny, Massachusetts Institute of Technology, Department of Brain and Cognitive Sciences, 43 Vassar Street, 46-4021, Cambridge, MA 02139, USA. (E-mail: mbedny@mit.edu).

We are grateful to the blind individuals, parents of blind children and the blind community for enabling the research described in this article. We would like to thank Lindsay Yazzolino for sharing her insightful reflections and Amy Skerry for comments on an earlier version of this draft. We would also like to thank the Packard Foundation and the NeuroDiscovery fund for their generous support of this research.

http://www.psypress.com/cogneuropsychology http://dx.doi.org/10.1080/02643294.2012.713342

Children learn about the world through sensations such as seeing shapes, feeling softness, and listening to sounds. Yet children think (and talk) in abstract terms that go way beyond sensory experience. Children categorize events as instances of *running*, whether the running is done by a boy, a turtle or a cheetah; and call running something different when it's done for the purpose of *chasing*, *racing*, or *escaping*. Children can distinguish between *falling* and *jumping* into the swimming pool and between *doubting* and *hoping* that they will get ice cream before dinner. Perhaps the most canonical human behaviour, language, is a feat of abstraction, both in the conceptual categories it picks out and the grammatical rules that govern its use. A fundamental question in cognitive science is how nature and nurture contribute to the development of such abstract representations. What innate learning mechanisms or conceptual "cores" do children bring to the problem of cognitive development (e.g., Spelke, 1998)? How does experience enable children to distinguish between *falling* versus *jumping*, *doubting* versus *hoping?*

Understanding how experience contributes to cognition is a formidable task. First, most people share the vast majority of their genes and important aspects of their environment. Almost all children experience sounds, sights, gravity, motion, language, and social interactions with other humans. Our shared nature and nurture make it difficult to separate the contributions of intrinsic biological constraints and experience, and to disentangle correlated dimensions of experience from each other. Individuals who grow up with *atypical* experiences provide rare insights into the causal mechanisms that shape cognition (Benzaquen, 2006; Gleitman & Newport, 1995).

Blindness in particular has long been a window into the developmental origins of the mind (Berkeley, 1709/1732; Hobbes, 1641/1984). Unlike sighted children, blind children do not see colours or faces, they do not follow the gaze of others, they do not see mountains, elephants, or a flickering fire, and the fact that two people are hugging near by is largely inaccessible to them. Blind infants have limited opportunities to observe objects, actions, and the perceptual states of other people. They have no access to facial expressions or eye gaze, and do not share first-person experiences of seeing with the sighted people around them. How does conceptual development differ, under these circumstances? How do blind children develop concepts of objects, actions, seeing, and thinking, and what are these concepts like in blind adults?

Cognitive scientists have investigated these philosophical puzzles by quantitatively studying the behaviour of blind individuals (Iverson & Goldin-Meadow, 1997; Landau, Gleitman & Spelke, 1981; Landau, Spelke & Gleitman, 1984; Shepard & Cooper, 1992). These studies have yielded illuminating, and sometimes surprising insights into the human mind. Most notably, aspects of cognition that were thought to depend heavily on vision, such as spatial reasoning, have turned out to develop quite typically in the absence of sight (Landau et al., 1981, 1984). Recently, the methods of cognitive neuroscience have opened up new opportunities to study the relationship between visual experience and neurocognitive development.

In this review we highlight insights from these neuroscientific studies of blindness. Studies of the neurobiology of concepts in blind people test some long held (and recently revived) claims about the sensory origins of cognition. Since the sensory experience of blind and sighted people is drastically different, does the neurobiology of concepts also differ in these populations? Augmenting behavioral findings, measures of brain function provide insights into whether blind and sighted people rely on similar cognitive mechanisms to solve the same behavioural tasks, not just "talking the talk". We centre our discussion on studies of several conceptual categories that are believed to depend heavily on vision: objects, actions, and perceptual states. We then consider the implications of these studies for theories on the organization of conceptual knowledge.

Studies of blindness also offer insights into how the mind is implemented in the brain. In particular, blindness offers a window into how nature and nurture contribute to human brain development. Congenital blindness causes a dramatic change to the typical developmental input of visual\cortex. Studies of the visual cortex in blind individuals thus offer an opportunity to explore the limits of neuroplasticity in the human brain. As we discuss below, these studies have begun to uncover how intrinsic constraints interact with experience during human brain specialization.

We begin by reviewing evidence of neuroplasticity in the visual system of blind individuals and then turn to studies of the neurobiology of concepts. We then juxtapose the effects of blindness on the visual system to its effects on conceptual systems. To foreshadow, while studies of the visual system in blind individuals reveal dramatic functional reorganization, studies on the neurobiology of concepts reveal resilience to blindness. The strikingly different effects of blindness on perceptual and conceptual systems inform our understanding of the distinctive nature and origins of such systems.

INSIGHTS INTO NATURE/ NURTURE QUESTIONS FROM NEUROPLASTICITY IN THE VISUAL SYSTEM

To what degree are the cognitive functions of neural circuits intrinsically constrained, even before receiving input from the environment (innate)? Prior to experience, human cortical areas differ from each other in the distribution and proportion of neuronal types as well as connectivity to other neural circuits. Do such neuroanatomical features ingrain a particular cognitive function (e.g., visuospatial discrimination, language, working memory)? Conversely, can lifetime experience qualitatively change the cognitive capacity of neural tissue? Studies of occipital cortex in blind individuals pit strong innate constraints against large-scale changes in experience.

The mammalian occipital cortex is believed to have evolved for vision. Comparative studies of brain anatomy across species suggest that those mammals that rely more on vision also have more elaborated occipital circuits (Barton, 2007; Kaas, 2008). The occipital cortex is anatomically tailored to the demands of sight: Primary visual cortex ("V1") has a disproportionately thick input layer (IV) and is massively dominated by input from the visual nucleus of the thalamus (the lateral geniculate nucleus). In sighted humans the visual system has a highly predictable functional organization both within visual cortical areas (e.g., retinotopy) and across cortical areas (e.g., motion, colour, object selectivity). Such consistency suggests the existence of strong innate biases. If any structure were to be resilient to changes in environmental input, it might be the visual system.

On the other hand, if experience could effect brain organization, total blindness should do so since it constitutes a massive change to typical developmental input. By contrast, most experiential changes in higher-cognitive domains are subtler, e.g., variation in socioeconomic status, reduced access to language due to deafness, or experimentally induced training. In all these cases typical experience is altered or reduced rather then removed entirely. Studies of total blindness therefore test the limits of cortical flexibility in the context of extreme changes in the environmental input. If the cognitive function of neural circuits is innately determined, absence of vision might lead occipital cortex to simply atrophy. By contrast, if neural circuits have the capacity to change function in the face of different input, the visual system of blind people would be likely to show this plasticity: losing visual functions, but possibly gaining other functions. If visual circuits do acquire new functions, we can ask how cognitively or computationally similar these functions are to vision?

Fifty years of neuroscientific research, in both humans and nonhuman animals, provides clear evidence for functional change in the visual system (Hubel & Wiesel, 1970; Wiesel & Hubel, 1963). First, blindness leads "visual" circuits to support vision less optimally. Removing visual input even temporarily during development leads to disorganization and loss of visual functions in the deprived cortex, and to corresponding visual deficits (Levin, Dumoulin, Winawer, Dougherty & Wandell, 2010; Wiesel & Hubel, 1963, 1965). For example, dark-reared ferrets do not develop classic direction selectivity in visual cortex (Li, Fitzpatrick, & White, 2006). In humans, temporary absence of pattern vision early in life (e.g., due to cataracts) leads to reduced acuity and persistent deficits in high-level vision even many years later (Fine et al., 2003; Levin et al., 2010; Maurer, Lewis, & Mondloch, 2005; Ostrovsky, Andalman & Sinha, 2006; Putzar, Goerendt, Lange, Rosler, & Roder, 2007). Just a few months of lost vision during infancy causes enduring impairments in adult face perception (Le Grand, Mondloch, Maurer, & Brent, 2003, 2004). Blind individuals who recover vision as adults (i.e., following years of blindness) have even more dramatic deficits and fail to show typical (category-specific) neural responses to faces and objects in visual cortex (Fine et al., 2003).

Second, in addition to loss of visual function, early blindness also enables occipital cortex to take on nonvisual functions. Animals who are deprived of vision early in life develop responses to touch and sound in occipital regions that would normally respond exclusively to vision (Kahn & Krubitzer, 2002; Rauschecker, 1995). Similarly, early neuroimaging studies with humans showed that occipital regions of blind people respond to touch and sound (Kujala et al., 1995; Uhl, Franzen, Lindinger, Lang & Deecke, 1991). For example, occipital regions are active when blind, but not sighted, individuals read Braille (Sadato et al., 1996; Uhl et al., 1991). Furthermore, transient disruption of occipital cortex by transcranial magnetic stimulation (TMS) impairs blind people's ability to recognize Braille letters by touch (Cohen et al., 1997; Hamilton, Keenan, Catala & Pascual-Leone, 2000), suggesting that crossmodal responses in the visual system are functionally relevant, not epiphenomenal.

Traditionally, these tactile and auditory responses in the visual system have been termed "crossmodal plasticity" because transfer of function is believed to occur from one sensory modality to another (e.g., from vision to touch) while preserving the underlying cognitive function (e.g. Merabet et al., 2004). For example, like vision, Braille reading requires fine-grained spatial discrimination (Sadato et al., 1996). Thus, although the modality of input to "visual" cortex is changed, the underlying cognitive function of visual cortex (i.e. spatial perception) might remain the same (Collignon et al., 2011). There are a number of similar examples where plasticity appears to preserves elements of the original cognitive function. For instance, the middle temporal complex (MT/MST) typically plays an important role in perception of visual motion (Dubner & Zeki, 1971; Tootell et al., 1995a, 1995b; Zeki, 1974). In congenitally blind individuals, this brain region responds to auditory motion (Bedny, Konkle, Pelphrey, Saxe, & Pascual-Leone, 2011b; Poirier et al., 2006; Saenz, Lewis, Huth, Fine & Koch, 2008; Wolbers, Zahorik & Giudice, 2011). In the cases of Braille and auditory motion, blindness changes the sensory modality that drives occipital circuits, but the underlying cognitive function may be preserved (Pascual-Leone, Amedi, Fregni & Merabet, 2005; Pascual-Leone & Hamilton, 2001; Rauschecker, 1995).

Other cases of plasticity provide clear examples of functional change that is more dramatic than crossmodal transfer. The most striking example is the acquisition of linguistic functions by occipital cortex. In most humans, the capacity for language depends on a neural system of left-lateralized brain regions in prefrontal and temporoparietal cortex. Like the visual system, the neurobiology of language is often resilient to environmental change. Children who grow up in different cultures and speak different languages (including both aural languages and sign languages) go on to develop similar fronto-temporal language systems (Bellugi, Poizner & Klima, 1983; Chee et al., 1999a; Chee, Tan & Thiel, 1999b). By contrast, adults who are blind from birth engage occipital (visual) cortex during language processing, in addition to classic language areas (Bedny, Pascual-Leone, Dodell-Feder, Fedorenko & Saxe, 2011c; Burton, Diamond & McDermott, 2003; Roder, Stock, Bien, Neville & Rosler, 2002).

Left-lateralized areas in the "visual" cortex respond not only during Braille reading (Buchel, Price, Frackowiak & Friston, 1998; Burton et al., 2002a; Hamilton & Pascual-Leone, 1998; Sadato et al., 1996), but also while blind individuals listen to aural speech (Amedi, Raz, Pianka, Malach & Zohary, 2003; Bedny et al., 2011c; Burton & McLaren, 2006) and covertly generate (i.e. think of) words (Amedi et al., 2003; Burton, Snyder, Diamond & Raichle, 2002b). Occipital cortex activity during language tasks is related to language processing specifically, and not to nonlinguistic aspects of verbal tasks such as general task difficulty or language-related imagery. Left occipital areas respond more during linguistic tasks than to difficult nonlinguistic perceptual and working memory tasks (Bedny et al., 2011c; Bedny, Pascual-Leone, Dravida & Saxe, 2011d). Various lines of evidence demonstrate that occipital activity during verbal tasks does not reflect spontaneous spatial imagery (Lakoff & Nunez, 2001). First, both in sighted and congenitally blind individuals, explicit imagery and language comprehension depend on distinct neural circuits (Vanlierde, De Volder, Wanet-Defalque, & Veraart, 2003). Second, the occipital response to sentences is not correlated with imagery ratings (Bedny, Dufour, Dravida, & Saxe, 2010) and is observed to linguistic stimuli that do not support visual imagery, including abstract words and Jabberwocky sentences (Amedi et al., 2003; Bedny et al., 2011c; Roder et al., 2002).

Like classic language areas, occipital regions in blind adults are sensitive to high-level linguistic information (i.e., compositional sentence structure and word meanings). Occipital brain regions respond more to Jabberwocky (containing compositional structure but no content words), and more to lists of words (content words with no compositional structure) as compared to lists of nonwords (low in both compositional structure and word meanings; Bedny et al., 2011c) (Figure 1). There is also evidence that occipital areas respond more to syntactically noncanonical than canonical sentences (Roder et al., 2002).

Even in the absence of a task (i.e., while simply resting), occipital activity in blind individuals is correlated with activity in prefrontal language areas (Bedny et al., 2011c; Liu et al., 2007; Watkins et al., 2012).

Finally, as in the case of Braille reading, occipital responses to language appear to be functionally relevant: TMS applied to the occipital pole leads to verb-generation errors in blind but not sighted individuals (Amedi, Floel, Knecht, Zohary & Cohen, 2004). Together these findings suggest that the visual system takes on language processing capacities as a result of blindness. These data imply that experience can induce human brain regions to change functions not only across sensory modalities, but also across cognitive domains (i.e., from vision to language).

While human cortical circuits appear to be highly flexible in the cognitive functions they can support, this flexibility declines and changes with age. Responses to nonvisual stimuli in occipital circuits are more robust and more widespread in people who are blind from birth (Burton et al., 2002a), and are also differentially localized in congenitally versus late blind people (Bedny et al., 2011d; Buchel et al., 1998; Burton et al., 2002a).

Age of blindness onset also affects which cognitive functions occipital circuits take on. While the visual system is active during verbal tasks (e.g., Braille reading, verb generation) in both late and congenitally blind people (Burton et al., 2002a), occipital regions contribute to language processing *per se* only in congenitally blind people. These differences in functional plasticity between late and congenitally blind people depend on the age of blindness onset, not the years of blindness. Even after decades of blindness, occipital areas respond equally to difficult linguistic and nonlinguistic tasks in late blind people (Bedny et al., 2011d). Also, TMS to the occipital pole impairs Braille reading only in congenitally blind individuals (Cohen et al., 1997). These data suggest that blindness during development specifically enables occipital circuits to participate in language processing.

We have recently begun studying the timecourse and mechanism of this language-related plasticity by working with blind children. Preliminary findings suggest that occipital cortex plasticity for language occurs during early

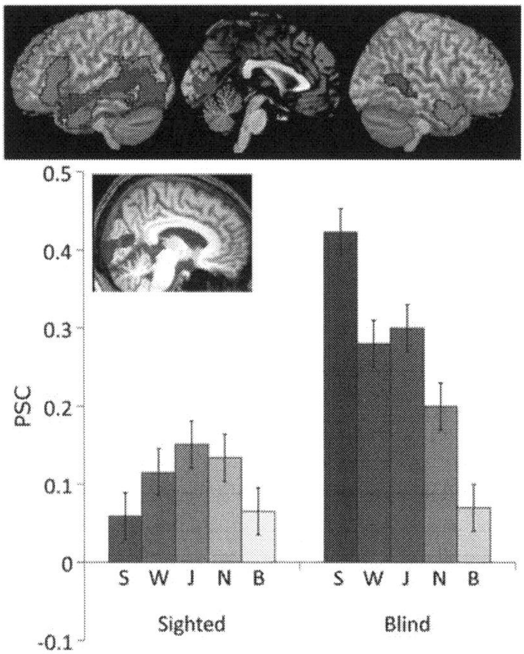

Figure 1. *Neural activity during sentence comprehension in sighted and blind individuals. Top panel shows results of a whole-brain analysis comparing sentences to backwards speech in sighted (red) and blind (blue) people. Whole-brain random-effects results are overlaid on a standardized template (corrected for multiple comparisons,* $p < .05$*). Bar charts show percent signal change (PSC) in pericalcarine cortex (approximate anatomical location of V1) while listening to sentences (S), word lists (W), Jabberwocky (J), nonword lists (N) and backwards speech (B). (For details see Bedny et al., 2011c.). To view a colour version of this figure, please see the online issue of the Journal.*

childhood. Occipital responses to language emerge in blind children by four years of age and appear to be independent of Braille learning (Bedny et al., 2012). These data suggest that occipital cortex takes on language functions during development, and possibly during language acquisition.

In sum, early blindness enables brain regions that evolved for vision to develop multiple nonvisual functions, including multimodal sensory responses and even high-level language functions. In the visual cortex innate predispositions coexist with the potential for large-scale experience-based change. These findings imply that developmental experience can qualitatively change the function of neural tissue across disparate cognitive domains. During development cortical areas are pluripotent: the same circuits can support both basic sensory and abstract cognitive functions.

Since experience in general and blindness in particular has the potential to reorganize neural systems, we can next ask how blindness affects the neurobiology of concepts. If sensory experience and concepts are tightly linked, changes to sensory systems should carry forward to conceptual representations. Conversely, preserved conceptual representations in the face of blindness would provide evidence for decoupling between sensation and concepts.

CONCEPTS AND BLINDNESS

The potential contribution of neuroscientific data to theories of concepts

Philosophers have long wondered what the concepts of blind people might be like. Many have concluded that the concepts of blind people must be very different from the concepts of sighted people, or at least missing a crucial piece (Hume, 1739/1978). Thomas Hobbes likened a blind person's knowledge of fire to a sighted person's knowledge of God (Hobbes, 1641/1984). The Anglo-Irish Empiricist George Berkeley similarly argued that blind people have drastically different concepts of everyday objects (Berkeley, 1709/1732). More recently, the psychologist Thomas Cutsforth wrote about the "unreality of words to the blind", asserting that terms such as "look" and "see" are meaningless to congenitally blind individuals and discouraging the use of such words by blind children (Cutsforth, 1932). These intuitions about blindness are founded on the premise that concepts are tightly linked to their perceptual origins. Similar empiricist commitments have been central to modern cognitive and neuroscientific theories (Allport, 1985; Paivio, 1971; Warrington & Shallice, 1984), including recent "embodied" theories of cognition (Barsalou, 1999; Gallese & Lakoff, 2005; Glenberg, 1997; Lakoff & Johnson, 1980; Prinz, 2002, 2005; Pulvermuller, 1999; Wilson, 2002). Since the sensory experience of blind people is very different from the experience of sighted people, these theories also predict that the concepts of blind people should be very different.

In sum, one view of conceptual development and organization is that concepts are largely sensory and thus modality-dependent. On this view, "visual" concepts can only be acquired normally through vision, and blind people should have large gaps in their concepts, compared to the concepts of sighted people. These gaps are most likely for concepts that in sighted people are putatively highly visual: concrete objects, actions, and experiences that specifically involve vision, such as seeing.

While modern empiricist theories are consistent with modality-dependence, they are also consistent with a weaker prediction, which we call the modality-flexible hypothesis. Embodied concepts must be sensory, but they need not be visual (Barsalou, 1999; Gallese & Lakoff, 2005; Glenberg, 1997; Lakoff & Johnson, 1980; Prinz, 2002; 2005; Pulvermuller, 1999; Wilson, 2002). Blind people could efficiently compensate for the absence of vision with images from other modalities. Concepts that sighted people acquire through vision and represent as visual images (e.g., *blue*, *bounce*, and *see*), could be acquired through touch or audition and represented as tactile and/or auditory images in the minds of people who are blind (Gallese & Lakoff, 2005; Meteyard, Cuadrado, Bahrami & Vigliocco, 2012). On this view, blind and sighted people might have similar knowledge and similar behaviour, but with different conceptual organization.

The third view we will consider here is the modality-invariant hypothesis. According to this proposal, in addition to knowing what things look like, people process a vast store of abstract conceptual information that allows them to make inferences, to categorize, and to communicate with others. On this view many concepts are largely abstract and modality-invariant, in both sighted and blind people. For example, action concepts might include abstract information about duration, causal structure, and agent intentions as well as spatial information, such as motion path, that is not modality-specific. This kind of conceptual information is modality-invariant in that the same information could just as well be acquired through vision, audition, or touch without any change to the underlying representations. This information might be acquired via innate "core" learning mechanisms that evolved for acquiring these abstract categories (Carey, 2009; Spelke, 1998; Spelke & Kinzler, 2007). Alternatively, these representations could be acquired by observing or inferring abstract structure from the environment (e.g., by observing causal interactions, intentional actions), and through language. For example, a child might learn that a giraffe is a type of animal that eats leaves either by hearing mom talking about giraffes or seeing a giraffe eating leaves in a zoo. Auditory versus visual means of learning this information may have no representational consequences. Similarly, learning what it means to see either by hearing others talk about seeing or by having first-person experiences of seeing might lead to qualitatively similar concepts.

The modality-dependent, modality-flexible and modality-invariant hypotheses outlined above serve as anchor points for our discussion of concepts in blind individuals. We end this section of the paper with some qualifications of these idealized theoretical position. The available behavioural and neuroscientific data on blindness contribute powerful evidence for disentangling these three positions. Decades of behavioural research weighs in against the modality-dependent view. The linguistic and reasoning behaviour of congenitally blind, and even deaf–blind individuals is largely similar to that of sighted people (Chomsky, 1986). Conceptual development is preserved in higher-cognitive domains that were thought to depend on vision (Iverson & Goldin-Meadow, 1997; Landau et al., 1981, 1984; Marmor & Zaback, 1976; Zimler & Keenan, 1983). Perhaps most strikingly, concepts of seeing are not hopelessly out of reach of blind adults and children (Bigelow, 1992; Landau & Gleitman, 1985; Peterson, Peterson, & Webb, 2000). Young blind children use terms such as "look" and "see" systematically to refer to visual perception in sighted people (and to tactile perception in themselves). They use colour words appropriately, to refer to a specific class of related perceptual qualities that cannot be perceived by touch but can be perceived through vision (Landau, 1983; Miller, 1983; Rosel, Caballer, Jara, & Oliver, 2005).

On the other hand, it can be difficult to distinguish between the modality-flexible and modality-invariant hypotheses using behavioural data alone. To illustrate this point, consider the conceptual category of colours. Blind children have no perceptual access to colour; there is no way to perceive colour other than through sight. Despite this, when blind adults are asked to make similarity judgements based on colour words, their ratings reflect a similarity space that resembles the Newtonian colour wheel (Marmor, 1978; Shepard & Cooper, 1992). Blind children begin to produce colour adjectives at approximately the same time as sighted children. Four-year-old blind children use colour names to refer to perceptual qualities of objects that cannot be felt by touch; and know that while concrete objects can all have colours, events and abstractions cannot have colours (Landau & Gleitman, 1985). By eight to 13 years of age blind children can name the colours of common objects (Connolly, Gleitman, & Thompson-Schill, 2007 for evidence in adults; Mills, 1983). There is also anecdotal evidence that blind children know other information about colours. A blind eight-year-old girl that recently visited our lab asked what the colour of her chair was. When told that the chair was blue, she politely asked if she might have a red or pink chair instead, "since blue is a boy colour".

On the other hand, there is also behavioural evidence that colour knowledge of blind people is not identical to that of sighted people. While the similarity judgements of all sighted people yield a Newtonian colour wheel, the ratings of blind people vary across individuals; some blind adults make judgements that do not reflect the Newtonian colour wheel (Shepard & Cooper, 1992). Blind people also tend to neglect colour information when making decisions about objects. Even when they can name the colours of common objects (e.g., fruits and vegetables), blind people do not use colour information to decide how similar a "banana" and a "lemon" are to each other (Connolly et al., 2007).

Behavioural evidence regarding colour concepts can thus be interpreted in two ways. The evidence that blind people on average acquire rich and accurate knowledge about colours, including associations to objects and cultural categories, demonstrates that even colour concepts can be acquired through non-sensory mechanisms, such as language. It seems possible that both blind and sighted children develop amodal representations of colour, consistent with the modality-independent hypothesis. Such representations might include information about how colour is perceived, gender correlations, and even the similarity of colours to each other. On the other hand, evidence that blind people's colour similarity space is heterogeneous and relatively underutilized supports the proposal that concepts are qualitatively distinct in blind and sighted people. In sighted people, colour concepts may be largely visual images, whereas for blind people they may be represented by analogy to other sensory modalities or in some other compensatory format, consistent with the modality-flexible hypothesis.

Even in cases where the behaviour of blind and sighted people is identical, it is still possible that different formats of representation are at play. For example, like sighted people, congenitally blind people take a longer time to perform mental rotation tasks as the angle of rotation between the two objects increases (Marmor & Zaback, 1976). This could be because both blind and sighted people are relying on a modality-independent spatial representation or because blind people use tactile representations where sighted people rely on visual representations (modality-flexible hypothesis). When the behaviour of blind and sighted people is generally similar, how can we tell whether blind and sighted people are relying on the same cognitive mechanisms, or whether blind people are efficiently compensating with alternative sensory modalities?

Measurements of neural activity can weigh in on the interpretive ambiguities left by behavioural findings. Information from different sensory modalities (e.g., vision versus touch) and different domains of knowledge (e.g., language versus space) is represented in distinct parts of the human cortex. As a result, the modality-flexible and modality-invariant hypotheses make different predictions for neural data. According to the modality-flexible view, for concepts whose organization is based on the sensory modality of acquisition, blind and sighted people achieve similar behavioural performance by depending on different formats of representation. Since we can distinguish brain regions that are dominated by different sensory modalities (e.g., auditory cortex and visual cortex), we can use neural data to ask whether blind and sighted people rely on similar or different cognitive mechanisms to solve the same behavioural tasks. In some cases, we can even make specific predictions about exactly which brain regions should be involved for each population (more on this below). We can also look for effects of blindness on the functional selectivity of those neural circuits that support conceptual tasks. If concepts are sensory, then blindness should change the functional profile of conceptual brain regions, as we know it changes the functional profile of visual brain regions. For concepts whose organization is independent of modality and structured around abstract features, blind and sighted people should achieve similar behavioural performance by appealing to the same neural mechanisms.

Concepts of objects and actions in blind individuals: Behavioural evidence and neural predictions

There is little doubt that sighted infants initially rely heavily on vision to learn about concrete objects and actions (Smith & Heise, 1992). Within the first year of life children use shape, pattern, and colour to individuate objects in their environment (Wilcox, 1999). Eleven-month-old infants use visual motion to parse actions and events along conceptually relevant boundaries (Baldwin, Baird, Saylor, & Clark, 2001) and infants infer intentional information based on visual cues (Woodward, 1998).

Blind children's experiences with objects and actions differ from those of sighted children both qualitatively and quantitatively. Qualitatively, blind infants learn about their environment through different sensory modalities—touch and audition rather than vision. This change in input modality also makes some kinds of information more accessible than other kinds. For example, perceptual information about texture and weight is more salient, whereas information about silhouettes, shape, and colour is less salient. Quantitatively, blind children also have less overall access to information about objects and actions in their environment. As a result, there is some evidence that blind children's behaviour is initially less directed towards external objects and events than the behaviour of sighted children. Blind children are delayed in reaching for distant objects (Adelson & Fraiberg, 1974). When blind children first begin to talk, they refer to other people's actions less frequently than to their own actions (compared to age-matched sighted children) (Andersen, Dunlea & Kekelis, 1984; Bigelow, 1987; Dunlea, 1989).

All three hypotheses about conceptual organization outlined above can be formulated specifically, regarding concepts of objects and events. First, if such concepts require vision for normal development, then blind children should be substantially (and in some cases, possibly permanently) delayed in acquisition of typical concepts of objects and actions (modality-dependent hypothesis) (Andersen et al., 1984; Cutsforth, 1932; Dunlea, 1989). Second, the modality-flexible hypothesis predicts that while sighted children's concepts are derived from visual experience, blind children efficiently compensate with sensory information from other modalities. For example, where sighted children acquire object concepts in the form of visual images of shape, blind children might represent shape information in a tactile format. Third, the modality-invariant hypothesis predicts that object and action concepts have key amodal components that are invariant with regard to modality of input. If so, blind children should acquire the very same concepts of objects and events as do sighted children.

Again, behavioural evidence clearly advocates against the modality-dependent hypothesis. Blind children's acquisition of words for objects and actions is largely unaffected (Johnson & Newport, 1989; Landau, 1983; Landau & Gleitman, 1985; Perez-Pereira & Castro, 1992; Urwin, 1983). Production of first words is only slightly, if at all, delayed (Bigelow, 1987; Landau & Gleitman, 1985; Urwin, 1983) and these first words consist mostly of names of objects and actions (Bigelow, 1987). By three years of age, blind children's lexical and grammatical development is largely indistinguishable from the development of sighted children (Landau & Gleitman, 1985).

The behavioural data leave open the two remaining hypotheses: that blind children compensate with sensory information from other modalities (modality-flexible hypothesis) or that concepts of objects and actions are invariant with regard to the sensory-modality of learning in both blind and sighted children (modality-independent hypothesis). Neuroscienctific studies of concepts in blind individuals can help distinguish between these possibilities. In particular, since there are specific brain regions that have been hypothesized to support object and event concepts respectively, we can ask how the development of these brain regions is affected by blindness.

Neural basis of object concepts in blind individuals

Knowledge of objects, such as animals and artifacts, is thought to depend in part on regions of the ventral temporal cortex. These areas are active when people listen to object names, and damage to this part of the brain causes deficits in knowledge about everyday objects (Caramazza & Shelton, 1998; Goldberg, Perfetti & Schneider, 2006; Hsu, Frankland & Thompson-Schill, in press; Kan, Barsalou, Solomon, Minor & Thompson-Schill, 2003; Martin, 2007; Simmons et al., 2007; Thompson-Schill, 2003; Tranel, Damasio & Damasio, 1997; Warrington & McCarthy, 1987; Warrington & Shallice, 1984). Within the ventral temporal cortex, there are also brain regions that support visual perception of objects such as animals, faces, and tools (e.g., Grill-Spector, 2003; Riesenhuber & Poggio, 2002). These brain regions are thought to represent modality-specific visual information about object shape, colour, and size. One interpretation of these findings is that ventral temporal representations of objects consist entirely or primarily of modality-specific visual images, and these same images are recruited as parts of the meanings of object words (Barsalou, Kyle Simmons, Barbey, & Wilson, 2003; Beauchamp & Martin, 2007; Martin, 2007; Pecher, Zeelenberg, & Barsalou, 2004; Pulvermuller, 1999; Pulvermuller & Hauk, 2006). This interpretation is consistent with the modality-dependent and modality-flexible hypotheses.

A related, but distinct proposal is that ventral temporal representations of object concepts are not themselves visual images but are derived from visual images. On this view, conceptual brain regions in the ventral temporal cortex are situated near visual brain regions because of their sensory history (Allport, 1985; Thompson-Schill, 2003). For example, because sighted people learn about objects primarily through vision, they might develop representations of object concepts near visual circuits involved in perceiving shape and colour.

Both of these interpretations of ventral temporal responses to objects in sighted people predict that these responses should be absent or at least organized differently in congenitally blind adults. When a blind person understands the word "giraffe", they cannot be recalling a visual image of a giraffe's shape. Contrary to this prediction, several studies have found ventral temporal responses to object concepts in congenitally blind adults (Noppeney, Friston, & Price, 2003). For example, Mahon and colleagues presented blind and sighted people with names of tools (e.g., hammer), non-manipulable artifacts (e.g., desk) and animals (e.g., giraffe) (Mahon, Anzellotti, Schwarzbach, Zampini & Caramazza, 2009). Participants made judgements about whether sequentially presented objects are similar in size. The neural pattern of response to animals and tools was similar in blind and sighted individuals. First, blind and sighted people both showed ventral temporal responses to both categories of objects. Second, the pattern of ventral temporal responses to tools versus animals was similar in blind and sighted people: Both groups showed a more medial response to tools and a more lateral response to animals (for converging evidence with nonverbal materials see Pietrini et al., 2004). Overall, there were no differences in the brain regions recruited for understanding object names (and making size judgements) in blind and sighted people. These findings suggest that some object-responsive regions in ventral temporal cortex do not depend on vision for normal development (see also Mahon, Schwarzbach, & Caramazza, 2010 for further evidence of preserved neurobiology of tool concepts).

One interpretation of these findings is that one set of regions in the ventral temporal cortex stores modality-independent information about objects (e.g., spatial shape representations or abstract information about animal ontogeny), and another, distinct group of regions stores modality-specific images of what objects look like. Within the modality-independent regions, the neural distribution of object information might not depend on sensory modality; instead, organization might depend on factors such as the relevance of function to category membership (Mahon et al., 2007). If so, we can infer that when people make semantic decisions based on object labels, they do so relying on modality-independent representations and not the visual images (which is why blind and sighted people show the same patterns of activation in such tasks). Visual images could still be retrieved for some detailed judgements about appearance (e.g., is a carrot darker than a stop sign?) (Thompson-Schill, 2003) but not, for example, as an automatic part of word comprehension. Seen in this light, studies of the neurobiology of objects provide evidence for the modality-invariant view (see below for a discussion of possible theoretical ambiguities).

However, these data remain open to alternative interpretations that are consistent with the modality-flexible view (Mahon et al., 2009). Ventral temporal object representations might be dominated by visual information in sighted people and compensated for by tactile or auditory information in blind people (Mahon et al., 2009; Meteyard et al., 2010). The similar patterns of neural activity in sighted and blind adults could reflect crossmodal plasticity, via which auditory and tactile information can come to activate typically visual areas (Sadato et al., 1996). For example, developmental blindness could strengthen weak tactile afferents to ventral temporal cortex. If the ventral temporal cortex additionally has some innate predisposition to represent shape information, it might then develop tactile shape representations in blind individuals (Amedi et al., 2007; Pascual-Leone & Hamilton, 2001) just as MT/MST represents motion from auditory input. Object representations could still be composed of sensory images in both blind and sighted people.

The available data fail to distinguish unambiguously between modality-invariance and modality-flexibility in the case of objects for another reason. The neural dissociations of the categories represented in ventral temporal cortex could be described either in abstract or in sensory terms. Are objects represented in ventral temporal cortex because of the particular relevance of visual shape and colour information to categorizing objects during development? Alternatively, have humans evolved neural mechanisms within ventral temporal cortex for picking out the ontological category of physical objects? Are artifacts and animals neurally dissociable because of abstract distinctions? Even preschoolers know that whether something is a chair depends to a large degree on the intent of the agent that made it, whereas whether something is a cow depends on its biological origins (Greif, Kemler Nelson, Keil, & Gutierrez, 2006). Alternatively, are these categories neurally dissociable because of sensory differences in their shape and size? As we argue below, the neurobiological evidence for modality-invariance is clearer in the case of action concepts.

Neural basis of action concepts in blind individuals

Actions make up another conceptual category that is believed to have a prominent visual component, especially from visual motion. People use patterns of visual motion to categorize events as "bouncing" versus "rolling", and to differentiate between "he jumped" versus "he was jumping" (Baldwin, Andersson, Saffran & Meyer, 2008; Baldwin et al., 2001; Zacks, Kumar, Abrams & Mehta, 2009). According to the modality-dependent hypothesis, action concepts are in part *comprised* of images of these visual motion patterns (Kable, Kan, Wilson, Thompson-Schill & Chatterjee, 2005; Kable, Lease-Spellmeyer, & Chatterjee, 2002; McClelland & Rogers, 2003; Pulvermuller, 1999). Apparently consistent with this prediction, multiple neuroimaging studies report that listening to action-verbs engages posterior lateral temporal regions, in or near visual motion areas (Chao, Haxby, & Martin, 1999; Kable et al., 2002, 2005; Kemmerer, Castillo, Talavage, Patterson & Wiley, 2008; Martin, Haxby, Lalonde, Wiggs & Ungerleider, 1995; Revill, Aslin, Tanenhaus, & Bavelier, 2008; Tettamanti et al., 2005; Tranel, Kemmerer, Adolphs, Damasio, & Damasio, 2003).

If action concepts of sighted people are composed in part of visual motion images, then the action concepts of blind individuals should be substantially different from those of the sighted. We tested this hypothesis by asking a group of congenitally blind individuals to perform a semantic similarity task with action-verbs and object-nouns. Participants judged pairs of action verbs or object-nouns on how related in meaning they were (e.g., "to kick" and "to run"; "the bush" and "the tree"). Behaviourally, blind people performed the similarity judgements just like sighted participants. The ratings of blind people were just as highly correlated with the ratings of sighted people as were the ratings of two different groups of sighted individuals. Blind and sighted people's ratings were just as highly correlated for manner of motion verbs (e.g., to kick, to roll) as for abstract mental state verbs (e.g., to think) (Bedny, Pascual-Leone, & Saxe, 2009; Koster-Hale, Saxe & Bedny, 2012). At least with regard to these simple kinds of semantic judgements, blind people appeared to have intact semantic representations of actions, providing evidence against the modality-dependent hypothesis.

Still, these behavioural data leave open both the modality-flexible and modality-invariant hypotheses. Where sighted people rely on visual images to decide how similar rolling is to bouncing, blind people might retrieve images in other modalities that efficiently compensate for lack of vision. Since vision, touch, and motor control are supported by distinct parts of cortex, neuroimaging studies could distinguish between these hypotheses. For example, the modality-flexible hypothesis predicts that sighted people activate visual motion circuits during action verb comprehension, whereas blind individuals rely on the motor and/or tactile system to a greater extent. By contrast, if blind and sighted people rely on similar neural circuits this would provide further evidence that these populations rely on similar cognitive mechanisms for understanding action verbs (modality-invariant hypothesis).

To test these hypotheses we scanned blind and sighted participants while they performed semantic similarity judgements with action verbs and object-nouns. As in Mahon's studies of object concepts, we found preserved neural responses to action-verbs (compared to object-nouns) in people who are blind. Like sighted people, congenitally blind individuals activated the left middle temporal gyrus (LMTG) when they made semantic decisions about action-verbs, but not when they made similar decisions about object-nouns (Bedny, Caramazza, Pascual-Leone & Saxe, 2012; Noppeney et al., 2003). The LMTG responses in blind people were similarly localized, of equal neuroanatomical extent, and equally robust. The presence of a typical LMTG response in people who have never seen makes it less likely that this brain region represents visual images of motion. More generally, there were no responses anywhere in the brain that were present in sighted people but missing in people who are blind, proving strong evidence against the modality-flexible hypothesis.

Importantly, we also found no evidence that blind individuals retrieved more motor or auditory–sensory information during action-verb comprehension, contrary to the predictions of the modality-flexible view.

Still, as in the case of objects, it is possible that the modality-flexible hypothesis is correct: Rather than relying on classic tactile and motor regions, blind people may have developed tactile and motor representations of motion in the same cortical location where sighted people represent visual motion, via crossmodal plasticity. For example, the LMTG might represent visual motion images of actions in sighted people, and tactile, auditory, or motor motion images of actions in people who are blind.

To test whether the representations of actions in LMTG are representations of motion patterns in any modality, we presented sighted and blind participants with noun and verb categories that varied in visual motion features. Visual motion brain regions that support seeing the movement of inanimate and animate objects all respond more to moving than to nonmoving visual stimuli (de Jong, Shipp, Skidmore, Frackowiak, & Zeki, 1994; Tootell et al., 1995a). If the LMTG stores perceptual motion information, it should also respond more to actions with than without motion.

Participants heard low-motion verbs (e.g., "to think"), medium-motion verbs (e.g., "to bleed"), and high-motion verbs (e.g., "to kick") as well as low-motion nouns (e.g., "the rock"), medium-motion nouns (e.g., "the broom"), and high-motion nouns (e.g., "the tiger"). Surprisingly, we found that the LMTG response is invariant with respect to motion information. The LMTG responds more to all verbs than to all nouns, irrespective of motion features. For example, the LMTG response was equally high for low-motion verbs such as "to think" and high-motion verbs such as "to kick." The LMTG response was equally low for high-motion nouns (e.g., "the tiger") and low-motion nouns (e.g., "the rock") (for converging evidence see Grossman et al., 2002; Rodriguez-Ferreiro, Gennari, Davies, & Cuetos, 2011). If anything the response of the LMTG was slightly higher for mental state verbs than action verbs. Furthermore, this response profile of the LMTG was identical in sighted and blind individuals across seven word categories. Finally, while we found robust effects of grammatical class on neural responses, we found no brain regions that responded more to high-motion verbs than to low-motion verbs (Figure 2, left panel).

These findings provide several different kinds of evidence for modality-invariant and abstract representations of actions. First, the LMTG, which was hypothesized to store visual images of motion, does not store visual information, does not store motion information and does not depend on early visual experience for normal development. In general, we find no evidence that visual motion associations predict neural responses to words anywhere in the brain. Nor is there any evidence that the neur'obiology of

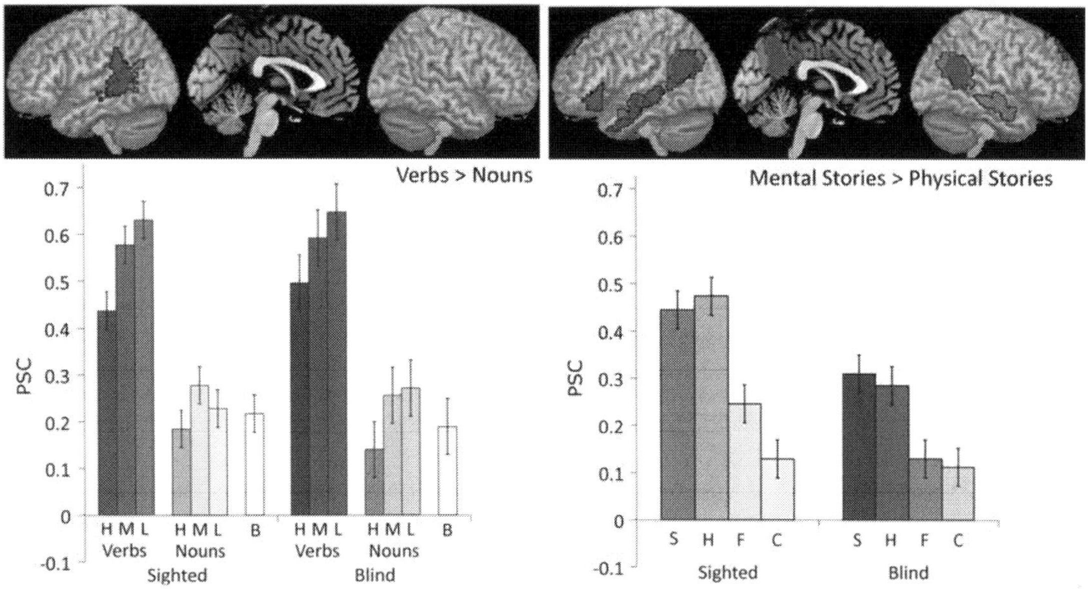

Figure 2. *Neural activity during verb and noun comprehension (left) as well as mentalizing (right) in blind and sighted individuals. Top left panel shows results of whole-brain random effects analyses for sighted (red) and blind (blue) groups, corrected for multiple comparisons, $p <$ .05. On the left are greater responses to verbs than nouns. Bottom left bar chart shows percent signal change (PSC) in the left middle temporal gyrus for verbs and nouns with varying degrees of visual motion information. Bars for higher motion words are displayed in darker colours: high motion (H), medium motion (M) low motion (L), backwards speech (B). Regions of interest were defined in individual subjects based on the verb > noun contrast (Bedny et al., 2011c). Top right panel shows neural response to stories about mental states as compared to stories about physical events. Right bar chart shows percent signal change in right temporoparietal junction for stories about mental states based on seeing (S), mental states based on hearing (H), bodily feelings, e.g., hunger (F), and control stories about physical events (C). To view a colour version of this figure, please see the online issue of the Journal.*

action concepts is different in congenitally blind individuals as compared to sighted people. By contrast, neural responses are sensitive to abstract features of words that are not reducible to perceptual primitives: namely their grammatical class (Hillis, Wityk, Barker & Caramazza, 2003; Shapiro & Caramazza, 2003; Yokoyama et al., 2006).

What exactly does LMTG represent about verbs? Based on our data, the LMTG could store abstract conceptual information relevant to verb meanings or grammatical information associated with verbs (Bedny et al., 2011a). Some evidence favours a role for the LMTG response in conceptual, rather than grammatical, processing. Several studies have reported LMTG responses to familiar actions in nonverbal tasks (Galati et al., 2008; Ricciardi et al., 2009) and damage to the LMTG impairs people's ability to match verbs to appropriate action videos (Kalenine, Buxbaum, & Coslett, 2010). In a recent experiment, we found that part of the LMTG responds not only to verbs, but also to event nouns (e.g., "the wedding") (Bedny, Dravida, & Saxe, 2012; see also Bedny & Thompson-Schill, 2006). Such findings suggest that the LMTG may store information relevant to lexicalized event categories (Frawley, 1992). Future studies of languages with distinct conceptual to linguistic mappings could yield important insights into the nature and developmental origins of the LMTG responses to verbs (e.g., De Bleser, 2003). Whatever the precise nature of LMTG representations, they are deployed during word comprehension and they develop independent of visual experience.

These findings suggest that action concepts retrieved during word comprehension and simple semantic judgements are modality-invariant. An interesting question concerns what kinds of tasks and stimuli engage these modality-invariant representations. There is some evidence that modality-invariant action representations are retrieved based on nonverbal materials. Congenitally blind individuals activate similar neural circuits to sighted people when they listen to action sounds (e.g., knocking or clapping) and remember action sequences. In both populations these kinds of tasks recruit not only lateral-temporal areas, such as the LMTG, but also left-lateralized areas in parietal and prefrontal cortex (Alaerts, Swinnen & Wenderoth, 2011; Fiehler, Burke, Bien, Roder, & Rosler, 2009; Lewis et al., 2011; Ricciardi et al., 2009).

In sum, blind and sighted people talk about actions and objects in similar ways and make similar semantic judgements about action and object categories. Drastic changes in sensory experience do not have equally drastic consequences for what people know about objects and actions (contrary to the modality-dependent hypothesis). Neuroscientific studies further suggest that similar behaviour of blind and sighted people is not masking qualitatively different formats of knowledge (contrary to the modality-flexible hypothesis). People who have never seen, and thus could not have learned concepts through vision, rely on neurobiologically similar representations of actions and objects. The same changes in sensory experience that reorganize the visual system have little, if any, consequence for the neurobiology of concepts. We hypothesize that these conceptual systems would show plasticity, and experience-dependence, in cases of qualitative change to the abstract experience relevant to those systems. Growing up isolated from objects or actions might lead to qualitatively different concepts. Finally, sensory dimensions that describe the neurobiological organization of the visual system (e.g., presence of motion) do not describe the organization of conceptual systems in either sighted or blind people. Instead, the neurobiology of concepts is organized along abstract dimensions (e.g., events versus entities). Humans possess modality-invariant and abstract conceptual representations of objects and actions, which are equally accessible to sighted and blind people.

Concepts of mental states: Behavioural and neuroscientific studies of Theory of Mind in blind individuals

The role of sensory experiences in conceptual development has also been hotly debated in a second domain: explicit thinking about other minds, or "Theory of Mind" (ToM). When we think about other people, we are often most interested in the abstract, invisible contents of their minds: their thoughts, motivations, hopes, dreams, and fears. Yet our own sensory experiences might be a gateway to understanding other minds: First, sensory experience gives us access to other people, allowing us to witness their actions and reactions; and second, our own sensory experience gives us a model for what it's like to have a mind, or experiences, that is "like me" (Meltzoff, 2005, 2007). For example, we might understand what it's like to learn through seeing because we ourselves can see. Since both of these sources of evidence are diminished for congenitally blind children, blind people might have very different concepts of other people's minds as compared to sighted people.

Development of ToM could depend on vision in at least two quite different (but not mutually exclusive) ways. First, vision is the dominant modality by which human infants learn about distal events, until they can use language. Other people's goal-directed actions, and attention, are frequently deployed in ways that are accessible by vision but not by other senses. For example, someone across the room might reach for a teddy bear, grab it, and smile, signalling successful completion of a goal-directed action; this whole sequence would be inaccessible for a blind child. There is extensive evidence that young sighted infants pay close attention to others' actions and facial expressions, and form rich expectations about how those actions will unfold. For example, sighted infants expect that people will reach for objects that they previously looked at

(Luo & Johnson, 2008), and that people's actions are oriented towards objects rather than places in space (Woodward, 1998). By age 10 months, infants also actively coordinate their direction of visual attention with an adult, using both gaze direction and (later) pointing to establish joint attention for communication. By age two years, infants expect an actor to reach for an object in the place where the actor last *saw* the object, showing that they track others' visual histories as well as current visual access (Baillargeon, Scott, & He, 2010; Luo & Baillargeon, 2007; Southgate, Senju, & Csibra, 2007). All of these early experiences with human actions feed into later conceptual developments; infants' visual expectations regarding goal-directed action at nine months predict their conceptual understanding of other people's beliefs three years later (Wellman, Lopez-Duran, LaBounty, & Hamilton, 2008).

Absence of visual access to others' actions is one limitation for blind children; another is the absence of visual experience itself. Given that other people's internal experiences are always inaccessible, one way children might learn about other minds is by assuming that other minds are similar to their own. That is, to figure out what an actor is experiencing, the observer could think: "What *would I* be experiencing, if I were in the actor's position?" This idea, known as the "like me hypothesis" (Meltzoff, 2007) or (relatedly) simulation theory, suggests that we understand others by assuming that they are similar to ourselves (Gallese, 2007). For example, preverbal sighted infants expect that other people's visual experiences are similar to their own; thus, after wearing an opaque blindfold and experiencing the absence of vision (but not before this experience), sighted infants expect that an adult wearing the same blindfold cannot see (Meltzoff & Brooks, 2008). If similar experiences are a necessary bridge for "simulating" other people's minds, then blind children would again be stymied, since the sighted people around them have many experiences that are fundamentally dissimilar from their own.

All of these reasons suggest that people who grow up blind might have a different understanding of other minds than sighted people do. By contrast, in explicit conversation and experiments, congenitally blind adults appear to have a very rich understanding of minds in general, and experiences of sight in particular. Landau and Gleitman (1985) asked a congenitally blind woman to define a range of verbs of seeing. Her definitions suggest a deep and subtle appreciation of the experience of sight. For example, she defined *to dazzle* as "to brighten, make it so bright that you can't see for a second, something sudden, like turning on a bright light in a dark room." We recently asked a group of congenitally blind adults to make semantic similarity judgements on verbs of perception (e.g., to spot, to peek) and visual quality (e.g., to sparkle, to flash). Remarkably, the judgements of congenitally blind individuals were highly similar to those of sighted people—just as similar as those of sighted people to each other. Judgements of congenitally blind individuals were also equally similar for visual verbs and for auditory (to boom, to crackle) and tactile verbs (to touch, to feel). Cluster analyses show that blind people distinguish verbs of visual perception from verbs of touch and verbs that are not tied to a particular modality (e.g., to investigate). In an experiment with narratives, we found that blind adults performed exactly as well as sighted adults on simple tests of understanding other minds (e.g., tracking what others believe, and predicting their emotions; Bedny et al., 2009).

These data raise the same challenge that we described above, for conceptual representations of actions and objects. If a blind adult can appropriately use words for, and answer questions about, mental states including visual experiences, does that mean that blind adults have the same concepts of beliefs, thoughts, and perceptions as sighted people? Or are verbal behaviours covering up fundamental differences in the ways that sighted and blind people think about the mind? As above, functional neuroimaging provides a complementary source of evidence to behavioural judgements. We can look "under the hood", and ask whether the neural circuits activated for thinking about the mind, in general, and experiences of seeing, in particular, are similar or different in sighted and blind adults.

We conducted a neuroimaging experiment to test these hypotheses. First, we asked sighted and blind adults to listen to stories about people's thoughts and beliefs, versus stories about other physical representations, such as maps, photographs, and audio recordings. Dozens of prior neuroimaging studies (Gallagher & Frith, 2003; Saxe & Kanwisher, 2003; Saxe & Wexler, 2005) had found that reading about people's thoughts leads to increased activity in a group of brain regions, including bilateral temporo-parietal junction (TPJ), medial prefrontal cortex (MPFC), and medial parietal cortex (precuneus, PC). Of these regions, the TPJ was specifically thought to depend on visual input. The TPJ is adjacent to brain regions recruited during visual observation of human bodies and actions (Downing, Jiang, Shuman, & Kanwisher, 2001; Grossman & Blake, 2002), and when considering others' gaze direction and visual perspectives (Aichhorn, Perner, Kronbichler, Staffen, & Ladurner, 2006; Pelphrey, Morris & McCarthy, 2004; Wyk, Hudac, Carter, Sobel & Pelphrey, 2009). Thus, it seemed plausible that the development of the TPJ might depend on visual input from its neuroanatomical neighbors during childhood. Contrary to this hypothesis, we found that all of the so-called "ToM regions" appeared identical in size and position in sighted and congenitally blind adults (Bedny et al., 2009). Thus, visual access to others' actions and gaze direction does not seem to be necessary for typical development of ToM brain regions (Figure 2, right panel).

Converging evidence for the same conclusion comes from Ma and colleagues (Ma & Han, 2011). Blind and sighted adults were asked to attribute traits to themselves and others (e.g., "lazy", "courageous"). Both blind adults (listening to trait words) and sighted adults (reading trait words) showed enhanced MPFC activity when attributing traits to themselves. Also, blind adults are actually better than sighted adults at recognizing emotional tone of voice and have increased neural markers of emotional response to voices (Klinge, Roder, & Buchel, 2010). Taken together, these three studies suggest that visual access is not necessary to develop typical "social" brain regions.

Second, we (Bedny et al., 2009) tested the "simulation" hypothesis that we understand other people's sensory and mental experiences by, in a sense, feeling what it would be like to have that experience in our own mind. Blind people have some of the same mental experiences as sighted people (e.g., hearing the sound of a baby laughing, hearing a friend's footsteps) but do not have other experiences (e.g., seeing a baby smiling, seeing a friend's handwriting). If blind and sighted people actually have fundamentally different representations of experiences of seeing, in spite of their similar language use, then we should see those differences in patterns of neural activation. By contrast, we again observed that blind adults' neural responses looked just like sighted adults'. Both blind and sighted adults showed robust activity in "ToM" brain regions when listening to stories about hearing and about seeing; there was no region anywhere in the brain that showed different responses to hearing versus seeing, in blind versus sighted people (Figure 2, right panel). These data could suggest that blind people treat seeing and hearing experiences as equivalent. That is, perhaps blind people interpret "to see" as "to perceive". Contrary to this interpretation we found that we could distinguish stories about seeing from stories about hearing based on the pattern of neural activity within the RTPJ (Koster-Hale, Bedny, & Saxe, 2012). Together, behavioural and neuroimaging data suggest that blind people have rich representations of seeing, despite never having seen.

Neuroimaging studies with blind adults thus provide evidence for preserved understanding of other minds despite differences in first person sensory experience. Apparently, by adulthood, understanding "running" does not necessarily involve a visual image of running, understanding "wanting" does not require watching someone reaching for an object, and even understanding "seeing" does not require first-person experiences of vision.

Interestingly, though, the developmental processes by which blind and sighted children arrive at an adult ToM may be different. Although blind adults appear to have unaffected ToM (at least on simple tasks), blind children are delayed in developing an understanding of visual perception (Bigelow, 1991, 1992; Millar, 1976). For example, the blind six-year-old, Kelli, understood that sighted people can see with their eyes. But she also claimed that if a sighted person closed their eyes, they could see through their mouth, provided there was no food in it (Landau & Gleitman, 1985). Blind children are also worse than age-matched sighted children at reasoning about line of sight and partial occlusion of one object by another (Bigelow, 1991, 1992; Millar, 1976). Delays in understanding visual experience may reflect the absence of first-person experience, and the analogy from other minds to my own experience (the "like me" hypothesis; Meltzoff, 2007).

More generally, blind children also show delays on standard milestones of ToM development, such as false-belief tasks, which tap children's understanding that other people can have incorrect beliefs about the state of the world, caused by misleading, incomplete or outdated evidence. Blind children are late to pass classic false-belief tasks, even those that do not require an understanding of visual perspective (McAlpine & Moore, 1995; Minter, Hobson, & Martin, 1998); and blind children continue to fail false-belief tasks after they catch up with sighted children on visual perspective-taking tasks (Peterson et al., 2000). Delays on false-belief tasks generalize across paradigms (e.g., the Sally Anne task) (Brambring & Asbrock, 2010; Green, Pring, & Swettenham, 2004; Peterson et al., 2000), and persist even when blind children reason about the mental states of other blind children (Peterson et al., 2000) and when tasks do not require visual knowledge of objects (Brambring & Asbrock). For example, in one auditory false-belief task, an experimenter played a familiar song to blind children. The song was stopped in the middle and the children were asked what they expected to hear when the player was turned on again. The children then heard an unexpected continuation of the song (e.g., the wrong phrase). Afterwards, children were asked: When I play the beginning of this song to your friend, what will *she* expect to hear? "Passing" the false-belief task requires children to predict that another child will expect to hear the correct continuation. Whereas almost all sighted children pass this task by five years of age, blind children do so by six years of age. On average, across 16 different ToM tasks specifically designed for blind children, blind children are delayed by 19 months relative to blindfolded sighted control children (Brambring & Asbrock, 2010).

Thus, losing visual access to other people does seem to delay development of children's ToM. One very interesting open question is *when* the delay occurs. Are blind infants delayed in developing initial nonverbal (perhaps implicit) expectations about others' actions, which then translate into later development of explicit conceptual understanding of mental states (Wellman et al., 2008)? Or do blind children show typical early stages of "theory of mind", including understanding of goals and desires, but then make a slower transition to a fully representational conception of beliefs? Future research with young blind children, and mental concepts beyond seeing and believing, is necessary to resolve this question.

Functional neuroimaging could be used to further investigate the origins of ToM deficits in blind children. Performing a false-belief task depends on many different cognitive abilities, including ToM, but also language and executive function (i.e., the ability to hold in mind and choose between multiple competing ideas (Flynn, O'Malley, & Wood, 2004; Rakoczy, 2009). Each of these cognitive capacities is associated with activity in different groups of neural regions (Botvinick, Cohen, & Carter, 2004; Friederici, 2002; Grodzinsky & Friederici, 2006; Miller & Cohen, 2001; Poeppel & Hickok, 2004; Price, 2000; Thompson-Schill, Bedny, & Goldberg, 2005). Thus, neuroimaging would allow us to test whether delays in ToM task performance in blind children are related to delayed development of domain-specific brain regions for ToM, or rather to differential development of the many other cognitive functions required for passing ToM tasks.

It may also be illuminating to compare the effects on ToM development of blindness versus deafness. Whereas blindness leads to a brief but significant delay in basic ToM milestones, deaf children show no delay in passing false-belief tasks, unless they are born to nonsigning parents. Absence of early *auditory* access to the world, *per se*, does not impair ToM; and the presence of early auditory access does not seem sufficient to support typical ToM development. These results converge to highlight the importance of early visual access to other people, at the first stages of ToM development.

On the other hand, early language deprivation can have longer lasting and more profound consequences for the development of ToM than blindness. Deaf children of non-native-signing parents can be delayed two to three years on standard ToM milestones (Peterson & Siegal, 1995; Pyers, 2006; Schick, de Villiers, de Villiers, & Hoffmeister, 2007; Woolfe, Want, & Siegal, 2002), and their performance, even on low-verbal versions of ToM tasks, is predicted by their parents' use of mental state verbs in sign language (Moeller & Schick, 2006). Strikingly, exposure to people talking about the mind appears to be a necessary gateway to a full ToM. Adults whose language does not contain mental state terms fail basic nonverbal false-belief tasks (Pyers & Senghas, 2009). When the content of the language changes, to include mental state terms, these adults show corresponding improvements on false belief tasks (Pyers & Senghas, 2009). It seems that visual access to other people cannot compensate for the evidence provided by language and conversation. By contrast, linguistic access can compensate for vision. Between age seven years and adolescence, blind children catch up with their sighted peers in performance on theory of mind tasks (Brambring & Asbrock, 2010).

Based on the developmental evidence, we hypothesize that learning about other minds proceeds in two phases. Prelinguistic infants learn about the minds of others primarily through visual access to human faces, eyes, and actions and through their own first-person experiences of seeing. With increased linguistic abilities, children rely heavily on language and in particular on learning from other people talking about the mind. As a result, lack of vision leads to slow initial development of social knowledge, but the resulting delays are eventually overcome by blind children—at least in part through evidence from language (see Urwin, 1983 for related ideas).

In sum, neuroimaging provides a new window into blind people's understanding of other minds. Corroborating behavioural evidence, neuroimaging results suggest that blind adults acquire complete and typical representations of other people's mental experiences, even experiences of seeing. On the other hand, blind children's development of mental state representations is slow. This slowing is not particular to representations of seeing, but likely results from reduced access to visual evidence of mental states. In the future, neuroimaging may facilitate discovering the cognitive origin of this delay.

Objects, actions, and thoughts in the minds of blind people: Some qualifications

Studies of blindness thus place an upper bound on the strength of the link between percepts and concepts. While the sensory experience of blind and sighted people is drastically different, behavioural and neuroimaging data show that conceptual representations of these two groups are strikingly similar. These similarities hold for conceptual categories that, in our view, are among the best candidates to show effects of blindness. Conceptual representations used to understand concrete words, categorize objects and actions, and think about the perceptual states of other people are not images of sensory experiences. Humans have a rich repertoire of abstract representations that capture the higher-order structure of their environment in terms of events, objects, agents, and their mental states. In this regard, neuroscience affirms rather than undercuts a basic tenet of modern cognitive science, that abstract representations are just as real in the mind and brain as representations of shape, colour, and orientation (Bedny & Caramazza, 2011; Caramazza & Mahon, 2003; Chatterjee, 2010;

Dove, 2009; Mahon & Caramazza, 2008; Potter & Faulconer, 1975; Potter, Valian, & Faulconer, 1977).

One question raised by this argument, however, is: Where is the boundary of a concept? In our experiments, and our review above, we have focused on abstract aspects of concepts that are necessary for understanding words and making simple inferences. In addition to this putative core, concepts are associated with lots of other information, including sensory images. In many conceptual tasks, sighted people can and do retrieve such visual knowledge (Thompson-Schill, 2003; Wilson, 2002). For example, visual information is used to make detailed judgements about the appearance of objects, such as their colours, shapes, and sizes (e.g., does a kangaroo have a long or short tail?) (Farah, Hammond, Levine, & Calvanio, 1988; Hsu et al., in press) and to answer questions about spatial layouts (e.g., how many windows are there in your kitchen?). We believe that the studies done to date have not tested blind individuals on tasks that are likely to depend on visual information in sighted individuals.

How do these phenomena relate to claims about amodal concepts? We expect that blind people *would* show differences from sighted people in how they performed image-based tasks, like counting their kitchen windows or deciding whether a stop sign is darker than a carrot. These differences would be manifest in their behaviour or neural responses or, more likely, both (Arditi, Holtzman, & Kosslyn, 1988). One interpretation is that amodal conceptual representations are distinct from sensory images, but both kinds of representations exist and can dynamically interact to support task performance. Similar interactions occur between different sensory systems. For example, auditory information affects both visual perception and processing in early visual areas of the human brain (Sadaghiani, Maier & Noppeney, 2009). A natural interpretation is that auditory and visual representations are distinct, but can interact and influence one another. In a similar way, sensory representations might contribute to conceptual tasks (Mandler, 2008).

Another possibility is that there is no clear distinction between conceptual and sensory representations; there is just a continuum of different kinds of knowledge. On this view, the data we have described show that blind and sighted people share one aspect of object and event concepts (the abstract features retrieved when understanding words and sentences), but other aspects of those same concepts (the sensory images used to make judgements about appearance) might be different. Data from blind individuals would then inform hypotheses about when these different aspects of knowledge are deployed: Whenever blind and sighted people show similar performance and similar brain activation, only the abstract features of conceptual knowledge are necessary for task performance.

These reflections also relate to another issue. Here we argue that blind and sighted people have roughly similar concepts of objects, actions, and sight, but the experiments to date have barely scratched the surface of these representations. When we probe in more detail, blind and sighted people will likely differ not only in the sensory images associated with their abstract knowledge, but in the fine-grained details of the abstract knowledge itself. Such differences might be analogous to differences between experts and non-experts in other cognitive domains (e.g., mechanics, marine biologists, and wine tasters) (Ballester, Patris, Symoneaux & Valentin, 2007; Goldberg & Thompson-Schill, 2009). The difference between a layman's and a marine biologist's representation of lobsters is not just that the former is gustatory while the latter's is visual. A marine biologist has significantly more detailed knowledge about lobsters: how they breathe, how they eat, and what their nervous system is like. Similarly a blind person might be less likely, on average, to know whether a hippopotamus has fur, and more likely to know about the cognitive capacities of guide dogs, the social networks of the blind community, and people's perception through touch. It may be particularly interesting to ask whether blind individuals differ in their fine-grained knowledge of sight (Heller & Kennedy, 1990). Do blind individuals have less detailed knowledge of occlusion, visual attention, line of sight, etc.? Neurally, such knowledge differences between blind and sighted people would likely be reflected in the information coded within similar brain regions, rather than in which brain regions store conceptual representations. Such conceptual differences across populations could be characterized by measuring behaviour and examining neural responses at higher spatial resolution, for example with multivoxel pattern analysis and fMRI adaptation (Druks & Froud, 2002; Pietrini et al., 2004). We hypothesize that conceptual differences between blind and sighted people are quantitative rather than qualitative. These differences, if they exist, are similar in kind to conceptual differences caused by other naturally occurring variation in life experiences, such as variation across cultures and professions. Just as we would say that the biologist and the layman share qualitatively similar concepts of lobsters, blind and sighted people share qualitatively similar concepts of objects, actions, and mental states.

CONCLUSIONS

Blindness has long been a window into the origins of the human mind, but often as a thought experiment. During the past century, cognitive scientists have tackled old philosophical puzzles by applying the methods of experimental psychology and neuroscience to the study of blindness. Rather than postulate what the minds of blind people should be like, cognitive scientists have collaborated with blind individuals to test theories of development. This effort has yielded a rich set of data that constrains cognitive and neuroscientific theories of development.

Studies of blindness reveal that brain regions with strong innate biases have a dramatic capacity for change. In children who grow up without sight, visual circuits develop drastically different cognitive functions. Contrary to what most theories of neurobiological development would predict, this neuroplasticity does not respect cognitive boundaries. The same brain regions that support visuospatial discrimination in sighted people participate in abstract cognitive functions, such as language, in blind individuals. Visual cortex plasticity demonstrates the pluripotency of human neural circuits during development.

While developmental blindness profoundly reorganizes brain regions that encode the surface structure of the visual world, it leaves the neurobiology of concepts largely unchanged. This neuroscientific observation augments behavioural evidence of preserved conceptual knowledge in people who are blind. Even in the case of concrete categories of objects and actions, blind people know similar information and this information is implemented in similar neural systems. Contrary to the suppositions of the empiricist philosophers, blindness does not qualitatively change the nature of concepts. In blind and sighted people alike, seemingly concrete concepts have core abstract components that develop independent from the sensory quality of experience.

REFERENCES

Adelson, E., & Fraiberg, S. (1974). Gross motor development in infants blind from birth. *Child Development*, *45*, 114–126.

Aichhorn, M., Perner, J., Kronbichler, M., Staffen, W., & Ladurner, G. (2006). Do visual perspective tasks need theory of mind? *NeuroImage*, *30*, 1059–1068.

Alaerts, K., Swinnen, S. P., & Wenderoth, N. (2011). Action perception in individuals with congenital blindness or deafness: How does the loss of a sensory modality from birth affect perception-induced motor facilitation? *Journal of Cognitive Neuroscience*, *23*, 1080–1087.

Allport, D. A. (1985). Distributed memory, modular subsystems and dysphasia. In S. K. Newman & R. Epstein (Eds.), *Current perspectives in dysphasia* (pp. 207–244). Edinburgh, UK: Churchill Livingstone.

Amedi, A., Floel, A., Knecht, S., Zohary, E., & Cohen, L. G. (2004). Transcranial magnetic stimulation of the occipital pole interferes with verbal processing in blind subjects. *Nature Neuroscience*, *7*, 1266–1270.

Amedi, A., Raz, N., Pianka, P., Malach, R., & Zohary, E. (2003). Early 'visual' cortex activation correlates with superior verbal memory performance in the blind. *Nature Neuroscience, 6,* 758–766.

Amedi, A., Stern, W. M., Camprodon, J. A., Bermpohl, F., Merabet, L., Rotman, S., Hemond, C., … Pascual-Leone, A. (2007). Shape conveyed by visual-to-auditory sensory substitution activates the lateral occipital complex. *Nature Neuroscience, 10,* 687–689.

Andersen, E. S., Dunlea, A., & Kekelis, L. S. (1984). Blind children's language: Resolving some differences. *Journal of Child Language, 11,* 645–664.

Arditi, A., Holtzman, J. D., & Kosslyn, S. M. (1988). Mental imagery and sensory experience in congenital blindness. *Neuropsychologia, 26,* 1–12.

Baillargeon, R., Scott, R. M., & He, Z. (2010). False-belief understanding in infants. *Trends in Cognitive Science, 14,* 110–118.

Baldwin, D., Andersson, A., Saffran, J., & Meyer, M. (2008). Segmenting dynamic human action via statistical structure. *Cognition, 106,* 1382–1407.

Baldwin, D. A., Baird, J. A., Saylor, M. M., & Clark, M. A. (2001). Infants parse dynamic action. *Child Development, 72,* 708–717.

Ballester, J., Patris, B., Symoneaux, R., & Valentin, D. (2007). Conceptual vs. perceptual wine spaces: Does expertise matter? *Food Quality and Preference, 19,* 267–276.

Barsalou, L. W. (1999). Perceptual symbol systems. *Behavioral and Brain Sciences, 22,* 577–609, discussion 610–560.

Barsalou, L. W., Kyle Simmons, W., Barbey, A. K., & Wilson, C. D. (2003). Grounding conceptual knowledge in modality-specific systems. *Trends in Cognitive Sciences, 7,* 84–91.

Barton, R. A. (2007). Evolutionary specialization in mammalian cortical structure. *Journal of Evolutionary Biology, 20,* 1504–1511.

Beauchamp, M. S., & Martin, A. (2007). Grounding object concepts in perception and action: evidence from fMRI studies of tools. *Cortex, 43,* 461–468.

Bedny, M., Dufour, N., Dravida, S., & Saxe, R. (2010). Item analysis of neural responses to sentences in visual cortex of congenitally blind adults. Unpublished raw data.

Bedny, M., & Caramazza, A. (2011). Perception, action, and word meanings in the human brain: the case from action verbs. *Annals of the New York Academy of Sciences, 1224,* 81–95.

Bedny, M., Caramazza, A., Pascual-Leone, A., & Saxe, R. (2012). Typical neural representations of action verbs develop without vision, *Cerebral Cortex, 22,* 286–293.

Bedny, M., Dravida, S., & Saxe, R. (2012). *Shindigs, brunches and rodeos: The neural basis of event words.* Unpublished manuscript.

Bedny, M., Konkle, T., Pelphrey, K., Saxe, R., & Pascual-Leone, A. (2011b). Sensitive period for a multimodal response in human visual motion area MT/MST. *Current Biology, 20,* 1900–1906.

Bedny, M., Pascual-Leone, A., Dodell-Feder, D., Fedorenko, E., & Saxe, R. (2011c). Language processing in the occipital cortex of congenitally blind adults. *Proceedings of the National Academy of Sciences of the United States of America, 108,* 4429–4434.

Bedny, M., Pascual-Leone, A., Dravida, S., & Saxe, R. (2011d). A sensitive period for language in the visual cortex: Distinct patterns of plasticity in congenitally versus late blind adults. *Brain and Language.* Manuscript submitted for publication.

Bedny, M., Pascual-Leone, A., & Saxe, R. R. (2009). Growing up blind does not change the neural bases of Theory of Mind. *Proceedings of the National Academy of Sciences of the United States of America, 106,* 11312–11317.

Bedny, M., Richardson, H. & Saxe, R. (2012). *"Visual" cortex is active during language processing in young blind children.* Unpublished manuscript.

Bedny, M., & Thompson-Schill, S. L. (2006). Neuroanatomically separable effects of imageability and grammatical class during single-word comprehension. *Brain and Language, 98,* 127–139.

Bellugi, U., Poizner, H., & Klima, E. S. (1983). Brain organization for language: Clues from sign aphasia. *Human Neurobiology, 2,* 155–170.

Benzaquen, A. S. (2006). *Encounters with wild children: Temptation And disappointment in the study of human nature.* McGill-Queen's University Press.

Berkeley, G. (1709/1732). *An essay towards a new theory of vision.* Dublin, Ireland: Aaron Rhames for Jeremy Pepyal.

Bigelow, A. (1987). Early words of blind children. *Journal of Child Language, 14,* 47–56.

Bigelow, A. (1991). Hiding in blind and sighted children. *Development and Psychopathology, 3,* 301–310.

Bigelow, A. (1992). The development of blind children's ability to predict what another sees. *Journal of Visual Impairment and Blindness, 86,* 181–184.

Botvinick, M. M., Cohen, J. D., & Carter, C. S. (2004). Conflict monitoring and anterior cingulate cortex: An update. *Trends in Cognitive Sciences, 8,* 539–546.

Brambring, M., & Asbrock, D. (2010). Validity of false belief tasks in blind children. *Journal of Autism and Developmental Disorders, 40,* 1471–1484.

Buchel, C., Price, C., Frackowiak, R. S., & Friston, K. (1998). Different activation patterns in the visual cortex of late and congenitally blind subjects. *Brain*, *121*(Pt 3), 409–419.

Burton, H., Diamond, J. B., & McDermott, K. B. (2003). Dissociating cortical regions activated by semantic and phonological tasks: a FMRI study in blind and sighted people. *Journal of Neurophysiology*, *90*, 1965–1982.

Burton, H., & McLaren, D. G. (2006). Visual cortex activation in late-onset, Braille naive blind individuals: An fMRI study during semantic and phonological tasks with heard words. *Neuroscience Letters*, *392*, 38–42.

Burton, H., Snyder, A. Z, Conturo, T. E., Akbudak, E., Ollinger, J. M., & Raichle, M. E. (2002a). Adaptive changes in early and late blind: A fMRI study of Braille reading. *Journal of Neurophysiology*, *87*, 589–607.

Burton, H., Snyder, A. Z, Diamond, J. B., & Raichle, M. E. (2002b). Adaptive changes in early and late blind: A fMRI study of verb generation to heard nouns. *Journal of Neurophysiology*, *88*, 3359–3371.

Caramazza, A., & Mahon, B. Z. (2003). The organization of conceptual knowledge: The evidence from category-specific semantic deficits. *Trends in Cognitive Sciences*, *7*, 354–361.

Caramazza, A., & Shelton, J. R. (1998). Domain-specific knowledge systems in the brain: The animate–inanimate distinction. *Journal of Cognitive Neuroscience*, *10*, 1–34.

Carey, S. (2009). *The origin of concepts*. Oxford, UK: Oxford University Press.

Chao, L. L., Haxby, J. V., & Martin, A. (1999). Attribute-based neural substrates in temporal cortex for perceiving and knowing about objects. *Nature Neuroscience*, *2*, 913–919.

Chatterjee, A. (2010). Disembodying cognition. *Language and Cognition*, *2*, 79–116.

Chee, M. W., Caplan, D., Soon, C. S., Sriram, N., Tan, E. W., Thiel, T., & Weekes, B. (1999a). Processing of visually presented sentences in Mandarin and English studied with fMRI. *Neuron*, *23*, 127–137.

Chee, M. W., Tan, E. W., & Thiel, T. (1999b). Mandarin and English single word processing studied with functional magnetic resonance imaging. *Journal of Neuroscience*, *19*, 3050–3056.

Chomsky, C. (1986). Analytic study of the Tadoma method: Language abilities of three deaf–blind subjects. *Journal of Speech and Hearing Research*, *29*, 332–347.

Cohen, L. G., Celnik, P., Pascual-Leone, A., Corwell, B., Falz, L., Dambrosia, J., ... Hallett, M. (1997). Functional relevance of cross-modal plasticity in blind humans. *Nature*, *389*, 180–183.

Collignon, O., Vandewalle, G., Voss, P., Albouy, G., Charbonneau, G., Lassonde, M., & Lepore, F. (2011). Functional specialization for auditory–spatial processing in the occipital cortex of congenitally blind humans. *Proceedings of the National Academy of Sciences of the United States of America*, *108*, 4435–4440.

Connolly, A. C., Gleitman, L. R., & Thompson-Schill, S. L. (2007). Effect of congenital blindness on the semantic representation of some everyday concepts. *Proceedings of the National Academy of Sciences of the United States of America*, *104*, 8241–8246.

Cutsforth, T. D. (1932). The unreality of words to the blind. *Teachers Forum*, *4*, 86–89.

De Bleser, R., & Kauschke, C. (2003). Acquisition and loss of nouns and verbs: Parallel or divergent patterns? *Journal of Neurolinguistics*, *16*, 213–229.

de Jong, B. M., Shipp, S., Skidmore, B., Frackowiak, R. S., & Zeki, S. (1994). The cerebral activity related to the visual perception of forward motion in depth. *Brain*, *117*, 1039–1054.

Dove, G. (2009). Beyond perceptual symbols: A call for representational pluralism. *Cognition*, *110*, 412–431.

Downing, P. E., Jiang, Y, Shuman, M., & Kanwisher, N. (2001). A cortical area selective for visual processing of the human body. *Science*, *293*, 2470–2473.

Druks, J., & Froud, K. (2002). The syntax of single words: Evidence from a patient with a selective function word reading deficit. *Cognitive Neuropsychology*, *19*, 207–244.

Dubner, R., & Zeki, S. M. (1971). Response properties and receptive fields of cells in an anatomically defined region of the superior temporal sulcus in the monkey. *Brain Research*, *35*, 528–532.

Dunlea, A. (1989). *Vision and the emergence of meaning: Blind and sighted children's early language*. New York, NY: Cambridge University Press.

Farah, M. J., Hammond, K. M., Levine, D. N., & Calvanio, R. (1988). Visual and spatial mental imagery: Dissociable systems of representation. *Cognitive Psychology*, *20*, 439–462.

Fiehler, K., Burke, M., Bien, S., Roder, B., & Rosler, F. (2009). The human dorsal action control system develops in the absence of vision. *Cerebral Cortex*, *19*, 1–12.

Fine, I., Wade, A. R., Brewer, A. A., May, M. G., Goodman, D. F., Boynton, G. M., ... MacLeod, D. I. A. (2003). Long-term deprivation affects visual perception and cortex. *Nature Neuroscience, 6,* 915–916.

Flynn, E., O'Malley, C., & Wood, D. (2004). A longitudinal, microgenetic study of the emergence of false belief understanding and inhibition skills. *Development Science, 7,* 103–115.

Frawley, W. (1992). *Linguistic semantics.* Hillsdale, NJ: Lawrence Erlbaum Associates.

Friederici, A. D. (2002). Towards a neural basis of auditory sentence processing. *Trends in Cognitive Science, 6,* 78–84.

Galati, G., Committeri, G., Spitoni, G., Aprile, T., Di Russo, F., Pitzalis, S., & Pizzamiglio, L. (2008). A selective representation of the meaning of actions in the auditory mirror system. *NeuroImage, 40,* 1274–1286.

Gallagher, H. L., & Frith, C. D. (2003). Functional imaging of 'theory of mind'. *Trends in Cognitive Science, 7,* 77–83.

Gallese, V. (2007). Before and below 'theory of mind': Embodied simulation and the neural correlates of social cognition. *Philosophical Transactions of the Royal Society of London B: Biological Sciences, 362,* 659–669.

Gallese, V., & Lakoff, G. (2005). The brain concepts: The role of the sensory-motor system in conceptual structure. *Cognitive Neuropsychology, 22,* 455–479.

Gleitman, L., & Newport, E. (1995). The invention of language by children: Environmental and biological influences on the acquisition of language. In L. Gleitman & M. Liberman (Eds.), *An invitation to cognitive science* (pp. 1–24). Cambridge, MA: MIT Press.

Glenberg, A. M. (1997). What memory is for. *Behavioral and Brain Sciences, 20,* 1–19, discussion 19–55.

Goldberg, R. F., Perfetti, C. A., & Schneider, W. (2006). Perceptual knowledge retrieval activates sensory brain regions. *Journal of Neuroscience, 26,* 4917–4921.

Goldberg, R. F., & Thompson-Schill, S. L. (2009). Developmental "roots" in mature biological knowledge. *Psychological Science, 20,* 480–487.

Green, S., Pring, L., & Swettenham, J. (2004). An investigation of first-order false belief understanding of children with congenital profound visual impairment. *British Journal of Developmental Psychology, 22,* 1–17.

Greif, M. L., Kemler, Nelson, D. G., Keil, F. C., & Gutierrez, F. (2006). What do children want to know about animals and artifacts? Domain-specific requests for information. *Psychological Science, 17,* 455–459.

Grill-Spector, K. (2003). The neural basis of object perception. *Current Opinion in Neurobiology, 13,* 159–166.

Grodzinsky, Y., & Friederici, A. D. (2006). Neuroimaging of syntax and syntactic processing. *Current Opinion in Neurobiology, 16,* 240–246.

Grossman, E. D., & Blake, R. (2002). Brain areas active during visual perception of biological motion. *Neuron, 35,* 1167–1175.

Grossman, M., Koenig, P., DeVita, C., Glosser, G., Alsop, D., Detre, J., & Gee, J. (2002). Neural representation of verb meaning: An fMRI study. *Human Brain Mapping, 15,* 124–134.

Hamilton, R., Keenan, J. P., Catala, M., & Pascual-Leone, A. (2000). Alexia for Braille following bilateral occipital stroke in an early blind woman. *NeuroReport, 11,* 237–240.

Hamilton, R. H., & Pascual-Leone, A. (1998). Cortical plasticity associated with Braille learning. *Trends in Cognitive Science, 2,* 168–174.

Heller, M. A., & Kennedy, J. M. (1990). Perspective taking, pictures, and the blind. *Perception & Psychophysics, 48,* 459–466.

Hillis, A. E., Wityk, R. J., Barker, P. B., & Caramazza, A. (2003). Neural regions essential for writing verbs. *Nature Neuroscience, 6,* 19–20.

Hobbes, T. (1641/1984). Meditations on first philosophy, objections with replies. In Robert Stoothoff & Douglas Murdoch (Eds.), *The Philosophical Writings of Descartes.* Cambridge, UK: Cambridge University Press.

Hsu, N. S., Frankland, S. M., & Thompson-Schill, S. L. (in press). Chromaticity of color perception and object color knowledge. *Neuropsychologia, 50,* 327–333.

Hubel, D. H., & Wiesel, T. N. (1970). The period of susceptibility to the physiological effects of unilateral eye closure in kittens. *Journal of Physiology, 206,* 419–436.

Hume, D. (1739/1978). *A treatise of human nature.* Oxford, UK: Oxford University Press.

Iverson, J. M., & Goldin-Meadow, S. (1997). What's communication got to do with it? Gesture in children blind from birth. *Development Psychology, 33,* 453–467.

Johnson, J. S., & Newport, E. L. (1989). Critical period effects in second language learning: The influence of maturational state on the acquisition of English as a second language. *Cognitive Psychology, 21,* 60–99.

Kaas, J. H. (2008). The evolution of the complex sensory and motor systems of the human brain. *Brain Research Bulletin, 75,* 384–390.

Kable, J. W., Kan, I. P., Wilson, A., Thompson-Schill, S. L., & Chatterjee, A. (2005). Conceptual representations of action in the lateral temporal cortex. *Journal of Cognitive Neuroscience, 17,* 1855–1870.

Kable, J. W., Lease-Spellmeyer, J., & Chatterjee, A. (2002). Neural substrates of action event knowledge. *Journal of Cognitive Neuroscience, 14,* 795–805.

Kahn, D. M., & Krubitzer, L. (2002). Massive cross-modal cortical plasticity and the emergence of a new cortical area in developmentally blind mammals. *Proceedings of the National Academy of Sciences of the United States of America, 99,* 11429–11434.

Kalenine, S., Buxbaum, L. J., & Coslett, H. B. (2010). Critical brain regions for action recognition: Lesion symptom mapping in left hemisphere stroke. *Brain, 133,* 3269–3280.

Kan, I. P., Barsalou, L. W., Solomon, K. O., Minor, J. K., & Thompson-Schill, S. L. (2003). Role of mental imagery in a property verification task: FMRI evidence for perceptual representations of conceptual knowledge. *Cognitive Neuropsychology, 20,* 525–540.

Kemmerer, D., Castillo, J. G., Talavage, T., Patterson, S., & Wiley, C. (2008). Neuroanatomical distribution of five semantic components of verbs: Evidence from fMRI. *Brain and Language, 107,* 16–43.

Klinge, C., Roder, B., & Buchel, C. (2010). Increased amygdala activation to emotional auditory stimuli in the blind. *Brain, 133,* 1729–1736.

Koster-Hale, J., Bedny, M., & Saxe, R. (2012). *Theory of Mind network encodes perceptual source information in both blind and sighted adults.* Unpublished manuscript.

Koster-Hale, J., Saxe, R., & Bedny, M. (2012). *To peek and to peer: "Visual" verb meanings are largely unaffected by congenital blindness.* Unpublished manuscript.

Kujala, T., Huotilainen, M., Sinkkonen, J., Ahonen, A. I., Alho, K., Hämäläinen, M. S., ... Näätänen, R. (1995). Visual cortex activation in blind humans during sound discrimination. *Neuroscience Letters, 183,* 143–146.

Lakoff, G., & Johnson, M. (1980). *Metaphors we live by.* Chicago, IL: University of Chicago Press.

Lakoff, G., & Nunez, R. (2001). *Where mathematics comes from: How the embodied mind brings mathematics into being.* New York, NY: Basic Books.

Landau, B. (1983). Blind children's language is not meaningless. In A.E. Mills (Ed.), *Language acquisition in the blind child: Normal and deficient* (pp. 62–76). San Diego, CA: College-Hill Press.

Landau, B., Gleitman, H., & Spelke, E. (1981). Spatial knowledge and geometric representation in a child blind from birth. *Science, 213,* 1275–1278.

Landau, B., & Gleitman, L. (1985). *Language and experience: Evidence from the blind child.* Cambridge, MA: Harvard University Press.

Landau, B., Spelke, E., & Gleitman, H. (1984). Spatial knowledge in a young blind child. *Cognition, 16,* 225–260.

Le Grand, R., Mondloch, C. J., Maurer, D., & Brent, H. P. (2003). Expert face processing requires visual input to the right hemisphere during infancy. *Nature Neuroscience, 6,* 1108–1112.

Le Grand, R., Mondloch, C. J., Maurer, D., & Brent, H. P. (2004). Impairment in holistic face processing following early visual deprivation. *Psychological Science, 15,* 762–768.

Levin, N., Dumoulin, S. O., Winawer, J., Dougherty, R. F., & Wandell, B. A. (2010). Cortical maps and white matter tracts following long period of visual deprivation and retinal image restoration. *Neuron, 65,* 21–31.

Lewis, J. W., Frum, C., Brefczynski-Lewis, J. A., Talkington, W. J., Walker, N. A., Rapuano, K. M., & Kovach, A. L. (2011). Cortical network differences in the sighted versus early blind for recognition of human-produced action sounds. *Human Brain Mapping, 32,* 2241–2255.

Li, Y., Fitzpatrick, D., & White, L. E. (2006). The development of direction selectivity in ferret visual cortex requires early visual experience. *Nature Neuroscience, 9,* 676–681.

Liu, Y., Yu, C., Liang, M., Li, J., Tian, L., Zhou, Y., ... Jiang, T. (2007). Whole brain functional connectivity in the early blind. *Brain, 130,* 2085–2096.

Luo, Y., & Baillargeon, R. (2007). Do 12.5-month-old infants consider what objects others can see when interpreting their actions? *Cognition, 105,* 489–512.

Luo, Y., & Johnson, S. C. (2008). Recognizing the role of perception in action at 6 months. *Developmental Science, 12,* 142–149.

Ma, Y., & Han, S. (2011). Neural representation of self-concept in sighted and congenitally blind adults. *Brain, 134,* 235–246.

Mahon, B. Z., Anzellotti, S., Schwarzbach, J., Zampini, M., & Caramazza, A. (2009). Category-specific organization in the human brain does not require visual experience. *Neuron, 63,* 397–405.

Mahon, B. Z., & Caramazza, A. (2008). A critical look at the embodied cognition hypothesis and a new proposal for grounding conceptual content. *Journal of Physiology, Paris, 102,* 59–70.

Mahon, B. Z, Milleville, S. C., Negri, G. A., Rumiati, R. I., Caramazza, A., & Martin, A. (2007). Action-related properties shape object representations in the ventral stream. *Neuron, 55,* 507–520.

Mahon, B. Z, Schwarzbach, J., & Caramazza, A. (2010). The representation of tools in the left parietal cortex is independent of visual experience. *Psychological Science.*

Mandler, J. M. (2008). On the birth and growth of concepts. *Philosophical Psychology, 21,* 207–230.

Marmor, G. S. (1978). Age at onset of blindness and the development of the semantics of color names. *Journal of Experimental Child Psychology, 25,* 267–278.

Marmor, G. S., & Zaback, L. A. (1976). Mental rotation by the blind: Does mental rotation depend on visual imagery? *Journal of Experimental Psychology: Human Perception and Performance, 2,* 515–521.

Martin, A. (2007). The representation of object concepts in the brain. *Annual Review of Psychology, 58,* 25–45.

Martin, A., Haxby, J. V., Lalonde, F. M., Wiggs, C. L., & Ungerleider, L. G. (1995). Discrete cortical regions associated with knowledge of color and knowledge of action. *Science, 270,* 102–105.

Maurer, D., Lewis, T. L., & Mondloch, C. J. (2005). Missing sights: Consequences for visual cognitive development. *Trends in Cognitive Sciences, 9,* 144–151.

McAlpine, L., & Moore, C. (1995). The development of social understanding in children with visual impairments. *Journal of Visual Impairment and Blindness, 89,* 349–358.

McClelland, J. L., & Rogers, T. T. (2003). The parallel distributed processing approach to semantic cognition. *Nature Reviews Neuroscience, 4,* 310–322.

Meltzoff, A. N. (2005). Imitation and other minds: The "Like Me" hypothesis. In S. Hurley & N. Chater (Eds.), *Perspectives on imitation: From neuroscience to social science* (pp. 55–77). Cambridge, MA: MIT Press.

Meltzoff, A. N. (2007). 'Like me': A foundation for social cognition. *Developmental Science, 10,* 126–134.

Meltzoff, A. N., & Brooks, R. (2008). Self-experience as a mechanism for learning about others: A training study in social cognition. *Developmental Psychology, 44,* 1257–1265.

Merabet, L., Thut, G., Murray, B., Andrews, J., Hsiao, S., & Pascual-Leone, A. (2004). Feeling by sight or seeing by touch? *Neuron, 42,* 173–179.

Meteyard, L., Cuadrado, S. R., Bahrami, B., & Vigliocco, G. (2012). Coming of age: A review of embodiment and the neuroscience of semantics. *Cortex, 48,* 788–804.

Millar, S. (1976). Spatial representation by blind and sighted children. *Journal of Experimental Child Psychology, 21,* 460–479.

Miller, E. K., & Cohen, J. D. (2001). An integrative theory of prefrontal cortex function. *Annual Review of Neuroscience, 24,* 167–202.

Miller, S. (1983). Language and active thought: Some aspects of reading and writing by blind children. In A.E. Mills (Ed.), *Language acquisition in the blind child: Normal and deficient* (pp. 167–186). San Diego, CA: College-Hill Press.

Mills, A. E. (1983). *Language acquisition in the blind child: Normal and deficient.* San Diego, CA: College-Hill Press.

Minter, M., Hobson, R. P., & Martin, B. (1998). Congenital visual impairment and 'theory of mind'. *British Journal of Developmental Psychology, 16,* 183–196.

Moeller, M. P., & Schick, B. (2006). Relations between maternal input and theory of mind understanding in deaf children. *Child Development, 77,* 751–766.

Noppeney, U., Friston, K. J., & Price, C. J. (2003). Effects of visual deprivation on the organization of the semantic system. *Brain, 126,* 1620–1627.

Ostrovsky, Y., Andalman, A., & Sinha, P. (2006). Vision following extended congenital blindness. *Psychological Science, 17,* 1009–1014.

Paivio, A. (1971). *Imagery and verbal processes.* New York, NY: Holt, Rinehart & Winston.

Pascual-Leone, A., Amedi, A., Fregni, F., & Merabet, L. B. (2005). The plastic human brain cortex. *Annual Review of Neuroscience, 28,* 377–401.

Pascual-Leone, A., & Hamilton, R. (2001). The metamodal organization of the bra. In C. Casanova & M. Ptito (Eds.), *Progress in brain research* (pp. 427–445). Amsterdam, The Netherlands: Elsevier Science.

Pecher, D., Zeelenberg, R., & Barsalou, L. W. (2004). Sensorimotor simulations underlie conceptual representations: Modality-specific effects of prior activation. *Psychonomic Bulletin & Review, 11,* 164–167.

Pelphrey, K. A., Morris, J. P., & McCarthy, G. (2004). Grasping the intentions of others: The perceived intentionality of an action influences activity in the superior temporal sulcus during social perception. *Journal of Cognitive Neuroscience, 16,* 1706–1716.

Perez-Pereira, M., & Castro, J. (1992). Pragmatic functions of blind and sighted children's language: A twin case study. *First Language, 12,* 17–37.

Peterson, C. C., Peterson, J. L., & Webb, J. (2000). Factors influencing the development of a theory of mind in blind children. *British Journal of Developmental Psychology, 18,* 431–447.

Peterson, C. C., & Siegal, M. (1995). Deafness, conversation and theory of mind. *Journal of Child Psychology and Psychiatry and Allied Disciplines, 36,* 459–474.

Pietrini, P., Furey, M. L., Ricciardi, E., Gobbini, M. I., Wu, W. H., Cohen, L., ... Haxby, J. V. (2004). Beyond sensory images: Object-based representation in the human ventral pathway. *Proceedings of the National Academy of Sciences of the United States of America, 101,* 5658–5663.

Poeppel, D., & Hickok, G. (2004). Towards a new functional anatomy of language. *Cognition, 92,* 1–12.

Poirier, C., Collignon, O., Scheiber, C., Renier, L., Vanlierde, A., Tranduy, D., ... De Volder, A. G. (2006). Auditory motion perception activates visual motion areas in early blind subjects. *NeuroImage, 31,* 279–285.

Potter, M. C., & Faulconer, B. A. (1975). Time to understand pictures and words. *Nature, 253,* 437–438.

Potter, M. C., Valian, V. V., & Faulconer, B. A. (1977). Representation of a sentence and its pragmatic implications: verbal, imagistic, or abstract? *Journal of Verbal Learning and Verbal Behavior, 16,* 1–12.

Price, C. J. (2000). The anatomy of language: Contributions from functional neuroimaging. *Journal of Anatomy, 197*(Pt 3), 335–359.

Prinz, J. (2002). *Furnishing the mind: Concepts and their perceptual bases.* Cambridge, MA: MIT Press.

Prinz, J. (2005). The return of concept empiricism. In H. Cohen & C. Lefebvre (Eds.), *Handbook of categorization in cognitive science.* New York, NY: Elsevier.

Pulvermuller, F. (1999). Words in the brain's language. *Behavioral and Brain Science, 22,* 253–279, discussion 280–336.

Pulvermuller, F., & Hauk, O. (2006). Category-specific conceptual processing of color and form in left fronto-temporal cortex. *Cerebral Cortex, 16,* 1193–1201.

Putzar, L., Goerendt, I., Lange, K., Rosler, F., & Roder, B. (2007). Early visual deprivation impairs multisensory interactions in humans. *Nature Neuroscience, 10,* 1243–1245.

Pyers, J. (2006). Constructing the social mind: Language and false-belief understanding. In N. J. Enfield & S. C. Levinson (Eds.), *Roots of human sociality: Culture, cognition and interaction* (pp. 207–228). New York, NY: Wenner-Gren Foundation of Anthropological Research.

Pyers, J. E., & Senghas, A. (2009). Language promotes false-belief understanding: Evidence from learners of a new sign language. *Psychological Science, 20,* 805–812.

Rakoczy, H. (2009). Executive function and the development of belief–desire psychology. *Developmental Science, 13,* 648–661.

Rauschecker, J. P. (1995). Compensatory plasticity and sensory substitution in the cerebral cortex. *Trends in Neurosciences, 18,* 36–43.

Revill, K. P., Aslin, R. N., Tanenhaus, M. K., & Bavelier, D. (2008). Neural correlates of partial lexical activation. *Proceedings of the National Academy of Sciences of the United States of America, 105,* 13111–13115.

Ricciardi, E., Bonino, D., Sani, L., Vecchi, T., Guazzelli, M., Haxby, J. V., ... Pietrini, P. (2009). Do we really need vision? How blind people "see" the actions of others. *Journal of Neuroscience, 29,* 9719–9724.

Riesenhuber, M., & Poggio, T. (2002). Neural mechanisms of object recognition. *Current Opinion in Neurobiology, 12,* 162–168.

Roder, B., Stock, O., Bien, S., Neville, H., & Rosler, F. (2002). Speech processing activates visual cortex in congenitally blind humans. *European Journal of Neuroscience, 16,* 930–936.

Rodriguez-Ferreiro, J., Gennari, S. P., Davies, R., & Cuetos, F. (2011). Neural correlates of abstract verb processing. *Journal of Cognitive Neuroscience, 23,* 106–118.

Rosel, J., Caballer, A., Jara, P., & Oliver, J. C. (2005). Verbalism in the narrative language of children who are blind and sighted. *Journal of Visual Impairment & Blindness, 99,* 413–425.

Sadaghiani, S., Maier, J. X., & Noppeney, U. (2009). Natural, metaphoric, and linguistic auditory direction signals have distinct influences on visual motion processing. *Journal of Neuroscience, 29,* 6490–6499.

Sadato, N., Pascual-Leone, A., Grafman, J., Ibanez, V., Deiber, M. P., Dold, G., & Hallett, M. (1996). Activation of the primary visual cortex by Braille reading in blind subjects. *Nature, 380,* 526–528.

Saenz, M., Lewis, L. B., Huth, A. G., Fine, I., & Koch, C. (2008). Visual motion area MT+/V5 responds to auditory motion in human sight-recovery subjects. *Journal of Neuroscience, 28,* 5141–5148.

Saxe, R., & Kanwisher, N. (2003). People thinking about thinking people: The role of the temporo-parietal junction in "theory of mind". *NeuroImage, 19,* 1835–1842.

Saxe, R., & Wexler, A. (2005). Making sense of another mind: The role of the right temporo-parietal junction. *Neuropsychologia, 43,* 1391–1399.

Schick, B., de Villiers, P., de Villiers, J., & Hoffmeister, R. (2007). Language and theory of mind: A study of deaf children. *Child Development, 78,* 376–396.

Shapiro, K., & Caramazza, A. (2003). Grammatical processing of nouns and verbs in left frontal cortex? *Neuropsychologia, 41,* 1189–1198.

Shepard, R. N., & Cooper, L. A. (1992). Representations of color in the blind, color-blind, and normally sighted. *Psychological Science, 3,* 97–104.

Simmons, W. K., Ramjee, V., Beauchamp, M. S., McRae, K., Martin, A., & Barsalou, L. W. (2007). A common neural substrate for perceiving and knowing about color. *Neuropsychologia, 45,* 2802–2810.

Smith, L. B., & Heise, D. (1992). Perceptual similarity and conceptual structure. In B. Burns (Ed.), *Percepts, concepts and categories: The representation and processing of information.* Amsterdam, The Netherlands: North-Holland Elsevier Science.

Southgate, V., Senju, A., & Csibra, G. (2007). Action anticipation through attribution of false belief by 2-year-olds. *Psychological Science, 18,* 587–592.

Spelke, E. S. (1998). Nativism, empiricism, and the origins of knowledge. *Infant Behavior and Development, 21,* 181–200.

Spelke, E. S., & Kinzler, K. D. (2007). Core knowledge. *Developmental Science, 10,* 89–96.

Tettamanti, M., Buccino, G., Saccuman, M. C., Gallese, V., Danna, M., ... Perani, D. (2005). Listening to action-related sentences activates fronto-parietal motor circuits. *Journal of Cognitive Neuroscience, 17,* 273–281.

Thompson-Schill, S. L. (2003). Neuroimaging studies of semantic memory: Inferring "how" from "where". *Neuropsychologia, 41,* 280–292.

Thompson-Schill, S. L., Bedny, M., & Goldberg, R. F. (2005). The frontal lobes and the regulation of mental activity. *Current Opinion in Neurobiology, 15,* 219–224.

Tootell, R. B., Reppas, J. B., Dale, A. M., Look, R. B., Sereno, M. I., Malach, R., ... Rosen, B. R. (1995a). Visual motion aftereffect in human cortical area MT revealed by functional magnetic resonance imaging. *Nature, 375,* 139–141.

Tootell, R. B., Reppas, J. B., Kwong, K. K., Malach, R., Born, R. T., Brady, T. J., ... Belliveau, J. W. (1995b). Functional analysis of human MT and related visual cortical areas using magnetic resonance imaging. *Journal of Neuroscience, 15,* 3215–3230.

Tranel, D., Damasio, H., & Damasio, A. R. (1997). A neural basis for the retrieval of conceptual knowledge. *Neuropsychologia, 35,* 1319–1327.

Tranel, D., Kemmerer, D., Adolphs, R., Damasio, H., & Damasio, A. R. (2003). Neural correlates of conceptual knowledge for actions. *Cognitive Neuropsychology, 20,* 409–432.

Uhl, F., Franzen, P., Lindinger, G., Lang, W., & Deecke, L. (1991). On the functionality of the visually deprived occipital cortex in early blind persons. *Neuroscience Letters, 124,* 256–259.

Urwin, C. (1983). Dialogue and cognitive functioning in the early language development of three blind children. In A.E. Mills (Ed.), *Language acquisition in the blind child: Normal and deficient* (pp. 142–161). San Diego, CA: College-Hill Press.

Vanlierde, A., De Volder, A. G., Wanet-Defalque, M. C., & Veraart, C. (2003). Occipito-parietal cortex activation during visuo-spatial imagery in early blind humans. *NeuroImage, 19,* 698–709.

Warrington, E. K., & McCarthy, R. A. (1987). Categories of knowledge: Further fractionations and an attempted integration. *Brain, 110*(Pt 5), 1273–1296.

Warrington, E. K., & Shallice, T. (1984). Category specific semantic impairments. *Brain, 107*(Pt 3), 829–854.

Watkins, K. E., Cowey, A., Alexander, I., Filippini, N., Kennedy, J. M., Smith, S. M., ... Bridge, H. (2012). Language networks in anophthalmia: Maintained hierarchy of processing in 'visual' cortex. *Brain, 135*(Pt 5), 1566–1577.

Wellman, H. M., Lopez-Duran, S., LaBounty, J., & Hamilton, B. (2008). Infant attention to intentional action predicts preschool theory of mind. *Developmental Psychology, 44,* 618–623.

Wiesel, T. N., & Hubel, D. H. (1963). Single-cell responses in striate cortex of kittens deprived of vision in one eye. *Journal of Neurophysiology, 26,* 1003–1017.

Wiesel, T. N., & Hubel, D. H. (1965). Comparison of the effects of unilateral and bilateral eye closure on cortical unit responses in kittens. *Journal of Neurophysiology, 28,* 1029–1040.

Wilcox, T. (1999). Object individuation: Infants' use of shape, size, pattern, and color. *Cognition, 72,* 125–166.

Wilson, M. (2002). Six views of embodied cognition. *Psychonomic Bulletin & Review, 9,* 625–636.

Wolbers, T., Zahorik, P., & Giudice, N. A. (2011). Decoding the direction of auditory motion in blind humans. *NeuroImage, 56,* 681–687.

Woodward, A. L. (1998). Infants selectively encode the goal object of an actor's reach. *Cognition, 69,* 1–34.

Woolfe, T., Want, S. C., & Siegal, M. (2002). Signposts to development: Theory of mind in deaf children. *Child Development, 73,* 768–778.

Wyk, B. C., Hudac, C. M., Carter, E. J., Sobel, D. M., & Pelphrey, K. A. (2009). Action understanding in the superior temporal sulcus region. *Psychological Science, 20,* 771–777.

Yokoyama, S., Miyamoto, T., Riera, J., Kim, J., Akitsuki, Y., Iwata, K., ... Kawashima, R. (2006). Cortical mechanisms involved in the processing of verbs: An fMRI study. *Journal of Cognitive Neuroscience, 18,* 1304–1313.

Zacks, J. M., Kumar, S., Abrams, R. A., & Mehta, R. (2009). Using movement and intentions to understand human activity. *Cognition, 112,* 201–216.

Zeki, S. M. (1974). Functional organization of a visual area in the posterior bank of the superior temporal sulcus of the rhesus monkey. *Journal of Physiology, 236,* 549–573.

Zimler, J., & Keenan, J. M. (1983). Imagery in the congenitally blind: How visual are visual images? *Journal of Experimental Psychology: Learning, Memory, and Cognition, 9,* 269–282.

Routes to short-term memory indexing: Lessons from deaf native users of American Sign Language

Elizabeth A. Hirshorn, Nina M. Fernandez, and Daphne Bavelier

Department of Brain and Cognitive Sciences, University of Rochester, Rochester, NY, USA

Models of working memory (WM) have been instrumental in understanding foundational cognitive processes and sources of individual differences. However, current models cannot conclusively explain the consistent group differences between deaf signers and hearing speakers on a number of short-term memory (STM) tasks. Here we take the perspective that these results are not due to a temporal order-processing deficit in deaf individuals, but rather reflect different biases in how different types of memory cues are used to do a given task. We further argue that the main driving force behind the shifts in relative biasing is a consequence of language modality (sign vs. speech) and the processing they afford, and not deafness, per se.

Keywords: Short-term memory; Deafness; Sign language; Phonological coding; Spatial–temporal coding.

Working memory (WM) supports the ability to maintain and manipulate representations in the service of cognition. One would be hard pressed to name any higher level cognitive ability that does not foundationally depend on holding information in memory and being able to manipulate and integrate it with knowledge from long-term memory. Cognitive constructs as varied as spatial navigation, mathematical calculations, or language processing, to name a few, all critically engage WM. Individual differences in WM have also proven quite critical to account for interindividual variability in a wide range of cognitive tasks, as well as fundamental group differences (Daneman & Carpenter, 1980; Engle, Kane, & Tuholski, 1999; Just & Carpenter, 1992). Here we consider a group difference consistently documented in the literature, the root of which has yet to be conclusively understood: lower serial span in deaf individuals.

The serial span in deaf populations

The extent literature since the early 1900s demonstrates that deaf individuals underperform compared to their hearing peers on serial recall of linguistic

Correspondence should be addressed to Elizabeth A. Hirshorn, Learning Research and Development Center, University of Pittsburgh, 3939 O'Hara St., Pittsburgh, PA 15213, USA. (E-mail: hirshorn@pitt.edu).

We would like to thank all of the subjects recruited from the National Technical Institute of the Deaf at the Rochester Institute of Technology, Rochester, NY, and from the University of Rochester, Rochester, NY. We would also like to thank C. Clark for subject recruitment, R. Harris for data collection, A. Sapre for computer programming, and T. Supalla for stimulus materials. This research was supported by the National Institutes of Health (DC04418 to D.B.) and the Charles A. Dana Foundation (to D.B.).

http://www.psypress.com/cogneuropsychology http://dx.doi.org/10.1080/02643294.2012.704354

material (Bellugi, Klima, & Siple, 1974–1975; Boutla, Supalla, Newport, & Bavelier, 2004; Conrad, 1970, 1972; Hall & Bavelier, 2011; Pintner & Patterson, 1917). In such tasks, participants are asked to recall a list of items in the exact order of presentation; the span is defined as the highest list length subjects can recall in the correct order. A typical example is the digit span task in which hearing English speakers exhibit a span of about 7 ± 2 whereas deaf individuals only reach about 5 ± 1 items. Although in early studies the lists to recall were presented in English print and thus relied on a language that may not have been native for many deaf individuals, the discrepancy in span was confirmed when testing deaf native signers in their native language, sign language. Lower span using signed stimuli has been demonstrated in American Sign Language (ASL; Logan, Maybery, & Fletcher, 1996), British Sign Language (Conrad, 1970; MacSweeney, Campbell, & Donlan, 1996), Italian Sign Language (Geraci, Gozzi, Papagno, & Cecchetto, 2008), Israeli Sign Language (Miller, 2007), and Swedish Sign Language (Rönnberg, Rudner, & Ingvar, 2004). Crucially, deaf participants in these studies were native users of the sign language used in the test. As it is known that deaf individuals raised in a signing community undergo the typical stages of language development (Mayberry & Squires, 2006; Newport & Meier, 1985; Schick, Marschark, & Spencer, 2005), their lower short-term memory (STM) performance cannot be easily attributed to poor language skills or lack of familiarity with the materials used. A role of poor language skills or deficient cognitive skills in the source of the span discrepancy has been further ruled out by the demonstration that *hearing* native signers also show a shorter span when tested in sign language (Boutla et al., 2004; Hall & Bavelier, 2011). Studies of hearing individuals fluent in both English and ASL demonstrate that the very same individuals show a normal span when tested in English but a reduced span when tested in ASL. Given the prevalence of the serial span in school settings and in clinical evaluations, the question arises of how to interpret lower serial span in deaf individuals. The current paper aims to gain understanding of these issues and, in doing so, reevaluate in a new light some of the foundational conceptions about WM and its underlying STM buffers.

Working memory and short-term memory buffers

A model of WM that has gained much traction over the last 40 years is the multicomponent model of Baddeley and Hitch (1974). This model describes two "slave STM buffers" that hold respectively visual/spatial (visuospatial sketchpad) and temporal/phonological (phonological loop) information for a limited amount of time, as well as a central executive that integrates and manipulates information available in these buffers along with that retrieved from long-term memory (Burgess & Hitch, 2005; Cowan, 2008). The visual–spatial sketchpad allows for the maintenance of visual–spatial information with a typical span of 4. The underlying mechanism involved with the visual–spatial sketchpad has been thought of as holding a mental imagery representation of the identity and the location of an object in memory (Kosslyn, 1981). The phonological loop, commonly compared to a "tape recorder in your head", has a span of about 7 ± 2 and is perhaps the most studied and well-understood component. It supports recoding of auditory and linguistic information and is especially efficient at maintaining verbal information, like remembering a phone number. The processes at play within the phonological loop have been characterized through a number of trademark effects including phonological similarity, word length, and articulatory suppression effects (Baddeley, 1992; Baddeley, Thomson, & Buchanan, 1975) that have shown how verbal STM can be affected (lowered) when items are phonologically similar, word length is longer, and articulation is suppressed by repeating an unrelated sound.

Evaluation in signers of the three landmark effects of the phonological loop has led Wilson and Emmorey to propose a sign-language-based rehearsal mechanism that parallels in many respects the phonological loop in speakers (Wilson, Bettger, Niculae, & Klima, 1997;

Wilson & Emmorey, 1997, 1998). These studies document an elegant parallel between phonological loop processes in sign language and spoken language. However, since they assume fundamentally similar underlying processing, phonological loop function in sign versus spoken language cannot explain the precise source of the performance differences in signers and speakers when using speech versus sign in STM tasks.

Over the years, two main classes of explanation have been put forward in the literature for this span discrepancy. First, we review explanations targeting the phonological loop and the possibility that sign language characteristics result in shorter spans within that buffer. Second, we consider explanations focused on the key role of auditory information and effects of deafness in shaping up temporal processing and the brain's ability at processing information serially.

Structural differences between speech and sign

An early explanation of the span difference between signers and speakers proposed that it could be due to fundamental properties of the different languages themselves. This was based on the observation that signs typically take longer to articulate than speech, either because of their complexity or because of the use of manual articulators that tend to be slower (Bellugi & Fischer, 1972). The serial span in speakers is known to get shorter as words get longer or more complex, and thus this explanation seemed quite coherent with the available pattern of data at the time. However, in 2004, Boutla et al. demonstrated that the discrepancy in span between signers and speakers fully remains even when the signed material is carefully matched in articulation length and complexity to speech materials (for further discussion, see Bavelier, Newport, Hall, Supalla, & Boutla, 2006; Wilson & Emmorey, 2006a, 2006b). Furthermore, individual differences in articulation are a good positive predictor of STM span in English, whereas there is no correlation between articulation rate and STM span in native signers (see Hall & Bavelier, 2010, Figure 30.2). Thus, a direct account of the span discrepancy in terms of articulation time differences or unequal phonological complexity across languages seemed unlikely.

A more recent proposal focuses on the internal structure of signs and argues that unlike speech, signs contain both simultaneous and sequential components that may result in "heavier" phonological units (Geraci et al., 2008; Gozzi, Geraci, Cecchetto, Perugini, & Papagno, 2011). Under this view, STM for sign material is hampered as compared to speech because the memory load associated with even the simplest syllable is likely to be higher in sign. In a recent work, Mann, Marshall, Mason, and Morgan (2010) noted that greater memory load in sign could stem from a higher number of formational parameters as well as from lesser constraints on the possible ways these can be combined (Mann et al., 2010). Indeed, it is well accepted that signers are faced with a much wider signing register than English speakers, having to adapt their comprehension and production of signs as the skill level of their interlocutor changes widely. Greater variability in sign does predict greater difficulty when encoding signs, especially rare items; however, it remains unclear how such views can explain lower STM span in signers when using signs as simple and overlearned as digits or letters, where hand shape alone is sufficient to represent each item. In addition, these explanations do not align well with the finding that sign language use hampers serial span performance at *presentation* and during memory *encoding*, but if anything *enhances* span when used at recall time (Hall & Bavelier, 2011). Such differences across memory stages call for more nuanced models.

A newer model of WM has argued that serial ordering processes in language *production* are a likely candidate for a maintenance mechanism in verbal WM, with particular emphasis placed on the process of phonological *encoding* (Acheson & MacDonald, 2009). Although a promising framework worth pursuing for future research, this proposal has not yet been fleshed out to consider possible differences in speech and sign production that are relevant for the current discussion.

Another model, termed the ease of language understanding (ELU), proposed by Rudner and Rönnberg (2008) also addresses working memory processes in the larger context of language production and comprehension. It acknowledges language-specific storage networks for speech and sign, respectively, as well as common phonological and semantic networks between speech and sign. It does not directly address the difference in serial spans between signers and speakers, but by considering the importance of multiple WM codes in the service of language processing, it provides a broader perspective on the importance and role of not only phonological representations in WM, but also semantic representations. It places a special emphasis on an episodic buffer, whose main role is to bind together information from different sources within a representation that uniquely refers to the item to be remembered. We return to the potential role of such episodic buffer after considering the alternative view that span discrepancy in hearing and deaf individuals can be understood as a consequence of auditory deprivation.

Temporal order deficits following auditory deprivation

The second class of explanation for shorter serial spans in deaf populations holds that early deafness hinders temporal processing. This view is driven by the fact that (a) most studies showing a smaller serial span have tested deaf individuals who were not necessarily signers, and (b) these studies used primarily English print rather than sign. The proposal that deafness may hinder temporal processing goes back to the early 1900s, largely stemming from studies comparing the short-term memory capacity of deaf individuals to that of hearing individuals (Bellugi et al., 1974–1975; Conrad, 1970, 1972; Pintner & Patterson, 1917). These results have often been understood in the context of the *deficiency theory of deafness,* which holds that integrative processes, such as multisensory integration, are essential for normal development. Previous research suggested a consistent sequence of development along sensory processes, starting with cutaneous, then vestibular, olfactory, auditory, and finally visual senses (Gottlieb, 1971). Such developmental scaffolding was seen as critical for "normal" development, with earlier senses creating a framework upon which senses with later onset could be built and incorporated (Radell & Gottlieb, 1992; Turkewitz & Kenny, 1982). Given the recognized role of audition in the processing of fine temporal distinction, this view predicted that deaf individuals would be at a disadvantage on tasks—especially visual ones—that require temporal ordering. This view is still prevalent, although often revised to contrast a disadvantage following auditory deprivation for memory tasks requiring temporal order but an advantage for those requiring spatial order (Bavelier, Newport, Hall, Supalla, & Boutla, 2008; Hanson, 1990; Wilson, 2001).

The contrast between spatial and temporal processing in the auditory versus visual modality finds support in studies showing that the auditory modality is better suited to process temporal order, whereas the visual modality is better equipped to process spatial information (e.g., Penney, 1989). For example, the auditory advantage in short-term memory recall tasks is typically attributed to such factors as a longer decay period for auditorily than for visually presented items, and to the automaticity of processing in the phonological loop (Baddeley, Lewis, & Vallar, 1984). The literature on STM and deafness reinforces this view as it documents a disadvantage for temporal order but better visuospatial memory in deaf individuals. In particular, several studies show better visuospatial skills in deaf signers than in hearing speakers (Emmorey, Kosslyn, & Bellugi, 1993). Tests of mental rotation (Emmorey & McCullough, 1998; McKee, 1988), memory for number in spatial arrays (Zarfaty, Nunes, & Bryant, 2004), and face recognition (Bellugi & Hickok, 1993) all reveal significant advantages in deaf signers. In addition, a strong preference for spatial coding has been reported in deaf children. When deaf and hearing children are asked to choose the "middle" digit from a group of three sequentially presented digits, but with a temporal order incongruent with the left-to-right spatial arrangement, deaf children choose the spatially middle digit whereas hearing children choose the temporally middle one (Hermelin & O'Connor, 1975; O'Connor & Hermelin, 1973). Additional evidence, albeit indirect, comes from a concentration/memory game study where subjects had to remember the spatial locations of pictures of faces or shoes and then find their matches in a matrix of cards (Arnold & Mills, 2001). When the use of a within-category set (all shoes or all faces) prevented efficient verbal tagging of the objects, deaf signers needed fewer attempts to find the matches than hearing nonsigners. Together, these results are suggestive of a visuospatial processing advantage in the deaf group and a temporal one in the hearing group.

However, in this case, evidence suggests that the visuospatial advantage may be due to sign language experience and not deafness, per se. For example, the Corsi Blocks Task, a paradigm often used to assess the spatial span, reveals higher spatial span in deaf than in hearing (Wilson et al., 1997). Interestingly, sign language experience (and not deafness) appears necessary and sufficient for this effect. Deaf children who have no exposure to sign language perform as well as, but not better than, hearing children on the Corsi Blocks Task (Parasnis, Samar, Bettger, & Sathe, 1996). Additionally, hearing adults or children (age 6 years) with non-native experience with sign languages exhibit increased spatial memory span on the Corsi Blocks Task as compared to their peers with no sign experience (Capirci, Cattani, Rossini, & Volterra, 1998; Keehner & Gathercole, 2007).

Nonetheless, the observation of a dichotomy between temporal and spatial memory in deaf and hearing individuals has led to two rather different claims about deafness and cognition. In line with the idea that temporal order and sequential processing is inherently facilitated in the auditory modality, the "auditory scaffolding hypothesis" proposes that experience with sound provides the proper foundation for the development of more general cognitive abilities related to representing temporal patterns (Conway, Pisoni, & Kronenberger, 2009). Under this hypothesis, deafness may lead to altered development of sequential or temporal order processing, which in turn may result in the decrease in learning, recalling and producing temporal information that are observed in deaf individuals. As temporal order processing is often acknowledged to be at the core of many cognitive abilities such as working memory, planning, language processing, and executive functioning, the auditory scaffolding hypothesis predicts that the decreased performance observed in deaf individuals on serial STM tasks will extend to a broad spectrum of cognitive tasks. In line with the claim that the auditory modality is inherently more suited to temporal order processing, there is some evidence from studies in hearing individuals that the auditory modality shows a quantitative advantage over visual and tactile modalities in statistical learning designs testing implicit sequence learning (Conway & Christiansen, 2005). Furthermore, Conway and colleagues also found that deaf children with cochlear implants, who have had degraded auditory input, showed disturbances in sequence-learning abilities in the visual domain (Conway, Pisoni, Anaya, Karpicke, & Henning, 2011) and in motor sequencing (Conway, Karpicke, et al., 2011), relative to the typically developing normal-hearing children. Data supporting the auditory scaffolding hypothesis should be qualified by pointing out that they mostly included hearing impaired individuals learning speech (with the aid of cochlear implants or hearing aids). These individuals are likely to have suffered from language delays and associated psychosocial challenges during development (Hauser, Lukomski, & Hillman, 2008; Hauser, Wills, & Isquith, 2006). Developmental delays, rather than auditory deprivation, per se, could be one major source of lower span in these populations. This concerns calls for a more systematic inclusion in future studies of deaf native signers.

The alternative view that we propose here is also consistent with the idea that the auditory modality affords direct access to temporal order information. However, unlike the auditory scaffolding hypothesis, it entertains the possibility that the lesser serial STM span noted in deaf individuals is not the result of a generalized impairment of temporal order processes with consequences for many aspects of cognition, but rather results from a lesser reliance in deaf populations on one form of temporal order information—that afforded by the rehearsal of phonologically encoded unit in the phonological loop. This view holds that differences between deaf and hearing are specific to tasks that require serial order recall of linguistic material, with little to no consequences for cognition at large. Accordingly, this view predicts that differences in memory between deaf and hearing individuals should be restricted to serial span tasks that rely heavily on rehearsal of linguistic materials. Working memory tasks, which diminish the contribution of rehearsal by requiring manipulation, rather than just maintenance of information, should alleviate the differences between deaf and hearing individuals. There is some evidence for this proposal. Boutla and collaborators (2004, Experiment 3) reported equivalent performance in deaf signers and hearing speakers on a working memory production span task, in which lists of words have to be recalled in a self-generated sentence. Temporal order is irrelevant in this task. Similarly, deaf and hearing individuals have been found to perform equally well when tested on free recall tasks that typically exceed the capacity of the phonological buffer and its rehearsal process (Bavelier, Newport, et al., 2008; Cumming & Rodda, 1985; Hanson, 1982, 1990; Krakow & Hanson, 1985). Thus, both the auditory scaffolding hypothesis and this latter view predict lesser performance in deaf than in hearing individuals on tasks that require serial order recall of verbal material. However, whereas the auditory scaffolding hypothesis predicts that such a deficit will have widespread effects throughout cognition, the latter view predicts differences only in tasks that actively engage the phonological loop and its rehearsal processes.

These alternative points of view have important implications for possible cognitive repercussions stemming from lack of audition. In addition, they pose a central question concerning cognition at large by forcing us to characterize the origins of temporal order processing. The ability to maintain temporal order may stem from various levels of representations. For example, the temporal order information afforded by verbal rehearsal does not encompass the same information as that afforded by motor movement or the visualization of a trajectory of a moving object. We consider below how these different types of information contribute to and alter the nature of sequential processing, as this issue remains largely unknown.

The case for an episodic buffer

A major contribution of several recent advances in modelling WM and language processing has been to acknowledge the importance of an episodic buffer, above and beyond the visuospatial and phonological buffer initially posited by Baddeley and Hitch (1974). The concept of episodic traces in memory was initially championed by Tulving (1983), based on the observation that in most cognitive tasks, whether sentence processing or scene understanding, the context of occurrence is necessary to uniquely qualify a memory trace (Potter, 1993; Tulving, 2002). One of the main roles of the episodic buffer is to integrate information across various encoding dimensions, including phonology, orthography, visual shape, or semantics, into a unique memory trace that refers to the to-be-memorized event (Bavelier, 1999; Kahneman, Treisman, & Gibbs, 1992; Pylyshyn, 1989). Thus a distinctive feature of the episodic buffer is to afford unique representations of the information in the outside world by providing a temporal, spatial, and semantic context in which the event occurred (Kahneman et al., 1992; Pylyshyn, 1989).

The importance of an episodic buffer during sentence processing is now recognized in several different models. To only cite a few, the model of Baddeley and Hitch (1974) considered earlier was revised in 2000 by Baddeley to include such a buffer on the grounds that some neuropsychological patients can recall a story despite an impaired phonological loop (Baddeley, 2000; Baddeley & Wilson, 2002). Similarly, the ELU argues for an episodic buffer that automatically combines multimodal information allowing for more efficient phonological processing and promoting language understanding.

Overall, neuropsychological data as well as work on language processing make it clear that language comprehension requires representations that go beyond those of the phonological loop. The episodic short-term memory buffer plays a key role in binding words to their context of occurrence and developing a rich sentence structure as sentence comprehension unfolds. Such a complex structure is not properly captured by serially sequencing words over time as the phonological loop does (Potter, 1983, 1999). Episodic memory traces are, thus, necessary to account for solving local ambiguity or reevaluation of meaning. In support of this view, recent work indicates that the type of order information necessary during sentence processing is different from serial order processing that mediates list recall (Bavelier, Newport, et al., 2008; Lewis, Vasishth, & Van Dyke, 2006; McElree, Foraker, & Dyer, 2003; Van Dyke & McElree, 2006). Reports that a semantic span measure is a better predictor of reading comprehension than the traditional serial span measures also highlight the greater role of conceptual representations in short-term memory than that suggested by research on serial span (Haarman, Davelaar, & Usher, 2003).

The importance of an episodic buffer holds not only for language processing but also when considering cognition at large. The need for memory traces that uniquely refer to events in the world is acknowledged throughout cognition. Spatiotemporal indexing has been proposed to support visual tracking over time as illustrated by the multiple object tracking paradigm where subjects are asked to track several moving objects amongst objects appearing identical (Pylyshyn, 1989). This proposed indexing also allows objects of attention to be represented as separate, enabling one to perceive two occurrences of the same object type as two entities rather than one (Kahneman et al., 1992; Kanwisher, 1987). Accordingly, such memory indexing has been proposed to provide the stepping stone for several aspects of cognitive development including object identification, knowledge of numerosity, and the understanding of causality (Carey & Xu, 2002). In the case of visual objects, this indexing mechanism has been proposed to engage the inferior intraparietal sulcus (Xu & Chun, 2005). Indexing events uniquely through their context of occurrence in space and time is therefore one of the main routes to WM.

The contribution of the episodic buffer to deaf/hearing differences in STM: An illustration of spatiotemporal individuation

With this background in place, we consider again the hearing/deaf differences for serial span tasks such as the digit span. We first illustrate how the deaf/hearing difference in serial span task may be understood in the context of WM models that posit not only a phonological loop and a visuospatial buffer, but also an episodic buffer (Figure 1). The view developed here is that deaf signers prefer episodic encoding and the spatiotemporal indexing it naturally embodies, whereas hearing speakers prefer the phonological loop and thus ordered phonological representations. We first assessed the possibility that deaf signers would outperform hearing speakers in memory tasks that require recall of temporal order information. In particular, our view proposes that deaf signers should excel on serial STM tasks that disable the contribution of ordered phonological representations but can be achieved through the spatial–temporal indexing afforded by the episodic buffer. We tested this prediction by asking participants to view a sequence of identical squares presented at different locations and to tell us about the temporal order of two of them at probe time (Figure 2). Importantly, the timing and presentation of the squares did not suggest one square moving from one location to another but rather implied several identical squares appearing one after the other at different locations. The presentation of the full array of squares at probe time was meant to reinforce such an interpretation of the display. These design features were carefully chosen to prevent the use of trajectories for the encoding of temporal information, unlike what is

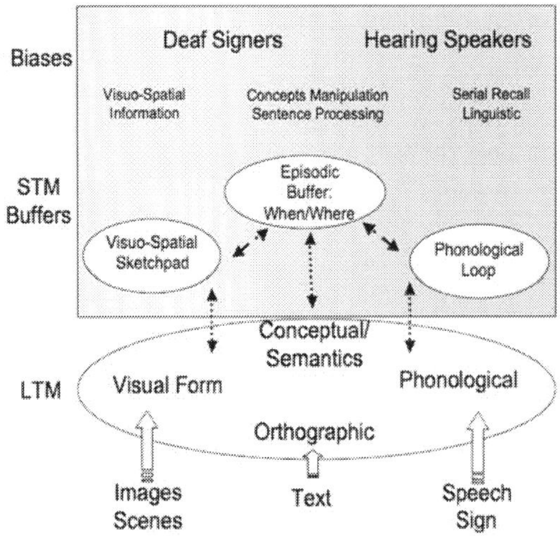

Figure 1. *The multiple component working memory model adapted from Baddeley (2000), which accounts for relative group biases. Incoming information first activates long-term memory (LTM) representations. This system permits the accumulation of long-term knowledge. In contrast, the short-term memory (STM) buffers represent dedicated temporary workspace, all under the control of the central executive (not shown here). The episodic buffer binds information from multiple codes and provide the richest input to the central executive, whereas the two slave systems are highly specialized for phonological versus visuospatial information, respectively. Moreover, the episodic system uniquely labels events with respect to their time and place of occurrence allowing individuation of "episode" or temporary memory trace that uniquely refer to one event in the world. In contrast, temporal information in the phonological loop is conveyed through the chaining of phonological units, and in the visual spatial sketchpad through trajectory through space. Experiment 1 was designed to require precise tagging of when/where as supported by the episodic buffer and favoured deaf signers. Experiment 2 allowed both when/where tagging and phonological codes. Such dual coding raised overall performance and led to equal performance across groups. Experiment 3 disabled when/where coding and favoured hearing speakers. To view a color version of this figure, please see the online issue of the Journal.*

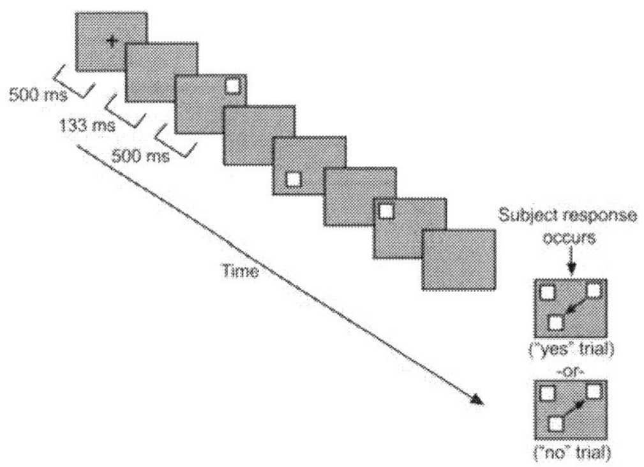

Figure 2. *In Experiment 1, participants had to perform a spatial short-term memory (STM) task and decide whether the two squares in the probe display were presented in the same location as squares in the sequence (Yes) or whether one of them was in a different location (No). The use of squares diminishes the contribution of the ordered phonological representations and ensures greater reliance on spatiotemporal indexing, predicting higher performance in deaf than in hearing.*

typically the case in Corsi block tasks. Thus, in this first version of this task (Experiment 1), once the sequence of squares had been presented, the probe display appeared containing all the squares at the spatial location at which they had appeared during the initial presentation phase. Two squares

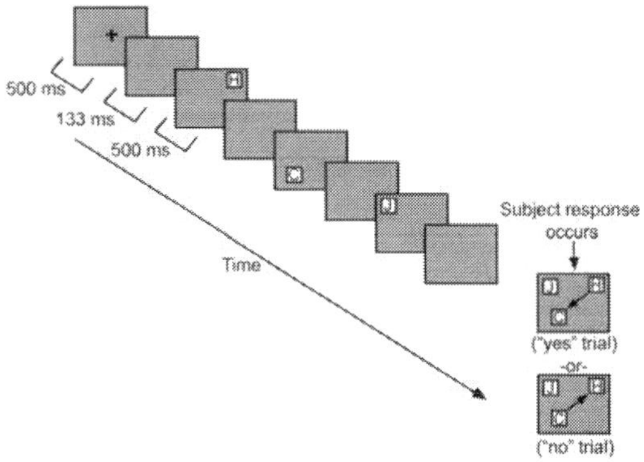

Figure 3. *The sequence of stimuli and types of probe displays used in Experiment 2 were identical to those in Experiment 1, except that each square was now labelled with a separate letter. As a result, spatiotemporal indexing and ordered phonological representations could both be efficiently used to encode and maintain information in short-term memory (STM) in Experiment 2.*

were linked by an arrow, and subjects had to decide whether the two squares had been presented in the temporal order suggested by the arrow (see Figure 2). As this task requires linking each square with its appropriate spatial and temporal index while reducing possible contributions from the phonological loop, we predicted that deaf signers would outperform hearing speakers.

In the second version of this task (Experiment 2, Figure 3), English and ASL letters were added on each of the squares respectively for the hearing and deaf groups (see Appendix, Figure A1, for ASL handshape letters). By providing each square with a separate, nameable label, we predicted improved performance in both populations as two different routes to STM indexing, rather than one, became available. In addition, we predicted a disproportional benefit to hearing as their preferred route of phonological encoding was enabled.

Finally, in a third version of this task (Experiment 3, Figure 4), the efficiency of spatiotemporal indexing was weakened, allowing us to test its relative contribution in deaf and hearing participants. Lettered squares were presented one at a time as in Experiment 2; however, at probe time, rather than presenting all the letters in their correct spatial position, only two letters

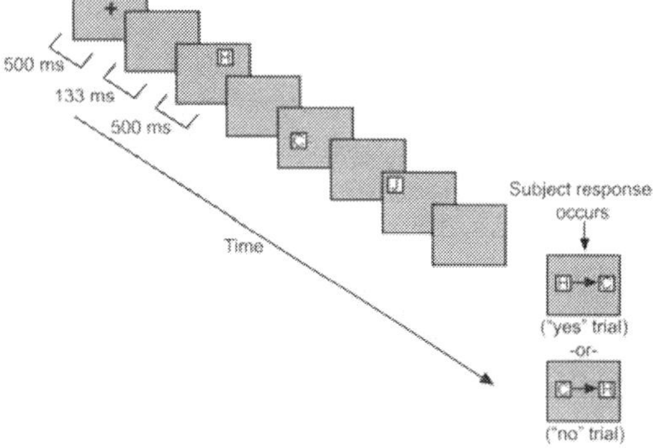

Figure 4. *The sequences of stimuli used in Experiment 3 were identical to those in Experiment 2. The only difference was in the probe displays in which the two probes were always displayed centrally, reducing the contribution of spatiotemporal indexing to the short-term memory (STM) task.*

were presented in the centre of the screen. Participants were to judge whether the letter on the left preceded that on the right; the two letters were linked by a corresponding arrow as in previous experiments. Because at probe time, the tested letters are presented at incongruent spatial locations with what was previously seen, this task renders spatiotemporal indexing inefficient, and the task is now best carried out by relying on ordered phonological representations (as in standard linguistic span tasks). By reducing the number of efficient memory codes that can be tapped, the task should be harder for both groups. However, it should be disproportionately so for the deaf signer group, as their preferred mode of STM coding is weakened. For all experimental conditions, the longest sequence length at which subjects performed at 67% was found for each subject. The span was defined as that length minus 1 in an analogy to the Wechsler Adult Intelligence Scale (WAIS; Wechsler, 1955, 1997) scoring procedure. The same congenitally deaf native signers and nonsigning hearing participants were run in all three versions of this task (see Method).

An omnibus 3 × 2 analysis of variance (ANOVA) with within-factor of experiment (1 vs. 2 vs. 3) and between-factor of group (deaf vs. hearing) revealed a significant main effect of experiment, $F(2, 40) = 11.733$, $p < .001$, $\eta_p^2 = .370$, no significant main effect of group, $F(1, 20) = 0.002$, $p = .968$, $\eta_p^2 = .00$, but importantly a significant interaction between experiment and group, $F(2, 40) = 5.367$, $p = .007$, $\eta_p^2 = .221$ (see Figure 5). Separate 2 × 2 ANOVAs show that when comparing Experiment 1 with Experiment 2, there was a marginal interaction, $F(1, 20) = 2.27$, $p = .096$, such that there was a deaf advantage in Experiment 1, which only allowed episodic/spatiotemporal coding ($\text{mean}_{\text{deaf}} = 5.23 \pm 0.32$, $\text{mean}_{\text{hearing}} = 4.32 \pm 0.42$), $t(20) = 1.732$, $p < .05$ (one-tailed), $d = 0.750$). The deaf advantage went away, and there was no group difference in Experiment 2 ($\text{mean}_{\text{deaf}} = 6.23 \pm 0.18$, $\text{mean}_{\text{hearing}} = 6.05 \pm 0.45$), $t(20) = 0.371$, $p = .714$, $d = 0.157$, when the additional cue of letter/phonological information was added. A 2 × 2 ANOVA comparing Experiments 2 and 3 also had a significant interaction, $F(1, 20) = 3.55$, $p < .05$, such that when spatial–temporal information was no longer relevant at the time of the probe in Experiment 3, there was greater decrease in span in the deaf signers compared to the hearing speakers than there was in Experiment 2 (Experiment 3: $\text{mean}_{\text{deaf}} = 4.59 \pm 0.43$, $\text{mean}_{\text{hearing}} = 5.64 \pm 0.24$), $t(20) = -2.11$, $p < .025$ (one-tailed), $d = 0.899$). When comparing Experiment 1 with Experiment 3 (the two tasks with just one memory code available), there was a significant interaction, $F(1, 20) = 10.15$, $p < .005$, such that deaf signers performed better when just spatiotemporal information was available (Experiment 1), and hearing speakers performed better when just phonological/verbal information was available (Experiment 3).

The main effect of experiment seemed attributable to greater spans when episodic and phonological codes both contributed useful memory information than when only one of them was available. Accordingly, the comparison of Experiments 1 and 2 showed that performance did improve from Experiment 1 to Experiment 2, as the use of the phonological loop was enabled ($\text{mean}_1 = 4.77 \pm 0.27$, $\text{mean}_2 = 6.14$

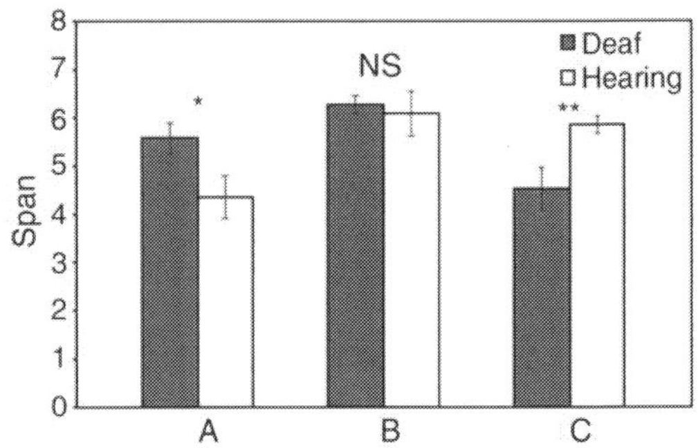

Figure 5. *Group differences in each experiment demonstrate different biases in deaf signers and hearing speakers. (A) There was a deaf advantage in Experiment 1, when only spatial–temporal coding could be used (*p < .05, one-tailed). (B) When both spatial–temporal and phonological coding could be used in Experiment 2, deaf and hearing spans did not differ. (C) When spatial–temporal coding at recall was disabled in Experiment 3, there was a hearing advantage (**p < .05, two-tailed).*

$\pm$ 0.24), $t(21) = -4.81, p < .001, d = 1.13$. The comparison of Experiments 2 and 3 allows us to examine the effect of disabling spatial–temporal indexing as the spatiotemporal congruity between presentation and probe was destroyed. As expected by weakening the efficiency of episodic coding, overall performance was worse in Experiment 3 than in Experiment 2 ($mean_2 = 6.14 \pm 0.24$, $mean_3 = 5.11 \pm 0.27$), $t(21) = 3.58$, $p = .002$, $d = 0.859$.

Taken together, Experiments 1, 2, and 3 support the view of dissociable routes to STM—spatiotemporal indexing and ordered phonological representations—that both coexist in deaf signers and hearing speakers, but with each population expressing a bias for one type of coding over the other. Each of these codes supports the processing of temporal order information, despite relying on rather different processes to do so. While the phonological store supports maintenance of ordered phonological representations, the episodic buffer is believed to be the main player when it comes to integrating spatial and temporal information into a richer STM trace including semantics and context of occurrence to uniquely refer to the event coded.

A weakness of this series of experiments is that it cannot cleanly distinguish between contributions of the episodic buffer versus the visuospatial sketchpad. The Corsi Blocks Task has a clear spatial component as the blocks are laid out in front of the subjects and remain in view throughout the task, and arguably it can be solved through the encoding of trajectories rather than temporal order, per se. The design features of the first experiment presented above were carefully chosen to weaken the potential use of trajectories for the encoding of temporal information. Yet, we acknowledge that these experiments cannot rule out the proposal that deaf signers more readily rely on the visuospatial sketchpad rather than on the episodic buffer, recognizing that such a view would require us to entertain the possibility of greater temporal information in the visuospatial sketchpad than is often assumed.

We would like to argue that a greater reliance on the episodic buffer in deaf signers affords a more parsimonious explanation as it captures data from experiments requiring just spatiotemporal indexing as shown here, as well as those manipulating sign language materials. The view here is that deaf signers and hearing speakers share a similar WM architecture, but that spoken language use readily entrains the phonological loop, making it a dominant device during most tasks, whereas sign language use readily entrains the episodic buffer, resulting in a rather weak signed phonological loop. Given the dominant role of the phonological loop in language acquisition (Baddeley, Gathercole, & Papagno, 1998), one could expect signers to exhibit language delays. Yet this is not the case (Mayberry & Squires, 2006; Meier, 1991), a result that we argue could be naturally explained by greater reliance on the episodic buffer in deaf signers.

Lastly, this work does not definitively distinguish between effects of deafness versus effects of sign language use in biasing preferred encoding in STM. Our view is that both signing and deafness may conspire to a weaker phonological loop, a weakness that would be compensated by greater reliance on the episodic buffer. This view predicts that strengthening the phonological loop, as oral training may do, would lead to higher spans, despite the individuals being profoundly deaf, whereas hearing signers would more readily rely on episodic coding during sign processing, despite a normal phonological loop for spoken materials. Future research that more systematically includes hearing signers and deaf orally trained, in addition to hearing speakers and deaf signers, would allow a finer evaluation of this view.

DISCUSSION

In closing, this paper argues for a greater consideration of the episodic buffer and its various roles when considering WM phenomenon. This is especially the case in clinical literatures, such as the deaf one, where the dominant model of WM typically only considers the phonological loop and the visuospatial sketchpad. It would seem a worthwhile path for WM research at large to consider the role of episodic STM in the development of executive skills and language processes. This conclusion rests on several observations outlined below.

Deaf signers' decreased STM span is isolated to a very specific subset of situations: serial order recall of linguistic material or material that can be recoded phonologically. Critically, the presented experiments show that deaf signers can perform equally (Experiment 2) or even better (Experiment 1) in serial span tasks than their peers who are hearing speakers. Thus, deaf signers are not poor at temporal order coding in general. In addition, this work highlights that equal performance on a given STM task does not mean equal processes at play. In Experiment 2, deaf signers and hearing speakers reached equal span performance. However, their spans were differentially affected by removing one memory cue versus another (in Experiments 1 and 3). Together, these results highlight two points: (a) *There is a need to differentiate between different mechanisms capable of supporting temporal order coding in WM.* On the one hand, the phonological loop certainly provides a very robust trace of the exact order of how the phonological information unfolds; on the other hand, the episodic buffer appears to allow for a richer contextual coding, binding together time and place of occurrence with multimodal information about the realization of the item and its meaning. The role of such richer, more contextually anchored representations in WM has been highlighted by research on sentence processing or scene understanding. (b) *This set of results argues for a WM model that takes into account relative biasing in STM processing that can be weighted by one's individual differences.*

This is not the first study to document a bias in hearing speakers for phonological encoding and relying on ordered phonological representations in the context of a serial STM task (Baddeley, 2003; Hollingworth, Richard, & Luck, 2008; Jiang, Olson, & Chun, 2000). This type of indexing into STM maintains the relative temporal order of the different phonemes in the memory trace and is extremely efficient for items that can contact with existing representations in long-term memory. The present results are more surprising in that they identify one population, deaf signers, in which such a strong bias for ordered phonological representations may not exist, and rather a bias for spatiotemporal indexing appears to be present. Although still quite speculative, a bias for such spatiotemporal indexing is likely to go hand in hand with a greater role for semantic information during memory tasks in deaf signers. Indeed, spatiotemporal indexing in most theoretical framework is seen as a way to individuate conceptual information in the support of action and cognition (Leslie, Xu, Tremoulet, & Scholl, 1998; Pylyshyn, 2001). This work should open new avenues of research as the role of spatiotemporal indexing and conceptual information in support of STM, at least in signers, gets better characterized.

Recent neuroimaging studies provide converging evidence for understanding working memory and the different STM buffers associated with it. STM tasks using spatial versus verbal stimuli have been contrasted to identify respectively the neural bases of the visual–spatial sketchpad and the phonological loop (Smith & Jonides, 1997; Smith, Jonides, & Koeppe, 1996; Smith et al., 1995). However, characterization of the episodic buffer and its possible neural bases has been hampered by the pervasiveness of verbal codes, and therefore the phonological loop, during any STM task that uses potentially nameable stimuli, whether pseudowords or new objects, in hearing individuals (Postle, D'Esposito, & Corkin, 2005). Thus, the notion that deaf signers are less reliant on phonological coding opens the possibility of studying deaf native signers for identifying unique neural underpinnings of STM components like the episodic buffer. Already, studies of the neural correlates of verbal working memory in signers versus speakers suggest important differences. Thus, although sign and spoken languages are linguistically similar by most accounts (Bellugi & Fischer, 1972; Bellugi, Poizner, & Klima, 1989), and both are proposed to similarly engage a linguistic-based phonological loop (Wilson & Emmorey, 1997), greater parietal activation has been systematically reported for sign than for speech. This was the case when considering hearing signers (Rönnberg et al., 2004), but also deaf signers (Bavelier, Newman, et al., 2008). Interestingly, recent work indicates a greater role for parietal areas in semantic processing and possibly episodic memory (Binder, Desai, Graves, & Conant, 2009; Wagner, Shannon, Kahn, & Buckner, 2005). Although only suggestive, further assessment of the parietal cortex and its subdivision as possible nodes within the episodic buffer should be a fruitful path for future work. Lastly, recent work highlights the advantage of examining separately the different phases of STM processing, such as encoding, maintenance, and recall, to refine our understanding of STM processes in deaf signers versus hearing speakers (Bavelier, Newman, et al., 2008; Hall & Bavelier, 2010, 2011). In one such study, while both groups engaged the same front-parietal network thought to be involved in working memory (Wager & Smith, 2003), deaf signers relied to a greater extent than hearing speakers on passive memory storage areas during encoding and maintenance, but relied more on executive process areas during recall (Bavelier, Newman, et al., 2008). Neuroimaging therefore affords a unique opportunity in further testing the relative contribution of distinguishable networks known to be involved in different components of working memory. Such an approach holds the promise of determining the relative engagement of one network versus another in each group despite equal STM performance, as in Experiment 2, where multiple codes are available for solving the task.

The current paper brings up important implications for future research on cognitive development and clinical and education practice. First, when studying effects of deafness on any cognitive processing, it is important to include deaf native signers, as to not conflate possible cognitive differences that are not due to deafness, such as language delays, or abnormal psychosocial development. Second, and most, relevant to clinical or educational assessment of deaf children, the digit span may not be an appropriate or representative assessment of WM/STM ability in deaf individuals. More generally, standard views derived from studies of hearing participants may not equally apply to deaf individuals. This is especially relevant when considering the development of literacy, as verbal STM is one of the main determinants of reading acquisition in hearing individuals (see Ramus and Ahissar, 2012 this issue). To the extent that the deaf child also relies on phonological representations of English to bootstrap reading, one may expect the work from hearing children to be relevant. Yet, when considering deaf native signers, the present work indicates that such assumptions may not hold, calling for a reevaluation anew of the factors that may foster reading in this population.

EXPERIMENT 1

Method

The same subjects were run on all three experimental conditions during the same session. Condition order was counterbalanced between subjects and did not affect the main results, and therefore it is not reported further.

Participants

Deaf group. Twelve adult congenitally deaf native signers were recruited from the National Technical Institute for the Deaf at the Rochester Institute of Technology, Rochester, NY (mean age = 24.08 years, *SEM* = 1.40, 7 females). All subjects reported having two deaf parents, and 11 subjects reported learning ASL from birth and using it daily. One subject reported learning German Sign Language at birth and learning ASL in school. For those subjects who knew their audiological information (7 out of 12 subjects), the average hearing loss was 90 dB (better ear average, range = 65–105 dB). Ten subjects were undergraduates, one subject was in graduate school, and one subject had completed a graduate degree. None of the subjects reported having any neurological impairment.

Hearing group. Twelve adult hearing speakers were recruited from the University of Rochester, Rochester, NY (mean age = 20.14 years, *SEM* = 0.90, 8 females). All subjects reported having normal hearing and no experience with signing (i.e., had not taken any classes in ASL and had no deaf friends or relatives). Ten subjects were undergraduates, one was in graduate school, and one had a graduate degree. None of the subjects reported having any neurological impairment.

Two outliers were identified, one in the hearing group and one in the deaf group, and were discarded. Both outliers were more than 2 standard deviations from their respective group's mean. Thus, the reported results are from 11 deaf subjects and 11 hearing subjects. All subjects were treated in accordance with the University of Rochester's Research Subjects Review Board guidelines and were paid for their participation in the study.

Stimuli, design, and procedure

Experimental trials were composed of a display sequence and a probe. The display sequence consisted of white squares flashed sequentially at different locations on a black background. Each square subtended approximately 2.1° of visual angle. The display sequence began with a fixation cross presented in the middle of the computer screen, followed by a 500-ms wait time and then a sequence of squares presented at a rate of 1 square per second as in other STM span studies (Figure 2). Each square was presented in a unique location on the computer screen so that no two squares touched or overlapped. The minimum distance allowed between squares was 1.25°. The to-be-encoded sequence of squares was then followed by a probe display containing all of the squares at the location they had appeared during the presentation sequence. An arrow linked two of the squares on the screen. One of the two squares was randomly chosen by the program, and the other one was temporally consecutive to the randomly chosen one. The two squares were then linked by an arrow, and the subjects' task was to decide whether the arrow indicated the correct temporal order between the two squares. In a "yes" trial, the square being pointed to came immediately after the square that the arrow was extending from. In a "no" trial, the direction of the arrow was reversed. In this way, the arrow always linked temporally consecutive squares, but indicated either the correct temporal order or the reverse order.

EXPERIMENT 2

Method

Participants

Participant were the same as those in Experiment 1.

Stimuli, design, and procedure

Experiment 2 is identical to Experiment 1 except that a distinct printed or finger-spelled letter was printed on each square (Figure 3). Thus, during the presentation phase, subjects viewed letters in a square frame presented one after the other at different locations, and then, during the probe phase, subjects viewed each letter where it had been presented before (Figure 3). An arrow linked two consecutive square-framed letters, and subjects had to decide whether the direction suggested by the arrow corresponded to the temporal order of presentation or not. Because each square could be uniquely individuated by its letter name, the task could now be carried out by relying on either spatiotemporal indexing or ordered phonological representations. As a result, the task should be easier for both groups, but disproportionately so for the hearing group.

The letter stimuli set consisted of 16 uppercase English letters, printed in Arial font, and 16 ASL handshape letters. The ASL handshape letters were made from high-quality photos of a deaf model's hand forming each hand shape (see supplementary information for the full set of handshape letters used). To minimize effects of phonological similarity, different letter sets were used for each language while keeping the letter set as close as possible. The English letters for this task were "B, C, D, F, G, H, J, K, L, M, Q, R, S, X, Y, Z", and the ASL handshape letters were "B, C, D, F, G, H, K, L, M, R, S, T, V, W, X, Y" (see Appendix Figure A1). Vowels were not included in either language's letter sets, in an attempt to minimize the production of words during the computer program's random presentation of the letters. In addition, polysyllabic English letters and ASL handshape letters that contained movement were also eliminated from the letter sets.

EXPERIMENT 3

Method

Participants

Participants were the same as those in Experiment 1.

Stimuli, design, and procedure

Stimuli and task were identical to those of Experiments 1 and 2, except the probe display. In Experiment 3, the probe display contained only two letters presented around the centre of the screen (Figure 4). The letters were consecutive ones, and subjects had to decide whether the arrow, which was always left to right, indicated the correct temporal order of presentation or not. The design and procedure was otherwise identical to those in Experiment 2.

REFERENCES

Acheson, D. J., & MacDonald, M. C. (2009). Verbal working memory and language production: Common approaches to the serial ordering of verbal information. *Psychological Bulletin*, *135*, 50.

Arnold, P., & Mills, M. (2001). Memory for faces, shoes and objects by deaf and hearing signers and hearing nonsigners. *Journal of Psycholinguistic Research*, *30*, 185–195.

Baddeley, A. (1992). Working memory. *Science*, *255*, 556–559.

Baddeley, A. D. (2000). The episodic buffer: A new component of working memory? *Trends in Cognitive Sciences*, *4*, 417–423.

Baddeley, A. (2003). Working memory and language: an overview. *Journal of Communication Disorders*, 36, 189–208.

Baddeley, A., Gathercole, S., & Papagno, C. (1998). The phonological loop as a language learning device. *Psychological Review*, *105*, 158.

Baddeley, A., & Hitch, G. J. (1974). Working memory. In G. Bower (Ed.), *Recent advances in learning and motivation* (Vol. VIII). New York, NY: Academic Press.

Baddeley, A. D., Lewis, V., & Vallar, G. (1984). Exploring the articulatory loop. *Quarterly Journal of Experimental Psychology*, *36A*, 233–252.

Baddeley, A., Thomson, N., & Buchanan, M. (1975). Word length and the structure of short-term memory. *Journal of Verbal Learning and Verbal Behavior*, *14*, 575–589.

Baddeley, A., & Wilson, B. A. (2002). Prose recall and amnesia: Implications for the structure of working memory. *Neuropsychologia*, *40*, 1737–1743.

Bavelier, D., Newman, A., Mukherjee, M., Hauser, P., Kemeny, S., Braun, A. R., et al. (2008). Neural correlates of short-term memory span in deaf native signers. *Cerebral Cortex*, *18*, 2263–2274.

Bavelier, D., Newport, E. L., Hall, M. L., Supalla, T., & Boutla, M. (2006). Persistent difference in short-term memory span between sign and speech: Implications for cross-linguistic comparisons. *Psychological Science*, *17*, 1090–1092.

Bavelier, D., Newport, E. L., Hall, M. L., Supalla, T., & Boutla, M. (2008). Ordered short-term memory differs in signers and speakers: Implications for models of short-term memory. *Cognition*, *107*, 433–459.

Bavelier, D. (1999). Role and nature of object representations in perceiving and acting. In V. Coltheart (Ed.), *Fleeting memories* (pp. 151–180). Cambridge, MA: MIT Press.

Bellugi, U., & Fischer, S. (1972). A comparison of sign language and spoken language. *Cognition*, *1*, 173–200.

Bellugi, U. & Hickok, G. (1995). Clues to the neurobiology of language. In R. Broadwell (Ed.), *Neuroscience, memory, and language: Decade of the Brain, Volume 1* (pp. 89–107). Washington, DC: Library of Congress.

Bellugi, U., Klima, E., & Siple, P. (1974–1975). Remembering in signs. *Cognition*, *3*, 93–125.

Bellugi, U., Poizner, H., & Klima, E. S. (1989). Language, modality and the brain. *Trends in Neuroscience*, *12*, 380–388.

Binder, J. R., Desai, R. H., Graves, W. W., & Conant, L. L. (2009). Where is the semantic system? A critical review and meta-analysis of 120 functional neuroimaging studies. *Cerebral Cortex*, *19*, 2767–2796.

Boutla, M., Supalla, T., Newport, L., & Bavelier, D. (2004). Short-term memory span: Insights from sign language. *Nature Neuroscience*, 7, 997–1002.

Burgess, N., & Hitch, G. (2005). Computational models of working memory: Putting long-term memory into context. *Trends in Cognitive Sciences*, *9*, 535–541.

Capirci, O., Cattani, A., Rossini, P., & Volterra, V. (1998). Teaching sign language to hearing children as a possible factor in cognitive enhancement. *Journal of Deaf Studies and Deaf Education*, *3*, 135–142.

Carey, S., & Xu, F. (2002). Infants' knowledge of objects: Beyond object files and object tracking. In B.J. Scholl (Ed.), *Objects and attention* (pp. 179–214). Boston, MA: MIT Press.

Conrad, R. (1970). Short-term memory processes in the deaf. *British Journal of Psychology*, *61*, 179–195.

Conrad, R. (1972). Short-term memory in the deaf: A test for speech coding. *British Journal of Psychology*, *63*, 173–180.

Conway, C. M., & Christiansen, M. H. (2005). Modality-constrained statistical learning of tactile, visual, and auditory sequences. *Journal of Experimental Psychology: Learning, Memory & Cognition*, *31*, 24–39.

Conway, C. M., Karpicke, J., Anaya, E. M., Henning, S. C., Kronenberger, W. G., & Pisoni, D. B. (2011). Nonverbal cognition in deaf children following cochlear implantation: Motor sequencing disturbances mediate language delays. *Developmental Neuropsychology*, *36*, 237–254.

Conway, C. M., Pisoni, D. B., Anaya, E. M., Karpicke, J., & Henning, S. C. (2011). Implicit sequence learning in deaf children with cochlear implants. *Developmental Science*, *14*, 69–82.

Conway, C. M., Pisoni, D. B., & Kronenberger, W. G. (2009). The importance of sound for cognitive sequencing abilities: The auditory scaffolding hypothesis. *Current Directions in Psychological Science*, *18*, 275–279.

Cowan, N. (2008). What are the differences between long-term, short-term and working memory? *Progress in Brain Research*, *169*, 323–338.

Cumming, C. E., & Rodda, M. (1985). The effects of auditory deprivation on successive processing. *Canadian Journal of Behavioral Science*, *17*, 233–245.

Daneman, M., & Carpenter, P. (1980). Individual differences in working memory and reading. *Journal of Verbal Learning and Verbal Behaviour*, *19*, 450–466.

Emmorey, K., Kosslyn, S. M., & Bellugi, U. (1993). Visual imagery and visual–spatial language: Enhanced imagery abilities in deaf and hearing ASL signers. *Cognition*, *46*, 139–181.

Emmorey, K., & McCullough, S. (1998). Mental rotation within linguistic and non-linguistic domains in users of American sign language. *Cognition*, *68*, 221–246.

Engle, R. W., Kane, M. J., & Tuholski, S. W. (1999). Individual differences in working memory capacity and what they tell us about controlled attention, general fluid intelligence, and functions of the prefrontal cortex. In A. Miyake & P. Shah (Eds.), *Models of working memory: Mechanisms of active maintenance and executive control* (pp. 102–134). New York, NY: Cambridge University Press.

Geraci, C., Gozzi, M., Papagno, C., & Cecchetto, C. (2008). How grammar can cope with limited short-term memory: Simultaneity and seriality in sign languages. *Cognition*, *106*, 780–804.

Gottlieb, G. (1971). Ontogenesis of sensory function in birds and mammals. In E. Tobach, L. Aronson, & E. Shaw (Eds.), *The biopsychology of development* (pp. 67–128). New York, NY: Academic Press.

Gozzi, M., Geraci, C., Cecchetto, C., Perugini, M., & Papagno, C. (2011). Looking for an explanation for the low sign span: Is order involved? *Journal of Deaf Studies and Deaf Education*, *16*, 101–107.

Haarman, H. J., Davelaar, E. J., & Usher, M. (2003). Individual differences in semantic short-term memory capacity and reading comprehension. *Journal of Memory and Language*, *48*, 320–345.

Hall, M. L., & Bavelier, D. (2010). Working memory, deafness, and sign language. In M. Marschark, P. E. Spencer, & P. E. Nathan (Eds.), *The Oxford handbook of deaf studies, language, and education* (Vol. 2, pp. 458–472). New York: Oxford University Press.

Hall, M. L., & Bavelier, D. (2011). Short-term memory stages in sign vs. speech: The source of the serial span discrepancy. *Cognition*, *120*, 54–66.

Hanson, V. L. (1982). Short-term recall by deaf signers of American Sign Language: Implications of encoding strategy for order recall. *Journal of Experimental Psychology: Learning, Memory & Cognition*, *8*, 572–583.

Hanson, V. L. (1990). Recall of order information by deaf signers: Phonetic coding in temporal order recall. *Memory and Cognition*, *18*, 604–610.

Hauser, P. C., Lukomski, J., & Hillman, T. (2008). Development of deaf and hard-of-hearing students' executive function. In M. H. Marschark & P. C (Eds.), *Deaf cognition: Foundations and outcomes* (pp. 286–308). Oxford, UK: Oxford University Press.

Hauser, P. C., Wills, K., & Isquith, P. K. (2006). Hard of hearing, deafness, and being deaf. In J. D. J. E. Farmer & S. Warschausky (Eds.), *Neurodevelopmental disabilities: Clinical research and*

practice (pp. 119–131). New York, NY: Guilford Publications.
Hermelin, B., & O'Connor, N. (1975). The recall of digits by normal, deaf and autistic children. *British Journal of Psychology*, *66*, 203–209.
Hollingworth, A., Richard, A. M., & Luck, S. J. (2008). Understanding the function of visual short-term memory: Transsaccadic memory, object correspondence, and gaze correction. *Journal of Experimental Psychology: General*, *137*, 163–181.
Jiang, Y., Olson, I. R., & Chun, M. M. (2000). Organization of visual short-term memory. *Journal of Experimental Psychology: Learning, Memory & Cognition*, *26*, 683–702.
Just, M. A., & Carpenter, P. A. (1992). A capacity theory of comprehension: Individual differences in working memory. *Psychological Review*, *99*, 122–149.
Kahneman, D., Treisman, A. M., & Gibbs, B. J. (1992). The reviewing of object files: Object-specific integration of information. *Cognitive Psychology*, *24*, 175–219.
Kanwisher, N. G. (1987). Repetition blindness: Type recognition without token individuation. *Cognition*, *27*, 117–143.
Keehner, M., & Gathercole, S. E. (2007). Cognitive adaptations arising from non-native experience of sign language in hearing adults. *Memory and Cognition*, *35*, 752–761.
Kosslyn, S. M. (1981). The medium and the message in mental imagery: A theory. *Psychological Review*, *88*, 46–66.
Krakow, R. A., & Hanson, V. L. (1985). Deaf signers and serial recall in the visual modality: Memory for signs, fingerspelling, and print. *Memory and Cognition*, *13*, 265–272.
Leslie, A. M., Xu, F., Tremoulet, P. D., & Scholl, B. J. (1998). Indexing and the object concept: Developing "what" and "where" systems. *Trends in Cognitive Sciences*, *2*, 10–18.
Lewis, R. L., Vasishth, S., & Van Dyke, J. A. (2006). Computational principles of working memory in sentence comprehension. *Trends in Cognitive Sciences*, *10*, 447–454.
Logan, K., Maybery, M., & Fletcher, J. (1996). The short-term memory of profoundly deaf people for words, signs, and abstract spatial stimuli. *Applied Cognitive Psychology*, *10*, 105–119.
MacSweeney, M., Campbell, R., & Donlan, C. (1996). Varieties of short-term memory coding in deaf teenagers. *Journal of Deaf Studies and Deaf Education*, *1*, 249–262.
Mann, W., Marshall, C. R., Mason, K., & Morgan, G. (2010). The acquisition of sign language: The impact of phonetic complexity on phonology. *Language Learning and Development*, *6*, 60–86.
Mayberry, R. I., & Squires, B. (2006). Sign language acquisition. In E. Lieven (Series Ed.) & K. Brown (Vol. Ed.). *Language acquisition*, *11*, 291–295.
McElree, B., Foraker, S., & Dyer, L. (2003). Memory structures that subserve sentence comprehension. *Journal of Memory and Language*, *48*, 67–91.
McKee, D. (1987) *An analysis of specialized cognitive functions in deaf and hearing signers* (Unpublished Doctoral dissertation). University of Pittsburgh, Pittsburgh, PA.
Meier, R. P. (1991). Language acquisition by deaf children. *American Scientist*, *79*, 60–70.
Miller, P. (2007). The role of spoken and sign languages in the retention of written words by prelingually deafened native signers. *Journal of Deaf Studies and Deaf Education*, *12*, 184–208.
Newport, E. L., & Meier, R. (1985). The acquisition of American Sign Language. In D. Slobin (Ed.), *The crosslinguistic study of language acquisition* (Vol. 1, pp. 881–938). Hillsdale, NJ: Lawrence Erlbaum Associates.
O'Connor, N., & Hermelin, B. M. (1973). The spatial or temporal organization of short-term memory. *Quarterly Journal of Experimental Psychology*, *25*, 335–343.
Parasnis, I., Samar, V. J., Bettger, J. G., & Sathe, K. (1996). Does deafness lead to enhancement of visual spatial cognition in children? *Journal of Deaf Studies and Deaf Education*, *1*, 145–152.
Penney, C. G. (1989). Modality effects and the structure of short-term verbal memory. *Memory & Cognition*, *17*, 398–422.
Pintner, R., & Patterson, D. (1917). A comparison of deaf and hearing children in visual memory for digits. *Journal of Experimental Psychology*, *2*, 76–88.
Postle, B. R., D'Esposito, M., & Corkin, S. (2005). Effects of verbal and nonverbal interference on spatial and object visual working memory. *Memory and Cognition*, *33*, 203–212.
Potter, M. C. (1983). Representational buffers: The see-mind hypothesis in picture perception, reading, and visual search. In K. Rayner (Ed.), *Eye movements in reading: Perceptual and language processes* (pp. 423–437). New York: Academic Press.

Potter, M. C. (1993). Very short-term conceptual memory. *Memory and Cognition*, *21*, 156–161.
Potter, M. C. (1999). Understanding sentences and scenes: The role of conceptual short-term memory. In V. Coltheart (Ed.), *Fleeting memories*. Cambridge, MA: MIT Press.
Pylyshyn, Z. W. (1989). The role of location indexes in spatial perception: A sketch of the FINST spatial-index model. *Cognition*, *32*, 65–97.
Pylyshyn, Z. W. (2001). Visual indexes, preconceptual objects, and situated vision. *Cognition*, *80*, 127–158.
Radell, P. L., & Gottlieb, G. (1992). Developmental intersensory interference: Augmented prenatal sensory experience interferes with auditory learning in duck embryos. *Developmental Psychology*, *28*, 795–803.
Ramus, F., & Ahissar, M. (2012 this issue). Developmental dyslexia: The difficulties of interpreting poor performance, and the importance of normal performance. *Cognitive Neuropsychology*, *29*, 104–122.
Rönnberg, J., Rudner, M., & Ingvar, M. (2004). Neural correlates of working memory for sign language. *Brain Research. Cognitive Brain Research*, *20*, 165–182.
Rudner, M., & Ronnberg, J. (2008). The role of the episodic buffer in working memory for language processing. *Cognitive Processing*, *9*, 19–28.
Schick, B. S., Marschark, M., & Spencer, P. E. (2005). *Advances in the sign language development of deaf children* (Vol. 15). New York, NY: Oxford University Press.
Smith, E., & Jonides, J. (1997). Working memory: A view from neuroimaging. *Cognitive Psychology*, *33*, 5–42.
Smith, E., Jonides, J., & Koeppe, R. (1996). Dissociating verbal and spatial working memory using PET. *Cerebral Cortex*, *6*, 11–20.
Smith, E. E., Jonides, J., Koeppe, R. A., Awh, E., Schumacher, E. H., & Minoshima, S. (1995). Spatial versus object working memory: PET investigations. *Journal of Cognitive Neuroscience*, *7*, 357–375.
Tulving, E. (1983). *Elements of episodic memory*. Oxford, UK: Clarendon Press.
Tulving, E. (2002). Episodic memory: From mind to brain. *Annual Review of Psychology*, *53*, 1–25.
Turkewitz, G., & Kenny, P. A. (1982). Limitations on input as a basis for neural organization and development. *Developmental Psychobiology*, *15*, 357–368.
Van Dyke, J. A., & McElree, B. (2006). Retrieval interference in sentence comprehension. *Journal of Memory and Language*, *55*, 157–166.
Wager, T., & Smith, E. E. (2003). Neuroimaging studies of working memory: A meta-analysis. *Cognitive, Affective and Behavioral Neuroscience*, *3*, 255–274.
Wagner, A. D., Shannon, B. J., Kahn, I., & Buckner, R. L. (2005). Parietal lobe contributions to episodic memory retrieval. *Trends in Cognitive Sciences*, *9*, 445–453.
Wechsler, D. (1955). *Wechsler Adult Intelligence Scale (WAIS)*. New York: The Psychological Corporation.
Wechsler, D. (1997). *Wechsler Adult Intelligence Scale (WAIS-III) 3*. New York: The Psychological Corporation.
Wilson, M. (2001). The case for sensorimotor coding in working memory. *Psychonomic Bulletin and Review*, *8*, 44–57.
Wilson, M., Bettger, J. G., Niculae, I., & Klima, E. S. (1997). Modality of language shapes working memory: Evidence from digit span and spatial span in ASL signers. *Journal of Deaf Studies and Deaf Education*, *2*, 150–160.
Wilson, M., & Emmorey, K. (1997). A visuospatial "phonological loop" in working memory: Evidence from American Sign Language. *Memory & Cognition*, *25*, 313–320.
Wilson, M., & Emmorey, K. (1998). A "word length effect" for sign language: Further evidence for the role of language in structuring working memory. *Memory & Cognition*, *26*, 584–590.
Wilson, M., & Emmorey, K. (2006a). Comparing sign language and speech reveals a universal limit on short-term memory capacity. *Psychological Science*, *17*, 682–683.
Wilson, M., & Emmorey, K. (2006b). No difference in short-term memory span between sign and speech. *Psychological Science*, *17*, 1093.
Xu, Y., & Chun, M. M. (2005). Dissociable neural mechanisms supporting visual short-term memory for objects. *Nature*, *440*, 91–95.
Zarfaty, Y., Nunes, T., & Bryant, P. (2004). The performance of young deaf children in spatial and temporal number tasks. *Journal of Deaf Studies and Deaf Education*, *9*, 139–181.

APPENDIX
Images of finger handshapes used in Experiments 2 and 3

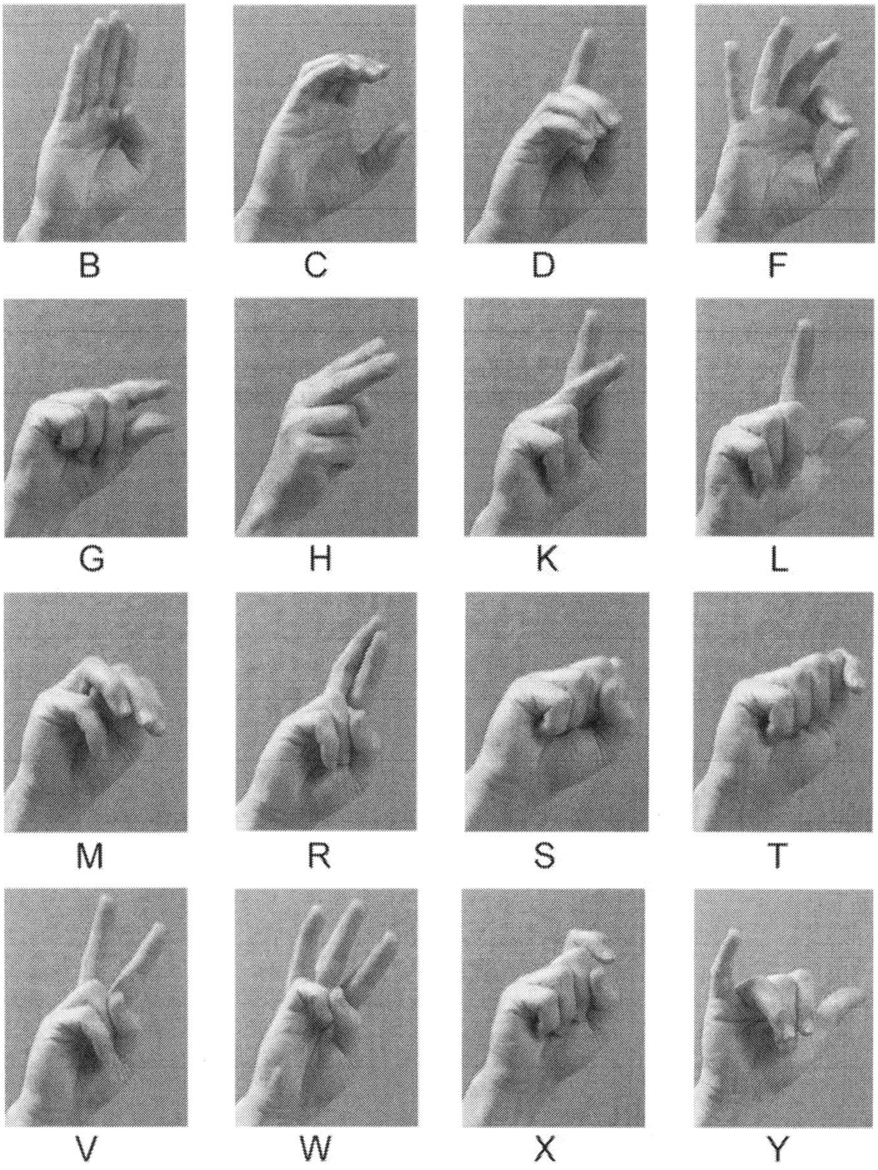

Figure A1. *Images of finger handshapes used in Experiments B and C.*

Developmental dyslexia: The difficulties of interpreting poor performance, and the importance of normal performance

Franck Ramus[1] **and Merav Ahissar**[2]

[1]Institut d'Etude de la Cognition, CNRS, EHESS, Ecole Normale Supérieure, Paris, France
[2]Department of Psychology and Edmond and Lily Safra Center for Brain Sciences, The Hebrew University of Jerusalem, Jerusalem, Israel

This paper provides a selective review of data on phonology, audition, vision, and learning abilities in developmental dyslexia, with a specific focus on patterns of normal alongside poor performance. Indeed we highlight the difficulties of interpreting poor performance, and we criticize theories of dyslexia that are exclusively suited to explaining poor performance, at the risk of overgeneralizing and predicting deficits in many more situations than are observed. We highlight a number of tasks and conditions where individuals with dyslexia seem to show perfectly normal performance, and we discuss the value of taking such data seriously into account and the difficulties of current theories to explain them. Finally, we discuss the experimental challenges for tasks investigating the nature of cognitive deficits in dyslexia and in other developmental disorders and the challenges for any proper theory of dyslexia aiming to explain cases of normal as well as poor performance.

Keywords: Cognitive development; Developmental dyslexia; Phonology; Anchoring; Sensory processing.

Developmental dyslexia is a common learning disorder affecting about 3–7% of the population (Lindgren, De Renzi, & Richman, 1985). It is defined as a specific deficit in reading acquisition that cannot be accounted for by low IQ, poor educational opportunities, or an obvious sensory or neurological damage (World Health Organization, 2008). It is quite remarkable that such a seemingly simple and circumscribed disorder has engendered a truly unique profusion of theories.

The first descriptions of developmental dyslexia viewed it as a "congenital word blindness" (Hinshelwood, 1900; Morgan, 1896; Stephenson, 1907), and indeed visual symptoms and hypotheses have dominated the best part of the 20th century (Dunlop, 1972; Hallgren, 1950; Orton, 1937). It is only in the 1970s, with the development of research on speech perception, in particular at Haskins Laboratories, that apparent visual confusions were reinterpreted as phonological ones,

Correspondence should be addressed to Franck Ramus, LSCP, 29 rue d'Ulm, 75005 Paris, France. (E-mail: franck.ramus@ens.fr).

F.R. is funded by Agence Nationale de la Recherche (Genedys), the European Commission (Neurodys), and the Fyssen Foundation. M.A. is funded by the Israeli Science Foundation.

http://www.psypress.com/cogneuropsychology http://dx.doi.org/10.1080/02643294.2012.677420

and that the theory of a phonological deficit emerged and gradually became predominant (Brady & Shankweiler, 1991; Liberman, 1973; Shankweiler & Liberman, 1972; Shankweiler, Liberman, Mark, & Fowler, 1979).

Around the year 2000, the theoretical landscape of dyslexia was a battleground between the hypothesis of a specific phonological deficit (Snowling, 2000; Vellutino, 1979), and alternative theories invoking either rapid temporal processing (Tallal, Miller, & Fitch, 1993), magnocellular function (Stein & Walsh, 1997), or the cerebellum (Nicolson & Fawcett, 1990; Nicolson, Fawcett, & Dean, 2001). These alternative theories have in return faced strong criticism (e.g., Amitay, Ahissar, & Nelken, 2002; Amitay, Ben-Yehudah, Banai, & Ahissar, 2002; Banai & Ahissar, 2006; Ben-Yehudah, Banai, & Ahissar, 2004; Ben-Yehudah, Sackett, Malchi-Ginzberg, & Ahissar, 2001; Ramus, 2001a, 2003, 2004; Ramus et al., 2003; Skottun, 2000; White, Frith, et al., 2006; White, Milne, et al., 2006).

However, far from establishing the supremacy of the specific phonological deficit theory, the unexpected consequence of this criticism has been the appearance of a profusion of new theoretical proposals, as diverse as sluggish attentional shifting (Hari & Renvall, 2001), a noise exclusion deficit (Sperling, Lu, Manis, & Seidenberg, 2005), a perceptual-centre perception deficit (Goswami, 2003), an anchoring deficit (M. Ahissar, 2007), procedural learning difficulties (Nicolson & Fawcett, 2007), a phonological access deficit (Ramus & Szenkovits, 2008), a visual attention deficit (Bosse, Tainturier, & Valdois, 2007; Vidyasagar & Pammer, 2010), and abnormal temporal sampling (Goswami, 2011). The abundance and diversity of these new theories partly stem from the fact that the large body of data on cognitive deficits in dyslexia fails to fit into a single coherent theoretical framework. It also partly reflects the limits of our current understanding of human cognition. Thus the relations between temporal auditory processing (or sampling) and the development of phonological representations are not well understood, and the notions of perceptual noise exclusion, anchoring, and access need to be more precisely defined and integrated into broader models of perception, attention, working, and long-term memory.

Additional factors of complexity include the fact that the disorder is heterogeneous, to the extent that several subtypes of dyslexia have been considered (Bakker, 1992; Boder, 1973; Bosse et al., 2007; Castles & Coltheart, 1993). Thus different theories might be correct for different subtypes. At the moment, the available data on deficits most proximal to reading are roughly consistent with the existence of a majority subtype characterized by a phonological deficit and one or several minority subtypes characterized by a visual deficit (Bosse et al., 2007). Additional subtypes of phonological and visual dyslexia might emerge from the consideration of underlying aetiologies. For instance, a certain proportion of dyslexic individuals have been shown to have broader deficits in the auditory domain: They might constitute a specific subtype of phonological dyslexia. Similarly, several hypotheses of visual dyslexia have been proposed, such as magnocellular dysfunction or reduced visual attention span: They might constitute distinct subtypes of visual dyslexia. However, apart from a few exceptions, most published studies rely on unselected groups of dyslexic participants. They typically report clear evidence that a majority of these cases have a phonological deficit. Thus their results must be skewed towards the cognitive profiles typical of the main phonological subtype. Yet these results show large inconsistencies between studies and remain compatible with multiple theories. We are not aware of any study successfully defining subtypes of dyslexia and providing evidence for distinct, reliable, cognitive (or biological) profiles associated with each subtype, although the study by Bosse et al. (2007) may be the best candidate so far.

It seems that the reason why so many different theories of dyslexia have been proposed is that deficits have been found in an astonishing variety of tasks. The dyslexia literature looks as if almost any new task investigated in dyslexic and control individuals were likely to show significantly poorer performance in the dyslexic group.

Sometimes, questions are raised as to what extent such poor performance may be due to below-average intellectual abilities (e.g., Amitay, Ahissar, et al., 2002; Hulslander et al., 2004). In the best controlled cases, however, poor performance occurs in a context of generally preserved or matched (at least nonverbal) intellectual ability. Ideally, normal performance is demonstrated on a control task measuring similar abilities under a condition that differs by a crucial parameter. Indeed, conditions under which performance is normal are crucial for the interpretation of conditions that yield poor performance, otherwise developmental dyslexia might be easily confounded with a minor intellectual disability or a generalized form of learning disability.

In the present paper, we argue that the greatest stumbling block for any theory of dyslexia is to explain both cases where dyslexic individuals perform poorly and cases where they perform normally. All too often, both phonological and domain-general theories of dyslexia are designed to fit patterns of poor performance exclusively, overlooking normal performance. In so doing, they run the risk of overgeneralizing—that is, of predicting poor performance in many more situations than are observed. Our argument is illustrated by a selective review of patterns of good and poor performance in dyslexia, which are still in need of a coherent explanation.

Patterns of normal and abnormal performance in developmental dyslexia

Phonology

Phonology refers to the mental representation and processing of speech sounds, both in perception and in production. Poor performance of dyslexic individuals has been consistently demonstrated in three broad areas involving phonology: phonological awareness (explicitly attending to, judging, and manipulating speech sounds), verbal short-term and working memory (short-term storage, manipulation, and repetition of words or pseudowords), and rapid automatized naming (RAN: speeded retrieval and naming of lists of digits, colours, or objects; Wagner & Torgesen, 1987). Whether these three components are independent or reflect a common underlying deficit remains an open question. The general consensus is that dyslexic individuals' phonological representations are degraded (a hypothesis that has been formulated in a number of different versions, e.g., noisy, sparsely coded, underspecified, with poor spectral or temporal resolution ...), and that this explains at least the first two components, and perhaps slowed rapid naming as well, at least to some extent.

As previously discussed by Ramus and Szenkovits (2008), tasks that involve phonology and that yield reliably poor performance of dyslexic individuals tend to require either explicit and complex mental manipulations of speech sounds or a high short-term or working memory load, or speeded conditions, or additional factors that make the task particularly difficult. There is no doubt that the hypothesis of degraded phonological representations, no matter the form that it takes, does predict poor performance in all these tasks. Our concern here is that it also predicts poor performance in a much broader range of tasks (see Ramus, 2001b) in which dyslexic individuals show far less obvious difficulties. We thus now focus on evidence for normal phonological performance in dyslexia.

Given that the primary function of phonology is to speak, using specific native-language phonemes and phonological processes, the most obvious prediction of the degraded phonological representations hypothesis should be that dyslexic individuals speak differently. However, there is very little evidence for that. There is broad agreement that dyslexic individuals speak perfectly normally. Informal clinical observations sometimes suggest a greater prevalence of word-finding difficulties and of slips of the tongue, but we are not aware that this has been confirmed experimentally (see C. R. Marshall, Harcourt-Brown, Ramus, & van der Lely, 2009, for evidence of normal word-finding abilities). Using word production tasks measuring the accuracy and distinctness of the pronunciation of target words, Elbro, Borstrom, and Petersen (1998) did provide data consistent with the idea that dyslexic children's lexical phonological representations might be underspecified. Furthermore, Lalain, Joly-Pottuz, and Habib (2003) have provided evidence for subtle deviations of certain aerodynamic parameters in dyslexic children's articulation of certain stop consonants. Fowler and Swainson (2004) replicated the observations of Elbro and colleagues, although it should be said that group differences were small and emerged in only some of the measures investigated. It remains unclear to what extent these results may be due to some individuals demonstrating a comorbidity between dyslexia and speech delay, speech sound disorder, or specific language impairment.

The degraded phonological representations hypothesis should also predict that lexical phonological retrieval should be slower and/or more prone to errors. However, while results from serial naming under speeded conditions (in RAN) clearly show slower performance, results from single picture naming typically do not (Elbro et al., 1998; McCrory, 2001). This therefore suggests that dyslexics' difficulties with RAN are due to the sequential aspects of the task, more than to the stage of phonological retrieval.

On the perception side, the degraded phonological representations hypothesis should predict widespread disruption of the categorical perception of phonemes. There has been a lot of research in this area, but the results are far from overwhelming. A number of studies have found significantly shallower curves for the categorical perception function of certain consonant contrasts, but these results seemed to hold only in a minority of dyslexic children (Adlard & Hazan, 1998; Breier et al., 2001; Manis et al., 1997; G. McArthur, Atkinson, & Ellis, 2009; Mody, Studdert-Kennedy, & Brady, 1997; Paul, Bott, Heim, Wienbruch, & Elbert, 2006; Rosen & Manganari, 2001) or only under specific conditions (e.g., with synthetic but not with natural speech; Blomert & Mitterer, 2004). Other studies failed to find significant group differences (Hazan, Messaoud-Galusi, Rosen, Nouwens, & Shakespeare, 2009; Ramus et al., 2003; Robertson, Joanisse, Desroches, & Ng, 2009; White, Milne et al., 2006).

Even under noise, which is assumed to magnify any subtle speech perception deficit, the evidence for a deficit is quite mixed (Brady, Shankweiler, & Mann, 1983; Chandrasekaran, Hornickel, Skoe, Nicol, & Kraus, 2009; Cornelissen, Hansen, Bradley, & Stein, 1996; Hazan et al., 2009; Inoue, Higashibara, Okazaki, & Maekawa, 2011; Robertson et al., 2009; Snowling, Goulandris, Bowlby, & Howell, 1986; Ziegler, Pech-Georgel, George, & Lorenzi, 2009). A comparison of studies that do and do not find group differences in speech perception in noise may suggest that differences are found only at very low signal/noise ratios (e.g., Ziegler et al., 2009) or under additional constraints (e.g., under high but not low presentation rate; Inoue et al., 2011).

Interestingly, lexical decision tasks sometimes reveal subtle differences between dyslexics and controls (Janse, de Bree, & Brouwer, 2010), although not compared to a reading-age control group (Poulsen, 2011). It remains an open question to what extent these small effects might be due to the metalinguistic demands of the lexical decision task ("is this a word or a nonword?"). Thus, for example, a cognitively less demanding lexical recognition task such as picture–word matching ("pear" or "bear"?) shows no group differences, even with chronological-age control children, whether in silence or in noise (C. R. Marshall, Ramus, & van der Lely, 2010).

The relative sparing of both input and output phonological processing is further confirmed in tasks involving both at the same time—for example, pseudoword repetition and various span tasks. Indeed, whereas a deficit in verbal short-term memory is well documented in dyslexia, it surfaces only when longer pseudowords or sequences are used. But the positive (and often overlooked) side of these results is that dyslexic individuals typically have no difficulty repeating 1- to 3-syllable pseudowords, thus showing no deficit in the accuracy of their perception and production (e.g., C. R. Marshall & van der Lely, 2009; Szenkovits & Ramus, 2005), which would not be expected if they misrepresented some aspects of phonological representations.

Another area that has received a lot of attention recently is prosody. Although there have been suggestions that the perception of certain acoustic cues to prosody may be impaired in dyslexia (Goswami et al., 2002; Goswami et al., 2011), these results do not seem to translate to speech prosody in a simple manner. In one study using a prosodic skills battery (Peppé & McCann, 2003), it has been found that children with dyslexia showed normal prosodic perception and production skills, and that their ability to use prosody for linguistic purposes (semantic or syntactic disambiguation) was at the level predicted by their linguistic abilities (C. R. Marshall et al., 2009). Another study did find that dyslexic children had difficulties with prosodic perception, but using a version of the DeeDee task, which involves making explicit judgements about prosody (Goswami, Gerson, & Astruc, 2010). This was confirmed in a similar study on dyslexic adults using a different, but still explicit, stress perception task (Leong, Hamalainen, Soltesz, & Goswami, 2011). Another study conducted on adult participants provided a partial replication, finding a striking dissociation between deficits in the awareness of prosodic patterns (using a version of the DeeDee task) and spared automatic processing of prosody, as measured by a task that did not explicitly bear on prosodic patterns, but that used speech material whose prosody was either congruent or incongruent (Mundy, 2011; Mundy & Carroll, in press). Finally, another study on adults reported difficulties in perceiving and producing foreign stress patterns, but that seemed to be entirely explained by the metaphonological nature of the task and by short-term memory load (Soroli, Szenkovits, & Ramus, 2010). Thus, it seems that deficits in prosody perception or production are found in individuals with dyslexia only to the extent that the tasks used involve metalinguistic judgements or other difficulty factors.

Another area where deficits might be expected in dyslexia is phonological grammar. These are regular, language- and context-dependent variations introduced by speakers in their fluent speech, which are taken into account by listeners for correct lexical recognition. If certain phonetic features (such as voicing or place of articulation) were less well represented by dyslexic individuals, they should produce less distinct phonological variations (such as assimilations, liaisons), in a manner that is less consistently dependent on phonological context. However, the few studies that have investigated the issue have consistently found normal perceptual compensation for assimilation processes in dyslexia (Blomert, Mitterer, & Paffen, 2004; C. R. Marshall et al., 2010; Szenkovits, Darma, Darcy, & Ramus, 2012). Another study investigating the sensitivity to well- and ill-formed consonant sequences in Hebrew reached the same conclusion (Berent, Vaknin, & Marcus, 2007; Berent, Vaknin-Nusbaum, Balaban, & Galaburda, 2012).

To mention one last area that has been recently investigated, Soroli and colleagues (2010) reported no evidence that dyslexic individuals might have more (or less) difficulty perceiving and producing foreign speech sounds than controls, again contrary to predictions made by the standard phonological deficit hypothesis.

Thus there is widespread evidence for normal performance of dyslexic individuals in many aspects of phonology, in tasks and conditions where most theories of the phonological deficit predict poor performance. The hypothesis of a deficit in the access to phonological representations was proposed to fill this gap (Ramus & Szenkovits, 2008); however, at this stage it is quite sketchy and underspecified. It remains a considerable challenge for theories of dyslexia to explain the specific pattern of poor and normal performance that is observed in the phonological domain.

Auditory processing

In a classic series of studies, Tallal and collaborators targeted the notion of "rapid" or "temporal" auditory processing in dyslexia and specific language impairment. For this purpose, they used the temporal order judgement task and its variants, and they manipulated the time interval between the two sounds whose order was to be judged. They reported poor performance of dyslexic children at short but not at long intervals (Tallal, 1980). This is precisely the sort of contrast between poor and normal performance that we are advocating here, and indeed this contrast played a crucial role in the broad influence of the temporal auditory processing theory. As is now well known, this theory has been criticized on the grounds that processing deficits for short intervals had a relatively low prevalence in dyslexia (e.g., Ramus, 2003; White, Milne, et al., 2006). What may be less well known is that the theory was also criticized on the side of normal performance at long intervals. Indeed, as pointed out by Rosen (2003), group differences vanished at long intervals because both groups reached ceiling performance. However, studies designed to avoid ceiling effects found group differences of the same magnitude at long and at short intervals (C. M. Marshall, Snowling, & Bailey, 2001; Nittrouer, 1999; Reed, 1989; Share, Jorm, MacLean, & Matthews, 2002; Waber et al., 2001). Other types of paradigms, such as frequency- or amplitude-modulation detection, did not find much evidence of a specificity of deficits at high temporal frequencies (Goswami et al., 2002; Lorenzi, Dumont, & Füllgrabe, 2000; Witton, Stein, Stoodley, Rosner, & Talcott, 2002; Witton et al., 1998). In a nutshell, manipulating the temporal dimension in auditory processing has produced inconsistent findings and has not yielded the clear pattern of poor and normal performance that was initially suggested.

M. Ahissar, Protopapas, Reid, and Merzenich (2000) largely replicated Tallal's (1980) findings in adult dyslexics. However, the same participants tended to also show difficulties in a series of other auditory discrimination tasks, such as frequency and duration discrimination. Moreover, the degree of difficulties was correlated across tasks. Namely, these were largely the same individuals who had the greatest difficulties across different dimensions (M. Ahissar et al., 2000; Banai & Ahissar, 2004). Furthermore, the individuals with the largest auditory difficulties also had broader verbal working memory deficits. Overall, these studies found no evidence for a *specific* deficit in the ability to identify rapidly varying stimuli. Thus, for example, the minimal duration needed for the detection of a gap in a continuous noise was not longer among dyslexics than among controls (M. Ahissar et al., 2000). Additionally, dyslexics did not show a deficit when brief stimuli were presented, and the frequency difference was "custom tailored" so that it was perceptually (rather than physically) equated across participants (Amitay, Ahissar, et al., 2002).

The observation that auditory deficits are largely correlated across tasks and dimensions links with other theories suggesting a contrast in the temporal domain, in a different temporal range. Indeed, it has been suggested that processing of larger temporal scales, important for speech segmentation at the syllabic level (Goswami et al., 2002) and for tracking the envelope of sentence amplitude modulation (4–16 Hz; E. Ahissar et al., 2001; Goswami, 2011; Goswami, Wang, et al., 2010; Hamalainen, Fosker, Szucs, & Goswami, 2011), is specifically impaired in dyslexia. Yet, when individuals' performance was measured in a variety of tasks tapping this relatively slow temporal processing as well as frequency discrimination, both were impaired to a similar extent (Huss, Verney, Fosker, Mead, & Goswami, 2011). It is difficult to explain why poor processing in this temporal range should lead to poor frequency discrimination. However, the implication of this lower frequency range potentially shifts the focus of the contrast from the perceptual to the attentional scale. Indeed, lower frequencies (~2 Hz) may characterize attentional processes required for perceptual integration and explicit object identification.

While the ability to identify stimuli that include rapid changes does not seem specifically impaired, many studies found difficulties in the ability to rapidly *identify* brief, serially presented stimuli. In other words, the temporal processing bottleneck, rather than being at a low level (ability to implicitly process fast modulations), seems to be situated at a higher level, where the limiting factor is the rate of explicit identification, perhaps due to a slowness of incorporation into explicit processes. The time scale that is relevant for the former is around 30 Hz—for example, the rate of transients that differ between /ba/ and /da/, whereas the time scale for the latter is around 3 Hz. The latter is relevant for fast serial object identification—for example, for identifying /ba/−/da/ as opposed to /da/−/ba/. Thus, Tallal's (1980) two-tone repetitions may in fact tap the latter time scale rather than the former, though the original interpretation was just the opposite. This interpretation is consistent with the finding that deficits in slow temporal processing are linked with poor performance in tasks requiring explicit judgements on the prosody of serially presented words or syllables (Goswami, Gerson, et al., 2010; Leong et al., 2011). In fact, many studies replicated difficulties in fast serial identification, of visual (e.g., Hari & Renvall, 2001) and auditory (e.g., Ben-Yehudah et al., 2004) stimuli. Many dyslexic participants need longer interstimulus intervals for reliable identification. This interpretation may also be in line with magnetoencephalography (MEG) data showing tracking difficulties around this temporal range. According to our revised interpretation, poor tracking is the outcome of slow identification, rather than revealing more basic segmentation processes (E. Ahissar et al., 2001). Our interpretation is also consistent with evidence of poor performance in auditory short-term memory tasks (Laasonen et al., in press).

In summary, on the one hand, there is substantial evidence for poor performance in a range of auditory tasks in dyslexia. On the other hand, attempts to delineate a simple contrast along a well-defined dimension—for example, along a particular frequency range (whether high or low)—fail to account for the whole body of data. A consistently repeated pattern is a difficulty in fast serial identification, which may not be specific to auditory stimuli. This description is compatible with both Tallal's (1980) classical findings and with Goswami's (2011) more recent investigations. However, we have offered a somewhat different interpretation of these results from that of either author.

Moreover, the nature of auditory difficulties may vary across subpopulations of dyslexics. Individuals with a broader profile of linguistic deficits tend to have a broader profile of auditory deficits (e.g., Heath, Hogben, & Clark, 1999; G. M. McArthur & Hogben, 2001), which is often concurrent with somewhat broader cognitive deficits. Our suggestion of a relatively selective deficit in fast serial identification may be more characteristic of individuals who are high academic achievers and tend to be overall slow yet accurate, both in their auditory identification and in their pattern of reading difficulties (Amitay, Ahissar, et al., 2002; Ben-Yehudah et al., 2004). Individuals with broader academic deficits may also have broader perceptual deficits.

Visual processing

As we have recalled in the introduction, dyslexia has long been believed to be a predominantly visual disorder. In the 1980s and 1990s, there were several attempts to explore the aetiology of dyslexia in visual pathways. Thus, Livingstone and colleagues (Livingstone, Rosen, Drislane, & Galaburda, 1991) suggested a specific impairment in the subsystem that processes faster changes in the visual modality, the magnocellular system. The conceptual link was the role that was attributed to the magnocellular system as inhibiting the parvocellular system during saccades and thus eliminating potential blur due to continuous activation of the sustained parvocellular system (e.g., Stein & Walsh, 1997). However, at about the same time it was found that the parvocellular system is not suppressed during saccades. Rather, the magnocellular system is (Burr, Morrone, & Ross, 1994). Yet, the elegant idea of a magnocellular dysfunction, which makes clear behavioural predictions, has inspired the majority of visual studies in the past 30 years.

Based on the few monkey studies that assessed the outcomes of lesions in the magnocellular layers of the lateral geniculate nucleus of the thalamus (Merigan, Byrne, & Maunsell, 1991; Schiller, Logothetis, & Charles, 1990), studies assessing the magnocellular hypothesis focused on contrast sensitivity to moving or flickering grating stimuli and on a variety of motion discrimination tasks (for a review, see Skottun, 2000). Most studies did not compare sensitivity within the magnocellular range with sensitivity in the non-magnocellular (i.e., parvocellular) range. When these were contrasted, for example, by comparing the impact of temporal frequency, or by comparing the consistency of the deficit across different magnocellular tasks, neither consistent nor specific magnocellular deficits were found (e.g., Amitay, Ben-Yehudah, et al., 2002).

The failure to find a specific magnocellular deficit led to two types of modification to the original hypothesis. One suggested that the deficit relates only to temporal aspects within the magnocellular range (McLean, Stuart, Coltheart, & Castles, 2011) and may affect both dorsal and ventral pathways that receive fast conducting neuronal fibres. Based on this conceptualization, several studies assessed the maximal temporal frequency at which participants still detect flicker (and do not experience a perceptual fusion), with isoluminant red–green flickers, which cannot be detected by the "colour-blind" magnocellular system, versus a flicker with an intensity contrast, which can be detected by the magnocellular system. This modified magnocellular hypothesis predicts a specific deficit in the latter condition. A marginal contrast was found in the expected direction. Yet performance thresholds were mainly correlated with generally slower response times, whose relations either with magnocellular performance (Skottun & Skoyles, 2007) or with specific reading skills are not clear.

Another rephrasing of the magnocellular hypothesis focuses on higher processing stages (spatial attention skills) of the dorsal stream, which receives most of its inputs from the magnocellular system (Stein & Walsh, 1997; Vidyasagar & Pammer, 2010). It suggests that the dorsal stream serially selects the positions of letters or letter sequences whose identity is subsequently determined by the ventral stream (Vidyasagar & Pammer, 2010). Furthermore, the idea is that mechanisms of serial search (on which visual reading procedures rely) are impaired in dyslexia, whereas parallel search for simple salient features, which does not require serial attention, is unimpaired. Yet, the claim for a contrast between unimpaired parallel search and impaired serial search has been challenged by other studies (e.g., Moores, Cassim, & Talcott, 2011) that reported other types of difficulties in the spatial allocation of attention—for example, an increased crowding effect (interference caused by a high density of similar neighbouring elements), as was already suggested years ago (Geiger & Lettvin, 1987). However, if dyslexics do have increased crowding effects, these seem to relate to their peripheral and not their foveal vision (Shovman & Ahissar, 2006), and thus their relevance to reading is not well understood.

The view of impaired serial attention was also promoted by Hari and colleagues, who suggested that dyslexics' attention is "sluggish"—namely, that it works somewhat more slowly and is perhaps less spatially refined (Hari & Renvall, 2001). This concept was supported by additional studies showing impaired serial visual identification (Ruffino et al., 2010) and a slower spatial cuing (Facoetti et al., 2010), particularly among dyslexic children with phonological difficulties. Although "sluggish" attention is a fuzzy description, it does make certain predictions. First, serial rather than parallel identification will be relatively more challenging for dyslexics. Second, the relevant time scale for dyslexics' difficulties is ~1–4 Hz (rather than faster time scales), and perhaps similar deficits will be found across modalities (see Facoetti et al., 2010). These predictions are consistent with our interpretation of the auditory findings described above. Moreover, they are consistent with visual studies that were aimed to assess serial versus parallel processing deficits, both in contrast detection (Ben-Yehudah et al., 2001) and in spatial discrimination tasks (spatial frequency discrimination between gratings; Ben-Yehudah & Ahissar, 2004; Ben-Yehudah et al., 2001). The interpretation of slower serial identification is also consistent with results of increased search time under challenging conditions, since these conditions require serial identifications and perhaps also serial comparisons with a template of the searched target (Sung, 2008). Which of the required stages for serial identifications poses the limiting bottleneck was not directly studied.

On the other hand, Valdois and colleagues have hypothesized that parallel rather than serial visual identification is impaired in dyslexia (e.g., Lassus-Sangosse, N'Guyen-Morel, & Valdois, 2008). However, in this case it seems fairly clear that they are talking about a distinct subtype of dyslexia. Indeed, they have found that visual attention span deficits can be dissociated from phonological deficits (Bosse et al., 2007), from magnocellular dysfunction (Prado, 2007; S. Valdois, personal communication, February 2012), and from sluggish attentional shifting (Lallier, Donnadieu, Berger, & Valdois, 2010; Peyrin, Demonet, N'Guyen-Morel, Le Bas, & Valdois, 2011), whereas both magnocellular dysfunction and sluggish attentional shifting tend to co-occur with phonological deficits (Lallier et al., 2009; Ramus, 2003). Thus, there may be no contradiction between the hypotheses of serial and parallel visual identification deficits; they may actually characterize different subtypes of dyslexia.

Learning

The failure to delineate a clear contrast between poor and normal performance along any specific auditory or visual dimension and the plethora of difficulties found across tasks and stimuli lead to the exploration of assessment procedures themselves. Thus, a subsequent line of studies focused on the dynamics of perception as a function of the context in which it was measured.

These studies manipulated the degree of cross-trial regularity rather than the tested stimulus dimensions or range of stimulus parameters. Since frequency discrimination was found impaired in dyslexia in several studies (described above), this dimension was explored using a series of different paradigms (M. Ahissar, Lubin, Putter-Katz, & Banai, 2006; Banai & Ahissar, 2006; Oganian & Ahissar, 2012). Notably, in one experiment, one of the two tones had a constant frequency across trials. This was intended to allow the auditory system to "anchor to" (implicitly detect) the repeated reference tone. The participant can thus perform the comparison by focusing on the variable tone and comparing it to the more stable memory trace of the reference tone formed across several trials, hence improving performance. Indeed, in another experiment, there was no repetition across trials, thus a "real" comparison, based on active working memory, had to be implemented on every trial, and performance was overall lower. Dyslexic participants, whether with (M. Ahissar et al., 2006) or without (Oganian & Ahissar, 2012) a broader language impairment, benefited to a smaller degree than controls from the tone repetition. Thus, in these studies, the degree of regularity was contrasted, and while increased regularity made the task "easier", this was not as effective for the dyslexic population.

Similar findings were obtained when speech perception in noise was tested using either a small set of items that were repeated across trials or a large set in which each word was repeated only once or twice. A significant group difference was found only with the small set, when listeners could gradually form implicit expectations about the repeated words. Ahissar and colleagues (M. Ahissar, 2007; Banai & Ahissar, 2010) proposed that this aspect of fast learning, "anchoring", is impaired in dyslexia: specifically, the detection of sound regularities within a window of several seconds to minutes—that is, longer than the 2–3-second window of working memory. They interpreted these findings as indicating that dyslexics' performance is limited neither by the stimulus dimension (e.g., tone frequency) nor by its complexity, but rather by the efficiency of anchoring to recently presented stimuli. Similar discrepancies were reported by Heath et al. (1999), who found deficits in a fast two-tone identification test (the Tallal repetition test) only when the temporal interval was reduced in a gradual, adaptive manner (which is the typical mode of administration), which allowed participants to form specific expectations about the interstimulus interval.

Similar findings were also reported by Nittrouer, Shune, and Lowenstein (2011), who tested the sensitivity to spectral glides and speech in noise in a population of children selected for having phonological deficits. They found no difference in sensitivity to either spectral cues or noise level. However, using an AX same–different paradigm, they found that children with phonological deficits had difficulties forming an internal reference for the repeated A stimulus and often had a higher tendency of answering "different" to an AA pair. Nittrouer et al. suggested that rather than having a basic perceptual deficit, these children may have difficulties forming categories based on consistently presented stimuli, which may affect the formation of phonological categories. Chandrasekaran et al. (2009) directly tested this hypothesis, by presenting syllables in noise under either a predictable, consistent context or a variable, inconsistent context. They found that repetition enhanced stimulus representation (subcortical auditory event-related potential, ERP, responses), but that this repetition effect was weakened in dyslexia. Similar results were found for poor readers (Strait, Hornickel, & Kraus, 2011). Oganian and Ahissar (2012) also measured the impact of repetition on reading rate and found that for controls, irregular words quickly become "regular" in a repeated context. However, dyslexics' reading rate was not "anchored" to local repetitions.

The relations between dyslexics' poor anchoring and their slower sequential identification described above are not clear. One option is that, as suggested by Kraus and colleagues (Chandrasekaran et al., 2009; Strait et al., 2011), repetition sharpens the representation (improves the signal to noise ratio) and hence facilitates the identification of repeated items. This sharpening being less efficient in dyslexia, identification is slower. Additionally, an effective detection of regularities may increase the effective size of perceptual units and hence decrease the number of required sequential identifications. For example, in two-tone identification, if the repeated tone is detected, only one identification is required in each trial (rather than two). Thus, when the reference tone is always lower than the nonreference (the standard psychophysical procedure), each of the two tones provides sufficient information for successful performance. If the reference is always presented first, it is sufficient to identify the second, nonreference, tone, which is indeed what good listeners do (Nahum, Daikhin, Lubin, Cohen, & Ahissar, 2010).

The ability to automatically detect regularities has been shown at very young ages for the case of word segmentation, based on transitional probabilities between syllables, (e.g., Saffran, Newport, Aslin, Tunick, & Barrueco, 1997). Anchoring may be needed for the ability to track such dependencies. Furthermore, difficulties with the detection of such regularities, for both speech and nonspeech sounds, has been associated with poor linguistic abilities, if not dyslexia per se (Evans, Saffran, & Robe-Torres, 2009).

Since the concept of anchoring has hardly been studied in the cognitive literature, the potential impact of poor anchoring within a window of seconds to minutes on the adequacy of long-term representations is not known and awaits further studies. Thus, in its initial formulation (M. Ahissar et al., 2006), the anchoring hypothesis did not predict poor phonological representations, only poor usage of these representations due to decreased benefit from the specific stimulation context (i.e., its regularities). Yet, it might be the case that poor anchoring could lead to poor long-term representations of those regularities (e.g., transitional probabilities) and hence might also lead to poor phonological representations.

In summary, the anchoring hypothesis proposes that dyslexics' "anchoring" memory is impaired, leading to inefficient usage of recent stimuli sequences and structures. Such impairment may lead to inefficient access to recently presented stimuli. Whether this putative deficit is expected to affect the adequacy of long-term representations—for example, phonology—should be the target of future research. More generally, our concern about overgeneralization and inaccurate prediction of poor performance potentially applies to the anchoring hypothesis as well. To this effect, it is important to emphasize that the anchoring hypothesis only applies to the auditory modality—indeed, attempts to find anchoring deficits in the visual modality have remained unsuccessful (M. Ahissar, unpublished data, 2012). Thus, the anchoring hypothesis specifically predicts that dyslexic individuals should perform poorly in all auditory tasks that require extracting regularities within time scales on the order of seconds and minutes, but not necessarily in other modalities or at other time scales, and not in conditions where no such regularities are available to enhance task performance.

Similar patterns in other developmental disorders

The interesting patterns of poor and normal performance that we have just reviewed in the case of dyslexia are not without counterpart in other developmental disorders. Of course, to the extent that a developmental disorder is characterized by a specific cognitive profile (as opposed to uniform intellectual disability), there have to be areas of normal or at least less impaired performance. But recent findings would seem to suggest that some deficits are not necessarily what they were long thought to be. We discuss two examples familiar to us, congenital amusia and autism, with the hope of drawing interest to these issues for a broader range of disorders.

In the case of congenital amusia, a consensus had gradually emerged that this was to be explained by a core deficit in the representation of pitch (Peretz, 2008). However, one study exploring pitch short-term memory found that amusics were impaired in pitch memory beyond what could be predicted from their simple pitch perception deficit (Gosselin, Jolicoeur, & Peretz, 2009), which sounds quite similar to verbal short-term memory deficits in dyslexia. Furthermore, a recent study exploring different levels of pitch processing found that, while amusic individuals showed typically poor performance in tasks involving judging melodies with either out-of-tune or out-of-key notes, their ERPs to the deviant notes revealed an interesting contrast. Indeed amusic participants showed normal early negativities to notes that were mistuned by a quarter-tone. At the same time they showed disrupted late positivities to both out-of-tune and out-of-key tones (Peretz, Brattico, Järvenpää, & Tervaniemi, 2009). Thus, in the authors' own words, and contrary to their expectations, "the presence of a mismatch negativity for mistuned pitches provides evidence that the amusic brain is sensitive to frequency of occurrence of fine-grained pitch differences in a musical context". They conclude that "the amusic brain appears to be more in tune than conscious perception reveals" (Peretz et al., 2009, p. 1283). In a striking parallel with Ramus and Szenkovits's (2008) analysis of the phonological deficit in dyslexia, it may well be that the problem in congenital amusia has more to do with accessing and manipulating pitch representations than with the representations themselves.

Turning to autism, there is a long tradition postulating that the core deficit lies in the representation of other people's mental states (Baron-Cohen, Leslie, & Frith, 1985; Leslie, 1987). Later theorizing has typically emphasized the existence of other deficits, but has not really challenged the existence of a metarepresentational deficit (Frith, 1989; Happé, 1999; Mottron, Dawson, Soulieres, Hubert, & Burack, 2006). Yet, many people have cautioned that poor performance in theory of mind (ToM) tests is open to multiple interpretations, including limitations in linguistic or executive abilities (e.g., Bloom & German, 2000). Most notably, studies on preverbal infants have shown the difficulty of inferring the absence of representations of others' mental states from poor performance in ToM tests (Onishi & Baillargeon, 2005; Southgate, Senju, & Csibra, 2007; Surian, Caldi, & Sperber, 2007), raising the very same methodological issues that we have highlighted here for dyslexia. Conversely, it has long been known that some individuals with high-functioning autism can eventually pass ToM tests, and again several interpretations have been offered for their normal performance (e.g., Happé, 1995).

In the meantime, other studies have provided evidence that people with autism show a diminished tendency to orient and attend to social stimuli (Dawson, Meltzoff, Osterling, Rinaldi, & Brown, 1998). In one notable study, adults with high-functioning autism were found to perform normally on an array of standard ToM tasks, yet their eye fixations revealed that they did not spontaneously anticipate an agent's actions based on her false belief (Senju, Southgate, White, & Frith, 2009). Furthermore, a recent study provided evidence that adolescents with autism display a form of anhedonia with respect to social stimuli, but not to other sources of pleasure (Chevallier, Grèzes, Molesworth, Berthoz, & Happé, in press). In addition, an increasing range of studies have shown that the poor performance of autistic individuals in social cognition tasks can be dramatically improved by explicitly drawing their attention to the relevant social stimuli (see review by Chevallier, in press). Thus, just like in the dyslexia literature, autism research may be on the verge of shifting explanations from a deficit of representations of mental states, to a lack of spontaneous orienting or access to those representations.

Discussion

This review has highlighted, across a large range of tasks and several developmental disorders, the difficulty of interpreting poor performance in a given task. Tasks are deceptive. No matter how simple they seem, they involve multiple levels of representation and types of processing. It is therefore difficult to unambiguously attribute variance in performance to a particular level of representation or type of processing.

This ambiguity problem potentially affects all tasks. Here we would like to particularly draw the attention to perceptual tasks. Indeed these tasks are often believed to purely tap perceptual representations, as if the very notion of a "pure" task made sense. Thus, even a task as seemingly simple as frequency discrimination (saying which of two pure tones is higher) raises interpretation problems. Beyond the sheer resolution of frequency representations, performance in such a task also involves at least: (a) overall vigilance; (b) focused attention; (c) understanding and automatizing the mapping between frequencies and "high" versus "low" labels (or keys); (d) attention/conscious access to auditory representations (i.e., metacognitive processes); (e) auditory echoic and/or short-term memory; (f) auditory long-term memory (when stimuli are familiar, for instance); (g) "anchoring"—that is, the ability to detect, learn, and exploit task structure and regularities to improve performance (for instance when one tone is kept constant).

In psychophysics, factors other than perceptual representations that may affect performance are not necessarily ignored, but they are at least experimentally neutralized, by selecting high-performing, well-behaving participants who are trained for hours (and who are able to focus their attention on a single task for that amount of time), so that in the end experimenters have reasonable grounds to assume that behavioural performance tells them something about participants' representations. But it is quite obvious that none of these conditions are met when testing pathological populations, let alone children. Thus a special group of participants may show poor performance by failing at a different locus from the one the task was designed to tap in normal participants. This is indeed what has been suggested in the case of categorical perception tasks, in which shallower identification curves and lower discrimination peaks in dyslexic participants may simply reflect more frequent lapses of attention (Davis, Castles, McAnally, & Gray, 2001; Roach, Edwards, & Hogben, 2004; Stuart, McAnally, & Castles, 2001).

Interpreting poor performance is difficult enough in the case of such a "simple" task as frequency discrimination; it may become inextricable in the case of more "complex" tasks such as those involving to a greater extent metacognition or working memory, which themselves are multilevel, multicomponent cognitive skills. What we are lacking at present are sufficiently precise models of these complex cognitive skills that would allow us to carry out careful task analyses and to determine which levels of representation and types of processing are shared by tasks and conditions in which patients perform poorly and are absent of tasks and conditions in which they perform normally. The notions of "phonological access" and of "anchoring" that we have previously proposed (M. Ahissar, 2007; Ramus & Szenkovits, 2008) should be seen as preliminary attempts in this respect, soon to be superseded by more precise hypotheses once suitable models of metacognition, attention, working memory, and learning will be available.

In the meantime, one logical consequence of this critique should be to study developmental disorders using simpler tasks—that is, tasks that involve as few levels of representation and types of processing as possible, or at least that allow a more precise manipulation and control of these factors. The risk is of course to find normal performance, as indeed has been the case in many studies reviewed in the first section. However, we have argued that, to the extent that normal performance is not just a consequence of insensitive tasks and low statistical power, but can be reliably proven, it is as informative as poor performance, even though the interpretation of normal performance can be deceptive too (Karmiloff-Smith, 1998).

It is sometimes argued that the deficit is "subtle" (e.g., in dyslexia, but also in some types of aphasia and many other acquired disorders), so that tasks that are too easy run the risk of "missing" the otherwise hidden deficit. Such considerations lead one to increase the difficulty of tasks, for instance by adding noise to the stimuli, by presenting them in sequence so as to increase the short-term memory load, or by adding time pressure. However, it seems to us that relatively little thought has been given to the extent to which such difficulty factors alter the very nature of the task and the levels of representation and types of processing involved.

If deficits are too subtle for our simple tasks, then maybe the proper response should be to increase the subtlety and the sensitivity of our techniques. One option is to keep using simple tasks while manipulating experimental factors of which participants are totally unaware and on which the task does not bear and to look for interactions between group and the manipulated factor. This is indeed precisely what a number of studies that we have reviewed have done, some yielding surprisingly null (but informative) results (e.g., C. R. Marshall et al., 2010), others yielding intriguingly positive ones (e.g., M. Ahissar et al., 2006). Another approach is to use brain imaging techniques to probe levels of representation or processing with minimal (if any) task demands—for instance, recordings of auditory cortical responses to sound under passive listening conditions (e.g., Lehongre, Ramus, Villiermet, Schwartz, & Giraud, 2011). The two approaches can, of course, be allied in order to measure modulations of brain responses by carefully chosen experimental factors, while again keeping task demands minimal. At any rate, the present review suggests that greater attention should be paid both to task difficulty factors that may degrade performance and to task regularities that may enhance it, and that when such factors are unavoidable, they should be explicitly manipulated, in order to uncover the specific role that they may play in task performance.

REFERENCES

Adlard, A., & Hazan, V. (1998). Speech perception in children with specific reading difficulties (dyslexia). *Quarterly Journal of Experimental Psychology*, *51A*(1), 153–177.

Ahissar, E., Nagarajan, S., Ahissar, M., Protopapas, A., Mahncke, H., & Merzenich, M. M. (2001). Speech comprehension is correlated with temporal response patterns recorded from auditory cortex. *Proceedings of the National Academy of Sciences, USA*, *98*(23), 13367–13372.

Ahissar, M. (2007). Dyslexia and the anchoring-deficit hypothesis. *Trends in Cognitive Sciences*, *11*(11), 458–465.

Ahissar, M. (2012). Unpublished raw data.

Ahissar, M., Lubin, Y., Putter-Katz, H., & Banai, K. (2006). Dyslexia and the failure to form a perceptual anchor. *Nature Neuroscience*, *9*(12), 1558–1564.

Ahissar, M., Protopapas, A., Reid, M., & Merzenich, M. M. (2000). Auditory processing parallels reading abilities in adults. *Proceedings of the National Academy of Sciences, USA*, *97*(12), 6832–6837.

Amitay, S., Ahissar, M., & Nelken, I. (2002). Auditory processing deficits in reading disabled adults. *Journal of the Association for Research in Otolaryngology*, *3*(3), 302–320.

Amitay, S., Ben-Yehudah, G., Banai, K., & Ahissar, M. (2002). Disabled readers suffer from visual and auditory impairments but not from a specific magnocellular deficit. *Brain, 125*(10), 2272–2285.

Bakker, D. J. (1992). Neuropsychological classification and treatment of dyslexia. *Journal of Learning Disabilities, 25*(2), 102–109.

Banai, K., & Ahissar, M. (2004). Poor frequency discrimination probes dyslexics with particularly impaired working memory. *Audiology and Neuro-Otology, 9*(6), 328–340.

Banai, K., & Ahissar, M. (2006). Auditory processing deficits in dyslexia: Task or stimulus related? *Cerebral Cortex, 16*(12), 1718–1728.

Banai, K., & Ahissar, M. (2010). On the importance of anchoring and the consequences of its impairment in dyslexia. *Dyslexia, 16*(3), 240–257.

Baron-Cohen, S., Leslie, A. M., & Frith, U. (1985). Does the autistic child have a "theory of mind"? *Cognition, 21*(1), 37–46.

Ben-Yehudah, G., & Ahissar, M. (2004). Sequential spatial frequency discrimination is consistently impaired among adult dyslexics. *Vision Research, 44*(10), 1047–1063.

Ben-Yehudah, G., Banai, K., & Ahissar, M. (2004). Patterns of deficit in auditory temporal processing among dyslexic adults. *Neuroreport, 15*(4), 627–631.

Ben-Yehudah, G., Sackett, E., Malchi-Ginzberg, L., & Ahissar, M. (2001). Impaired temporal contrast sensitivity in dyslexics is specific to retain-and-compare paradigms. *Brain, 124*(7), 1381–1395.

Berent, I., Vaknin, V., & Marcus, G. F. (2007). Roots, stems, and the universality of lexical representations: Evidence from Hebrew. *Cognition, 104*(2), 254–286.

Berent, I., Vaknin-Nusbaum, V., Balaban, E., & Galaburda, A. M. (2012). *Dyslexia impairs speech recognition but spares phonological competence*, Manuscript submitted for publication.

Blomert, L., & Mitterer, H. (2004). The fragile nature of the speech-perception deficit in dyslexia: Natural vs synthetic speech. *Brain and Language, 89*(1), 21–26.

Blomert, L., Mitterer, H., & Paffen, C. (2004). In search of the auditory, phonetic and/or phonological problems in dyslexia: Context effects in speech perception. *Journal of Speech, Language, and Hearing Research, 47*(5), 1030–1047.

Bloom, P., & German, T. P. (2000). Two reasons to abandon the false belief task as a test of theory of mind. *Cognition, 77*(1), B25–B31.

Boder, E. (1973). Developmental dyslexia: A diagnostic approach based on three atypical reading–spelling patterns. *Developmental Medicine & Child Neurology, 15*(5), 663–687.

Bosse, M. L., Tainturier, M. J., & Valdois, S. (2007). Developmental dyslexia: The visual attention span deficit hypothesis. *Cognition, 104*, 198–230.

Brady, S., & Shankweiler, D. (1991). *Phonological processes in literacy.* Hillsdale, NJ: Lawrence Erlbaum Associates.

Brady, S., Shankweiler, D., & Mann, V. (1983). Speech perception and memory coding in relation to reading ability. *Journal of Experimental Child Psychology, 35*(2), 345–367.

Breier, J. I., Gray, L., Fletcher, J. M., Diehl, R. L., Klaas, P., Foorman, B. R., et al. (2001). Perception of voice and tone onset time continua in children with dyslexia with and without attention deficit/hyperactivity disorder. *Journal of Experimental Child Psychology, 80*(3), 245–270.

Burr, D. C., Morrone, M. C., & Ross, J. (1994). Selective suppression of the magnocellular visual pathway during saccadic eye movements. *Nature, 371*(6497), 511–513.

Castles, A., & Coltheart, M. (1993). Varieties of developmental dyslexia. *Cognition, 47*(2), 149–180.

Chandrasekaran, B., Hornickel, J., Skoe, E., Nicol, T., & Kraus, N. (2009). Context-dependent encoding in the human auditory brainstem relates to hearing speech in noise: Implications for developmental dyslexia. *Neuron, 64*(3), 311–319.

Chevallier, C. (in press). Theory of mind and autism: Beyond Baron-Cohen et al.'s Sally-Anne study. In A. Slater & P. Quinn (Eds.), *Refreshing developmental psychology: Beyond the classic studies.* London, UK: Sage.

Chevallier, C., Grèzes, J., Molesworth, C., Berthoz, S., & Happé, F. (in press). Brief report: Selective social anhedonia in high functioning autism. *Journal of Autism and Developmental Disorders.*

Cornelissen, P. L., Hansen, P. C., Bradley, L., & Stein, J. F. (1996). Analysis of perceptual confusions between nine sets of consonant–vowel sounds in normal and dyslexic adults. *Cognition, 59*(3), 275–306.

Davis, C., Castles, A., McAnally, K., & Gray, J. (2001). Lapses of concentration and dyslexic performance on the Ternus task. *Cognition, 81*(2), B21–B31.

Dawson, G., Meltzoff, A. N., Osterling, J., Rinaldi, J., & Brown, E. (1998). Children with autism fail to orient to naturally occurring social stimuli. *Journal of Autism and Developmental Disorders, 28*(6), 479–485.

Dunlop, P. (1972). Dyslexia: The orthoptic approach. *Australian Journal of Orthoptics, 12,* 16–20.
Elbro, C., Borstrom, I., & Petersen, D. K. (1998). Predicting dyslexia from kindergarten: The importance of distinctness of phonological representations of lexical items. *Reading Research Quarterly, 33*(1), 36–60.
Evans, J. L., Saffran, J. R., & Robe-Torres, K. (2009). Statistical learning in children with specific language impairment. *Journal of Speech Language and Hearing Research, 52*(2), 321–335.
Facoetti, A., Trussardi, A. N., Ruffino, M., Lorusso, M. L., Cattaneo, C., Galli, R., et al. (2010). Multisensory spatial attention deficits are predictive of phonological decoding skills in developmental dyslexia. *Journal of Cognitive Neuroscience, 22*(5), 1011–1025.
Fowler, A. E., & Swainson, B. (2004). Relationships of naming skills to reading, memory, and receptive vocabulary: Evidence for imprecise phonological representations of words by poor readers. *Annals of Dyslexia, 54*(2), 247–280.
Frith, U. (1989). *Autism: Explaining the enigma.* Oxford, UK: Blackwell.
Geiger, G., & Lettvin, J. Y. (1987). Peripheral vision in persons with dyslexia. *New England Journal of Medicine, 316*(20), 1238–1243.
Gosselin, N., Jolicoeur, P., & Peretz, I. (2009). Impaired memory for pitch in congenital amusia. *Annals of the New York Academy of Sciences, 1169,* 270–272.
Goswami, U. (2003). Why theories about developmental dyslexia require developmental designs. *Trends in Cognitive Sciences, 7*(12), 534–540.
Goswami, U. (2011). A temporal sampling framework for developmental dyslexia. *Trends in Cognitive Sciences, 15*(1), 3–10.
Goswami, U., Gerson, D., & Astruc, L. (2010). Amplitude envelope perception, phonology and prosodic sensitivity in children with developmental dyslexia. *Reading and Writing, 23*(8), 995–1019. doi:10.1007/s11145-009-9186-6
Goswami, U., Thomson, J., Richardson, U., Stainthorp, R., Hughes, D., Rosen, S., et al. (2002). Amplitude envelope onsets and developmental dyslexia: A new hypothesis. *Proceedings of the National Academy of Sciences, USA, 99*(16), 10911–10916.
Goswami, U., Wang, H. L., Cruz, A., Fosker, T., Mead, N., & Huss, M. (2010). Language-universal sensory deficits in developmental dyslexia: English, Spanish, and Chinese. *Journal of Cognitive Neuroscience, 23*(2), 325–337.
Goswami, U., Wang, H. L. S., Cruz, A., Fosker, T., Mead, N., & Huss, M. (2011). Language-universal sensory deficits in developmental dyslexia: English, Spanish, and Chinese. *Journal of Cognitive Neuroscience, 23*(2), 325–337.
Hallgren, B. (1950). Specific dyslexia (congenital word-blindness); a clinical and genetic study. *Acta Psychiatrica et Neurologica. Supplementum., 65,* 1–287.
Hamalainen, J. A., Fosker, T., Szucs, D., & Goswami, U. (2011). N1, P2 and T-complex of the auditory brain event-related potentials to tones with varying rise times in adults with and without dyslexia. *International Journal of Psychophysiology, 81*(1), 51–59.
Happé, F. (1995). The role of age and verbal ability in the theory of mind task performance of subjects with autism. *Child Development, 66*(3), 843–855.
Happé, F. (1999). Autism: Cognitive deficit or cognitive style? *Trends in Cognitive Sciences, 3*(6), 216–222.
Hari, R., & Renvall, H. (2001). Impaired processing of rapid stimulus sequences in dyslexia. *Trends in Cognitive Sciences, 5*(12), 525–532.
Hazan, V., Messaoud-Galusi, S., Rosen, S., Nouwens, S., & Shakespeare, B. (2009). Speech perception abilities of adults with dyslexia: Is there any evidence for a true deficit? *Journal of Speech Language and Hearing Research, 52*(6), 1510–1529.
Heath, S. M., Hogben, J. H., & Clark, C. D. (1999). Auditory temporal processing in disabled readers with and without oral language delay. *Journal of Child Psychology and Psychiatry, 40*(4), 637–647.
Hinshelwood, J. (1900). Congenital word blindness. *Lancet,* 1506–1508.
Hulslander, J., Talcott, J., Witton, C., DeFries, J. C., Pennington, B. F., Wadsworth, S., et al. (2004). Sensory processing, reading, IQ, and attention. *Journal of Experimental Child Psychology, 88*(3), 274–295.
Huss, M., Verney, J. P., Fosker, T., Mead, N., & Goswami, U. (2011). Music, rhythm, rise time perception and developmental dyslexia: Perception of musical meter predicts reading and phonology. *Cortex, 47*(6), 674–689.
Inoue, T., Higashibara, F., Okazaki, S., & Maekawa, H. (2011). Speech perception in noise deficits in Japanese children with reading difficulties: Effects of presentation rate. *Research in Developmental Disabilities, 32*(6), 2748–2757.
Janse, E., de Bree, E., & Brouwer, S. (2010). Decreased sensitivity to phonemic mismatch in spoken word processing in adult developmental dyslexia. *Journal of Psycholinguistic Research, 39*(6), 523–539.

Karmiloff-Smith, A. (1998). Development itself is the key to understanding developmental disorders. *Trends in Cognitive Sciences*, *2*(10), 389–398.

Laasonen, M., Virsu, V., Oinonen, S., Sandbacka, M., Salakari, A., & Service, E. (in press). Phonological and sensory short-term memory are correlates and both affected in developmental dyslexia. *Reading and Writing*.

Lalain, M., Joly-Pottuz, B., & Habib, M. (2003). Dyslexia: The articulatory hypothesis revisited. *Brain and Cognition*, *53*(2), 253–256.

Lallier, M., Donnadieu, S., Berger, C., & Valdois, S. (2010). A case study of developmental phonological dyslexia: Is the attentional deficit in the perception of rapid stimuli sequences amodal? *Cortex*, *46*(2), 231–241. doi:10.1016/j.cortex.2009.03.014

Lallier, M., Thierry, G., Tainturier, M. J., Donnadieu, S., Peyrin, C., Billard, C., et al. (2009). Auditory and visual stream segregation in children and adults: An assessment of the amodality assumption of the "sluggish attentional shifting" theory of dyslexia. *Brain Research*, *1302*, 132–147.

Lassus-Sangosse, D., N'Guyen-Morel, M. A., & Valdois, S. (2008). Sequential or simultaneous visual processing deficit in developmental dyslexia? *Vision Research*, *48*(8), 979–988. doi:10.1016/j.visres.2008.01.025

Lehongre, K., Ramus, F., Villiermet, N., Schwartz, D., & Giraud, A. L. (2011). Altered low-gamma sampling in auditory cortex accounts for the three main facets of dyslexia. *Neuron*, *72*(6), 1080–1090.

Leong, V., Hamalainen, J., Soltesz, F., & Goswami, U. (2011). Rise time perception and detection of syllable stress in adults with developmental dyslexia. *Journal of Memory and Language*, *64*(1), 59–73. doi:10.1016/j.jml.2010.09.003

Leslie, A. M. (1987). Pretense and representation: The origins of "theory of mind". *Psychological Review*, *94*(4), 412–426.

Liberman, I. Y. (1973). Segmentation of the spoken word and reading acquisition. *Bulletin of the Orton Society*, *23*, 65–77.

Lindgren, S. D., De Renzi, E., & Richman, L. C. (1985). Cross-national comparisons of developmental dyslexia in Italy and the United States. *Child Development*, *56*, 1404–1417.

Livingstone, M. S., Rosen, G. D., Drislane, F. W., & Galaburda, A. M. (1991). Physiological and anatomical evidence for a magnocellular defect in developmental dyslexia. *Proceedings of the National Academy of Sciences*, *88*, 7943–7947.

Lorenzi, C., Dumont, A., & Füllgrabe, C. (2000). Use of temporal envelope cues by children with developmental dyslexia. *Journal of Speech, Language and Hearing Research*, *43*, 1367–1379.

Manis, F. R., McBride-Chang, C., Seidenberg, M. S., Keating, P., Doi, L. M., Munson, B., et al. (1997). Are speech perception deficits associated with developmental dyslexia? *Journal of Experimental Child Psychology*, *66*(2), 211–235.

Marshall, C. M., Snowling, M. J., & Bailey, P. J. (2001). Rapid auditory processing and phonological ability in normal readers and readers with dyslexia. *Journal of Speech, Language and Hearing Research*, *44*(4), 925–940.

Marshall, C. R., Harcourt-Brown, S., Ramus, F., & van der Lely, H. K. J. (2009). The link between prosody and language skills in children with specific language impairment (SLI) and/or dyslexia. *International Journal of Language and Communication Disorders*, *44*(4), 466–488.

Marshall, C. R., Ramus, F., & van der Lely, H. (2010). Do children with dyslexia and/or specific language impairment compensate for place assimilation? Insight into phonological grammar and representations. *Cognitive Neuropsychology*, *27*(7), 563–586.

Marshall, C. R., & van der Lely, H. K. J. (2009). Effects of word position and stress on onset cluster production: Evidence from typical development, specific language impairment, and dyslexia. *Language*, *85*(1), 39–57.

McArthur, G., Atkinson, C., & Ellis, D. (2009). Atypical brain responses to sounds in children with specific language and reading impairments. *Developmental Science*, *12*(5), 768–783.

McArthur, G. M., & Hogben, J. H. (2001). Auditory backward recognition masking in children with a specific language impairment and children with a specific reading disability. *Journal of the Acoustical Society of America*, *109*(3), 1092–1100.

McCrory, E. (2001). *A neurocognitive investigation of phonological processing in dyslexia* (Unpublished doctoral dissertation). University College London, London, UK.

McLean, G. M., Stuart, G. W., Coltheart, V., & Castles, A. (2011). Visual temporal processing in dyslexia and the magnocellular deficit theory: The need for speed? *Journal of Experimental Psychology: Human Perception & Performance*, *37*(6), 1957–1975.

Merigan, W. H., Byrne, C. E., & Maunsell, J. H. R. (1991). Does primate motion perception depend on the magnocellular pathway? *Journal of Neuroscience, 11*, 3422–3429.

Mody, M., Studdert-Kennedy, M., & Brady, S. (1997). Speech perception deficits in poor readers: Auditory processing or phonological coding? *Journal of Experimental Child Psychology, 64*(2), 199–231.

Moores, E., Cassim, R., & Talcott, J. B. (2011). Adults with dyslexia exhibit large effects of crowding, increased dependence on cues, and detrimental effects of distractors in visual search tasks. *Neuropsychologia, 49*(14), 3881–3890.

Morgan, W. P. (1896). A case of congenital word blindness. *British Medical Journal*, 2, 1378.

Mottron, L., Dawson, M., Soulieres, I., Hubert, B., & Burack, J. (2006). Enhanced perceptual functioning in autism: An update, and eight principles of autistic perception. *Journal of Autism and Developmental Disorders, 36*(1), 27–43.

Mundy, I. R. (2011). *The conscious awareness and underlying representation of syllabic stress in skilled adult readers and adults with developmental dyslexia*, (Unpublished PhD dissertation). Warwick University, Coventry, UK.

Mundy, I. R., & Carroll, J. M. (in press). Speech prosody and developmental dyslexia: Reduced phonological awareness in the context of intact phonological representations. *Journal of Cognitive Psychology*.

Nahum, M., Daikhin, L., Lubin, Y., Cohen, Y., & Ahissar, M. (2010). From comparison to classification: A cortical tool for boosting perception. *Journal of Neuroscience, 30*(3), 1128–1136.

Nicolson, R. I., & Fawcett, A. J. (1990). Automaticity: A new framework for dyslexia research? *Cognition, 35*(2), 159–182.

Nicolson, R. I., & Fawcett, A. J. (2007). Procedural learning difficulties: Reuniting the developmental disorders? *Trends in Neurosciences, 30*(4), 135–141.

Nicolson, R. I., Fawcett, A. J., & Dean, P. (2001). Dyslexia, development and the cerebellum. *Trends in Neurosciences, 24*(9), 515–516.

Nittrouer, S. (1999). Do temporal processing deficits cause phonological processing problems? *Journal of Speech, Language, and Hearing Research, 42*(4), 925–942.

Nittrouer, S., Shune, S., & Lowenstein, J. H. (2011). What is the deficit in phonological processing deficits: Auditory sensitivity, masking, or category formation? *Journal of Experimental Child Psychology, 108*(4), 762–785.

Oganian, Y., & Ahissar, M. (2012). *Poor anchoring limits dyslexics' perceptual, memory, and reading skills*, Manuscript submitted for publication.

Onishi, K. H., & Baillargeon, R. (2005). Do 15-month-old infants understand false beliefs? *Science, 308*(5719), 255–258.

Orton, S. (1937). *Reading, writing and speech problems in children*. New York, NY: Norton.

Paul, I., Bott, C., Heim, S., Wienbruch, C., & Elbert, T. R. (2006). Phonological but not auditory discrimination is impaired in dyslexia. *European Journal of Neuroscience, 24*(10), 2945–2953. doi:10.1111/j.1460-9568.2006.05153.x

Peppé, S., & McCann, J. (2003). Assessing intonation and prosody in children with atypical language development: The PEPS-C test and the revised version. *Clinical Linguistics & Phonetics, 17*(4–5), 345–354. doi:10.1080/0269920031000079994

Peretz, I. (2008). Musical disorders: From behavior to genes. *Current Directions in Psychological Science, 17*, 329–333.

Peretz, I., Brattico, E., Järvenpää, M., & Tervaniemi, M. (2009). The amusic brain: In tune, out of key, and unaware. *Brain, 132*(5), 1277–1286.

Peyrin, C., Demonet, J. F., N'Guyen-Morel, M. A., Le Bas, J. F., & Valdois, S. (2011). Superior parietal lobule dysfunction in a homogeneous group of dyslexic children with a visual attention span disorder. *Brain and Language, 118*(3), 128–138.

Poulsen, M. (2011). Do dyslexics have auditory input processing difficulties? *Applied Psycholinguistics, 32*(2), 245–261.

Prado, C. (2007). *Mouvements oculaires, empan visuo-attentionnel et théorie magnocellulaire* [Ocular movements, visual-attention span and magnocellular theory] (Unpublished PhD dissertation). Université Pierre Mendès-France, Grenoble, France.

Ramus, F. (2001a). Dyslexia—Talk of two theories. *Nature, 412*, 393–395.

Ramus, F. (2001b). Outstanding questions about phonological processing in dyslexia. *Dyslexia, 7*, 197–216.

Ramus, F. (2003). Developmental dyslexia: Specific phonological deficit or general sensorimotor dysfunction? *Current Opinion in Neurobiology, 13*(2), 212–218.

Ramus, F. (2004). Neurobiology of dyslexia: A reinterpretation of the data. *Trends in Neurosciences, 27*(12), 720–726.

Ramus, F., Rosen, S., Dakin, S. C., Day, B. L., Castellote, J. M., White, S., et al. (2003). Theories of developmental dyslexia: Insights from a multiple case study of dyslexic adults. *Brain, 126*(4), 841–865.

Ramus, F., & Szenkovits, G. (2008). What phonological deficit? *Quarterly Journal of Experimental Psychology, 61*(1), 129–141.

Reed, M. A. (1989). Speech perception and the discrimination of brief auditory cues in reading disabled children. *Journal of Experimental Child Psychology, 48,* 270–292.

Roach, N. W., Edwards, V. T., & Hogben, J. H. (2004). The tale is in the tail: An alternative hypothesis for psychophysical performance variability in dyslexia. *Perception, 33*(7), 817–830.

Robertson, E. K., Joanisse, M. F., Desroches, A. S., & Ng, S. (2009). Categorical speech perception deficits distinguish language and reading impairments in children. *Developmental Science, 12*(5), 753–767.

Rosen, S. (2003). Auditory processing in dyslexia and specific language impairment: Is there a deficit? What is its nature? Does it explain anything? *Journal of Phonetics, 31,* 509–527.

Rosen, S., & Manganari, E. (2001). Is there a relationship between speech and nonspeech auditory processing in children with dyslexia? *Journal of Speech, Language, and Hearing Research, 44*(4), 720–736.

Ruffino, M., Trussardi, A. N., Gori, S., Finzi, A., Giovagnoli, S., Menghini, D., et al. (2010). Attentional engagement deficits in dyslexic children. *Neuropsychologia, 48*(13), 3793–3801.

Saffran, J. R., Newport, E. L., Aslin, R. N., Tunick, R. A., & Barrueco, S. (1997). Incidental language learning: Listening (and learning) out of the corner of your ear. *Psychological Science, 8*(2), 101–105.

Schiller, P. H., Logothetis, N. K., & Charles, E. R. (1990). Role of the color-opponent and broad-band channels in vision. *Visual Neuroscience, 5,* 321–346.

Senju, A., Southgate, V., White, S., & Frith, U. (2009). Mindblind eyes: An absence of spontaneous theory of mind in Asperger syndrome. *Science, 325*(5942), 883–885.

Shankweiler, D. P., & Liberman, I. Y. (1972). Misreading: A search for causes. In J. F. Kavanagh & I. G. Mattingly (Eds.), *Language by ear and by eye: The relationships between speech and reading* (pp. 293–317). Cambridge, MA: MIT Press.

Shankweiler, D. P., Liberman, I. Y., Mark, L. S., & Fowler, C. A. (1979). The speech code and learning to read. *Journal of Experimental Psychology: Human Learning and Memory, 5,* 531–545.

Share, D. L., Jorm, A. F., MacLean, R., & Matthews, R. (2002). Temporal processing and reading disability. *Reading and Writing: An Interdisciplinary Journal, 15,* 151–178.

Shovman, M. M., & Ahissar, M. (2006). Isolating the impact of visual perception on dyslexics' reading ability. *Vision Research, 46*(20), 3514–3525.

Skottun, B. C. (2000). The magnocellular deficit theory of dyslexia: The evidence from contrast sensitivity. *Vision Research, 40*(1), 111–127.

Skottun, B. C., & Skoyles, J. R. (2007). A few remarks on relating reaction time to magnocellular activity. *Journal of Clinical and Experimental Neuropsychology, 29*(8), 860-866. doi: 10.1080/13803390601147637

Snowling, M. J. (2000). *Dyslexia* (2nd ed.). Oxford, UK: Blackwell.

Snowling, M. J., Goulandris, N., Bowlby, M., & Howell, P. (1986). Segmentation and speech perception in relation to reading skill: A developmental analysis. *Journal of Experimental Child Psychology, 41*(3), 489–507.

Soroli, E., Szenkovits, G., & Ramus, F. (2010). Exploring dyslexics' phonological deficit: III. Foreign speech perception and production. *Dyslexia, 16,* 318–340.

Southgate, V., Senju, A., & Csibra, G. (2007). Action anticipation through attribution of false belief by 2-year-olds. *Psychological Science, 18*(7), 587–592. doi:10.1111/j.1467-9280.2007.01944.x

Sperling, A. J., Lu, Z. L., Manis, F. R., & Seidenberg, M. S. (2005). Deficits in perceptual noise exclusion in developmental dyslexia. *Nature Neuroscience, 8*(7), 862–863.

Stein, J. F., & Walsh, V. (1997). To see but not to read; The magnocellular theory of dyslexia. *Trends in Neurosciences, 20*(4), 147–152.

Stephenson, S. (1907). Six cases of congenital word-blindness affecting three generations of one family. *Ophthalmoscope, 5,* 482–484.

Strait, D. L., Hornickel, J., & Kraus, N. (2011). Subcortical processing of speech regularities underlies reading and music aptitude in children. *Behavioral and Brain Functions, 7,* 44. doi: 10.1186/1744-9081-7-44

Stuart, G. W., McAnally, K. I., & Castles, A. (2001). Can contrast sensitivity functions in dyslexia be explained by inattention rather than a magnocellular deficit? *Vision Research, 41,* 3205–3211.

Sung, K. (2008). Serial and parallel attentive visual searches: Evidence from cumulative distribution functions of response times. *Journal of Experimental Psychology: Human Perception and Performance, 34*(6), 1372–1388.

Surian, L., Caldi, S., & Sperber, D. (2007). Attribution of beliefs by 13-month-old infants. *Psychological Science, 18*(7), 580–586. doi:10.1111/j.1467-9280.2007.01943.x

Szenkovits, G., Darma, Q., Darcy, I., & Ramus, F. (2012). *Exploring dyslexics' phonological deficit: II. Phonological grammar*, Manuscript submitted for publication.

Szenkovits, G., & Ramus, F. (2005). Exploring dyslexics' phonological deficit: I. Lexical vs. sub-lexical and input vs. output processes. *Dyslexia, 11*(4), 253–268.

Tallal, P. (1980). Auditory temporal perception, phonics, and reading disabilities in children. *Brain and Language, 9*(2), 182–198.

Tallal, P., Miller, S., & Fitch, R. H. (1993). Neurobiological basis of speech: A case for the pre-eminence of temporal processing. *Annals of the New York Academy of Sciences, 682*, 27–47.

Vellutino, F. R. (1979). *Dyslexia: Research and theory.* Cambridge, MA: MIT Press.

Vidyasagar, T. R., & Pammer, K. (2010). Dyslexia: A deficit in visuo-spatial attention, not in phonological processing. *Trends in Cognitive Sciences, 14*(2), 57–63.

Waber, D. P., Weiler, M. D., Wolff, P. H., Bellinger, D., Marcus, D. J., Ariel, R., et al. (2001). Processing of rapid auditory stimuli in school-age children referred for evaluation of learning disorders. *Child Development, 72*(1), 37–49.

Wagner, R. K., & Torgesen, J. K. (1987). The nature of phonological processing and its causal role in the acquisition of reading skills. *Psychological Bulletin, 101*, 192–212.

White, S., Frith, U., Milne, E., Rosen, S., Swettenham, J., & Ramus, F. (2006). A double dissociation between sensorimotor impairments and reading disability: A comparison of autistic and dyslexic children. *Cognitive Neuropsychology, 23*(5), 748–761.

White, S., Milne, E., Rosen, S., Hansen, P. C., Swettenham, J., Frith, U., et al. (2006). The role of sensorimotor impairments in dyslexia: A multiple case study of dyslexic children. *Developmental Science, 9*(3), 237–255.

Witton, C., Stein, J. F., Stoodley, C. J., Rosner, B. S., & Talcott, J. B. (2002). Separate influences of acoustic AM and FM sensitivity on the phonological decoding skills of impaired and normal readers. *Journal of Cognitive Neuroscience, 14*(6), 866–874.

Witton, C., Talcott, J. B., Hansen, P. C., Richardson, A. J., Griffiths, T. D., Rees, A., et al. (1998). Sensitivity to dynamic auditory and visual stimuli predicts nonword reading ability in both dyslexic and normal readers. *Current Biology, 8*(14), 791–797.

World Health Organization (2008). *International statistical classification of diseases and related health problems–tenth revision* (2nd ed.). Geneva, Switzerland: Author.

Ziegler, J. C., Pech-Georgel, C., George, F., & Lorenzi, C. (2009). Speech-perception-in-noise deficits in dyslexia. *Developmental Science, 12*(5), 732–745.

Genes, language, and the nature of scientific explanations: The case of Williams syndrome

Julien Musolino[1] and Barbara Landau[2]

[1]Psychology and Cognitive Science, Rutgers University, Piscataway, NJ, USA
[2]Cognitive Science, Johns Hopkins University, Baltimore, MD, USA

In this article, we discuss two experiments of nature and their implications for the sciences of the mind. The first, Williams syndrome, bears on one of cognitive science's holy grails: the possibility of unravelling the causal chain between genes and cognition. We sketch the outline of a general framework to study the relationship between genes and cognition, focusing as our case study on the development of language in individuals with Williams syndrome. Our approach emphasizes the role of three key ingredients: the need to specify a clear level of analysis, the need to provide a theoretical account of the relevant cognitive structure at that level, and the importance of the (typical) developmental process itself. The promise offered by the case of Williams syndrome has also given rise to two strongly conflicting theoretical approaches—modularity and neuroconstructivism—themselves offshoots of a perennial debate between nativism and empiricism. We apply our framework to explore the tension created by these two conflicting perspectives. To this end, we discuss a second experiment of nature, which allows us to compare the two competing perspectives in what comes close to a controlled experimental setting. From this comparison, we conclude that the "meaningful debate assumption", a widespread assumption suggesting that neuroconstructivism and modularity address the same questions and represent genuine theoretical alternatives, rests on a fallacy.

Keywords: Williams syndrome; Language; Modularity.

Simply put, the goal of science is to understand the natural world. Often though, nature only reluctantly lets us peer behind the curtain, forcing scientists to deploy ingenious measures to take a peek at its true face. Occasionally, nature is more charitable and reveals itself by orchestrating its own experiments. Such experiments of nature, as they are called, are cherished by scientists because they can bear on questions that would be practically or ethically impossible for them to answer otherwise. For scientists interested in the structure and development of the human mind, few puzzles are as tantalizing as the question of the relationship between genes and cognition. A little over 20 years ago, a fascinating natural experiment was brought to the attention of the cognitive science community with the potential to begin unravelling the causal chain linking genes and cognition.

This experiment of nature was Williams syndrome—a relatively rare genetic disorder that

Correspondence should be addressed to Julien Musolino, Psychology and Cognitive Science, Rutgers University, 152 Frelinghuysen Road, Piscataway, NJ 08854, USA. (Email: jumusolino@gmail.com).

This work was partially funded by grant R01 NS050876 to B. Landau.

http://www.psypress.com/cogneuropsychology http://dx.doi.org/10.1080/02643294.2012.702103

results in a highly unusual cognitive profile, with individuals showing severe impairments in a range of spatial functions but strikingly fluent and well-structured language. This profile has placed Williams syndrome at the centre of a major controversy within cognitive science over some of its foundational questions, including the modularity of mind, the nature and role of innate knowledge in language acquisition, and the relationship between language and other aspects of cognition. What makes Williams syndrome so interesting is that the unusual cognitive profile arises as a consequence of a well-defined genetic condition, with about 25 genes missing from chromosome 7. Perhaps not too surprisingly given the issues at stake, accounts of the cognitive profile of individuals with Williams syndrome and its implications for the sciences of the mind tell the tale of two strongly conflicting viewpoints.

One set of conclusions regarding the cognitive phenotype of individuals with Williams syndrome is that knowledge of language—and in particular syntax—is "spared" or "intact" relative to other cognitive systems and therefore that Williams syndrome represents one side of a double dissociation between language and general intelligence. To quote Pinker (1999): "The genes of one group of children [children with specific language impairment] impair their grammar while sparing general intelligence; the genes of another group of children [children with Williams syndrome] impair their intelligence while sparing their grammar" (p. 262). Thus, Williams syndrome is often cited as a compelling demonstration of the modularity of mind (Jackendoff, 1994; Piatelli-Palmarini, 2001; Pinker, 1999).

A radically different position holds that knowledge of language—and in particular syntax—is not "spared" or "intact" in this atypical population, and therefore that Williams syndrome does *not* provide evidence for modularity. Moreover, scientists holding this position conclude that the linguistic profile of people with Williams syndrome (WS) shows exactly the opposite—that even a distinct genetic disorder cannot result in cognitive systems cleaving along the lines suggested by modular theories of mind. This competing view, most closely associated with a broader framework known as neuroconstructivism, holds specifically that knowledge of language in individuals with Williams syndrome is only superficially good because it is achieved through the use of cognitive mechanisms different from those operating in normal individuals (Karmiloff & Karmiloff-Smith, 2001; Karmiloff-Smith, 1998; Karmiloff-Smith et al., 1997; Thomas & Karmiloff-Smith, 2003). To quote Karmiloff and Karmiloff-Smith (2001): "It has become increasingly clear, therefore, that the superficially impressive language skills of individuals with WS may be due to good auditory memory rather than an intact grammar module" (pp. 202–203).

What shall we make of such contradictory claims and conclusions? And, more generally, how should we approach the relationship between genes and cognition in the first place? In this article, we address these questions as follows: As a first step, we articulate the outline of a framework that we believe represents a productive way of approaching these questions. In doing so, we highlight three important components of such an approach. First, we ask how we should think about the relationship between genes and cognition, focusing on the question of what it might mean for genes to *cause* a particular cognitive profile. Here we argue that because the causal link between genes and cognition is extremely complex and indirect, it is crucial to proceed by selecting a clear level of analysis as our focus. Specifically, we argue for the importance of the *cognitive* level in understanding the WS cognitive phenotype. Second, in order to address the question of how a specific cognitive system—in this case language—may get damaged in WS, we need a *theory* of the cognitive structure in question, or at least a theory of the empirical phenomena under investigation. Third, we emphasize the role of development itself—in this case typical development—as a crucial benchmark against which to evaluate the atypical profile found in WS (Landau, 2011; Landau & Hoffman, 2012). These ideas may not be new, but we believe that they are important and thus worth emphasizing.

After developing this framework, we use it to explore the nature of the conflicting perspectives described earlier. What is new, here, is what follows from the proposed framework. By far the most common assumption is that the tension between the modular and neuroconstructivist approaches stems from a meaningful debate between two sides (e.g., Brock, 2007; Mervis & Becerra, 2007; Zukowski, 2009). A recent formulation of this thesis holds that interpretations conflict because the data themselves are ambiguous: Look at them through a generative/modular lens and you will reach one set of conclusions; put on neuroconstructivist goggles and you will reach a radically different set of conclusions (Thomas, Karamenis, & Knowland, 2010). Implicit in this perspective are the assumptions that the two competing frameworks address the same questions and that they provide explanatorily equivalent accounts of the relevant empirical phenomena.

Here, we turn the tables on the "meaningful debate assumption", which underpins much of the literature on this topic, and we show that this assumption rests on a fallacy. In doing so, we focus on the status of *grammatical knowledge* in individuals with Williams syndrome—perhaps the most contentious issue within this "debate". We argue that there is "the illusion of a debate" between the two views described above, and we pinpoint the factors that give rise to this illusion. We identify two main sources: The first is substantial and has to do with what constitutes a scientific explanation in the first place (Musolino & Landau, 2010). The second, which is a direct consequence of the first, is semantic in nature and involves the use of the same terms—for example, "selective sparing", "impaired", "intact"—with different intended meanings.

With these important distinctions and clarifications in place, we revisit the empirical terrain, showing that the data are no longer ambiguous. Instead, the data strongly support the conclusion that grammar—qua *knowledge* of core linguistic rules and representations—is, in its essentials, present and engaged in individuals with Williams syndrome, just as it is in typically developing and mature individuals. This conclusion, in turn, raises a serious challenge for neuroconstructivism, as acknowledged by some of its proponents (Thomas et al., 2010), which, so far, has not been met (Musolino & Landau, 2010). Finally, we propose a new solution to an apparent paradox that has been claimed to undermine conclusions regarding "intact" syntactic knowledge in individuals with Williams syndrome (Thomas et al., 2010).

Our framework

In this section, we introduce the key ideas underlying our framework. We begin by asking how we should think about the relationship between genes and cognition, focusing on the question of what it might mean for genes to *cause* a particular cognitive profile as in the case of WS. Next, we discuss the need to select a clear level of analysis as our focus, in this case the cognitive level, and the need to have a *theory* of the cognitive structure in question, or at least a theory of the empirical phenomenon under investigation. Finally, we discuss the role of development itself—in this case typical development—as a crucial benchmark against which to evaluate the atypical profile found in WS.

Genes and cognition

Williams syndrome (WS) is a relatively rare genetic disorder (prevalence of about 1 in 7,500 live births; Strømme, Bjørnstad, & Ramstad, 2002), which is due to a microdeletion of approximately 25 genes on chromosome 7 (Ewart et al., 1993). WS gives rise to physical abnormalities, which include cardiac anomalies and unusual facial features, as well as cognitive abnormalities. What makes the WS cognitive phenotype so interesting for cognitive scientists is that it is characterized by a strikingly uneven profile with areas of relative strength, such as language, alongside severe weaknesses in domains such as space, number, planning, and problem solving (e.g., Bellugi, Marks, Bihrle, & Sabo, 1988; Karmiloff-Smith et al., 1997). Consider the classic example (Galaburda, Wang, Bellugi, & Rossen, 1994) of an 18-year-old individual with Williams syndrome

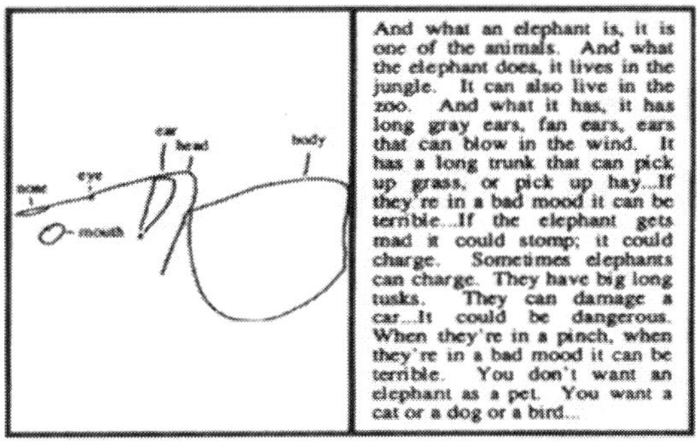

Figure 1. *Contrast between visuospatial and language abilities in Williams syndrome (WS). The dramatic contrast between language and visuospatial functions in a WS subject, age 18 years, IQ 49. He was asked to draw an elephant and tell what he knows about an elephant. Notice the Impoverished drawing as opposed to the embellished grammatically complex language. From* Atypical cognitive deficits in developmental disorders: Implications for brain function *by Broman, Sarah H.; Grafman, Jordan. Copyright 1994. Reproduced with permission of Taylor & Francis Group LLC - Books in the format Journal via Copyright Clearance Center.*

who was asked to draw a picture of an elephant and describe what he knows about elephants (Figure 1, reproduced from Bellugi, Wang, & Jernigan, 1994).

On first glance, there is a glaring asymmetry between the verbal description of the elephant—fluent, with well-formed sentences that convey coherent thoughts—and the impoverished drawing, which preserves virtually nothing of the spatial structure of parts and only the barest structure of spatial relationships among parts. Could such a striking example represent a clear case of a direct link between genes and cognition? In other words, is it possible—as conjectured by Bellugi and colleagues (Bellugi et al., 1988, 1994)—that the absence of 25 genes on a chromosome can cause the derailment of one major system of knowledge (spatial cognition) while leaving another one (language) intact? More generally, how should we approach the relationship between genes and cognition in the first place?

As Marcus (2004) explains, it is patently clear that genes do shape our mental lives, just like they can predispose us to cancer or diabetes. In the case of Williams syndrome, it is also trivially true that the missing genes somehow cause the attested uneven cognitive profile. However, there is a chasm between individual genes, or strands of DNA, and the fine details of syntactic structure or spatial representations at the cognitive level. How, then, should we approach the study of cognitive deficits caused by a genetic disorder?

In his important book *Understanding Developmental Disorders: A Causal Modeling Approach*, John Morton (2004) offers some important suggestions. He begins by asking us to consider the nature of explanation, using as an example the question of what caused Romeo's death. Consider the hypothesis in (1).

1. Romeo was killed by the poison that he took.

This hypothesis is a priori plausible and constitutes a valid scientific explanation given what we know about poisons and human bodies. In principle, gaps in the causal chain can be filled by finding out which poison Romeo took and how it acted on his body. However, Morton argues that people would not consider this to be a very good explanation because, in a sense, it is too specific and thus not very informative. Consider now the hypothesis in (2).

2. Romeo's genes caused him to commit suicide.

In this case, Morton suggests that even if we were to assume that suicides run in Romeo's family, (2) would be a deeply unsatisfying explanation because it leaves far too many gaps in the causal chain. It is unlikely that anyone would want to posit that the act of committing suicide is coded in Romeo's genes, and the hypothesis in (2) does little to specify the details of the causal chain between genes and the act of suicide.

The same argument applies to the relationship between genes and the cognitive profile of people with WS. If we simply say that the missing genes are causing the uneven cognitive profile, this account would be deeply unsatisfying, even if it is trivially true, because it is uninformative and therefore lacks scientific usefulness. It is also clear that the link between genes and cognition is indirect and enormously complex. Moreover, at present, the causal chain between the genetic and cognitive levels is massively underspecified at many points. Given this state of affairs, how then should we proceed to study the link between genes and cognition? Many writers have suggested that in order to fully understand the effects of genes on cognition, scientists in different disciplines will need to coordinate their efforts as they focus on different ends of the causal chain.

At the genetic end, we need to understand what genes do at the molecular level and how this affects the development of the brain and mind (Marcus, 2004). At the cognitive level, we need a cartography that is as detailed and precise as possible. As Ramus (2006) points out, while the causal chain is clearly anchored in both ends, the genetic analysis of any disorder "can only be as good as the characterization of the phenotype, and cognitive phenotyping is (or should be) in the hands of cognitive scientists (p. 249)". Thus, at the cognitive end, progress can be made by being clear about exactly what part of the causal chain is being studied—and at what level of analysis—and by laying out as clearly as possible the structures and mechanisms involved.

Levels of analysis and the importance of theories at each level

In this regard, it has become commonplace in work on the theoretical foundations of cognitive science to distinguish among three levels of analysis at which information processing systems may be described. In his influential book *Vision*, David Marr (1982) dubbed these levels the *computational*, the *algorithmic*, and the *implementational*. Pylyshyn (1984) calls these levels the semantic, syntactic, and physical, and they are also sometimes called the levels of content, form, and medium (Glass, Holyoak, & Santa, 1979). Roughly speaking, the computational level corresponds to the level at which the system's goal is described (in terms of mental representations); the algorithmic level corresponds to the level at which the system's method can be described (in terms of cognitive processes); and finally, the implementational level specifies the physical means by which the representations and algorithms are realized (e.g., neurons in the case brains, or silicon chips for computers).

This division of labour, in turn, entails that one should strive to formulate, or at least use, explanatory theories *at the relevant level of analysis*. This point should be obvious, but, as we discover later, it is often overlooked, leading to unnecessary confusion. For example, if the goal is to try to understand *language* abilities in individuals with Williams syndrome at the *computational level*, as is the case here, we need to use theoretical concepts from linguistic theory—for example, noun, verb, quantifier scope, and so on—and not notions such as plasticity, interactivity, or redundancy, which may very well apply at a different level of analysis.[1] Likewise, no one would seriously try to explain how chess pieces move on a board by using quantum-mechanical rules and justifying such a move by pointing out that, after all, chess sets are made out of atoms.

The importance of development

We now have discussed two of the three ingredients in the proposed approach: the need to identify a clear level of analysis in the causal chain between genes and behaviour, and the related need to rely on explanatory theories at the chosen level of analysis. The third ingredient that we believe plays an important role in our understanding of genetically induced developmental disorders such as Williams syndrome is the role of development itself, and in particular *typical* development. Since Williams syndrome is a genetic deficit that is present at birth, the syndrome is, by definition, developmental. The fact that cognition unfolds over developmental time entails that hypotheses regarding the nature of a linguistic deficit—or lack thereof—will have to take into account aspects of the developmental process (Karmiloff-Smith, 1998).

There are two views on precisely why development matters. One view is that to the extent that the mind is modular, it doesn't start that way,

[1] Or at least, we should not do so until one set of concepts can be meaningfully reduced to the other.

but rather, becomes modular as a result of the developmental process itself (Elman et al., 1996; Karmiloff-Smith, 1998, 2007). However, if the developmental process operates within an atypical brain, as in the case of Williams syndrome, then this altered brain, in turn, will lead to altered learning mechanisms and, ultimately, qualitatively different knowledge representations at the cognitive level (Karmiloff-Smith, 1998).

An alternative view is that while studies of developmental deficits must certainly take into account the developmental process itself, and not prejudge representation solely by what is known about adult brain damage studies, there are nevertheless very strong constraints on what a given cognitive system—such as language—could look like. This view is rooted in the idea that cognitive systems normally develop from origins that themselves embody strong constraints on their architecture. This idea stems from the notion that there are core aspects of human knowledge such as object, space, language, number, and social understanding that emerge very early in development, without formal instruction or otherwise highly specific experiential constraints (Carey, 2009; Spelke, 1998).

These two views can be empirically tested. For example, one can examine in detail whether the language that is produced and comprehended by people with WS is best understood as a system that is characterized by the same underlying linguistic structures as those that are thought to characterize normal language; or alternatively, whether that language is best characterized by missing components of the theoretical system and/or completely different units, structures, and rules. Indeed, this has been at the heart of the debate about language in people with WS, and we provide a concrete example of how this debate gets played out in the literature.

Note that the focus on linguistic structure can be separated from the question of whether language in people with WS (or any special population) is "normal"—by which we usually mean, on a par quantitatively and qualitatively, with typically developing children and normal adults of the same age. But this is not the only question about the endpoint of development that one can ask, nor even, perhaps, the most interesting. For example, it is possible (as we discuss in more detail later) that people with WS develop the same linguistic system as normally developing individuals, but do so at a much slower rate, and undergo developmental arrest at some point, perhaps around adolescence (Landau, 2011; Landau & Hoffman, 2012). This would generate a language profile that looks qualitatively the same as a normally developing person *at a much younger age*. If a normally developing 4-year-old child has control of rich linguistic structures, then under the scenario of slow development and arrest at an early functional level, so too could a person with Williams syndrome.

We return to this hypothesis later in our paper. For now, suffice it to say that the hypothesis is a likely candidate not only for many aspects of language, but also for many aspects of spatial representation, ranging from object recognition to perception of motion coherence to some aspects of navigation (Landau & Hoffman, 2012). If it proves true for language as well, it would solve the problem of how one can have a system that emerges under tight constraints—not disrupted under even conditions of genetic deletion—but at the same time, does not reach the functional level of a chronological age-mate.

To review, in our framework, we emphasize the importance of the cognitive level in understanding the cognitive phenotype in Williams syndrome; the importance of choosing theoretical frameworks pegged appropriately to the particular aspect of cognition being considered; and the importance of considering developmental trajectories in thinking about whether and how the theoretical entities under investigation emerge. Let us now move to a discussion of the two conflicting perspectives with which we opened our paper. In the third part, we focus on a concrete example, apply the notions we explained in our framework, and compare the two views.

Two conflicting perspectives: Modularity and neuroconstructivism

On a general level, the two views described earlier—namely, the generative/modular view and neuroconstructivism—illustrate a perennial controversy over the structure and development of the human mind. These conflicting viewpoints have led to important disagreements in the case most relevant to us here, the acquisition of language. One view, most famously articulated by Noam Chomsky and Jerry Fodor, maintains that the mind contains a domain-specific set of principles dedicated to the acquisition of language—a language "module" or language "organ" to use classic metaphors. Mental modules, in Fodor's (1983) seminal formulation, are taken to meet a number of criteria. The ones most relevant to the study of language in Williams syndrome are domain specificity and ontogenetic invariance (Musolino, Chunyo, & Landau, 2010).[2] Many evolutionary psychologists have also come to view modularity as a form of functional specialization, a concept borrowed from biology (Pinker, 1997, 2005; Sperber, 1994, 2005; Tooby & Cosmides, 1992). For example, Pinker (1997) suggests that modules ought to be understood in terms of the operations they perform on domain-relevant information, rather than through a list of necessary features (see Barrett & Kurzban, 2006, for a discussion of these ideas).

Another common assumption, underlying much work in theoretical linguistics, is that the language module itself has a modular structure and that it contains at least two submodules: a lexicon and a computational system. The former can be thought of as a mental dictionary containing a list of stored forms specifying category membership for entities such as nouns, verbs, and so on, along with other idiosyncratic information. The latter is a set of rules used to combine lexical entries in order to construct larger structures such as words, phrases, and sentences (Chomsky, 1995). On this view of linguistic organization, advocates of modularity have suggested that WS differentially affects the lexicon and the computational system in the sense that the former is adversely affected while the latter is spared (Clahsen & Almazan, 1998; Clahsen & Temple, 2003; Pinker, 1999). For example, Clahsen and Temple (2003) express this view as follows: "They [Clahsen & Almazan, 1998] argued that these two core modules of language are dissociated in WS such that the computational (rule-based) system for language is selectively spared, while lexical representations and/or their access procedures are impaired" (p. 324).

Within the past couple of decades, an alternative to modularity has emerged, growing from work by Elman et al. (2001). This new perspective has been applied to neurodevelopmental disorders under a framework known as neuroconstructivism (Karmiloff & Karmiloff-Smith, 2001; Karmiloff-Smith, 1997, 1998; Thomas, 2008; Thomas & Karmiloff-Smith, 2005; Westermann et al., 2007). One prominent case that has been used to illustrate this approach is Williams syndrome. Two central tenets of neuroconstructivism are that individuals with WS learn language using cognitive mechanisms that are different from the ones used by typically developing individuals and that, as a consequence, *knowledge* of grammar is compromised in this disordered population.

The following quotes illustrate these two claims:

- In sum . . . Williams Syndrome also displays an abnormal cognitive phenotype in which, even where behavioural scores are equivalent to those of normal controls, the cognitive processes by which such proficiency is achieved are different. (Karmiloff-Smith, 1998, p. 395)
- The results of the two present studies . . . challenge the often cited claim that the particular interest of Williams Syndrome for cognitive science lies in the fact that morphosyntactic *rules* are intact [our emphasis]. (Karmiloff-Smith et al., 1997, p. 257).
- The final semantic and conceptual *representations* [our emphasis] formed in individuals

[2] Fodor's full set of criteria includes: domain specificity, obligatory firing, inaccessibility to consciousness, speed, encapsulation, shallow outputs, localization, ontogenetic invariance, and characteristic breakdown patterns.

with WS appear to be shallower, with less abstract information and more perceptually based detail. (Thomas & Karmiloff-Smith, 2003, p. 652)

Neuroconstructivism therefore explicitly rejects, on empirical, theoretical, and methodological grounds, the central conclusions expressed by advocates of the modularity view. To quote Karmiloff-Smith (1998), "this change in perspective means that atypical development should not be considered in terms of a catalogue of impaired and intact functions, in which non-affected modules are considered to develop normally, independently of the others. Such claims are based on the static, adult neuropsychological model which is inappropriate for understanding the dynamics of developmental disorders" (p. 390).

Instead, neuroconstructivism contends that language abilities in WS only *appear* to be impressive, mainly because individuals with WS have good auditory memory skills. This claim can be illustrated by the following quote from Karmiloff and Karmiloff-Smith (2001): "It has become increasingly clear, therefore, that the superficially impressive language skills of individuals with WS may be due to good auditory memory rather than an intact grammar module" (pp. 202–203). Furthermore, neuroconstructivism highlights the role of rote learning in WS and suggests that individuals in this population have difficulty extracting underlying regularities and forming linguistic generalizations. The following two quotes from Karmiloff-Smith et al. (1997) illustrate these points.

- This suggests that if WS children go about language acquisition differently from normal children . . . they will end up—as they indeed do—with large vocabularies but relatively poor system building. (p. 257)
- We challenge these claims [about modularity] and hypothesize that the mechanisms by which people with WS learn language do not follow the normal path. We argue that the language of WS people, although good given their level of mental retardation, will not turn out to be "intact". (p. 247)

To support their conclusions, neuroconstructivists often point to empirical studies by Karmiloff-Smith et al. (1997) suggesting that the comprehension of embedded clauses in English-speaking individuals is an area of weakness and that French-speaking individuals with WS experience difficulty with certain aspects of grammatical gender. Volterra, Capirci, Pezzini, Sabbadini, and Vicari (1996), as well as Capirci, Sabbadini, and Volterra (1996), who studied Italian-speaking individuals with WS, also report unusual syntactic and morphological errors. However, as Brock (2007) points out, further investigation is needed in order to determine the implications of such findings.

In more recent neuroconstructivist work, Thomas and Karmiloff-Smith (2003) discuss two additional hypotheses regarding potential sources of atypicality in WS language. According to what these authors call the conservative hypothesis, " . . . it is argued that the language we see in WS is merely the product of delayed development combined with low IQ" (p. 652). Alternatively, Thomas and Karmiloff-Smith (2003) introduce the semantics–phonology imbalance hypothesis according to which language development in WS takes place under altered constraints. Specifically, individuals with WS rely on a particular strength in auditory short-term memory while lexical semantics is a relative weakness. As a consequence of this imbalance, it is argued, individuals with WS are more reliant on phonological than on semantic information in language processing tasks, which may lead to certain patterns of atypical behaviour.

It is worth pointing out that other investigators have found little empirical evidence supporting the semantics–phonology imbalance hypothesis. For example, this is the conclusion reached by Brock (2007) after an extensive review of the literature on language development in WS. Instead, Brock reports that, by and large, the available evidence is consistent with the "conservative hypothesis", a conclusion echoed by Thomas (2008) who acknowledges, citing Brock's (2007) study, that as research on WS progressed, the "conservative hypothesis" seems to have eclipsed the "imbalance hypothesis". It is also of interest here that other investigators have arrived at essentially the same conclusion, as illustrated by the following quote from Tager-Flusberg, Plesa-Skwerer, Faja, and Joseph (2003): "Despite claims to the contrary (Karmiloff-Smith et al., 2002), there is no evidence that children with WMS acquire language any differently than other children, although they may be delayed in the onset of first words and phrases, as would be expected given their mental retardation (Morris & Mervis, 1999)" (p. 20).

A concrete case of cognitive phenotyping

So far, we have sketched the outline of a general framework to study the relationship between genes and cognition, focusing as our case study on the development of language in individuals with Williams syndrome. Our approach emphasizes the role of three main factors: the need to specify a clear level of analysis, the need to provide a theoretical account of the relevant cognitive structure at that level, and the importance of the (typical) developmental process itself. In order to apply these ideas, and make good on our promise to shed some light on the controversy surrounding the linguistic abilities of individuals with Williams syndrome, we now turn to a concrete case of cognitive phenotyping. In doing so, we focus on knowledge of grammar in this disordered population, arguably the most controversial issue, as discussed above. Specifically, we discuss an interpretive generalization involving the interaction of negation and the disjunction operator, *or*. By focusing on what might at first glance look like an arcane generalization, we not only illustrate the general approach advocated here, but, more importantly, we show that it can illuminate much broader issues in the study of syntax and semantics in typical and atypical development.

Following the approach outlined in the previous sections, we begin by specifying a clear level of analysis for the phenomenon under investigation: the *computational* level in Marr's (1982) sense. Next, we provide an independently motivated theoretical account of our phenomenon and highlight the core grammatical principles at play. We then discuss the results of a set of experiments designed to test knowledge of these core grammatical principles in individuals with Williams syndrome. In doing so, we underscore the role played by typical development, our third factor, in accounting for the observed behavioural patterns. Finally, we bring those results to bear on the two conflicting views discussed above and show that the "meaningful debate assumption", which underpins much of the literature on this topic, rests on a fallacy.

The phenomenon

Consider the sentences in (1–2).

1. All of my friends liked the movie.
2. Some of my friends liked the movie.

Notice that whenever (1) is true, (2) is also necessarily true. In other words, if it is true that all my friends liked the movie, it must also be true that some did. Consequently, we say that (1) *entails* (2) but not vice versa (that is, if it is true that some of my friends liked the movie, it doesn't necessarily follow that all of them did). More generally, we can say that propositions containing *all* entail equivalent propositions containing *some*, as shown in (3).

(3) ALL A are B $\Rightarrow$ SOME A are B

Now consider the examples in (4–5)

4.a. John bought a house
  b. John bought an expensive house
5.a. John didn't buy a house
  b. John didn't buy an expensive house

Notice that (4a) does not entail (4b). That is, if it is true that John bought a house, it does not follow that it must have been an expensive one. John could very well have bought a cheap house. Interestingly, however, when the sentences are negated, as in (5), (5a) now entails (5b). In other words, if it is true that John didn't buy a house, it must also be true that he didn't buy an expensive house. Notice further that the entailment patterns created by the presence of negation have a directionality. That is, negation licenses inferences from sets (the set of houses) to subsets (the set of expensive houses), and for that reason it is called a downward entailing expression.

Linguists have noticed that downward entailing expressions, such as negation, have an interesting set of properties. One such property concerns the way downward entailing expressions affect the interpretation of other logical operators, such as the disjunction operator, *or*. First, notice that in a declarative sentence like (6), *or* typically receives what is called a *disjunctive* or *exclusive* interpretation. That is, the most natural interpretation of (6) is that John bought one kind of car or the other, but not both. Another way to say this is that (6) does not entail (7). To see this, imagine that John bought a BMW. This would clearly make (6) true, but it would also make (7) false. In other words, it is not the case that whenever (6) is true, (7) must also be true—(6) does not entail (7).

6. John bought a BMW or a Mercedes
7. John bought a BMW and John bought a Mercedes

Consider now what happens when (6) and (7) are negated, as in (8) and (9).

8. John didn't buy a BMW or a Mercedes
9. John didn't buy a BMW and John didn't buy a Mercedes

In the presence of negation, disjunction, *or*, is now interpreted conjunctively, or inclusively. What this means is that (8) is interpreted to mean that John bought neither a BMW nor a Mercedes. Crucially, unlike in the case of (6) and (7), when negation is present, (8) entails (9). This interpretive pattern, relating statements containing disjunction, *or*, to equivalent statements containing conjunction, *and*, is captured by one of De Morgan's famous laws of propositional logic, as shown in (10). In plain English, (10) states that the negation of the disjunction of two propositions is logically equivalent to the conjunction of their negations, (11).

10. $\neg (P \vee Q) \Leftrightarrow (\neg P) \wedge (\neg Q)$
11. not (P or Q) ⇔ (not P) and (not Q)

Consider now the examples in (12) and (13) and the apparent problem they pose. Both examples contain negation and the disjunctive operator, *or*, and yet only (12) obeys De Morgan's law. In other words, (13a) entails (13b), but (12a) does not entail (12b). That is, we get a disjunctive reading of *or* in (12) and a conjunctive reading in (13). In order to understand why this should be, and how exactly negation interacts with disjunction, we now provide a theoretical account of the phenomenon.

12.a. The man who didn't get a pay raise bought a BMW or a Mercedes.
b. The man who didn't get a pay raise bought a BMW and the man who didn't get a pay raise bought a Mercedes.

13.a. The man who got a pay raise didn't buy a BMW or a Mercedes.
b. The man who got a pay raise didn't buy a BMW and the man who got a pay raise didn't buy a Mercedes.

The theoretical account

In order to understand how negation interacts with disjunction, we need to introduce three important and independently motivated theoretical notions: syntactic structure, c-command, and scope. The notion of syntactic structure should be fairly familiar. The idea is that linguistic representations of sentences are hierarchical and that the rules of grammar make reference to this hierarchal organization. Thus, a sentence like (14) is not just a string of words but rather can be represented as being hierarchically organized, as shown in (15a–15b).

14. The man danced with the woman.

15.a. (S {NP The man} {VP danced [PP with (NP the woman)]})
where S = sentence, NP = noun phrase, VP = verb phrase, PP = prepositional phrase
b. (See Figure 2.)

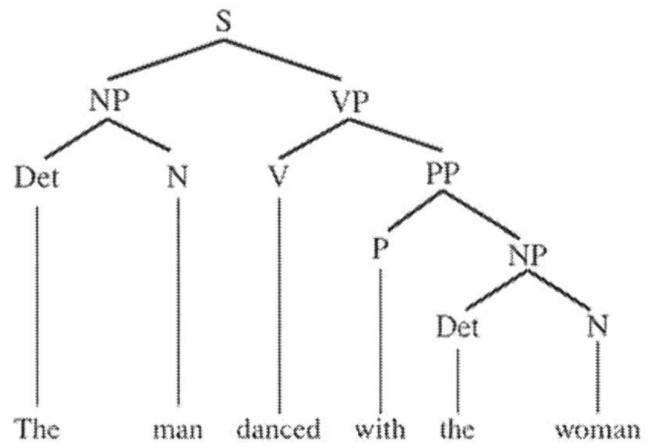

Figure 2. *Example 15b. S = sentence, NP = noun phrase, VP = verb phrase, PP = prepositional phrase, Det = determiner.*

C-command is a structural relation defined over hierarchical structure, and it is defined as follows.

(15) *x* c-command *y* iff:
a. $x \neq y$
b. Neither *x* dominates *y* nor *y* dominates *x*
c. The first branching node that dominates *x* also dominates *y*

A useful rule of thumb to calculate the c-command domain of an expression, for example the c-command domain of the verb *danced* in (15), is to start at the V node in the tree diagram, go up to the first branching point (i.e., VP), and then follow the descending path in all directions. Everything contained within the descending path from the first branching node (the dotted box in the diagram in 16) falls within the c-command domain of the expression under consideration.

16. (See Figure 3.)

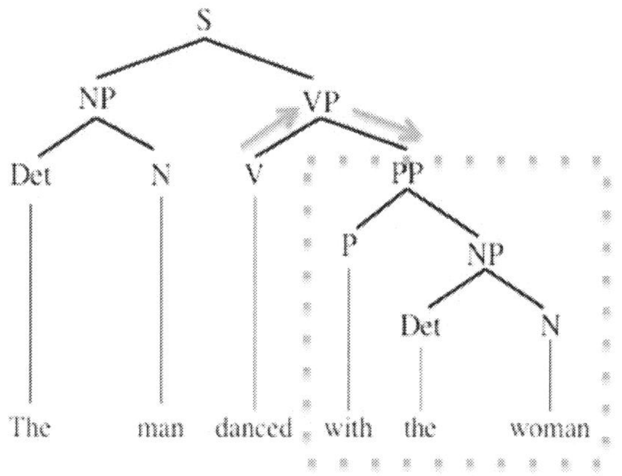

Figure 3. *Example 16. S = sentence, NP = noun phrase, VP = verb phrase, PP = prepositional phrase, Det = determiner. To view a colour version of this figure, please see the online issue of the Journal.*

Hierarchical structure and c-command, in turn, play a crucial role in the notion of scope. In order to illustrate the notion of scope, we can use a simple mathematical analogy. Consider the expressions $3 \times (2 + 1)$ and $(3 \times 2) + 1$. The scope of $3 \times$ (the number 3 followed by the multiplication sign) can be thought of as its domain of application. Thus, in $3 \times (2 + 1)$, the expression $(2 + 1)$ falls within the scope of the expression $3 \times$. However, in $(3 \times 2) + 1$, the number 2 falls within the scope of the expression $3 \times$ but the number 1 falls outside of its scope. Finally notice that different scope relations yield different results when the expressions are computed—that is, $3 \times (2 + 1) = 9$ whereas $(3 \times 2) + 1 = 7$.

Let us now consider the notion of scope as it applies to language. Certain expressions, such as negation, for example, are "scope-bearing expressions". Scope, in turn, is defined in terms of the notion of c-command, as given in (17).

17. Scope principle: An expression *X* takes scope over an expression *Y* iff *X* c-commands Y.

Going back to the diagram in (16) then, (17) simply means that the verb *danced* takes scope over the prepositional phrase *with the woman*, as indicated by the c-command relation. Returning to the way negation and disjunction interact, we can now say that *or* receives a conjunctive interpretation—that is, that De Morgan's law applies—if *or* falls within the scope of negation—that is, if it falls within the c-command of negation. We can now return to the examples in (11) and (12), repeated here as (18), and see that negation, which is too deeply embedded within the subject NP, does not c-command *or* in (18a) but that it does c-command *or* in (18b). This explains why only (18b) obeys De Morgan's law. The reader can verify that for himself/herself by looking at the tree diagrams provided in (19a) and (19b) and applying the informal (or the formal) definition given for c-command.

18.a. {IP [NP The man who didn't get a pay raise] [I' (VP bought a BMW or a Mercedes)]}

where IP = inflectional phrase, I' = I-bar

b. {IP [NP The man who got a pay raise] [I' didn't (VP buy a BMW or a Mercedes)]}

19.a. (See Figure 4.)
b. (See Figure 5.)

To recap, negation, a downward-entailing operator, can interact with disjunction, *or*, to give rise to a pattern of entailment relations known as De Morgan's laws of propositional logic. Whether or not the interpretation of negation and disjunction is subject to De Morgan's laws, in turn, depends on

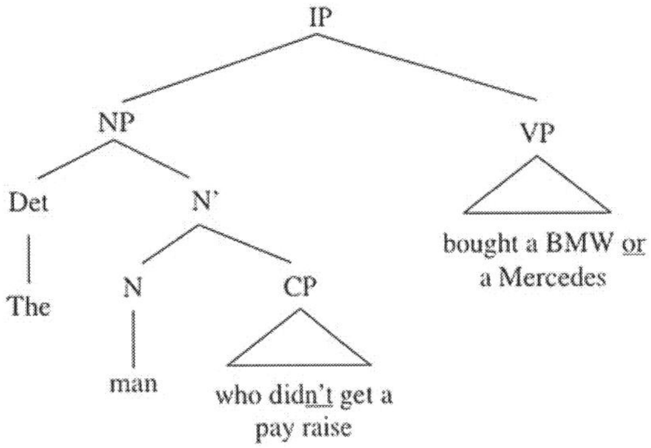

Figure 4. *Example 19a. IP = inflectional phrase, NP = noun phrase, VP = verb phrase, CP = complementizer phrase, Det = determiner.*

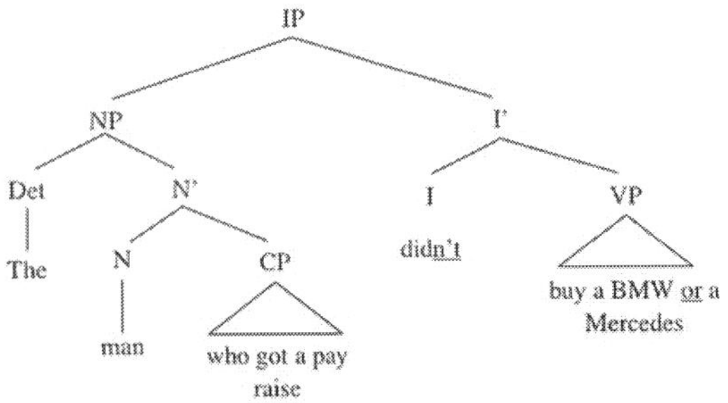

Figure 5. *Example 19b. IP = inflectional phrase, NP = noun phrase, VP = verb phrase, CP = complementizer phrase, Det = determiner.*

the kind of syntactic relation holding between these two elements. Specifically, for De Morgan's law to hold, *or* must occur in the scope—that is, the c-command domain—of negation.

Testing the linguistic knowledge of people with WS
Given the ideas outlined in the previous two sections, we developed an experiment designed to test two issues (Musolino et al., 2010). First, we wanted to know whether, at the *computational level* of analysis, there is evidence for the *theoretical* constructs described in the previous section in individuals with Williams syndrome. To the extent that this is the case, we then can ask the second question: How does the functional level reached by individuals with WS compare to the absolute levels of performance reached by normally developing children of different ages? This, in turn, will directly bear on the hypothesis of "slow development followed by arrest", which we introduced earlier. The prediction from this view is that people with WS should, even as adults, show a quantitative and qualitative profile similar to that of normally developing children who are much younger.

More specifically, in our experiment we sought to determine whether knowledge of scope, c-command, and De Morgan's law is present and engaged in individuals with Williams syndrome. We therefore devised an experiment to assess how such individuals interpret sentences containing negation and disjunction. The basic idea behind the experiment is this: Sentences such as the following are very similar to each other but have quite different meanings:

- *The cat who meowed will not be given a fish or milk*
- *The cat who does not meow will be given a fish or milk*

These sentences contain virtually identical sets of words, including negation and disjunction, and both have relativized subjects. As discussed above, however, these two sentences have different truth conditions. How then can someone know that one sentence is true in a situation in which the cat is given fish or milk while the other sentence is false in the same situation? The answer is that when people interpret such sentences, they engage the rules and principles outlined above (or their theoretical equivalent). In other words, it is *because* people have tacit knowledge of scope, c-command, and de Morgan's law of propositional logic that they can assign the correct meanings to closely related pairs of sentences containing negation and disjunction. Thus, to the extent that experimental participants can correctly distinguish such sentences, one can then infer that they must possess knowledge of the abstract principles described above.

Using a computerized truth value judgement task, we tested individuals with Williams syndrome on their interpretation of sentences containing both negation and disjunction. As mentioned above, our primary goal was to determine whether knowledge of scope, c-command, and De Morgans' law is present in individuals with Williams syndrome and appropriately engaged during language comprehension. To that end, we tested participants on their interpretation of sentences like the ones in (20) and (21), in two experimental conditions. In the precede condition, participants heard sentences in which negation only precedes disjunction—but does not c-command it—(21). In the c-command condition, participants heard sentences in which negation both precedes and c-commands disjunction, (20).

20. The cat who meows will *not* be given a fish *or* milk
21. The cat who does *not* meow will be given a fish *or* milk.

Participants heard prerecorded versions of the sentences used, as descriptions of animated vignettes were displayed on a computer screen. Figure 6 illustrates our procedure and the fact that sentences like (20) and (21) have different truth conditions.

Our experiment also included four control conditions designed to isolate each of the elements that interacted in the experimental sentences. Specifically, being able to correctly calculate the truth conditions of sentences such as (20) and (21) also involves understanding (a) the meaning of negation (*not*), (b) the meaning of *or*, (c) being able to parse a relative clause, and (d) knowledge of De Morgan's laws. The four control conditions were therefore designed to independently test for knowledge of (a–d).

We tested 12 individuals with Williams syndrome (mean age as year, month, 16;4; age range, 11;10–21;11), a group of typically developing children matched to the individuals with WS on the basis of mental age (MA; mean age, 6;1), a group of younger typically developing children (mean age, 4;3), and a group of 12 typical adult native speakers of English.

We found that the WS and MA control groups did not differ from each other on the control conditions and that both groups performed close to

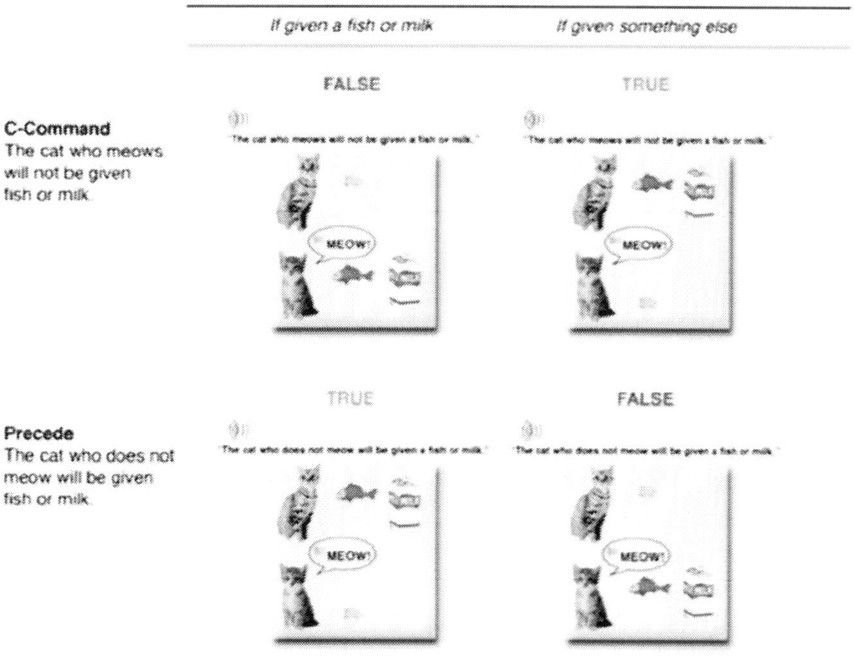

Figure 6. *Sample truth conditions for precede and c-command statements. To view a colour version of this figure, please see the online issue of the Journal.*

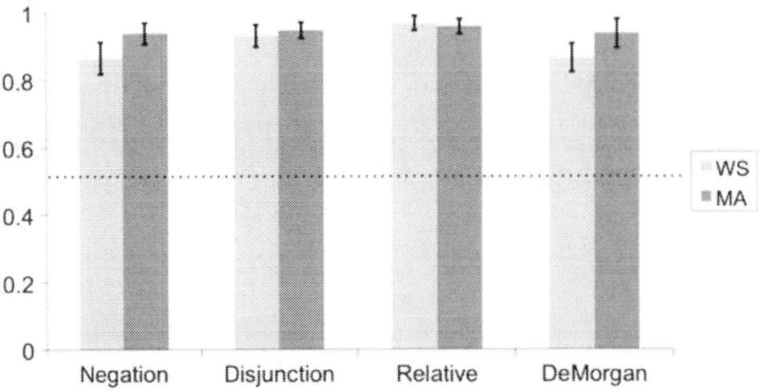

Figure 7. *Proportion of correct responses in control conditions. To view a colour version of this figure, please see the online issue of the Journal.*

ceiling (90.8% vs. 94.5% correct responses on average, respectively; see Figure 7). In the experimental conditions, both groups performed above what would be predicted by chance; however, in this case, MA controls significantly outperformed the WS group (89.5% vs. 76% correct, respectively, averaging between the two conditions; see Figure 8). Thus, the analysis revealed a group (WS vs. MA) by condition (control vs. experimental) interaction.

From these results, one can draw two important conclusions. The first concerns the above-chance performance on the experimental conditions; this demonstrates that individuals with WS as well as MA controls have knowledge of the abstract principles of scope, c-command, and de Morgan's law of propositional logic.[3] Without these, they could not have drawn correct inferences about the meanings in the two types of experimental sentence, which had virtually the same lexical items, but in different syntactic configurations. The second conclusion is that whatever gives rise to the difference in performance between WS and MA controls in the experimental conditions is unlikely to be due to lack of knowledge of the individual elements interacting in the experimental conditions. This is because, on the control conditions, specifically designed to test for such knowledge, the performance of individuals with WS did not differ from that of MA controls.

One possible explanation for the fact that WS and MA differed only in the experimental conditions is that interpreting sentences which contain negation, disjunction, and a relativized subject—as opposed to having to interpret these elements one at a time in the control conditions—leads to more processing difficulties for WS than for MA. By this, we mean that increased

[3] One of the reviewers raises the possibility that individuals with WS may interpret our sentences correctly not because they know about c-command, scope, and so on, but rather because they are using simpler "heuristics", such as, "cat meows → no food" and "cat not meow → food". First, notice that because we used 16 different target sentences in our experimental conditions (precede and c-command), all using different combinations of lexical items, you would need 16 separate "heuristics" like the one proposed here to account for the facts we report (e.g., a policeman/doughnut heuristic, a pirate/jewel one, etc.; see Musolino et al.'s (2010) original article for a list of the stimuli). Second, the proposed heuristic would not actually work in the "cat meowing" case. Indeed, in the case of a sentence like (20) *The cat who meows will not be given a fish or milk*, it is not simply that the sentence will be true if the meowing cat gets no food. To be sure, the sentence will be true if the meowing cat gets neither a fish nor milk; however, it would also be true if the meowing cat gets food *other* than a fish or milk. In order to appreciate that, one needs to understand the meaning of disjunction, *or*, and how it interacts with negation. So one could try to construct a more detailed heuristic to take that into account, and also make that heuristic abstract enough to account for cases involving policemen and doughnuts, pirates and jewels, and so on. Doing so, however, would amount to formulating the kind of abstract notions that linguists take to be underlying people's ability to correctly interpret sentences containing negation and disjunction (e.g., scope, c-command, etc.). For a more detailed discussion of this point, see Musolino et al. (2010; p. 150).

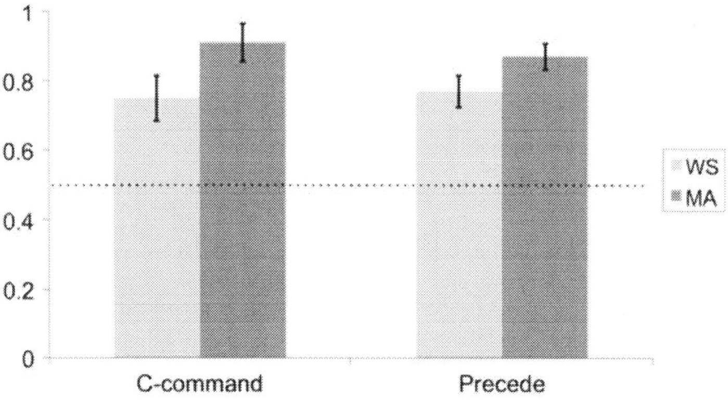

Figure 8. *Proportion of correct responses in experimental conditions. WS = Williams syndrome. MA = mental age controls. To view a colour version of this figure, please see the online issue of the Journal.*

syntactic complexity might result in increased burden on processes such as working memory, which are required to hold parts of a sentence in mind while computing the meaning over all parts. We know that people with WS have verbal working memory limitations (Clarke & Clarke, 1974; Ellis, 1978; Hulme & Mackenzie, 1992; McDade & Adler, 1980; Vicari, Carlesimo, Albertini, & Caltagirone, 1994; Vicari, Brizzolara, Carlesimo, Pezzini, & Volterra, 1996; Vicari, Carlesimo, & Caltagirone, 1995) and that normally developing children show systematic increases in verbal working memory during early and later childhood. Assuming that working memory does contribute to processing complex sentences, we would predict that certain combinations of operations could depress performance for both individuals with WS and normally developing children.

To further investigate this question, we used a multiple regression analysis to assess the contribution of each of the control variables to overall performance in the experimental conditions. We found that for both MA matched children and individuals with WS, performance on the control conditions was significantly related to performance on the experimental conditions. Moreover, in both cases, negation is a significant predictor of overall performance. We also found that the combination of negation and disjunction seems to create more processing difficulty for people with WS than for the MA matched group. One way to interpret these results is that individuals with WS can handle processing complexity—and therefore perform like MA controls—but that working memory limitations will at some point limit the WS individual to a greater degree than the normally developing mental age matches. Once that limit is crossed, performance deteriorates more rapidly for individuals with WS than for MA controls.

This hypothesis, in turn, makes an interesting prediction: namely, that individuals with less mature processing skills—such as younger typically developing children (i.e., children younger than our mental age matches, who were on average 6 years old)—should, like individuals with WS, experience more difficulty with the experimental conditions than with the control conditions. In order to test this prediction, we compared the performance of individuals with WS with that of a group of typically developing 4-year-olds . Recall that comparing the performance of individuals with WS and MA controls revealed a group by condition interaction. In other words, while the two groups did not differ on the four control conditions (each of which tested a single property), individuals with WS did not perform as well as MA controls on the experimental conditions.

As predicted, the comparison between individuals with WS and normally developing 4-year-olds uncovered no such group by condition interaction.

To the extent that the difference in performance between individuals with WS and 4-year-olds on the one hand and MA matches (6-year-olds) on the other reflects the greater complexity of the experimental conditions than of the control conditions, we reasoned that we might be able to observe this effect when comparing the normal 4- and 6 year-olds directly. Indeed, this is precisely what we found: The 4-year-olds behaved disproportionately worse than the 6-year-olds on the experimental conditions compared to the control conditions.

This pattern—rough equivalence of individuals with WS and 4-year-old normally developing children—is predicted by the theory of slow growth followed by developmental arrest that we discussed earlier (and is spelled out in more detail in Landau & Hoffman, 2012). Specifically, if people with WS show very slow development coupled with developmental arrest at an early functional level, their language should look very similar to normally developing children at a much younger age. It is noteworthy that an extensive review of findings on syntax and semantics in people with WS have shown just this pattern, with one exception—overall vocabulary (Landau & Hoffman, 2012). Indeed, standardized measures of vocabulary do show growth in people with WS through adolescence, leading to the common observation that people with WS have strong vocabularies, relative to other skills. This is not surprising, given that vocabulary in normal individuals continues to grow throughout the lifetime. By contrast, much of syntax and formal semantics—such as we have tested here—show effects of age at which they are learned. As is well known, young children acquire many properties of syntax, semantics, and morphology in their preschool years, but children and adults who start learning a second language later in life struggle to achieve native fluency (Munnich & Landau, 2010; Newport, 1990).

Comparing the two frameworks

As discussed earlier, studies of the linguistic abilities of individuals with WS have led to strongly conflicting conclusions regarding the nature of the cognitive profile in this disordered population. By far the most common assumption is that this tension stems from a meaningful debate between two sides (e.g., Brock, 2007; Mervis & Becerra, 2007; Zukowski, 2004). A recent formulation of this thesis holds that interpretations conflict because the data themselves are ambiguous: Look at them through a generative/modular lens, and you will reach one set of conclusions; put on neuroconstructivist goggles, and you will reach a radically different set of conclusions (Thomas et al., 2010). Implicit in this perspective are the assumptions that the two competing frameworks address the same questions and that they provide explanatorily equivalent accounts of the relevant empirical phenomena.

Another natural experiment, this one occurring through a set of publications and played out in the pages of the journal *Language Learning and Development*, gives us an opportunity to compare the two competing set of ideas in the equivalent of a controlled environment. Along with the publication of Musolino et al.'s (2010) study came a detailed commentary by Michael Thomas and his group, which spells out the neuroconstructivist perspective. For Thomas et al. (2010), the data presented by Musolino et al. (2010) were ambiguous and contained aspects that could be viewed to support one theory or the other. To quote Thomas et al. (2010): "the behavioural data had aspects that could be viewed by both Position 1 and Position 2 [generative/modular vs. neuroconstructivist] as supporting their theories, depending on the assumptions used in interpreting the results. The MCL [Musolino, Chunyo, & Landau] study, therefore, revolved around a particular way of interpreting the data, rather than arbitrating between hypotheses from competing theories" (p. 163). Moreover, Thomas et al. present their approach as an *alternative* to the one developed by Musolino et al.: "In this article, we consider the theoretical assumptions necessary to draw conclusions such as those of Musolino, Chunyo, and Landau (henceforth MCL) from the observed behavioural data and place them in the context of *alternative theoretical assumptions* that would lead to a different conclusion [our emphasis]" (p. 163).

Let us now turn to the behavioural data that are claimed to have different possible interpretations depending on one's theoretical inclinations. What exactly are they? Recall that in our experimental conditions, we (Musolino, Chunyo, & Landau, 2010; MCL) made two observations. The first is that both groups of participants (WS and MA controls) were able to distinguish between statements in the precede and c-command conditions at levels above what would be predicted by chance. Let us call this Observation 1. The second observation is that participants in the MA control group performed better, by about 13%, than individuals with WS. Let us call this Observation 2 (Figure 9).

Thomas et al.'s (2010) claim now translates as follows: Depending on whether one decides to focus on Observation 1 or Observation 2, one will reach different conclusions. Specifically, Observation 1 suggests the presence of knowledge in both groups whereas Observation 2, because of the differences in behavioural levels, suggests that the two groups are different. Hence Thomas et al.'s conclusion that: "Given a certain set of theoretical assumptions (e.g., generative/modular), fairly poor performance can nevertheless be viewed as indicating typical development. Given other theoretical assumptions (e.g., a neuroconstructivist view of constrained development), the same data can be viewed as indicative of atypicality" (p. 162).[4]

One can indeed worry about labels here—that is, whether we should say that WS development is typical or atypical—but this would be missing the whole point. Of course development is in some ways atypical in individuals with WS; nobody has ever claimed otherwise. The real question is not how we should label the data, but how we should *explain* them.

Let us begin with Observation 1. How can we account for above-chance performance? On the account that we developed (MCL, 2010), there is a very precise reason for why both groups are able to distinguish c-command and precede statements: At the computational level, they possess and engage the detailed knowledge outlined in our theoretical section. This account is explanatory because it is not a mere restatement of the fact that precede and c-command statements are different. Instead, it specifies precisely *what* the difference is in terms of abstract and independently motivated principles and *how* such a difference yields the observed interpretive patterns.

Recall now that Thomas et al. (2010) argue that neuroconstructivism provides an alternative explanation of the phenomenon under investigation. In this regard, it is informative to consider what these authors propose. According to Thomas et al., the neuroconstructivism approach emphasizes: "both (to) the use of particular methodological approaches . . . and (to) the formulation of explanations with certain characteristics (e.g., theories that features concepts such as *plasticity*, *adaptation*, *interactivity*, *redundancy*, and *compensation*; see Thomas, 2005)" (p. 165) and "Such an account might presumably appeal to lexical or semantic/pragmatic compensatory mechanisms, comprise processes that contain some but not all of the grammatical properties outlined in the generative theory, or employ computational mechanisms that approximate formal syntactic systems under some processing conditions but not others (Christiansen & Chater, 2001; Rumelhart & McClelland, 1986)" (p. 168).

So instead of concepts such as scope, c-command, and entailment patterns, Thomas et al. (2010) argued that we should use notions such as plasticity, adaptation, interactivity, and lexical or semantic/pragmatic compensatory mechanisms. What is important about concepts such as scope, c-command, and entailment

[4] It should be pointed out that accuracy levels for our WS group were 76% correct in the experimental conditions (compared to 89.5% for mental age controls) and 90.8% in the control conditions (compared to 94.5% for MA controls). Describing these results as "fairly poor performance" might be useful for rhetorical purposes, but it is hard to see how this performance is "poor", as it must reflect possession of a highly abstract knowledge system. From that point of view, we find it misleading to characterize the performance as "poor".

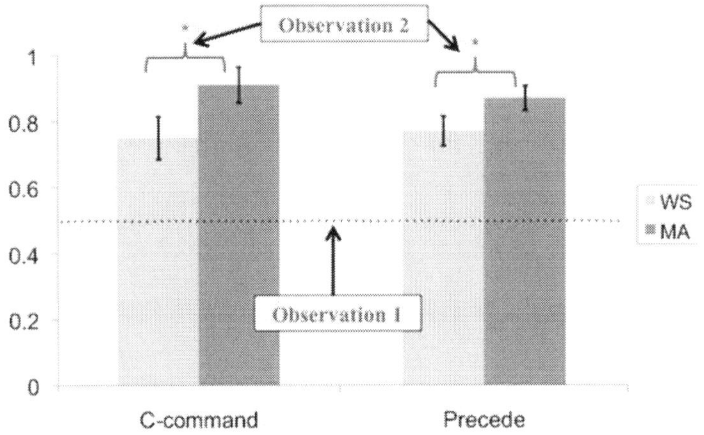

Figure 9. *Performance of the WS and MA control groups on the experimental conditions. WS = Williams syndrome. MA = mental age controls. To view a colour version of this figure, please see the online issue of the Journal.*

relations is that they can be shown to play an explanatory role at what Marr (1982) called the computational level of analysis. Indeed, we devoted a whole section showing precisely how such an account works. On the other hand, notions such as plasticity, adaptation, and interactivity, because they are so vaguely defined in this context, are not useful at the computational level. To be sure, nobody knows how one could account for say, the interpretive contrast between the examples in (22) and (23) in terms of plasticity or interactivity.

22. The cat who meows will *not* be given a fish *or* milk
23. The cat who does *not* meow will be given a fish *or* milk.

One could of course always argue that notions such as plasticity, interactivity, and the like were never meant to apply at the computational level, but perhaps at the algorithmic or the physical levels. If so, one could not say that they represent an alternative account of what was proposed at the computational level, as Thomas et al. (2010) seem to imply. More importantly, however, one would still be left with the nontrivial task of showing precisely how notions such as plasticity or interactivity at, say, the physical or algorithmic levels meaningfully relate to notions such as scope and c-command at the computational level.

We can now come back to our two observations. Take Observation 1 again (above-chance behaviour in the experimental conditions). One can now see that while one side has an explanatory account of that observation, the other side does not. On the account developed here, participants can distinguish very similar pairs of sentences containing negation and disjunction precisely *because* of their knowledge of syntactic structure, scope, c-command, and de Morgan's law of propositional logic. In contrast, notions like plasticity and interactivity explain nothing about this finding. Turning to Observation 2, Musolino et al. (2010) proposed that the small differences in behavioural levels between individuals with WS and MA controls on the experimental conditions do not stem from problems with linguistic knowledge since the two subject groups do not differ on the control conditions, which test for knowledge of the individual components interacting in the experimental conditions. Rather, Musolino et al. concluded that the combined complexity of the elements involved is what is likely to give rise to the difference between WS and MA. Furthermore, they speculated that this may have to do with differences in computational resources such as working memory and showed that the same behavioural pattern emerges in younger, typically developing individuals (whose working memory capacity is not as developed as that of MA controls). This explanation is consistent with our emphasis on the role of development and with our hypothesis of slow development followed by arrest at the functional level of younger, typically developing children (roughly 5-year-olds). While this may not be the right explanation, or even the best one, here too, it is a testable hypothesis, and the data are consistent with it. We do not believe that neuroconstructivism offers a meaningful alternative for this set of empirical facts.

Evaluating the meaningful debate assumption

In the previous section, we focused on the details of the account developed by Musolino et al. (2010) and the neuroconstructivist alternative proposed by Thomas et al. (2010). Doing so allowed us to uncover a number of clues that have important implications for the "meaningful debate assumption" put forth by Thomas et al. (2010) and found in most of the literature on this topic (see Brock, 2007; Mervis & Becerra, 2007; Zukowski, 2009, inter alios). Recall that this hypothesis rests on two key assumptions, namely that (a) the two competing frameworks address the same questions, and (b) that they provide explanatorily equivalent accounts of the relevant empirical phenomenon. The upshot of our discussion is that these two assumptions are untenable. Regarding (a), neuroconstructivism seems to be concerned with appropriate labelling—should we call this or that behaviour (a)typical?—whereas Musolino et al. (2010) asked a different question—a standard one in the field of language acquisition—about the presence of linguistic knowledge. Regarding the second assumption, (b), our discussion reveals, as we have taken great pains to show, that the two frameworks *do not* provide explanatorily equivalent accounts of the relevant empirical phenomena.

This difference has profound implications for a range of issues surrounding the "debate" over language abilities in individuals with Williams syndrome. For one thing, if one does not have a theory of the relevant empirical phenomenon (e.g., the interaction of negation and disjunction, relative clauses, etc.) at the relevant level of analysis (in this case Marr's, 1982, computational level), then one cannot say anything meaningful about questions pertaining to linguistic knowledge. Returning to our earlier analogy, this would amount to trying to understand the behaviour of chess players (engaged in chess playing, of course) without an account of what the rules of chess are. And so instead, as we have seen, Thomas et al. (2010) reframe the debate in terms of a different question about (a)typicality.

In this regard, another important point of contention between competing accounts of language development in individuals with Williams syndrome is the question of whether language, or aspects thereof, are "intact" in this disordered population. In their discussion of these issues, Musolino et al. (2010) point out that the notion of "intact" grammar in WS can be defined in at least two ways:

Grammar is intact in WS if:

a. *Grammatical knowledge* is present and has the same structure as posited in the typical system, or
b. *Behavioural* levels on language tasks are at least as good as those of the relevant comparison group (e.g., individuals matched for chronological age, mental age, etc.).

Moreover, Musolino et al. argue that (a) should be relevant criterion for the area of cognitive science that is concerned with knowledge representations, while (b) is relevant for a different set of questions, perhaps concerning limits on working memory available to use grammatical knowledge. Thus, in mentalistic terms, a claim that grammar is intact is a claim that at the computational level of analysis, the mental representations found in, say, individuals with WS, are the same structures as those posited in the typical, mature system. To quote Zukowski (2008): "The question of whether WS language is intact or not is most meaningful with respect to *grammatical knowledge* [our emphasis]. If people with WS are able to acquire normal grammars despite the fact that their brain development is slightly atypical, this would contradict expectations that have been articulated by some researchers working within a neuroconstructivist framework (Karmiloff-Smith, 1998; Thomas et al., 2001). On the other hand, if poor comprehension of relative clauses by people with WS is due to difficulty processing structures that are nevertheless part of the grammatical competence system, this would not bear on the debate" (pp. 3–4).

Returning to our chess analogy, the question of whether knowledge of chess is "intact" is most meaningful when asked about knowledge of the rules of chess. Imagine, for example, two populations that differed in chess-playing behaviour. Population A, compared to Population B, would take much longer to play each move, would wipe each piece before putting it back on the board, would always use the same opening, and would never castle. Such differences in chess-playing behaviour between Population A and Population B might be informative at some level and for some purposes, but they do not bear on the question of whether knowledge of the rules of chess is compromised in Population A. In fact, such differences may very well have nothing to do with knowledge of chess itself. In contrast, suppose that Population A, compared to Population B, was found to move its rooks along diagonals or its bishops along straight lines.[5] Here too, one would observe a difference in chess-playing behaviour between the two populations, but it would have a very different meaning. In this case, such behaviour would indicate that knowledge of the rules of chess is compromised in Population A. Finally, notice that without a theory of what the rules of chess are, one would have no way of distinguishing the two examples above, both of which involve differences in "chess-playing behaviour" between two populations.

What this means for our current purposes is that without a theory of the relevant linguistic knowledge at the relevant level of analysis (two of our core desiderata) one cannot meaningfully ask the question of whether grammar is "intact". One could of course attempt to do so and counter claims that knowledge is present and engaged by observing that behavioural levels between the groups of participants are different. However, as our previous analogy illustrates, and as Zukowski (2009) points out, this would amount to comparing generative apples with neuroconstructivist oranges, thereby only giving rise to the "illusion" of a meaningful debate. Thus, in addition to different standards regarding what constitutes a scientific explanation, explored at length in the previous section, the "debate" over language abilities in WS has been fuelled by confusion over the meaning of terms such as "intact" and the level of analysis at which they ought to apply.

To summarize, we have shown that the "meaningful debate assumption" rests on a fallacy that stems from the use of different explanatory standards and the associated confusion over key notions (e.g., "intact") that follows from such a difference. This conclusion, in turn, follows from the application of the criteria discussed as part of the approach advocated here. Recall now that in addition to being presented as theoretical "alternatives", the generative/modular approach and neuroconstructivism also make competing empirical claims regarding the status of grammatical knowledge in individuals with Williams syndrome. However, an important, albeit undesirable, consequence of the "meaningful debate assumption" is that it has the effect of rendering theories immune from empirical falsification in spite of clearly incompatible empirical claims.

This is because any data presented as a potential refutation of neuroconstructivist claims regarding language abilities in WS (e.g., that knowledge of grammar isn't "intact"—that is, is only superficially good, etc.), as in the case of Musolino et al. (2010), for example, can be countered by the objection that those data are relevant *only when viewed from a particular theoretical perspective*. As we have seen, this is indeed the strategy adopted by Thomas et al. (2010). Thus, the "meaningful debate assumption", in our view, has been a major

[5] For readers unfamiliar with the rules of chess, rooks move along straight lines and bishops along diagonals.

contributor to the unproductive, polarized discussion found in the literature on language in Williams syndrome. However, our conclusion that the "meaningful debate assumption" is untenable suggests a way out of the impasse described above. Following the approach developed here, we now have a clear criterion that can be used to assess competing empirical claims regarding the nature of language abilities in individuals with Williams syndrome.

As discussed earlier, in order decide whether grammar is spared or impaired in this disordered population, we need to empirically determine whether (a) is true. In other words, we need to ask whether *grammatical knowledge* is present in people with WS and has the same structure as that posited in the typical system. Returning to our chess analogy, what we want to know is whether individuals with Williams syndrome believe that they should move their bishops along straight lines and their rooks along diagonals (which would violate the rules of chess). To the extent that (a) is true, then neuroconstructivist claims about impaired grammar would be falsified (Musolino et al., 2010; Zukowski, 2009). On the other hand, if (a) is false, then generative/modular claims would need to be revised.

The results of Musolino et al.'s (2010) study demonstrate that knowledge of core syntactic and semantic principles (e.g., scope, c-command, de Morgan's laws of propositional logic) is indeed present and engaged in individuals with WS, as it is in typically developing and normal, mature individuals. In other words, the results support the conclusion that (a) is true. More generally, there is evidence that the same conclusion holds for knowledge of a number of other core grammatical principles that have been investigated in people with WS, including knowledge of the principles underlying the production and comprehension of relative clauses (Zukowski, 2004, 2009), binding and passives (Bellugi et al., 1990; Clahsen & Almazan, 1998; Ring & Clahsen, 2005; Perovic & Wexler, 2007), regular morphology (Bromberg, Ullman, Marcus, Kelly, & Levine, 1995; Clahsen & Almazan, 1998; Clahsen, Ring, & Temple, 2004; Penke & Krause, 2004; Pléh, Lukács, & Racsmány, 2003; Zukowski, 2005), and core aspects of the syntax and semantics of spatial language (Landau, 2011; Landau & Hoffman, 2012).

Moreover, in his extensive review of the literature on language in individuals with Williams syndrome, Brock (2007) finds no significant evidence that would suggest that (a) is not true. This conclusion contradicts neuroconstructivist claims that language in Williams syndrome is only superficially good, that such individuals are unable to extract underlying regularities, or that they rely excessively on rote learning (Karmiloff & Karmiloff-Smith, 2001; Karmiloff-Smith, 1998). To quote Brock (2007): "In general, there is also very little evidence that syntax or morphology develop atypically. . . . There is also little firm evidence to support the claim that individuals with Williams syndrome rely excessively on rote learning when acquiring grammatical structures" (p. 116).

Finally, we would like to explore two additional consequences of the approach developed here or the "debate" over language in people with WS. The first has to do with our discussion of levels of analysis. A central tenet of the neuroconstructivist approach, as explained by Karmiloff-Smith (1998), is that because individuals with WS start out with a different set of genes, compared to typically developing individuals, and therefore slightly different brains, this must entail that structures at the cognitive level must also be qualitatively different in the two populations. In other words, missing genes give rise to abnormal brains, abnormal brains lead to altered learning mechanisms, and altered learning mechanisms yield different grammars. To quote Karmiloff-Smith (1998): "In sum, brain volume, brain anatomy, brain chemistry, hemispheric asymmetry, and the temporal patterns of brain activity are all atypical in people with WS. How could the resulting cognitive system be described in terms of normal brains with parts intact and parts impaired, as the popular view holds? Rather, the brains of infants with WS develop differently from the outset, which has subtle widespread repercussions at the cognitive level. . . . " (p. 393).

Notice that the same argument could be made by replacing "genes" with "environment"—both of which obviously matter—in the Karmiloff-Smith (1998) equation. So environmental differences should lead to different brains, which in turn should lead to different learning mechanisms, leading, once again, to different grammars. However, it is obvious that such a statement should not be regarded as an a priori truth, but rather as an empirical question. In fact, one of the central conclusions of half a century of research on language acquisition is that widely different environmental conditions can lead to strikingly similar cognitive structures in the case of language (Goldin-Meadow, 2003; Landau & Gleitman, 1985; Gleitman & Newport, 1995). Likewise, whether different genes and altered brains lead to different grammars should be settled empirically rather than given as a necessary a priori conclusion.

What this means, in terms of levels of analysis, is that the mapping between the implementational, algorithmic, and computation levels, to come back to Marr's (1982) distinctions, cannot be as simple and rigidly deterministic as Karmiloff-Smith (1998) suggests. Besides, since different devices can implement the same algorithm, and the same computational outcome can be achieved via different algorithmic procedures (Marr, 1982), there is no a priori reason to believe that differences at one level of analysis will automatically lead to differences at the next level. Rather, the need to specify a clear level of analysis and engage in theory-driven cognitive phenotyping, as we have argued here, compels one to not prejudge this issue and treat the question of whether genetic differences may ultimately give rise to different cognitive structures as an empirical one.

The second consequence of the approach developed here that we would like to discuss involves our third criterion—namely, the importance of considering the trajectory of typical development in attempt to understand atypical populations. In their commentary on Musolino et al.'s (2010) work, Thomas et al. (2010) point out that even if one were to endorse the set of theoretical assumptions made by Musolino et al., one could nevertheless arrive at opposite conclusions regarding the status of grammatical knowledge in people with WS. To quote Thomas et al. (2010): "We have argued that the authors' conclusion is partly dependent on a set of assumptions regarding how the experimental data should be interpreted. Nevertheless, even with similar assumptions and methods, other researchers have recently come to the opposite conclusion, that is, that aspects of syntax develop atypically in WS" (p. 168). This kind of alleged theoretical inconsistency, in turn, invites the conclusion that the data are in fact ambiguous, as the "meaningful debate assumption" suggests.

To support their conclusion, Thomas et al. (2010) point to a study by Perovic and Wexler (2007) on the acquisition of passives in individuals with Williams. Specifically, Perovic and Wexler report an interesting asymmetry between passives of actional and psychological verbs. While the former are handled well by individuals with WS, the latter prove to be much more challenging. These authors conclude that certain aspects of syntax develop atypically in people with WS. And that, according to Thomas et al. (2010), is a problem for the generative/modular approach. However, Perovic and Wexler's findings are in fact perfectly compatible with the approach developed here. The key, as we argued earlier, is to take typical development into account when interpreting the behaviour documented by Perovic and Wexler in individuals with WS. Doing so reveals that the asymmetry observed in people with WS regarding passives of actional and psychological verbs is also found in typically developing children. Indeed, as Perovic and Wexler themselves point out, while passives of actional verbs are generally mastered by typically developing 5-year-olds, the same is not true for passives of psychological verbs, which take an additional two or three years to mature. If we are correct in assuming that people with WS undergo overall slow development, followed by early developmental arrest at the functional level of a 4- or 5-year-old child, as discussed throughout this paper, then we are in fact predicting exactly what Perovic and Wexler report—namely, that passives of actional verbs will be handled well by people with WS (because they are also handled well by typically developing 5-year-olds) but that passives of psychological verbs will prove to be a challenge (because they are also a challenge for typically developing 5-year-olds).

Conclusions

In this article, we discussed an experiment of nature and its implications for the sciences of the mind. The case of Williams syndrome bears on one of cognitive science's holy grails: the possibility of unravelling the causal chain between genes and cognition. Here, we have sketched the outline of a general framework to study the relationship between these two domains (the genetic and the mental), focusing as our case study on the development of language in individuals with Williams syndrome. In light of the complexity of the issues at stake, our approach emphasizes the role of three key factors: the need to specify a clear level of analysis, the need to provide a theoretical account of the relevant cognitive structure at that level, and the importance of the (typical) developmental process itself.

Perhaps not too surprisingly given the issues at stake, the discovery of Williams syndrome has also given rise to two strongly conflicting theoretical approaches—modularity and neuroconstructivism—themselves offshoots of a perennial debate between nativism and empiricism. Here, we applied our proposed framework to explore the tension created by these two conflicting perspectives. To this end, we turned to a second experiment of nature—a published paper and reactions to it—which afforded us the rare opportunity of being able to compare the two competing perspectives in what comes close to a controlled experimental setting. From this comparison, we concluded that the "meaningful debate assumption"—a widespread assumption suggesting that neuroconstructivism and modularity address the same questions and represent genuine theoretical alternatives—rests on a fallacy.

REFERENCES

Barrett, H. C., & Kurzban, R. (2006). Modularity in cognition: Framing the debate. *Psychological Review, 113,* 628–647.

Bellugi, U., Marks, S., Bihrle, A. M., & Sabo, H. (1988). Dissociation between language and cognitive functions in Williams syndrome. In D. Bishop & K. Mogford (Eds.), *Language development in exceptional circumstances.* London, UK: Churchill Livingstone.

Bellugi, U., Bihrle, A., Jernigan, T., Trauner, D., & Doherty, S. (1990). Neuropsychological, neurological, and neuroanatomical profile of Williams syndrome. *American Journal of Medical Genetics, 37,* 115–125.

Bellugi, U., Wang, P., & Jernigan, T. L. (1994). Williams syndrome: An unusual neuropsychological profile. In S. Broman & J. Graffman (Eds.), *Atypical cognitive deficits in developmental disorders: Implications for brain function* (pp. 23–56). Hillsdale, NJ: Lawrence Erlbaum Associates.

Brock, J. (2007). Language abilities in Williams syndrome: A critical review. *Development and Psychopathology, 19,* 97–127.

Broman, S., & Graffman, J. (Eds.) (1994). *Atypical cognitive deficits in developmental disorders: Implications for brain function.* Hillsdale, NJ: Lawrence Erlbaum Associates.

Bromberg, H. S., Ullman, M., Marcus, G., Kelly, K. B., & Levine, K. (1995). A dissociation of lexical memory and grammar in Williams syndrome: Evidence from inflectional morphology. *Genetic Counseling, 6,* 166–167.

Capirci, O., Sabbadini, L., & Volterra, V. (1996). Language development in Williams syndrome: A case study. *Cognitive Neuropsychology, 13,* 1017–1039.

Carey, S. (2009). *The origin of concepts.* New York: Oxford University Press.

Chomsky, N. (1995). *The minimalist program.* Cambridge, MA: MIT Press.

Clahsen, H., & Almazan, M. (1998). Syntax and morphology in Williams syndrome. *Cognition, 68,* 167–198.

Clahsen, H., Ring, M., & Temple, C. M. (2004). Lexical and morphological skills in English-speaking children with Williams syndrome. In S. Bartke & J. Siegmüller (Eds.), *Williams syndrome across languages* (pp. 222–244). Amsterdam, The Netherlands: John Benjamins.

Clahsen, H., & Temple, C. M. (2003). Words and rules in children with William's syndrome. In Y. Levy & J. Schaeffer (Eds.), *Language competence across populations: Toward a definition of specific language impairment* (pp. 323–352). Hillsdale, NJ: Lawrence Erlbaum Associates.

Clarke, A. M., & Clarke, A.D. B. (1974). *Readings from mental deficiency: The changing outlook* (3rd ed.). London, UK: Methuen.

Ellis, N. R. (1978). Do the mentally retarded have poor memory? *Intelligence, 2,* 41–54.

Elman, J. L., Bates, E., Johnson, M. H., Karmiloff-Smith, A., Parisi, D., & Plunkett, K. (1996). *Rethinking innateness: Connectionism in a developmental framework.* Cambridge, MA: The MIT Press.

Elman, J. L., Bates, E. A., Johnson, M. H., Karmiloff-Smith, A., Parisi, D., & Plunkett, K. (2001). *Rethinking innateness: A connectionist perspective on development.* Cambridge, MA: MIT Press.

Ewart, A. K., Morris, C. A., Atkinson, D., Jin, W., Sternes, K., Spallone, P., et al. (1993). Hemizygosity at the elastin locus in a developmental disorder, Williams syndrome. *Nature Genetics, 5,* 11–16.

Fodor, J. (1983). *The modularity of mind.* Cambridge, MA: MIT Press.

Galaburda, A. M., Wang, P. P., Bellugi, U., & Rossen, M. (1994). Cytoarchitectonic anomalies in a genetically based disorder: Williams Syndrome. *Neuroreport, 5,* 753–7.

Glass, A., Holyoak, K., & Santa, J. (1979). *Cognition.* Reading, MA: Addison-Wesley.

Gleitman, L. R., & Newport, E. L. (1995). The invention of language by children: Environmental and biological influences on the acquisition of language. In L. Gleitman & M. Liberman (Eds.), *Language: An invitation to cognitive science* (pp. 1–24). Cambridge, MA: MIT Press.

Goldin-Meadow, S. (2003). *The resilience of language: What gesture creation in deaf children can tell us about how all children learn language.* New York: Psychology Press.

Hulme, C., & Mackenzie, S. (1992). *Working memory and severe learning disabilities.* Hove, UK: Lawrence Erlbaum Associates.

Jackendoff, R. (1994). *Patterns in the mind.* New York: Basic Books.

Karmiloff, K., & Karmiloff-Smith, A. (2001). *Pathways to language.* Cambridge, MA: Harvard University Press.

Karmiloff-Smith, A. (1997). Crucial differences between developmental cognitive neuroscience and adult neuropsychology. *Developmental Neuropsychology, 13,* 513–524.

Karmiloff-Smith, A. (1998). Development itself is the key to understanding developmental disorders. *Trends in Cognitive Sciences, 2,* 389–398.

Karmiloff-Smith, A. (2007). Atypical epigenesis. *Developmental Science, 10,* 84.

Karmiloff-Smith, A., Grant, J., Berthoud, I., Davies, M., Howlin, P., & Udwin, O. (1997). Language and Williams syndrome: How intact is "intact"? *Child Development, 68,* 246–262.

Landau, B. (2011). The organization and development of spatial cognition: Insights from Williams syndrome. In J. Burack, R. M. Hodapp, G. Iarocci, & E. Zigler (Eds.), *Handbook of intellectual disabilities and development* (2nd ed.). New York, NY: Oxford University Press.

Landau, B., & Gleitman, L. R. (1985). *Language and experience: Evidence from the blind child.* Cambridge, MA: Harvard University Press.

Landau, B., & Hoffman, J. E. (2012). *Spatial representation: From gene to mind.* New York, NY: Oxford University Press.

Marcus, G. F. (2004). *The birth of the mind: How a tiny number of genes creates the complexities of human thought.* New York: Basic Books.

Marr, D. (1982). *Vision.* San Francisco: W. H. Freeman & Co.

McDade, H. L., & Adler, S. (1980). Down syndrome and short-term memory impairment: A storage or retrieval deficit? *American Journal of Mental Deficiency, 84,* 561–567.

Mervis, C., & Becerra, A. (2007). Language and communicative development in Williams Syndrome. *Mental Retardation and Developmental Disabilities Research Reviews, 13,* 3–15.

Morton, J. (2004). *Understanding developmental disorders: A causal modelling approach.* Malden, MA: Blackwell Publishing.

Munnich, E., & Landau, B. (2010). Developmental decline in the acquisition of spatial language. *Language Learning and Development, 6,* 32–59.

Musolino, J., Chunyo, G., & Landau, B. (2010). Uncovering knowledge of core syntactic and semantic principles in individuals with Williams syndrome. *Language Learning and Development, 6,* 126–161.

Musolino, J., & Landau, B. (2010). When theories don't compete: Response to Thomas, Karaminis, and

Knowland's commentary on Musolino, Chunyo, and Landau. *Language Learning and Development*, *6*(2), 170–178.

Newport, E. L. (1990). Maturational constraints on language learning. *Cognitive Science*, *14*, 11–28.

Penke, M., & Krause, M. (2004). Regular and irregular inflectional morphology in German Williams syndrome. In S. Niedeggen-Bartke & J. Siegmüller (Eds.), *Williams syndrome across languages* (pp. 245–270). Amsterdam, The Netherlands: Benjamins.

Perovic, A., & Wexler, K. (2007). Complex grammar in Williams syndrome. *Clinical Linguistics & Phonetics*, *21*, 729–745.

Perovic, A., & Wexler, K. (2010). Development of verbal passive in Williams syndrome. *Journal of Speech, Language, and Hearing Research*, *53*, 1294–1306.

Piatelli-Palmarini, M. (2001). Speaking of learning: How do we acquire our marvelous facility for expressing ourselves in words? *Nature*, *411*, 887–888.

Pinker, S. (1997). *How the mind works*. New York, NY: Norton.

Pinker, S. (1999). *Words and rules: The ingredients of language*. New York, NY: Basic Books.

Pinker, S. (2005). So how does the mind work? *Mind & Language*, *20*, 1–24.

Pléh, C., Lukács, A., & Racsmány, M. (2003). Morphological patterns in Hungarian children with Williams syndrome and the rule debates. *Brain and Language*, *86*, 377–383.

Pylyshyn, Z. W. (1984). *Computation and cognition: Towards a foundation for cognitive science*. Cambridge, MA: MIT Press.

Ramus, F. (2006). Genes, brain, and cognition: A roadmap for the cognitive scientist. *Cognition*, *101*, 247–269.

Ring, M., & Clahsen, H. (2005). Distinct patterns of language impairment in Down's Syndrome and Williams Syndrome: The case of syntactic chains. *Journal of Neurolinguistics*, *18*, 479–501.

Spelke, E. S. (1998). Nativism, empiricism, and the origins of knowledge. *Infant Behavior and Development*, *21*(2), 181–200.

Sperber, D. (1994). The modularity of thought and the epidemiology of representations. In L. A. Hirschfeld & S. A. Gelman (Eds.), *Mapping the mind: Domain specificity in cognition and culture* (pp. 39–67). New York, NY: Cambridge University Press.

Sperber, D. (2005). Modularity and relevance: How can a massively modular mind be flexible and context-sensitive? In P. Carruthers, S. Laurence, & S. Stich (Eds.), *The innate mind: Structure and content* (pp. 53–68). Oxford, UK: Oxford University Press.

Strømme, P., Bjørnstad, P. G., & Ramstad, K. (2002). Prevalence estimation of Williams syndrome. *Journal of Child Neurology*, *17*, 269–271.

Tager-Flusberg, H., Plesa-Skwerer, D., Faja, S., & Joseph, R. M. (2003). People with Williams syndrome process faces holistically. *Cognition*, *89*, 11–24.

Thomas, M. S. C. (2008). L'acquisition du langage dans les pathologies du diveloppement [Language development in developmental disorders]. In M. Kail, M. Fayol, & M. Hickmann (Eds.), *L'apprentissage des langues* (pp. 451–475). Paris: CNRS Editions.

Thomas, M. S. C., Karamenis, T. N., & Knowland, V. C. P. (2010). What is typical language development? *Language Learning and Development*, *6*, 162–169.

Thomas, M. S. C., & Karmiloff-Smith, A. (2003). Modeling language acquisition in atypical phenotypes. *Psychological Review*, *110*, 647–682.

Thomas, M. S. C., & Karmiloff-Smith, A. (2005). Can developmental disorders reveal the component parts of the language faculty? *Language Learning and Development*, *1*, 65–92.

Tooby, J., & Cosmides, L. (1992). The psychological foundations of culture. In J. H. Barkow, L. Cosmides, & J. Tooby (Eds.), *The adapted mind: Evolutionary psychology and the generation of culture* (pp. 19–136). New York, NY: Oxford University Press.

Vicari, S., Brizzolara, D., Carlesimo, G., Pezzini, G., & Volterra, V. (1996). Memory abilities in children with Williams syndrome. *Cortex*, *32*, 503–514.

Vicari, S., Carlesimo, A., Albertini, G., & Caltagirone, C. (1994, January). *Qualitative profiles of memory abilities in persons with Down syndrome and with mental retardation*, Poster presented at the 12th European Workshop on Cognitive Neuropsychology, Brixen, Italy.

Vicari, S., Carlesimo, A., & Caltagirone, C. (1995). Short-term memory in persons with intellectual disabilities. *Journal of Intelligence Disorders Research*, *39*, 532–537.

Volterra, V., Capirci, O., Pezzini, G., Sabbadini, L., & Vicari, S. (1996). Linguistic abilities in Italian children with Williams syndrome. *Cortex*, *32*, 663–677.

Westermann, G., Mareschal, D., Johnson, M. H., Sirois, S., Spratling, M. W., & Thomas, M. S. C. (2007). Neuro-constructivism. *Developmental Science*, *10*, 75–83.

Zukowski, A. (2004). Investigating knowledge of complex syntax: Insights from experimental studies of Williams syndrome. In M. Rice & S. Warren (Eds.), *Developmental language disorders: From phenotypes to etiologies*. Mahwah, NJ: Lawrence Erlbaum Associates.

Zukowski, A. (2005). Knowledge of constraints on compounding in children and adolescents with Williams Syndrome. *Journal of Speech, Language and Hearing Research*, *48*, 79–92.

Zukowski, A. (2009). Elicited production of relative clauses reflects intact grammatical knowledge in Williams syndrome. *Language and Cognitive Processes*, *24*, 1–43.

The origins and structure of quantitative concepts

Cory D. Bonn, and Jessica F. Cantlon

Brain & Cognitive Sciences Department, University of Rochester, Rochester, NY, USA

"Number" is the single most influential quantitative dimension in modern human society. It is our preferred dimension for keeping track of almost everything, including distance, weight, time, temperature, and value. How did "number" become psychologically affiliated with all of these different quantitative dimensions? Humans and other animals process a broad range of quantitative information across many psychophysical dimensions and sensory modalities. The fact that adults can rapidly translate one dimension (e.g., loudness) into any other (e.g., handgrip pressure) has been long established by psychophysics research (Stevens, 1975). Recent literature has attempted to account for the development of the computational and neural mechanisms that underlie interactions between quantitative dimensions. We review evidence that there are fundamental cognitive and neural relations among different quantitative dimensions (number, size, time, pitch, loudness, and brightness). Then, drawing on theoretical frameworks that explain phenomena from cross-modal perception, we outline some possible conceptualizations for how different quantitative dimensions could come to be related over both ontogenetic and phylogenetic time scales.

Keywords: Numerosity; Development; Magnitude; fMRI.

Humans and other animals process information from many continuous psychophysical dimensions across sensory modalities and perceptual variables, including number, size, event duration, speed, visual and auditory brightness, pitch, and loudness. These dimensions constitute "quantities" or "magnitudes"[1] because they are (at least roughly) interpretable as amounts, as in the case of number, size, and duration, visual brightness, and loudness, or because changes in stimulus values can be readily interpreted as amounts, as in the case of auditory brightness and pitch. Discrimination data collected from many such dimensions conform to Weber's law: successful discrimination of two stimuli along a given continuum depends on their ratio rather than absolute values. This is the principal signature of analog magnitude representations, in which values of increasing quantity are correlated with an increase in uncertainty (Gallistel, 1990; Gallistel & Gelman, 1992, 2000; Moyer & Landauer, 1967; Stevens, 1975; see also Cantlon, Platt, & Brannon, 2009, for

Correspondence should be addressed to: Jessica F. Cantlon, University of Rochester – Brain & Cognitive Sciences, Box 270268, Rochester, NY 14607, USA (E-mail: jcantlon@rcbi.rochester.edu).

The authors wish to thank Bradford Z. Mahon for comments and discussion on earlier drafts of the manuscript and support from NSF Graduate Research Fellowship to C.B. and NIH R01HD064636 to J.C.

[1] We use "magnitude" and "quantity" interchangeably in this paper.

http://www.psypress.com/cogneuropsychology http://dx.doi.org/10.1080/02643294.2012.707122

review). This commonality in psychophysical performance suggests that, at some level, the neural computations required of each dimension are similar. In fact, a growing body of evidence suggests that different magnitudes—even those that might not be intuitively grouped at first glance—are related.

We begin by presenting the historical origins of currently discussed proposals for functional and neural architectures of magnitude representation. We then consider evidence that many dimensions of magnitude are related in the adult mind and brain, including space, time, number, pitch, and brightness. We include a brief overview and critique of the evidence discussed in previous reviews (Bueti & Walsh, 2009; Cantlon, Platt, & Brannon, 2009; Lourenco & Longo, 2011) as well as more recent, related findings; in addition, we include potentially related literature not previously discussed to illustrate the scope and complexity of the evidence to be explained.

The section that follows describes biologically plausible computational analogies for processes that could account for the development of composite or overlapping magnitude representations. Because little is known about the development of these representations, we base our discussion on theoretical frameworks that have shaped investigations of multisensory integration and cross-modal transfer. Previous characterizations of the development of composite magnitude representations leave many assumptions and linking hypotheses unstated. We lay out some assumptions and predictions of the candidate hypotheses to frame current evidence and guide future research. This allows us to illustrate that some of the implicit assumptions about relations among magnitudes may not be valid. In particular, we show that asymmetries of interference between two dimensions of magnitude (e.g., space interferes with time more than time interferes with space) are consistent with *many* conceptualizations of magnitude relations and therefore do not offer a way of adjudicating among them.

In the final portion of the paper, we consider how either evolution or learning and development may implement these processes and the multiple representational levels at which composite representations may occur, incorporating evidence from developmental studies as well as highlighting areas where research is needed.

Origins of current debates

The question of how quantitative cognition is functionally organized in the brain began with neuropsychological investigations of patients with numerical and arithmetic impairments (e.g., Gerstmann, 1940). Neurological patients with parietal lesions can be impaired in making numerical judgments, while other cognitive abilities such as object categorization and recognition remain intact (Cipolotti, Butterworth, & Denes, 1991; Dehaene & Cohen, 1997). Furthermore, studies of patients with semantic dementia (and anterior temporal lobe atrophy) have shown that numerical skills can be spared in cases where other semantically demanding tasks such as picture categorization or picture naming are impaired (Cappelletti, Kopelman, Morton, & Butterworth, 2005). Those data show that it is possible to isolate numerical cognition from other components of cognition through damage to one (albeit large) part of the brain: the parietal cortex. Because those initial studies did not test magnitude representations for dimensions other than number, the question of whether the dissociation between "number" and other semantic domains is unique to *numerical* magnitudes cannot be resolved at present. In fact, it is not always the case that numerical deficits neatly segregate from other deficits: individuals with relatively focal lesions to intraparietal cortex commonly exhibit simultaneous deficits in arithmetic, spatial, and abstract perceptual judgments (Figure 1) (Gerstmann, 1940; Takayama, Sugishita, Akiguchi, & Kimura, 1994). The functional relationships among those associated impairments have not been studied, and so it cannot be concluded that there is representational interdependence between arithmetic and visuospatial judgments. However, a long tradition of cognitive-science research supports the possibility that judgments of other perceptual intensities or

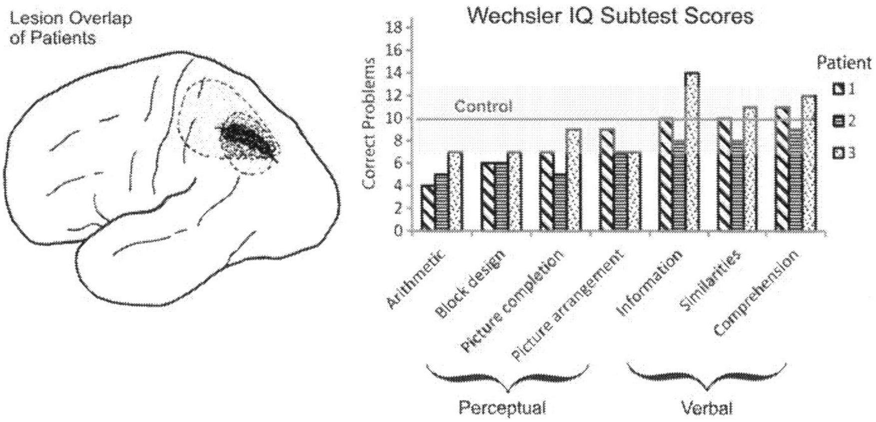

Figure 1. *Left: Lesion overlap at the intraparietal sulcus of three patients with isolated acalculia. Right: Performance of acalculic patients on subtests of Wechsler Adult Intelligence Scale demonstrates impairment to arithmetic ability, as well as more subtle impairments in perceptual and spatial reasoning, but no impairment on verbal tasks. From: "Isolated acalculia due to left parietal lesion" by Y. Takayama, M. Sugishita, I. Akiguchi, & J. Kimura, 1994,* Archives of Neurology, 51, *p. 290. Copyright 1994 by the American Medical Association. Reprinted with permission from the American Medical Association.. To view a colour version of this figure, please see the online issue of the Journal.*

magnitudes (e.g., size, time, brightness, loudness) could exhibit a similar pattern of impairment to numerical performance in these cases of neural impairment.

The idea that other magnitudes might share a common neural code was initially proposed by Gallistel and Gelman (2000). In their review of behavioural data from humans and other animals, they argued that discrete number should be represented with an analog magnitude code. Because animals must combine discrete number with continuous quantities in making decisions (e.g., in assessing food patches based on the number of potential food items and the space over which the food is spread), reconciling these incompatible formats necessitates conversion to a common code: the analog format.

Drawing on this suggestion, Walsh (2003) proposed that space, time, and other quantities—primarily number—share an abstract, undifferentiated magnitude code present at birth. His key claim is that an interconnected magnitude representation of time, space, and number emerges because of the critical role of magnitude information in the action system. The argument is that the common neural location of magnitude information and motor control in parietal cortex is what binds those computations. Although neural location could be an important factor in determining what cognitive representations are associated, a potentially more important factor is their functional origins in development. According to Walsh, the generalized magnitude system becomes differentiated in postnatal development, developing into specialized magnitude subsystems that share neural resources (in parietal cortex), though exactly *how* they are shared over development and to what extent each dimension is functionally differentiated remains unspecified.

One problem for understanding how magnitude dimensions are related over development is that a substantial amount of behavioural and neural evidence from human adults and non-human animals is consistent with a number of theoretical possibilities for how magnitude relations developed or evolved. These possibilities include innate relations, learned correlational relationships, and both verbal/cultural and nonverbal analogies. We review the evidence in the next section.

Inferences about the canonical domains of space, time, and number

Evidence for interactions among representations of space, time, and number comes from tasks that elicit representations in two of these dimensions simultaneously. In a now classic study of the interaction between time and number, Meck and Church (1983) found that rats are similarly sensitive to both number and duration (holding the other variable constant). In addition, they found that administration of methamphetamines increases the speed of the mechanism governing judgments of both dimensions, indicating that the animals' representations of time and number are subject to common constraints at some level of processing (Figure 2). Similarly, a recent study in human adults suggests that a click train can accelerate a common internal clock in sequential line, duration, and numerosity bisection tasks (Droit-Volet, 2010). Experiments in pigeons (Roberts, 1995; Roberts, Coughlin, & Roberts, 2000) and Stroop-like experiments in humans (Dormal, Seron, & Pesenti, 2006) have shown similar behavioural signatures (but see Roitman, Brannon, Andrews, & Platt, 2007, for evidence of a possible asymmetry in representations of number and duration). Taken together, these findings suggest that a common mechanism underlies judgments of both dimensions in these nonverbal tasks.

Reaction-time experiments also provide evidence of the interaction between number and space. In one early study, Henik and Tzelgov (1982) showed that when Arabic numerals are pitted against physical size (e.g., 9 5), judgments of which numeral is larger (in size or number) showed congruency effects between the attended and unattended dimensions. Another classic signature is the so-called SNARC effect (Spatial–Numerical Association of Response Codes; Dehaene, Bossini, & Giraux, 1993). According to the most popular construal, adults map representations of number onto a horizontal mental number line, explaining the observation of faster processing times for larger numerical values on the right side of the line. This type of mapping between space and number is also evident in cases of spatial neglect, wherein adult neurological patients with parietal cortex damage can exhibit

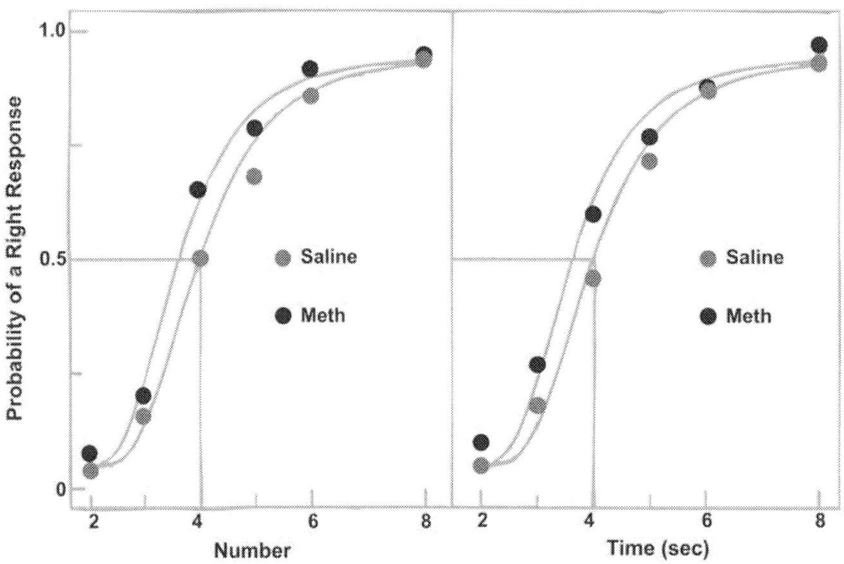

Figure 2. *Psychophysical functions from Meck & Church (1983). Median probability of a right response as a function of number (left) and duration (right). The methamphetamine condition (black circles) shifted the curves above the baseline (saline—red circles) condition by about 10% for judgments of both number and duration. From "A mode control model of counting and timing processes" by W. H. Meck & R. M. Church, 1983,* Journal of Experimental Psychology: Animal Behavior Processes, *9(3), p. 328. Copyright 1983 by the American Psychological Association. Reprinted with permission as granted in the republishing guidelines of the American Psychological Association. To view a colour version of this figure, please see the online issue of the Journal.*

asymmetries in their estimates of the "centre" during both line bisection and numerical bisection tasks (Zorzi, Priftis, & Umiltà, 2002). Thus the neural origin of space–number association appears to depend on parietal cortex. However, this is at least partly a learned association. The space–number mapping is known to emerge following exposure to counting behaviours and formal training in school (Berch, Foley, Hill, & Ryan, 1999; Opfer, Thompson, & Furlong, 2010; van Galen & Reitsma, 2008) and is flexible in bilinguals who learn two different spatial writing directions (Shaki & Fischer, 2008), strongly implicating culture in shaping this type of representation. However, it is unclear whether the culturally mediated mapping of number onto space builds on a biological disposition to preferentially map number onto space (e.g., de Hevia & Spelke, 2010). One recent set of experiments suggests that space does not have a privileged psychological relationship with number in adulthood. Nuñez, Doan, and Nikoulina (2011) tested how well adult participants mapped number to non-spatial formats. In these experiments, participants mapped number onto non-spatial formats such as squeezing, bell striking, and vocalizing as well as spatial ones. Though the non-spatial mappings were found to be slightly different from the spatial mappings (they were logarithmically rather than linearly spaced and less precise), the authors suggest that there might not be anything biologically or conceptually special about the space–number relationship. However, an open issue is whether higher precision in the spatial judgments relative to non-spatial judgments is due to innate biases or extensive cultural experience with mapping dimensions onto space.

Much of the recent evidence for an interaction between representations of time and space in adults and animals comes from experiments that explore how language use might shape the development of concepts. Across languages, the use of spatial language to describe time suggests that conceptualization of time is dependent on physical conceptions of space, though the exact way in which languages tend to conceptualize time in terms of space varies across cultures. For instance, according to Boroditsky (2000, 2001), Mandarin speakers are more likely to think about time in a vertical orientation than are English speakers, in line with the metaphors present in the language. Failures to replicate these results have rendered the original findings controversial (Chen, 2007; January & Kako, 2007; see Boroditsky, Fuhrman, & McCormick, 2011, for a response). Nonetheless, evidence from linguistic metaphors (e.g., Lakoff & Johnson, 1980, 1999) may suggest a link between space and time independently of whether the link is at a deep representational level or a superficial linguistic response level.

Results from tasks that presumably do not depend on language use suggest that the dependence of representations of time on space extends beyond the domain of language. Nonverbally presented magnitudes with no temporal component (i.e., static stimuli) modulate estimates of duration; larger, brighter, and more numerous stimuli are perceived to last longer than smaller stimuli of equal duration (Xuan, Zhang, He, & Chen, 2007). Eagleman (2008) suggests that these heuristic estimates of duration from size, brightness, and number directly reflect the amount of neural energy required for visual stimulus encoding, implying that the perception of interval duration is heavily influenced by aspects of stimulus encoding that are only *indirectly* related to timing (see also Pariyadath & Eagleman, 2007). The implications of those studies are not settled: either duration perception largely piggy-backs on the computational machinery of other magnitudes or the weight given to other magnitudes in overlapping representations is so large that it masks the input from true timing mechanisms. Under either interpretation, interactions between time, brightness, number, and size are fundamental.

A possibly related behavioural signature is an asymmetry of interference: in adult humans, judgments of line length interfere with judgments of duration more than duration judgments interfere with judgments of line length (Casasanto & Boroditsky, 2008). In one recent study, Merritt, Casasanto, and Brannon (2010) found that while adults' nonverbal judgments of duration are affected by the simultaneous representation of line length in a dual task, the effect of duration on judgments of line length are considerably smaller, consistent with previous findings. In rhesus macaques, duration and line length seem to interfere with each other equally, suggesting that the magnitude code the monkeys accessed is equally distributed between spatial and temporal representations. Thus there appears to be a spatially biased temporal representation in humans but not in monkeys. However, even though both the humans and the monkeys were trained to complete the task without verbal labels, human participants may still have linguistically encoded the durations (subvocally or otherwise) into English spatial terms (i.e., "short" and "long"). So, the uniquely human pattern of interference might arise at the level of lexical representation or response selection rather than a language-independent magnitude system. The results from the monkeys show that this asymmetry between time and size is a uniquely human phenomenon and therefore is unlikely to be purely a signature of interval timing as proposed by Eagleman (2008). Thus, we potentially can rule out the claim that the use of size, brightness, and number as a proxy for interval duration (described earlier) is the root cause of asymmetrical interference effects between space and time in humans.

The relationship between space and time has also been found at the neural level. Single-neuron data from neurophysiology studies of monkeys broadly indicate that the same neural substrate represents space, time, and number (Leon & Shadlen, 2003; Nieder, 2005; Roitman, Brannon, & Platt, 2007). Moreover, some data even suggest that a single parietal neuron can represent more than one type of magnitude. In one study (Tudusciuc & Nieder, 2007), monkeys were trained to perform a line length-matching task and a numerical matching task. During stimulus presentation or a subsequent delay, single neurons in ventral intraparietal cortex (VIP) responded selectively to visual stimuli based on their numerosity or length. Although some neurons responded only to numerosity and others only to line length, a subset of cells (~20%) responded to the magnitudes of both the line lengths and the numerical values. In an adjacent parietal region, lateral intraparietal cortex (LIP), single neurons have been shown to be sensitive to quantities such as duration and number (Leon & Shadlen, 2003; Roitman et al., 2007). These and other studies, including fMRI studies of adults, have led some researchers to argue for a "distributed but overlapping" representation of different magnitudes at the neural level (Pinel, Piazza, Le Bihan, & Dehaene, 2004; Tudusciuc & Nieder, 2007). Moreover, Pinel et al. (2004) found that the amount of functional overlap between brain regions recruited during Stroop-like tasks predicted the size of the interference effects observed (Figure 3). Simply put, different types of magnitude representation including size, number, and time (and possibly brightness) share *some* neural resources in parietal cortex but not others.

Taken together, these findings tend to emphasize the relations between the dimensions of space, time, and number. The fact that there are so many studies that report a relationship between those dimensions (and not others) has led to arguments that there is a biologically privileged relationship among the dimensions of space, time, and number (Dehaene, Izard, Spelke, & Pica, 2008; Dehaene, Spelke, Pinel, Stanescu, & Tsivkin, 1999; Srinivasan & Carey, 2010; Walsh, 2003). However, as mentioned above, there is some evidence for fundamental interactions among quantitative dimensions beyond space, time, and number, such as interactions between time and brightness (Xuan et al., 2007). In the next section we review further evidence.

Beyond space, time, and number

There is some evidence that dimensions such as loudness, brightness, and pitch—dimensions other than those that are allegedly privileged (space, time, and number)—interact at the representational level. For example, adults are equally facile at scaling any kind of continuum to digital number as they are with scaling to loudness (Stevens, 1975). Furthermore, we already

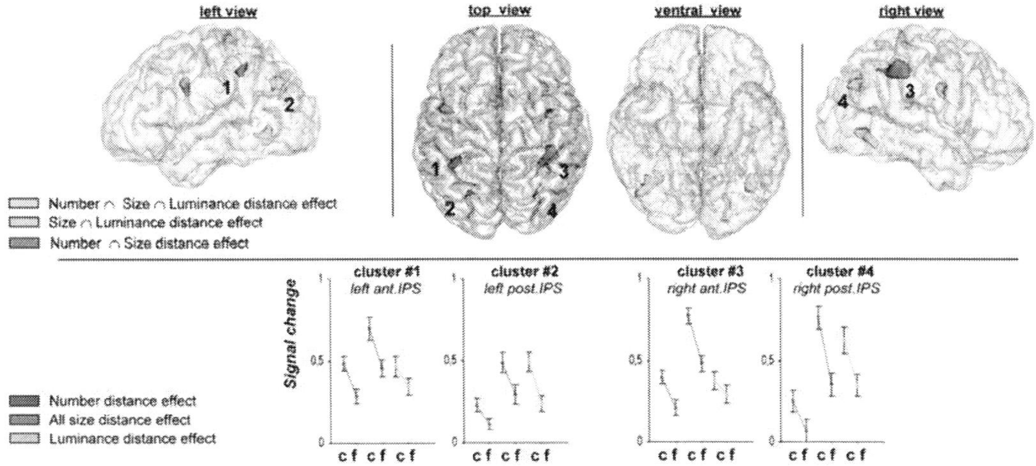

Figure 3. *Top: Neural overlap among combinations of the dimensions of number, size and luminance. Bottom: The distance effect: neural signal differences in the intraparietal sulcus (IPS) between close (c) and far (f) pairs of number stimuli, size stimuli, and luminance stimuli. Adapted from "Distributed and overlapping cerebral representations of number, size, and luminance during comparative judgments" by P. Pinel, M. Piazza, D. Le Bihan, & S. Dehaene, 2004,* Neuron, 41, *p. 6. Copyright 2004 by Cell Press. Reprinted with permission from Cell Press. To view a colour version of this figure, please see the online issue of the Journal.*

described evidence that among adult humans, brighter stimuli (in addition to larger and more numerous stimuli) are mistakenly estimated as lasting longer in duration than darker stimuli (Xuan et al., 2007). In addition, cross-dimensional mapping effects show up in Stroop-like paradigms for dimensions beyond space, time, and number. Marks (1987) showed that presentation of irrelevant auditory pitch information in visual brightness judgments (dark vs. light) and irrelevant visual brightness information in auditory pitch judgments (low vs. high) affects adults' reaction times. In that experiment, irrelevant stimuli that were congruent (dark and low; light and high) facilitated responses, and those that were incongruent (dark and high; light and low) interfered with responses. In this section, we focus in particular on interactions found between non-canonical domains (e.g., auditory pitch and luminance) and canonical domains (number, space, and time).

Interactions with non-canonical domains

i. Luminance/brightness and loudness. Pinel et al. (2004) report interactions between stimulus luminance and the canonical domains of number and space in magnitude comparison tasks. Irrelevant luminance information interfered with Arabic numeral and size comparisons, as indicated by a significant increase in response times on trials where the irrelevant dimension was incongruent with the relevant dimension. In addition, irrelevant information about physical size (but not number) interfered with luminance comparisons. The authors report that symmetrical interference only occurred between size and luminance. In combination with the finding that the amount of functional overlap in activation in parietal cortex parallels the size of interference effects (see Figure 2), this study suggests that size, number, and luminance share computational resources and that, at least in the adult state, the representations of some pairs of magnitudes might be more closely related than others. Although it might not be intuitive that number and size should interact with luminance, one line of vision research suggests that they should: of two objects at equal depth, the brighter object will be perceived as closer (e.g., Farnè, 1977). This presumably is because the amount of retinal surface area stimulated by light reflected from an object increases as an object approaches. Thus, representations of subjective size and luminance may be linked to the perception of object distance.

Luminance interacts with perceived duration as well. With absolute duration held constant, humans, pigeons, and rats perceive bright lights as lasting longer than dim lights (Brigner, 1986; Kraemer, Brown, & Randall, 1995; Kraemer, Randall, & Brown, 1997; Wilkie, 1987; Xuan et al., 2007). Goldstone, Lhamon, & Sechzer (1978) report an effect of loudness on perceived tone duration as well as brightness on light duration in a magnitude comparison task (Figure 4). These results do not provide evidence for whether duration might also modulate brightness or loudness perception. However, at a broad level, these findings from pigeons, rats, and humans implicate fundamental interactions between time and brightness.

ii. Pitch. A mapping similar to the SNARC effect occurs in the mapping of pitch height onto vertical space in adults (aptly dubbed the "SMARC effect"; Rusconi, Kwan, Giordano, Umiltà, & Butterworth, 2006). In this experiment, subjects were required to indicate whether a given pitch was lower or higher than a standard by pressing the space bar or the 6 key; each key stood for the "higher" response half the time. For example, pressing 6 for a "lower" response would result in longer response times, while pressing the same key for a "higher" response would result in faster responses. A similar signature of pitch–space representation has been observed in infants (Walker et al., 2009). Mapping of pitch height onto vertical space in infants, musicians, and non-musicians alike may also result from peripheral filtering of the acoustic signal by the pinnae; shifting pitch height corresponds to shifting spectral peaks in the head-related transfer function (HRTF) for vertical space (Butler, 1969, 1971; Roffler & Butler, 1967; for an explanation relating these results to the HRTF, see Moore, 2003). Thus, the mapping of pitch height onto space might be explained at more than one level of representation—a consequence of learning the fundamental acoustic cues to object height or a higher-level, shared magnitude code.

Other evidence for the mapping of pitch onto a spatial representation, through either a common magnitude code or some other mechanism, comes from individuals with congenital amusia. Congenital amusia is an impairment of fine-grained pitch discrimination and of pitch-change direction (Ayotte, Peretz, & Hyde, 2002; Peretz & Hyde, 2003) and impaired short-term memory for nonverbal, auditory sequences (Tillmann, Schulze, & Foxton, 2009; Williamson, McDonald, Deutsch, Griffiths, & Stewart, 2010). It has been found to be correlated with impaired performance on spatial tasks (Douglas & Bilkey, 2007). In addition, impaired memory for changes in pitch-height direction reduces interference with spatial judgments in dual tasks in which both pitch and spatial judgments are made, suggesting that the representation of pitch height may share computational resources in individuals with typical pitch-processing capabilities (Douglas & Bilkey, 2007; but see Tillmann et al., 2010).

Some studies also report interactions between duration and pitch. In the auditory kappa effect, tones are perceived as longer when their pitch is higher (Brigner, 1988; Cohen, Hansel, & Sylvester, 1954; see also Lourenco & Longo, 2011). In addition, the pitch difference between two tones increases both the perceived duration of the silence between them (Crowder & Neath, 1995; Shigeno, 1986) and the length of an intervening tone (Henry & McAuley, 2009). Moreover, amusics fail to show an auditory kappa effect at small pitch intervals (<4 semitones; Pfeuty & Peretz, 2010). In the auditory tau effect, the pitch of the second tone in a three-tone sequence is affected by its timing; for example, when the middle tone is closer in time to the first tone, it is also perceived as closer in pitch (Christensen & Huang, 1979; Cohen et al., 1954; Henry, McAuley, & Zaleha, 2009; Shigeno, 1986). These studies indicate interactions between representations of pitch, space, and time.

Neuropsychological data that address the issue of neural overlap between representations of pitch and other magnitudes are currently sparse.

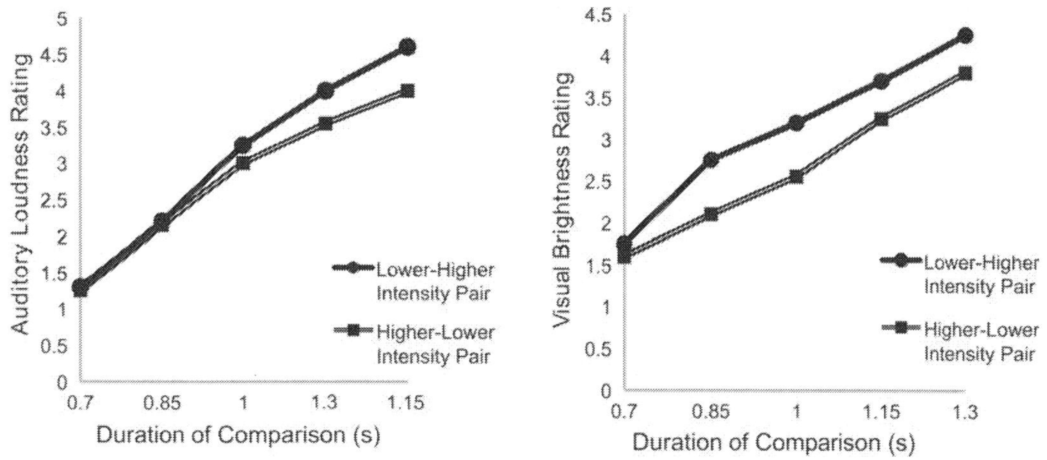

Figure 4. *The y-axis is the "average category response" rating, where 1 = "shorter" and 5 = "longer" than a 1-s standard duration. The x-axis indicates the duration of the comparison value (in seconds). Higher–lower intensity in the figure legend refers to the order of brightness or loudness value presentation. High–Low pairs induce a bias to rate durations slightly lower, on average, than do Low–High pairs. Figures redrawn from "Light intensity and judged duration", by S. Goldstone, W. T. Lhamon, & J. Sechzer, 1978,* Bulletin of the Psychonomic Society, 12*(1), p. 84. Copyright 1978 by the Psychonomic Society. Adapted with permission from the Psychonomic Society.*

Ideally, such tests would be administered within-subjects in cases of focal damage to a parietal locus that has caused a magnitude-related, performance impairment. One study that was conducted in that way showed that patients with damage to right posterior parietal cortex can exhibit impairments in judging the relative duration of two tones but remain unimpaired in judging tone pitch (Harrington, Haaland, & Knight, 1998). However, 2 out of the 10 patients in that study presented with comorbid impairments of pitch and duration judgment. The study shows that pitch and duration judgment are neurally dissociable processes in individuals with right posterior parietal lesions but that mutual impairment can occur in some of those cases. Interestingly, in patients with more anterior lesions, more than half of the individuals exhibited mutual impairment of pitch and duration judgments. Thus, pitch and duration judgments are commonly dissociated following posterior cortical lesions, but they are associated in cases of more anterior lesions. However, since the pitch judgment task was intended as a control task in that study, it is difficult to determine the nature of the association between duration and pitch judgments in the group with anterior lesions. Future studies that are intended to test for comorbid impairments in magnitude judgments would ideally include control tasks that allow performance to be functionally dissected.

iii. Melodic contour. Ordinal relations among exemplars from one dimension are easily compared to ordinal relations from another dimension. In the domain of pitch height, ordinal relations among successive musical notes form melodic contour (Marvin & Laprade, 1987). A more imprecise definition of contour is the "up" and "down" motion between successive notes (Dowling, 1978; Dowling & Fujitani, 1971). One study reports that similar contour relations may be found in other auditory patterns such as loudness and brightness, which is correlated with the portion of the frequency spectrum with the greatest concentration of energy (McDermott, Lehr, & Oxenham, 2008). Adults can match contours across auditory dimensions and recognize familiar melodies in dimensions other than pitch. The authors suggest that contour extraction is a generalized feature of auditory memory and may have a centralized processing mechanism. Further work is needed to assess whether contour extraction is based on ordinal computations from a generalized analog magnitude system such as the one that may underlie the processing of ordinal relations for space, time, and number. The representation of ordinal relations, including relative judgments of number, size, time, loudness, brightness, and pitch (i.e., mental comparisons) might be functionally interdependent and share mechanisms, or they could be functionally parallel and rely on mechanisms that are not shared but, rather, operate in a similar way. In fact, this conclusion could also apply to much of the data that shows associations among dimensions such as number, space, and time: the data are often ambiguous as to whether their relationship is one of functional interdependence or a functional parallel.

Summary of evidence from human adults and animals

Based on the above evidence, several open but empirically tractable issues can be identified. One issue is the extent to which the representations of different magnitudes and their associated computations are distinct. Another issue is to define what a more comprehensive description of the functional architecture of the magnitude system(s) should look like. A final issue is at what level of representation interference effects arise and whether asymmetries of interference reflect unequal distribution of computational resources. Most extant studies are consistent with many views of magnitude relations, including innate constraints on certain magnitude relations and statistical, correlational, or associative learning or tuning of abstract magnitude representation during learning.

In order to understand what taxonomic distinctions exist among magnitudes, it is important to consider how associations among magnitudes might originate and develop in the mind and brain and therefore what their functional relations could be. In the following section, we consider existing ideas about magnitude representation within the larger context of theories of "abstraction" in development. We extend frameworks from cross-modal perception to the conceptual structure of abstract relations among magnitudes. The frameworks presented here are not mutually exclusive and could even be complementary. Here, we describe two broad mechanisms for how magnitude dimensions could become related.

The formation of magnitude relations

Little is known about the development of generalized magnitude representations. We borrow hypotheses and evidence from research on the development of multisensory perception to help frame research questions concerning the relations between magnitudes. This approach is justifiable because multisensory representations of abstract percepts (e.g., object location, typically modelled as a weighted combination of visual and auditory cues) are similar to generalized magnitudes in the sense that information from separate sources can be bound together and/or influence composite representations that factor in information from more than one source.

A. Types of relationships among magnitudes

In principle, there are two possible types of cross-dimensional magnitude representation: (1) connections between pairs or groups of magnitudes that arise from simple association, and (2) more general, abstract, higher-level representations. In the multisensory-integration and cross-modal perception literature, these higher-level representations are often referred to as *amodal* because they refer to a property that does not belong to any one sensory modality alone. In the case of magnitudes, we refer to this type of representation as *adimensional* because information is abstracted away from magnitude dimensions rather than stimulus modalities. Both types of representation may be present at birth or built and tuned across development.

i. Simple associations or conditional probabilities. The binding of correlated events across senses and cognitive domains (assumed to be innately separate) has been the historically dominant explanation of the development of multisensory percepts and abstract concepts (e.g., Piaget, 1952, 1954). At a minimum, an associative account requires that infants and children construct representations of correlations among percepts via a direct connection: stimulation of one dimension at a certain magnitude leads to activation of a regular value of magnitude in another dimension, and this mapping is established on the basis of previous observations. At the computational level, this is analogous to the storage of the conditional probabilities among individual instances of magnitude observations. In the simplest case, this would be stored as the probability of observing a magnitude level on dimension Y given the observed magnitude on dimension X, $p(Y|X)$, and/or the reverse, $p(X|Y)$. As we alluded to earlier, postnatal learning need not be the only process that explains the construction of such mappings; infants may come with innate, prior expectations about any given conditional probability. Conditional probabilities can also explain asymmetrical relations between any two variables: $p(Y|X)$ may not be equal to $p(X|Y)$. This means that, contrary to general assumptions in the literature, an associative account of this type does not require symmetrical associations between dimensions.

How plausible is this type of mechanism? There is no doubt that infants possess powerful associative-learning and statistical-learning mechanisms that build representations of conditional probabilities. Infant methodologies that use reinforcement schedules, like the conditioned head-turn procedure (see Werker, Polka & Pegg, 1997, for a review) and paradigms that involve anticipatory eye movements (McMurray & Aslin, 2004), would not work without associative learning. Infants' (and adults') sensitivity to transitional probabilities between adjacent and non-adjacent syllables and tones provides evidence that associations can be used to abstract conditional rules and auditory patterns (Aslin, Saffran, & Newport, 1998; Creel, Newport, & Aslin, 2004; Newport & Aslin, 2004; Saffran, Aslin, & Newport, 1996; Saffran, Johnson, Aslin, & Newport, 1999). Some studies suggest that similar signatures of transitional-probability learning can be found within a variety of modalities (e.g., visual sequences of objects, Kirkham, Slemmer, & Johnson, 2002), and across modalities (Yu & Smith, 2011), and that this type of learning can apply to multiple perceptual and cognitive domains (Thiessen, 2011).

Although associative learning is a powerful mechanism that can result in complex representations in infants, it has limitations for explaining more abstract ordinal and arithmetic interactions among magnitudes. As mentioned earlier, in order for different magnitude dimensions to be related or compared to one another, the process must require abstraction from the stimuli themselves (Gallistel & Gelman, 2000). A process of abstracting magnitudes also would allow different dimensions to be combined together—for example, to compute rate from number and time, or density from number and surface area. The abstraction away from absolute magnitude to normalized, relative magnitude implies the use of a code or representation that is common to all magnitude dimensions, which could arise in the second type of model: abstract, adimensional representations.

ii. Amodal and adimensional representations. An abstract magnitude representation can be thought of as a representation in which the intensity of a stimulus is represented as "a lot" or "a little", independently of the dimension from which the intensity initially derives. Current conceptualizations of analog magnitude representation assume that type of abstractness wherein the values of a given dimension are encoded as relative (normalized) values, such as "a lot" or "a little", in addition to absolute values (e.g., see Cantlon, Platt, & Brannon, 2009, for review; Srinivasan & Carey, 2010). By virtue of being encoded in a common analog magnitude format, intensities and quantities theoretically provide the necessary level of abstraction for encoding the correlations or redundancies among various magnitudes in the natural environment. At the computational level, generalized representations of the correlations among multiple dimensions might be tuned as one or more composite variables that receive weighted inputs from each individual dimension. We base our conceptualization of these adimensional variables on various descriptions and models of amodal representations from the multisensory-integration and cross-modal perception literature.

A large body of evidence suggests that amodal representations of multisensory inputs exist early in development. Eleanor Gibson (1969) sought to explain cross-modal matching behaviour in multiple domains (e.g., for intensity across several modalities, Stevens, Mack, & Stevens, 1960; for higher-order figural properties, Rudel & Teuber, 1964; and for case studies of letter identification after vision restoration, Gregory & Wallace, 1963) and cross-modal transfer (e.g., for non-conventional shape, Caviness, 1964). Her approach assumes initial separateness of modalities and dimensions but asserts the possibility that more abstract representations of information presented across multiple modalities or dimensions also are present early in infant development and may be (at least initially) more important than modality-specific representations. In this view, an abstract, amodal representation of intensity or amount of stimulation is present from birth or very early in infancy and thus represents an innate component of multisensory perception. Gibson thought of amodal representations as dividing into two possible types, both of which rely on information redundancy. Her discussion of amodal relations includes two types: (1) intersensory redundancy (e.g., timing information about hammer strikes can be sampled from both the auditory and visual modalities) and also (2) relative intensity (e.g., "sharpness, bluntness, and jerkiness"; Gibson, 1969, p. 219).

Since Gibson, evidence for amodal representations in infancy has come from demonstrations of information transfer across modalities in infants (from oral to visual, Gottfried, Rose, & Bridger, 1977; from tactile to visual, Gottfried et al., 1977; Meltzoff & Borton, 1979; though see Maurer, Stager, & Mondloch, 1999) as well as demonstrations of cross-modal equivalence (e.g., continuity/discontinuity and ascendancy/descendency, Wagner, Winner, Cicchetti, & Gardner, 1981). Across those demonstrations of amodal representation, the transfer of information from one modality to the next is not necessarily equally strong in either direction (e.g., in visual–tactile transfer, Bushnell & Weinberger, 1987). As for correlational representations between magnitudes, this finding indicates that symmetrical relationships between different dimensions need not be assumed for adimensional magnitude representations. An asymmetry in mappings between magnitudes also does not indicate that one dimension is more or less fundamental than the other, since we see that asymmetrical relations emerge among basic sensory modalities.

Some studies suggest that similar behavioural signatures from cross-modal perception exist for various types of magnitude. For example, Jordan and Baker (2010) found that 3- to 5-year-old children succeed at number matching tasks when given redundant auditory and visual numerical information, but they perform at chance levels when given only unimodal information. In addition, redundant, multisensory information increases the precision of 6-month-olds' numerical discrimination (Jordan, Suanda, & Brannon, 2008). These data demonstrate that redundant, multimodal information about magnitude dimensions is more powerful than unimodal information. Moreover, Lewkowicz and Turkewitz (1980) demonstrated that 3- and 4.5-week-old infants respond to matched relative intensity levels of auditory loudness and visual brightness. These data are important because they show that very young infants find correspondences between different magnitude dimensions, even across modalities. The result supports the argument that adimensional representations of magnitude (in this case, loudness and brightness) are fundamental in development.

Little is known about the computations that underlie the development of amodal representations or the format of their original state. To address the hypothesis that multisensory representations are tuned over time from unisensory inputs, Yildirim and Jacobs (2012) developed a nonparametric Bayesian model with multisensory feature variables (without specifying the number of features in advance) that are tuned in the course of learning. These multisensory feature variables are latent in the sense that they are unobserved: they must be estimated from the values of the observed unisensory inputs. As higher-level representations are tuned to integrate information from unisensory inputs, they allow for improved inference in both the latent variable(s) and the unisensory domains. Moreover, training with multisensory input leads to better performance in simulated unisensory tasks than training in unisensory input only, and it can predict values of missing unisensory inputs from latent variables. These results match known benefits of multisensory perception and training in multisensory environments.

If adimensional variables are computed in the same manner, we might expect similar benefits to arise in unidimensional judgments following learning. If subjects train on a task with multiple magnitudes, this will lead to improved inference in tasks involving only one magnitude. In addition, such an account would predict transfer of stimulation from one magnitude dimension to all magnitude dimensions tied to the same adimensional magnitude. This account also predicts the existence of neurons that respond to multiple magnitudes at birth (an innate capacity to represent correlational information) and that mature, adimensional neurons are tuned to weight unidimensional inputs relative to their precision.

A way of conceptualizing how adimensional variables of this sort might be constructed at the representational level is principle component analysis (PCA), a method that reduces high-dimensional data sets to low-dimensional sets of composite variables by grouping clusters of correlated variables. Groups of correlated unidimensional variables are mapped onto one principal component to implement dimensionality reduction. Each individual dimension's contribution to the value on the principal component is weighted relative to its distance from the principal component. The functional implication of this PCA-type representation is that a large amount of unrelated but structurally similar magnitude information could be compressed into a smaller amount of related magnitude information in which any commonalities among magnitude dimensions are represented only once. Interference effects arise naturally in this architecture from the information loss associated with collapsing correlated dimensions onto the same principal component. Asymmetries in interference would arise from the different amount of weight given to each dimension in estimating a particular stimulus' value on the principal component.

Artificial neural networks, which implement PCA (Oja, 1982) and its variants, have modelled emergent properties of real neurophysiological systems. In one example, a recent type of neural network used for dimensionality reduction called deep networks (Hinton & Salakhutdinov, 2006) has successfully modelled neurophysiological and behavioural data from visual numerosity estimation and comparison tasks (Stoianov & Zorzi, 2012). However, like Yildirim and Jacobs's model (2012), PCA and its more sophisticated variants have important limitations. For example, in classical PCA, the researcher must specify the number of principal components to find in advance of performing the computation. In short, every model must start with *some* constraints in the form of specifying prior information about the latent components to be found. This suggests that part of the challenge of investigating the development of generalized magnitude representations is the specification of the initial state of the representations.

B. *Current evidence and predictions*

Current behavioural evidence that supports either an associative or an amodal/adimensional view of magnitude relations is limited. Independently of hypotheses concerning the precise nature of an abstract magnitude code, it has been proposed that certain dimensions map spontaneously onto some dimensions but not others in infancy and childhood because they share a privileged relationship from birth (e.g. Dehaene et al., 2008; de Hevia & Spelke, 2010; Srinivasan & Carey, 2010). In particular, these studies have argued for privileged relations between space and number and space and time. These studies do not aim to distinguish among associations, statistical correlations, or adimensional representations of magnitudes, though the developmental primacy and generality of the findings suggest that at least one of these processes is engaged within the first months of life. Identical thresholds across space, time, and number in 6-month-olds suggest the development of a shared substrate for time, size, and number (Brannon, Lutz & Cordes, 2006; vanMarle & Wynn, 2009; reviewed in Cantlon, Platt, & Brannon, 2009, and Feigenson, 2007). Similar results have been reported for older children (5 and 8 yrs) and adults (Droit-Volet, Clément, & Fayol, 2008). However, it is clear from the psychophysics of magnitude estimation (Stevens, 1975) that adults can, at the very least, map relational information from any one dimension onto any other dimension. How do infants reach that adult state?

In children, the precision of numerical discrimination judgments gets finer from ages 6 to 8 years; quantitative comparisons in non-numerical magnitudes (e.g., luminance and bar height) follow this same developmental trajectory (Holloway & Ansari, 2008). Similar results, mentioned above, have been found among infants for the discrimination trajectories of size, time, and number over the first year of development (see Feigenson, 2007). These data suggest that the mechanism and/or constraints underlying the development of these comparisons are common across continua.

Beyond shared constraints, there is evidence that different types of magnitudes are encoded relationally as early as infancy. Infants seem to spontaneously map stimuli from one of these magnitude dimensions to another. In one example, infants showed evidence of this spontaneous mapping when habituated to positively correlated number/line-length pairs (de Hevia & Spelke, 2010). One recent study showed that 9-month-olds were equally likely to transfer an experimentally learned association between one dimension and colour-pattern cues to another dimension (Lourenco & Longo, 2010). For example, if infants learned that large objects were black and had stripes while small objects were white with dots, they expected a congruent association between those colour/shape patterns and the dimensions of number and duration. The generality of these effects with other continuous dimensions such as brightness, loudness, duration, or density is not yet known, though one study suggests that it may not hold across all magnitude dimensions. Srinivasan and Carey (2010) show that 9-month-old infants more easily bind line length to tone duration than to tone amplitude when such mappings are positively correlated.

To explain these findings, Srinivasan and Carey (2010) propose that two dimensions may share some degree of computational and neural resources. At one extreme—termed *functional overlap*—two dimensions may innately share computational and neural resources such that cross-dimensional mapping should be spontaneous even in infancy and early childhood. At the other extreme—termed *structural similarity* (borrowed from Gentner & Markman, 2005)—the two dimensions may share a representational format (e.g., ordered analog magnitude) and may therefore be mapped analogically; however, these dimensions cannot (or may not yet appear to) map onto each other spontaneously in children and infants because they share minimal computational and neural resources at those developmental time points.

Innately privileged relations between certain magnitudes are also indicated in the universality of their association. The ability to map numbers onto space (number lines), for example, is widespread among human cultures. The Mundurucu, an Amazonian people who lack a rich linguistic system of discrete number, can map nonverbal numerical magnitude onto horizontal lines just as do Western subjects (Dehaene et al., 2008). The finding supports the conclusion that mappings between space and number are not culturally determined, because Mundurucu do not generally use numerical symbols in reading and reciting. However, this finding does not necessarily indicate the presence of an innate bias to map numbers to space in humans (Cantlon, Cordes, Libertus, & Brannon, 2009; van Dijck & Fias, 2011), and it could represent an underlying preference for spatial representations in general.

Fundamental interactions between space and number are also observed in Stroop-like effects between magnitudes throughout development. Monkeys and 3-year-old children simultaneously and automatically represent both number and cumulative surface area in judgments of visual dot arrays (Cantlon & Brannon, 2007; Cantlon, Safford, & Brannon, 2010). Performance for both groups is better when number and cumulative area are congruent between the arrays than when they are incongruent, suggesting a convergence of the dimensions at some point in the processing stream. Similar results of congruity effects between number and area have been found in Stroop-like tasks with 5-year-old children and adults (Gebius, Cohen Kadosh, de Haan, & Henik, 2009; Hurewitz, Gelman, & Schnitzer, 2006). These data from monkeys and young children demonstrate convergence of magnitude representations for number and space during stimulus processing. However, the data do not indicate at what level of representation mappings between dimensions occur.

Some evidence from childhood suggests that the full array of conceptual mappings between dimensions emerges gradually over development. For example, 3-year-olds reliably match high-pitched sounds to smaller and brighter balls in a categorization task (Mondloch & Maurer, 2004). At the age of 3 and 4 years, but not at 2 years, children match louder sounds with larger visual stimuli; however, mapping between the dimension of surface darkness (as distinct from luminance) and size is less consistent (Smith & Sera, 1992). Children of age 6 and 8 years can spontaneously map higher-order relational patterns among objects between different dimensions (e.g., *small–big–small* to *light–dark–light*); 4-year-olds can perform such mappings, but only following within-dimension mapping trials (Gentner & Medina, 1998; Kotovsky & Gentner, 1996). Broadly speaking, these studies suggest that some higher-order relations that depend on the ordinal nature of different magnitudes can be accessed at young ages. Performance-competence issues related to the explicit nature of the mapping task render the poor performance of young children on mapping between certain dimensions difficult to interpret. Moreover, some data from infants showing early mappings between dimensions such as pitch and space (Walker et al., 2009) and loudness and brightness (Lewkowicz & Turkewitz, 1980) are at odds with a conclusion of gradual mappings between dimensions over development. However, at face value, the data implicate experience-related changes in cross-dimensional mapping concepts during childhood.

In summary, some evidence from interdimensional mapping in infancy and across cultures is consistent with the existence of innate relations between magnitudes. However, there is currently a question as to which dimensions are related to one another and when. Moreover, further evidence is needed to show whether these relations are amodal/adimensional, or separate but associated. In an experimental setting, an amodal/adimensional architecture predicts that training in multiple dimensions will result in improved inference in the unidimensional domains. Finally, some evidence described above indicates that infants and children benefit from redundant magnitude information, and it is generally known that congruent magnitude information (such as surface area and number) results in better performance than incongruent magnitude information in children, adults, and non-human primates. However, whether there is a *critical* role for redundant cross-dimensional magnitude information in the development of magnitude concepts is not known.

Trajectory of developing magnitude representations

In previous studies, the developmental origins of relations among magnitudes have been studied independently of the mechanisms that are responsible for altering those relations over the course of development. In this section, we describe mechanisms that are hypothesized to influence the developmental course of "abstract", amodal representations during infancy, and we discuss their significance for the development of magnitude representation. Virtually no evidence from cross-sectional studies is available concerning the time-course of magnitude mappings across development. However, we can make predictions about what the course of development might look like based on evidence from the time-course of cross-modal perception—if, in fact, the neural underpinnings of coordinating information across magnitudes are principally similar to those of cross-modal perception (as suggested in Spector & Maurer, 2009).

Neonates and very young infants seem to successfully coordinate information from different modalities, fail at similar tasks in the following months, and gradually regain those computational capacities before the end of the first year of life (Figure 5) (e.g., face–voice synchrony, Pickens et al., 1994; tactile to visual transfer as demonstrated by novelty preference, Streri, 1987, and Streri & Pêcheux, 1986). Maurer and colleagues claim that this U-shaped function characterizing the development of multi-modal integration and cross-modal matching cannot be fully explained by either coordination of innately separate unisensory inputs or a progression from undifferentiated to differentiated representations of redundant information across the senses alone (Maurer & Maurer, 1988; Maurer & Mondloch, 2004).

To explain those phenomena, it has been proposed that infants experience something akin to synesthesia near birth; this hypothesis has been formulated in strong (Maurer & Maurer, 1988; Spector & Maurer, 2009) and weak (reviewed in

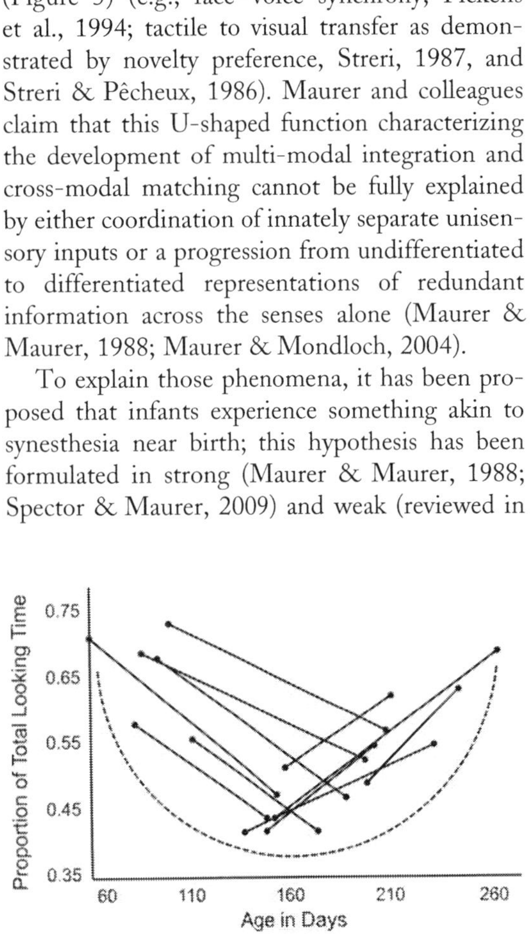

Figure 5. *Figure demonstrates a U-shaped curve (drawn for illustrative purposes) for cross-modal matching of synchronized faces and voices in infants studied longitudinally. Dependent measure on the* y-axis *is the proportion of total looking time to matching/synchronized face–voice pairs. Figure redrawn from "Full-term and pre-term infants' perception of face–voice synchrony" by J. Pickens, T. Field, T. Nawrocki, A. Martinez, D. Soutullo, & J. Gonzalez, 1994,* Infant Behavior and Development, 17, *p. 451. Copyright 1994 by Elsevier. Reproduced with permission from Elsevier.*

Maurer & Mondloch, 2004) versions. Originally motivated in part by evidence for increased differentiation among sensory areas associated with neural pruning in the first year of life (Neville, 1995), the strong version claims that a percept experienced in one modality automatically stimulates a parallel percept in another modality. Over the course of the first year of life, these synesthetic percepts become weaker as overabundant neural connections between different functional areas of the brain become either pruned or inhibited, but they form the basis for systematic (quasi-synesthetic) associations in non-synesthetic adults (Spector & Maurer, 2009). Magnitudes, under a similar conceptualization, might be related via cross-activation of dimension-dedicated mechanisms. The weak version of the hypothesis, traceable to a much older proposal (e.g., Hayek, 1952; von Hornbostel, 1938), states that newborn infants do not differentiate between senses; however, over time, infants begin to differentiate information coming from different senses and subsequently learn to coordinate information from each modality. Importantly, the strong and weak versions are not necessarily mutually exclusive. Whatever the case, the neural process hypothesized to underlie differentiation is pruning, and the process hypothesized to underlie subsequent coordination of information from separate senses is coordination. By extension, under a process such as this, magnitude representations would initially be neurally undifferentiated at birth; across development, pruning would lead to increased differentiation among magnitude dimensions and to subsequent coordination.

Researchers have supported the neonatal synesthesia hypothesis either with evidence for infant mappings of dimensions that do not have a straightforward, information-redundancy explanation or by explicitly documenting the decrease in synesthetic associations over development. For example, the presence of particular shapes influences the colour preferences of infants at 2 months but not at 8 months, consistent with the predictions of neural pruning or inhibition of connections between the areas that process shape and colour (Wagner & Dobkins, 2011). Associations between continuous psychophysical dimensions are also present early in life and may be supported by an innate, synesthesia-like component. For instance, infants at 4 months of age prefer to look at a ball that is bouncing in congruent motion with an auditory pitch (the ball goes up when the pitch goes up) over a ball that is bouncing incongruently with pitch; in addition, they prefer to look at a shape that is getting sharper as the pitch paired with it gets higher (Figure 6) (Walker et al., 2009).

The proposal that differentiation among magnitudes is mediated by processes of pruning or inhibition predicts (1) neural changes (e.g., in functional connectivity and white-matter integrity in relevant brain regions such as intraparietal cortex) correlated with behavioural changes across the first year of life and into childhood and (2) that occasionally adults would demonstrate vestigial associations among the magnitude dimensions hypothesized to be intimately connected at birth. There is at least some evidence for the second prediction: digit–colour synesthetes show a decrease in the subjective brightness of the induced colour experience as the magnitude of the

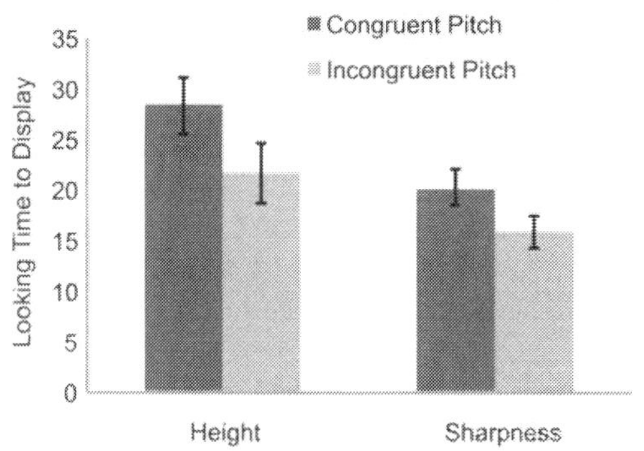

Figure 6. *Mean total looking times to displays with a bouncing ball (congruent or incongruent pitch height to object height mapping) or an object decreasing or increasing in sharpness (congruent or incongruent pitch height to sharpness mapping). Measurements taken from Walker et al. (2009). Error bars* ±*1* SE. *From "Preverbal infants' sensitivity to synaesthetic cross-modal correspondences" by P. Walker, J. G. Bremner, U. Mason, J. Spring, K. Mattock, A. Slater, & S. P. Johnson, 2009,* Psychological Science, *21(1), p. 23. Copyright 2009 by the authors. Drawn with permission from P. Walker.*

numerical inducer increases (Cohen Kadosh, Henik, & Walsh, 2009); this is similar to reports of a connection between luminance and number in non-synesthetes (Cohen Kadosh, Cohen Kadosh, & Henik, 2007). Moreover, there is some evidence that the mechanism underlying spatial-sequence synesthesia, in which tokens from number sequences, alphabets, and other series take on explicit spatial locations, parallels the SNARC effect in non-synesthetes (Eagleman, 2009).

Evolutionary perspectives on adimensional magnitude representation

Ultimately, any account of generalized, adimensional magnitudes must be placed in an evolutionary context. If these adimensional representations of magnitude are innate, where did they come from? Both the developmental and the evolutionary history of the relations between magnitude systems will have important consequences for interactions among magnitudes in adults. Walsh's (2003) view of the differentiation of space, time, and number leaves the job only to development. However, both descent with modification—the gradual differentiation of dedicated modules across evolution from more primitive ones originally dedicated to other purposes (e.g., Marcus, 2006)—and culturally mediated repurposing of cortical areas designed to perform related computations during development (Dehaene & Cohen, 2007) may play a role in shaping how adults process magnitude information.

Perceptual and cognitive systems are shaped by natural selection to address the demands of interacting with and representing the natural world. So, evolution could shape those systems in such a way that innate mechanisms are in place to encode environmental statistics that are stable across long periods of time, and more fluid mechanisms are in place for learning across shorter timescales such as development (Simoncelli & Olshausen, 2001; Yang & Purves, 2004). If a process like correlational learning among magnitudes is to be tuned across evolution, then correlations among magnitudes should exist in the natural environment. We can think of a few intuitive examples: long travel distances are generally associated with greater travel durations; in natural light, close and/or large objects impact the brightness of a visual scene more than do objects that are small and/or far away; greater numbers are loosely associated with greater spatial extent, and (for foragers) number of fruit to be harvested is correlated with greater foraging time. However, it is unclear how to go about collecting statistics from the natural environment to characterize the empirical correlations among magnitudes.

One potentially informative first question to ask about evolution is, how did different but related magnitudes emerge in the first place? According to descent with modification, separate, but closely related, magnitude representations may have emerged via duplication, expansion, or other modifications of previously existing machinery. One view of the functional organization of magnitudes that maps onto this idea is that space serves as the foundational domain for all other magnitudes, particularly those that are hypothesized to be more conceptually abstract—such as number and time. This view finds some loose correspondence in metaphor theory, in which linguistic metaphors that use "space" to talk about other domains are taken as indirect evidence of "space's" conceptual primacy (e.g., Clark, 1973; Lakoff & Johnson, 1980, 1999). Piaget (1969) also proposed that children conceptualize duration solely in terms of space and only later differentiate duration from space. Other investigators have failed to find sufficient evidence to support such a strong claim in toddlers and pre-schoolers (e.g., Friedman & Seely, 1976; Levin, 1977; Levin, Israeli, & Darom, 1978; Levin & Gilat, 1983). Yet, these findings do not rule out the possibility that spatial representations are evolutionarily primary.

The notion that "space" could ground other continuous magnitude representations is not far-fetched from an evolutionary perspective. Location and motion are among the only dimensions that can be represented by the most primitive forms of vertebrate "eyes". Depressed sheets of light-sensitive cells—the most primitive "eye"—can get very little form or object information; however, they get a good representation of location and motion direction (Lamb, Collin, & Pugh, 2007; Land & Fernald, 1992). Numerical information, in contrast, would require some ability to segregate objects. A similar argument for the primacy of space can be made from an even more primitive sensory system than vision: chemoreception. Modern animals can use this sense to represent simple one-dimensional spatial maps of chemical gradients without access to object form or individuation (Adams-Hunt & Jacobs, 2007).

Evolutionary forces could have caused relations among magnitudes to form in the sense that one dimension evolved from another, leaving functional similarities in their neural and computational operations. If many magnitude representations emerged from modification of the functional substrates that code for space, we might expect functional parallels between the spatial module and its evolutionary descendants as well as parallels among the descendants, although the degree of overlap would likely be heterogeneous and difficult to quantify. Confirmation of such an evolutionary process would require comparative work across multiple species of non-human primates as well as more distantly related animals and the possibility of genetic anomalies that selectively impair processing of multiple magnitudes thought to be dependent on, or genetically descended from, spatial processing. Congenital disorders affecting the evolutionarily primary magnitude system could also cluster with impairments of related magnitude systems if genetic physical and functional interdependencies from a common evolutionary history still remain. For instance, people with developmental dyscalculia, who have difficulty processing number magnitudes, show weaker interference effects from the physical size of the number than do normal controls (Rubinsten & Henik, 2006), suggesting an impaired ability to relate digital number and physical size. In addition, this population performs less well on time discrimination tasks, with lower scores on a standardized screening test (Cappelletti, Freeman, & Butterworth, 2011). However, more work is needed to determine whether a broader set of magnitude abilities is impaired.

Adjudicating among theories and conclusion

The most important point that we hope to have captured in this review is that questions regarding the source and functions of different types of magnitude representation in the mind and brain are tractable for the fields of cognitive neuroscience and development, thanks to the empirical and theoretical foundation that was laid by prior cognitive and neuropsychological research. Increasingly detailed models of associational or adimensional architectures will help adjudicate among hypotheses about the development and organization of magnitude representations. These two conceptualizations of magnitude relations are based on literature from cross-modal perception, which has relevance in the domain of magnitude representation. This way of framing magnitude representation offers amendments to existing interpretations of behavioural signatures, such as asymmetries in cross-dimensional mappings, and new predictions for the interactions among dimensions as a function of learning.

Current evidence demonstrates the existence of interactions or neural overlap among magnitudes and that these interactions vary in strength. This evidence is consistent with theories of interaction and overlap that emphasize either a strong innate component or a strong learned component. Under our characterization of associational or correlational representations of magnitudes, innate mappings may be subject to modification by early experience, and learned mappings are likely subject to innate constraints. The evolution of relations among magnitudes and the trajectory of magnitude relations across development require specification to paint a richer picture of the underlying computations and neural architecture.

Building on these models, future experiments could clarify the extent of functional overlap among dimensions and the relative contributions of pruning and construction to the developmental course of overlapping magnitude representations. Such knowledge will help constrain and refine explicit models of representation. Clarification of the possible levels at which interactions between dimensions might arise will help evaluate the assumptions underlying interpretations of mapping "strength" and symmetry.

First, we have to understand the degree to which neural processes and representational content are shared among dimensions. Measurements of neural overlap are helpful for distinguishing whether magnitude representations with the same behavioural signatures (e.g., Weber's law) are functionally interdependent (same behaviour, same neural substrate) or functionally parallel (same behaviour, different neural substrate). Furthermore, without linking overlapping neural signatures to more explicit models of representation, it is impossible to fully understand the functional origins of those neural signatures.

The development of neural processes for magnitude processing can also uniquely reveal functional distinctions and relations between dimensions. For example, a lack of neural overlap between dimensions in adulthood does not imply a lack of neural overlap in infancy. If a lack of neural overlap is to be taken as evidence for distinct magnitude representations, it would have to be shown that it is also lacking in development. Otherwise, the possibility that non-overlapping magnitude representations have a common developmental foundation remains open. Overlap early in development (even if absent in adulthood) will likely have functional consequences for the structure of the non-overlapping adult representations. And, of course, even if magnitude representations do not overlap in infancy, the possibility remains that they had a common evolutionary origin (perhaps still evident in non-human animals). The developmental and evolutionary origins of relations among magnitudes are thus critical for understanding the origins of magnitude representations, and they too represent different levels at which interactions among magnitude representations could have arisen (Tinbergen, 1963).

In terms of the development of magnitude relations, future research could determine the relative contributions of pruning and construction to the overlap among representations of different magnitudes. Pruning (or masking) would predict decreased associations among magnitudes with increased precision for discriminating within and between dimensions over development. Construction would predict increased associations among magnitudes over development. A combination of the forces of pruning and construction on development could take the form of a U-shaped trajectory of magnitude discrimination wherein associations among magnitudes initially decrease (pruning) and then subsequently increase (construction), as is found for cross-modal perception.

Second, at what level of processing do interactions between magnitudes occur, and what are the evolutionary and cultural influences that shape that level? The levels at which magnitude representations can interact and the number and types of continua to which such an underlying magnitude code applies beyond space, time, and number—for example, brightness, loudness, and pitch—are currently underspecified. At the algorithmic level of analysis, "levels" can refer to stages of processing such as encoding, comparison, and response selection in the Sternbergian sense (Sternberg, 1966, 1969a, 1969b, 2011). At these levels of processing, interactions among magnitude representations occur that may also be subject to varying evolutionary and cultural influences—for example, as we discussed above regarding Casasanto and Boroditsky (2008) and Merritt et al. (2010), higher-level, linguistic re-encoding of line durations with the terms "long" and "short" could account for some of the interference effects reported in adult humans. In principle, different types of behavioural signatures of interactions may have come from different levels of processing—for example, the interaction between space and number might occur during working memory for the SNARC effect (van Dijck & Fias, 2011) but at encoding for Stroop-like interference.

The salience of each dimension on its own, as shaped by cultural forces, also can influence the nature of the observed overlap at different levels of processing. For example, if number and space are each culturally prominent dimensions in the human experience, then they might appear to have a stronger mapping than space and brightness, given that brightness is less prominent than are space or number in this example. The salience of each individual dimension can influence the symmetry of the relations between magnitudes, and the natural clustering of dimensions in the environment can also influence the symmetry of the correlations. Therefore, it is important to consider subjects' sensitivity to mapping each dimension alone in assessments of cross-dimensional magnitude representations. Given the above points, the existence or non-existence of asymmetries of interference or facilitation between magnitude representations may not be enough to adjudicate among competing hypotheses of the origins of magnitude relations.

We have described two general frameworks for clarifying and building hypotheses about overlapping magnitude representations: associations among absolute magnitudes and composite, abstract magnitudes. A benefit of their generality is that these types of representation can be implemented across both evolutionary and developmental timescales. Moreover, they lend themselves to computationally precise predictions about behaviour and neural activity.

REFERENCES

Adams-Hunt, M. M., & Jacobs, L. F. (2007). Cognition for foraging. In D. W. Stephens & R. C. Ydenberg (Eds.), *Foraging: Behavior and ecology* (pp. 105–138). Chicago, IL: University of Chicago Press.

Aslin, J. R., Saffran, J. R., & Newport, E. L. (1998). Computation of conditional probability statistics by human infants. *Psychological Science*, *9*, 321–324.

Ayotte, J., Peretz, I., & Hyde, K. (2002). Congenital amusia: A group study of adults afflicted with a music-specific disorder. *Brain*, *125*, 238–251.

Berch, D. B., Foley, E. J., Hill, R. J., & Ryan, P. M. (1999). Extracting parity and magnitude from arabic numerals: Developmental changes in number processing and mental representation. *Journal of Experimental Child Psychology*, *74*, 286–308.

Boroditsky, L. (2000). Metaphoric structuring: Understanding time through spatial metaphors. *Cognition*, *75*, 1–28.

Boroditsky, L. (2001). Does language shape thought? English and Mandarin speakers' conceptions of time. *Cognitive Psychology*, *43*, 1–22.

Boroditsky, L., Fuhrman, O., & McCormick, K. (2011). Do English and Mandarin speakers think about time differently? *Cognition, 118,* 123–129.

Brannon, E. M., Lutz, D., & Cordes, S. (2006). The development of area discrimination and its implications for numerical abilities in infancy. *Developmental Science, 9*(6), F59–F64.

Brigner, W. L. (1986). Effect of perceived brightness on perceived time. *Perceptual & Motor Skills, 63,* 427–430.

Brigner, W. L. (1988). Perceived duration as a function of pitch. *Perceptual & Motor Skills, 67,* 301–302.

Bueti, D., & Walsh, V. (2009). The parietal cortex and the representation of time, space, number, and other magnitudes. *Philosophical Transactions of the Royal Society B, 364,* 1831–1840.

Bushnell, E. W., & Weinberger, N. (1987). Infants' detection of visual–tactual discrepancies: Asymmetries that indicate a directive role of visual information. *Journal of Experimental Psychology: Human Perception and Performance, 13*(4), 601–608.

Butler, R. A. (1969). Monaural and binaural localization of noise bursts vertically in the medial sagittal plane. *Journal of Auditory Research, 3,* 230–235.

Butler, R. A. (1971). The monaural localization of tonal stimuli. *Attention, Perception, & Psychophysics, 9,* 99–101.

Cantlon, J. F., & Brannon, E. M. (2007). How much does number matter to a monkey (*Macaca mulatta*). *Journal of Experimental Psychology: Animal Behavior Processes, 33,* 32–41.

Cantlon, J. F., Cordes, S., Libertus, M. E., & Brannon, E. M. (2009). Comment on "Log or linear: Distinct intuitions of the number scale in Western and Amazonian indigene cultures". *Science, 323,* 38b.

Cantlon, J. F., Platt, M. L., & Brannon, E. M. (2009). Beyond the number domain. *Trends in Cognitive Sciences, 13*(2), 83–91.

Cantlon, J. F., Safford, K. E., & Brannon, E. M. (2010). Spontaneous analog number representations in three-year-old children. *Developmental Science, 13*(2), 289–297.

Cappelletti, M., Freeman, E. D., & Butterworth, B. L. (2011). Time processing in dyscalculia. *Frontiers in Psychology, 2,* 1–10.

Cappelletti, M., Kopelman, M. D., Morton, J., & Butterworth, B. (2005). Dissociations in numerical abilities revealed by progressive cognitive decline in a patient with semantic dementia. *Cognitive Neuropsychology, 22,* 771–793.

Casasanto, D., & Boroditsky, L. (2008). Time in the mind: Using space to think about time. *Cognition, 106,* 579–593.

Caviness, J. A. (1964). *Visual and tactual perception of solid shape* (Doctoral dissertation). Cornell University, Ithaca, NY.

Chen, J. Y. (2007). Do Chinese and English speakers think about time differently? Failure of replicating Boroditsky (2001). *Cognition, 104,* 427–436.

Christensen, I. P., & Huang, Y. L. (1979). The auditory tau effect and memory for pitch. *Perception & Psychophysics, 26,* 489–494.

Cipolotti, L., Butterworth, B., & Denes, G. (1991). A specific deficit for numbers in a case of dense acalculia. *Brain, 114,* 2619–2637.

Clark, E. V. (1973). What's in a word? On the child's acquisition of semantics in his first language. In T.E. Moore (Ed.), *Cognitive development and the acquisition of language* (pp. 65–110). New York: Academic Press.

Cohen, J., Hansel, C. E. M., & Sylvester, J. D. (1954). Interdependence of temporal and auditory judgments. *Nature, 174,* 642–644.

Cohen Kadosh, R., Cohen Kadosh, K., & Henik, A. (2007). The neuronal correlate of bidirectional synesthesia: A combined event-related potential and functional magnetic resonance imaging study. *Journal of Cognitive Neuroscience, 19,* 2050–2059.

Cohen Kadosh, R., Henik, A., & Walsh, V. (2009). Synesthesia: Learned or lost? *Developmental Science, 12,* 484–491.

Creel, S. C., Newport, E. L., & Aslin, R. N. (2004). Distant melodies: Statistical learning of non-adjacent dependencies in tone sequences. *Journal of Experimental Psychology: Learning, Memory, and Cognition, 30,* 1119–1130.

Crowder, R. G., & Neath, I. (1995). The influence of pitch on time perception in short melodies. *Music Perception: An Interdisciplinary Journal, 12,* 379–386.

Dehaene, S., Bossini, S., & Giraux, P. (1993). The mental representation of parity and number magnitude. *Journal of Experimental Psychology: General, 122,* 371–396.

Dehaene, S., & Cohen, L. (1997). Cerebral pathways for calculation: Double dissociation between rote verbal and quantitative knowledge of arithmetic. *Cortex, 33,* 219–250.

Dehaene, S., & Cohen (2007). Cultural recycling of cortical maps. *Neuron, 56,* 384–398.

Dehaene, S., Izard, V., Spelke, E., & Pica, P. (2008). Log or linear? Distinct intuitions of the number

scale in Western and Amazonian indigene cultures. *Science, 320,* 1217–1220.
Dehaene, S., Spelke, E., Pinel, P., Stanescu, R., & Tsivkin, S. (1999). Sources of mathematical thinking: Behavioral and brain-imaging evidence. *Science, 284,* 970–974.
de Hevia, M. D., & Spelke, E. S. (2010). Number-space mapping in human infants. *Psychological Science, 21,* 653–660.
Dormal, V., Seron, X., & Pesenti, M. (2006). Numerosity-duration interference: A Stroop experiment. *Acta Psychologica, 121,* 109–124.
Douglas, K. M., & Bilkey, D. K. (2007). Amusia is associated with deficits in spatial processing. *Nature Neuroscience, 10,* 915–921.
Dowling, W. J. (1978). Scale and contour: Two components of a theory of memory for melodies. *Psychological Review, 85,* 341–354.
Dowling, W. J., & Fujitani, D. S. (1971). Contour, interval, & pitch recognition in memory for melodies. *Journal of the Acoustical Society of America, 49,* 524.
Droit-Volet, S. (2010). Speeding up a master clock common to time, number, and length? *Behavioral Processes, 85,* 126–134.
Droit-Volet, S., Clément, A., & Fayol, M. (2008). Time, number and length: Similarities and differences in discrimination in adults and children. *Quarterly Journal of Experimental Psychology, 61,* 1827–1846.
Eagleman, D. M. (2008). Human time perception and its illusions. *Current Opinion in Neurobiology, 18,* 131–136.
Eagleman, D. M. (2009). The objectification of overlearned sequences: A new view of spatial sequence synesthesia. *Cortex, 45,* 1266–1277.
Farnè, M. (1977). Brightness as an indicator of distance: Relative brightness per se or contrast with the background? *Perception, 6,* 287–293.
Feigenson, L. (2007). The equality of quantity. *Trends in Cognitive Sciences, 11*(5), 185–187.
Friedman, W. J., & Seely, P. B. (1976). The child's acquisition of spatial and temporal word meanings. *Child Development, 47,* 1103–1108.
Gallistel, C. R. (1990). *The organization of learning.* Cambridge, MA: MIT Press.
Gallistel, C. R., & Gelman, R. (1992). Preverbal and verbal counting and computation. *Cognition, 44,* 43–74.
Gallistel, C. R., & Gelman, R. (2000). Non-verbal numerical cognition: From reals to integers. *Trends in Cognitive Sciences, 4*(2), 59–65.
Gebius, T., Cohen Kadosh, R., de Haan, E., & Henik, A. (2009). Automatic quantity processing in 5-year-olds and adults. *Cognitive Processes, 10,* 133–142.
Gentner, D., & Markman, A. B. (2005). Defining structural similarity. *Journal of Cognitive Science, 6,* 1–20.
Gentner, D., & Medina, J. (1998). Similarity and the development of rules. *Cognition, 65,* 263–297.
Gerstmann, J. (1940). Syndrome of finger agnosia, disorientation for right and left, agraphia and acalculia. *Archives of Neurology and Psychiatry, 44,* 398–408.
Gibson, E. J. (1969). *Principles of perceptual learning and development.* New York, NY: Appleton-Century-Crofts.
Goldstone, S., Lhamon, W. T., & Sechzer, J. (1978). Light intensity and judged duration. *Bulletin of the Psychonomic Society, 12,* 83–84.
Gottfried, A. W., Rose, S. A., & Bridger, W. H. (1977). Cross-modal transfer in human infants. *Child Development, 48,* 118–123.
Gregory, R. L., & Wallace, J. G. (1963). Recovery from early blindness: A case study. *Experimental Psychology Society Monographs, 2,* Cambridge: Heffers.
Harrington, D. L., Haaland, K. Y., & Knight, R. T. (1998). Cortical networks underlying mechanisms of time perception. *The Journal of Neuroscience, 18,* 1085–1095.
Hayek, F. A. (1952). *The sensory order.* Chicago, IL: University of Chicago Press.
Henik, A., & Tzelgov, H. (1982). Is three greater than five: The relation between physical and semantic size in comparison tasks. *Memory & Cognition I, 10,* 389–395.
Henry, M. J., & McAuley, J. D. (2009). Evaluation of an imputed pitch velocity model of the auditory kappa effect. *Journal of Experimental Psychology: Human Perception and Performance, 35,* 551–564.
Henry, M. J., McAuley, J. D., & Zaleha, M. (2009). Evaluation of an imputed pitch velocity model of the auditory tau effect. *Attention, Perception, & Psychophysics, 71,* 1399–1413.
Hinton, G. E., & Salakhutdinov, R. R. (2006). Reducing the dimensionality of data with neural networks. *Science, 313,* 504–507.
Holloway, I. D., & Ansari, D. (2008). Domain-specific and domain-general changes in children's development of number comparison. *Developmental Science, 11,* 644–649.
Hurewitz, F., Gelman, R., & Schnitzer, B. (2006). Sometimes area counts more than number. *Proceedings of the National Academy of Sciences, 103,* 19599–19604.

January, D., & Kako, E. (2007). Re-evaluating evidence for the linguistic relativity hypothesis: Response to Boroditsky (2001). *Cognition, 104*, 417–426.

Jordan, K. E., & Baker, J. (2010). Multisensory information boosts numerical matching abilities in young children. *Developmental Science, 14*, 205–213.

Jordan, K. E., Suanda, S. H., & Brannon, E. M. (2008). Intersensory redundancy accelerates preverbal numerical competence. *Cognition, 108*, 210–221.

Kirkham, N. Z., Slemmer, J. A., & Johnson, S. P. (2002). Visual statistical learning in infancy: Evidence for a domain general learning mechanism. *Cognition, 83*, B35–B42.

Kotovsky, L., & Gentner, D. (1996). Comparison and categorization in the development of relational similarity. *Child Development, 67*, 2797–2822.

Kraemer, P. J., Brown, R. W., & Randall, C. K. (1995). Signal intensity and duration estimation in rats. *Behavioural Processes, 34*, 265–268.

Kraemer, P. J., Randall, C. K., & Brown, R. W. (1997). The influence of stimulus attributes on duration of matching-to-sample in pigeons. *Animal Learning and Behavior, 25*, 148–157.

Lakoff, G., & Johnson, M. (1980). *Metaphors we live by*. Chicago, IL: University of Chicago Press.

Lakoff, G., & Johnson, M. (1999). *Philosophy in the flesh: The embodied mind and its challenge to Western thought*. Chicago, IL: University of Chicago Press.

Lamb, T. D., Collin, S. P., & Pugh, E. N. (2007). Evolution of the vertebrate eye: Opsins, photoreceptors, retina and eye cup. *Nature Reviews Neuroscience, 8*, 970–976.

Land, M. F., & Fernald, R. D. (1992). The evolution of eyes. *Annual Review of Neuroscience, 15*, 1–29.

Leon, M. I., & Shadlen, M. N. (2003). Representation of time by neurons in the posterior parietal cortex of the macaque. *Neuron, 38*, 317–327.

Levin, I. (1977). The development of time concepts in young children: Reasoning about duration. *Child Development, 48*, 435–444.

Levin, I., & Gilat, I. (1983). A developmental analysis of early time concepts: The equivalence and additivity of the effect of interfering cues on duration comparisons of young children. *Child Development, 54*, 78–83.

Levin, I., Israeli, E., & Darom, E. (1978). The development of time concepts in young children: The relations between duration and succession. *Child Development, 49*, 755–764.

Lewkowicz, D. J., & Turkewitz, G. (1980). Cross-modal equivalence in early infancy: Auditory–visual intensity matching. *Developmental Psychology, 16*, 597–607.

Lourenco, S. F., & Longo, M. R. (2010). General magnitude representation in human infants. *Psychological Science, 21*, 873–881.

Lourenco, S. F., & Longo, M. R. (2011). Origins and development of generalized magnitude representation. In S. Dehaene & E. Brannon (Eds.), *Space, time, and number in the brain: Searching for the foundations of mathematical thought* (pp. 225–244). Waltham, MA: Academic Press.

Marcus, G. F. (2006). Cognitive architecture and descent with modification. *Cognition, 101*, 443–465.

Marks, L. E. (1987). On cross-modal similarity: Auditory–visual interactions in speeded discrimination. *Journal of Experimental Psychology: Human Perception and Performance, 13*, 384–394.

Marvin, E. W., & Laprade, P. A. (1987). Relating musical contours: Extensions of a theory for contour. *Journal of Music Theory, 31*, 225–267.

Maurer, D., & Maurer, C. (1988). *The world of the newborn*. New York: Basic Books.

Maurer, D., & Mondloch, C. J. (2004). Neonatal synesthesia: A reevaluation. In L. Robertson & N. Sagiv (Eds.), *Attention on synesthesia: Cognition, development and neuroscience* (pp. 193–213). New York, NY: Oxford University Press.

Maurer, D., Stager, C. L., & Mondloch, C. J. (1999). Cross-modal transfer of shape is difficult to demonstrate in one-month-olds. *Child Development, 70*, 1047–1057.

McDermott, J. H., Lehr, A. J., & Oxenham, A. J. (2008). Is relative pitch specific to pitch? *Psychological Science, 19*, 1263–1271.

McMurray, B., & Aslin, R. N. (2004). Anticipatory eye movements reveal infants' auditory and visual categories. *Infancy, 6*, 203–229.

Meck, W. H., & Church, R. M. (1983). A mode control model of counting and timing processes. *Journal of Experimental Psychology: Animal Behavior Processes, 9*, 320–334.

Meltzoff, A. N., & Borton, R. W. (1979). Intermodal matching by human neonates. *Nature, 282*, 403–404.

Merritt, D. J., Casasanto, D., & Brannon, E. M. (2010). Do monkeys think in metaphors? Representations of space and time in monkeys and humans. *Cognition, 117*, 191–202.

Mondloch, C. J., & Maurer, D. (2004). Do small white balls squeak? Pitch–object correspondences in young children. *Cognitive, Affective, & Behavioral Neuroscience, 4*, 133–136.

Moore, B.C. J. (2003). *An introduction to the psychology of hearing* (5th ed.). Bingley, UK: Emerald Group.

Moyer, R. S., & Landauer, T. K. (1967). Time required for judgments of numerical inequality. *Nature, 215,* 1519–1520.

Neville, H. (1995). Developmental specificity in neurocognitive development in humans. In M. Gazzaniga (Ed.), *The cognitive neurosciences* (pp. 219–231). Cambridge, MA: Bradford Books.

Newport, E. L., & Aslin, R. N. (2004). Learning at a distance: I. Statistical learning of non-adjacent dependencies. *Cognitive Psychology, 48,* 127–162.

Nieder, A. (2005). Counting on neurons: The neurobiology of numerical competence. *Nature Reviews Neuroscience, 6*(3), 177–190.

Nuñez, R., Doan, D., & Nikoulina, A. (2011). Squeezing, striking, and vocalizing: Is number representation fundamentally spatial? *Cognition, 120,* 225–235.

Oja, E. (1982). A simplified neuron model as a principal component analyzer. *Journal of Mathematical Biology, 15,* 267–273.

Opfer, J. E., Thompson, C. A., & Furlong, E. E. (2010). The early development of spatial–numeric associations: Evidence from spatial and quantitative performance of preschoolers. *Developmental Science, 13,* 761–771.

Pariyadath, V., & Eagleman, D. (2007). The effect of predictability on subjective duration. *PLoS ONE, 11,* e1264.

Peretz, I., & Hyde, K. L. (2003). What is specific to music processing? Insights from congenital amusia. *Trends in Cognitive Sciences,* 7(8), 362–367.

Pfeuty, M., & Peretz, I. (2010). Abnormal pitch–time interference in congenital amusia: Evidence from an implicit test. *Attention, Perception, & Psychophysics, 72,* 763–774.

Piaget, J. (1952). *The child's conception of number.* London, UK: Routledge.

Piaget, J. (1954). *The construction of reality in the child.* New York, NY: Basic Books.

Piaget, J. (1969). *The child's conception of time.* London, UK: Routledge and Kegan Paul.

Pickens, J., Field, T., Nawrocki, T., Martinez, A., Soutullo, D., & Gonzalez, J. (1994). Full-term and pre-term infants' perception of face–voice synchrony. *Infant Behavior and Development, 17,* 447–455.

Pinel, P., Piazza, M., Le Bihan, D., & Dehaene, S. (2004). Distributed and overlapping cerebral representations of number, size, and luminance during comparative judgments. *Neuron, 41,* 1–20.

Roberts, W. A. (1995). Simultaneous numerical and temporal processing in the pigeon. *Current Directions in Psychological Science, 4*(2), 47–51.

Roberts, W. A., Coughlin, R., & Roberts, S. (2000). Pigeons flexibly time or count on cue. *Psychological Science, 11*(3), 218–222.

Roffler, S. K., & Butler, R. A. (1967). Localization of tonal stimuli in the vertical plane. *The Journal of the Acoustical Society of America, 43,* 1260–1266.

Roitman, J. D., Brannon, E. M., Andrews, J. R., & Platt, M. L. (2007). Nonverbal representation of time and number in adults. *Acta Psychologica, 124,* 296–318.

Roitman, J. D., Brannon, E. M., & Platt, M. L. (2007). Monotonic coding of numerosity in macaque lateral intraparietal cortex. *PLoS Biology, 5*(8), e208.

Rubinsten, O., & Henik, A. (2006). Double dissociation of functions in developmental dyslexia and dyscalculia. *Journal of Educational Psychology, 98,* 854–867.

Rudel, R. G., & Teuber, H. L. (1964). Crossmodal transfer of shape discrimination by children. *Neuropsychologia, 2,* 1–8.

Rusconi, E., Kwan, B., Giordano, B. L., Umiltà, C., & Butterworth, B. (2006). Spatial representation of pitch height: The SMARC effect. *Cognition, 99,* 113–129.

Saffran, J. R., Aslin, R. N., & Newport, E. L. (1996). Statistical learning by 8-month-old infants. *Science, 274*(5294), 1926–1928.

Saffran, J. R., Johnson, E. K., Aslin, R. N., & Newport, E. L. (1999). Statistical learning of tone sequences by adults and infants. *Cognition, 70,* 27–52.

Shaki, S., & Fischer, M. H. (2008). Reading space into numbers: A cross-linguistic comparison of the SNARC effect. *Cognition, 108,* 590–599.

Shigeno, S. (1986). The auditory tau and kappa effects for speech and nonspeech stimuli. *Perception & Psychophysics, 40,* 9–19.

Simoncelli, E. P., & Olshausen, B. A. (2001). Natural image statistics and neural representation. *Annual Reviews of Neuroscience, 24,* 1193–1216.

Smith, L. B., & Sera, M. D. (1992). A developmental analysis of the polar structure of dimensions. *Cognitive Psychology, 24,* 99–142.

Spector, F., & Maurer, D. (2009). Synesthesia: A new approach to understanding the development of perception. *Developmental Psychology, 45,* 175–189.

Srinivasan, M., & Carey, S. (2010). The long and the short of it: On the nature and origin of functional overlap between representations of space and time. *Cognition, 116,* 217–241.

Sternberg, S. (1966). High-speed scanning in human memory. *Science, 153,* 652–654.

Sternberg, S. (1969a). Memory-scanning: Mental processes revealed by reaction-time experiments. *American Scientist, 57,* 421–457.

Sternberg, S. (1969b). The discovery of processing stages: Extensions of Donders' method. In W.G. Koster (Ed.), *Attention and Performance II* (pp. 276–315), Acta Psychologica, 30. Amsterdam, The Netherlands: North Holland Publishing.

Sternberg, S. (2011). Modular processes in mind and brain. *Cognitive Neuropsychology, 28,* 156–208.

Stevens, J. C., Mack, J. D., & Stevens, S. S. (1960). Growth of sensation on seven continua as measured by force of handgrip. *Journal of Experimental Psychology, 59,* 60–67.

Stevens, S. S. (1975). *Psychophysics: Introduction to its perceptual, neural, and social prospects.* New York, NY: Wiley.

Stoianov, I., & Zorzi, M. (2012). Emergence of a "visual number sense" in hierarchical generative models. *Nature Neuroscience, 15,* 194–196.

Streri, A. (1987). Tactile discrimination of shape and intermodal transfer in 2- to 3-month-old infants. *British Journal of Developmental Psychology, 5,* 213–220.

Streri, A., & Pêcheux, M. G. (1986). Tactual habituation and discrimination of form in infancy: A comparison with vision. *Child Development, 57,* 100–104.

Takayama, Y., Sugishita, M., Akiguchi, I., & Kimura, J. (1994). Isolated acalculia due to left parietal lesion. *Archives of Neurology, 51,* 286–291.

Thiessen, E. D. (2011). Domain general constraints on statistical learning. *Child Development, 82,* 462–470.

Tillmann, B., Jolicœur, P., Ishihara, M., Gosselin, N., Bertrand, O., Rossetti, Y., et al. (2010). The amusic brain: Lost in music, but not in space. *PLoS ONE, 5*(4), e10173.

Tillmann, B., Schulze, K., & Foxton, J. M. (2009). Congenital amusia: A short-term memory deficit for non-verbal, but not verbal sounds. *Brain and Cognition, 71,* 259–264.

Tinbergen, N. (1963). On aims and methods of ethology. *Zeitschrift für Tierpsychologie, 20,* 410–433.

Tudusciuc, O., & Nieder, A. (2007). Neuronal population coding of continuous and discrete quantity in the primate posterior parietal cortex. *Proceedings of the National Academy of Sciences, 104*(36), 14513–14518.

van Dijck, J., & Fias, W. (2011). A working memory account for spatial–numerical associations. *Cognition, 119,* 114–119.

van Galen, M. S., & Reitsma, P. (2008). Developing access to number magnitude: A study of the SNARC effect in 7- to 9-year-olds. *Journal of Experimental Child Psychology, 101,* 99–113.

vanMarle, K., & Wynn, K. (2009). Infants' auditory enumeration: Evidence for analog magnitudes in the small number range. *Cognition, 111,* 302–316.

von Hornbostel, E. M. (1938). Selection 17: The unity of the senses (E. Koffka & W. Vinton, Trans.). In W. D. Ellis (Ed.), *A source book of Gestalt psychology* (pp. 210–216). New York, NY: Harcourt-Brace.

Wagner, K., & Dobkins, K. R. (2011). Synesthetic associations decrease during infancy. *Psychological Science, 22,* 1067–1072.

Wagner, S., Winner, E., Cicchetti, D., & Gardner, H. (1981). "Metaphorical" mapping in human infants. *Child Development, 52,* 728–731.

Walker, P., Bremner, J. G., Mason, U., Spring, J., Mattock, K., Slater, A., et al. (2009). Preverbal infants' sensitivity to synaesthetic cross-modal correspondences. *Psychological Science, 21*(1), 21–25.

Walsh, V. (2003). A theory of magnitude: Common cortical metrics of time, space, and quantity. *Trends in Cognitive Sciences, 7*(11), 483–488.

Werker, J. F., Polka, L., & Pegg, J. E. (1997). The conditioned head turn procedure as a method for testing infant speech perception. *Early Development and Parenting, 6,* 171–178.

Williamson, V. J., McDonald, C., Deutsch, D., Griffiths, T. D., & Stewart, L. (2010). Faster decline of pitch memory over time in congenital amusia. *Advances in Cognitive Psychology, 6,* 15–22.

Wilkie, D. M. (1987). Stimulus intensity affects pigeons' timing behavior: Implications for an internal clock model. *Animal Learning and Behavior, 15,* 35–39.

Xuan, B., Zhang, D., He, S., & Chen, X. (2007). Larger stimuli are judged to last longer. *Journal of Vision, 7,* 1–5.

Yang, Z., & Purves, D. (2004). The statistical structure of natural light patterns determines perceived light intensity. *Proceedings of the National Academy of Sciences, 101,* 8745–8750.

Yildirim, I., & Jacobs, R. A. (2012). A rational analysis of the acquisition of multisensory representations. *Cognitive Science, 36,* 305–332.

Yu, C., & Smith, L. B. (2011). What you learn is what you see: Using eye movements to study infant cross-situational word learning. *Developmental Science, 14,* 165–180.

Zorzi, M., Priftis, K., & Umiltà, C. (2002). Brain damage: Neglect disrupts the mental number line. *Nature, 417,* 138–139.

A critical review of the development of face recognition: Experience is less important than previously believed

Elinor McKone[1,3], Kate Crookes[2], Linda Jeffery[3,4], and Daniel D. Dilks[5]

[1]Department of Psychology, Australian National University, Canberra, ACT, Australia
[2]Department of Psychology, University of Hong Kong, Hong Kong, China
[3]ARC Centre of Excellence in Cognition and its Disorders, Australia
[4]School of Psychology, The University of Western Australia, Crawley, WA, Australia
[5]McGovern Institute for Brain Research, Massachusetts Institute of Technology, Cambridge, MA, USA

Historically, it has been argued that face individuation develops very slowly, not reaching adult levels until adolescence, with experience being the driving force behind this protracted improvement. Here, we challenge this view based on extensive review of behavioural and neural findings. Results demonstrate qualitative presence of all key phenomena related to face individuation (encoding of novel faces, holistic processing effects, face-space effects, face-selective responses in neuroimaging) at the earliest ages tested, typically 3–5 years of age and in many cases even infancy. Results further argue for quantitative maturity by early childhood, based on an increasing number of behavioural studies that have avoided the common methodological problem of restriction of range, as well as event-related potential (ERP), but not functional magnetic resonance imaging (fMRI) studies. We raise a new possibility that could account for the discrepant fMRI findings—namely, the use of adult-sized head coils on child-sized heads. We review genetic and innate contributions to face individuation (twin studies, neonates, visually deprived monkeys, critical periods, perceptual narrowing). We conclude that the role of experience in the development of the mechanisms of face identification has been overestimated. The emerging picture is that the mechanisms supporting face individuation are mature early, consistent with the social needs of children for reliable person identification in everyday life, and are also driven to an important extent by our evolutionary history.

Keywords: Face recognition; Development; Age of maturity; Behaviour; Functional magnetic resonance imaging; Event-related potential.

Adults can identify a specific individual face, distinguishing this person from hundreds of others despite wide variations in facial appearance that result from changes in viewpoint, lighting, emotional expression, and hairstyle. This typically requires a mere glance, belying the substantial computational

Correspondence should be addressed to Elinor McKone, Department of Psychology, Australian National University, Canberra, ACT 0200, Australia. (E-mail: Elinor.McKone@anu.edu.au).

Preparation of this article was supported by Australian Research Council Grants DP0984558 to E.M. and DP0770923 to L.J., plus salary funding for K.C. from Hong Kong Research Grants Council (HKU7440/08H, William Hayward), salary funding for L.J. from ARC Centre of Excellence Grant (CE110001021), and salary funding for D.D. from Ellison Medical Foundation (Nancy Kanwisher). We thank Laura Germine for her unpublished data referred to in Footnote 9.

http://www.psypress.com/cogneuropsychology http://dx.doi.org/10.1080/02643294.2012.660138

demands that must underlie the ability. The importance of face identification skills in everyday life is highlighted by the social difficulties encountered when these skills are compromised (e.g., in developmental prosopagnosia or autism spectrum disorder; Schultz, 2005; Yardley, McDermott, Pisarski, Duchaine, & Nakayama, 2008). Adult ability to individuate thousands of faces is supported by specialized perceptual processes, typically applied to faces but not other visual objects, and by specialized neural mechanisms including face-selective regions of cortex (McKone, Kanwisher, & Duchaine, 2007). How do these processes develop?

Traditionally, our exquisite face identification skills have been viewed primarily as the result of extensive experience during infancy, childhood, and adolescence, with adult-like abilities emerging relatively late in development. From the 1970s to the mid-1990s, an extreme version of this late maturity view was dominant (*encoding switch hypothesis*; Carey & Diamond, 1977), which proposed that specialized mechanisms of face perception were not even qualitatively present until 10 years of age, and that extended lifetime experience with faces was driving this slow development (Carey & Diamond, 1994). This was taken as consistent with claimed evidence that, with enough experience (e.g., 10 years) of making within-class discriminations, other object classes (e.g., dogs) could become "special" and processed like faces (Diamond & Carey, 1986; but see Brants, Wagemans, & Op de Beeck, 2011; Harel, Gilaie-Dotan, Malach, & Bentin, 2010; McKone, et al., 2007; Robbins & McKone, 2007). From the mid-1990s on, new evidence that many aspects of face processing were qualitatively present at younger ages forced a modification of the late maturity view, with theoreticians proposing only late quantitative maturity of a subset of aspects of face perception (Mondloch, Le Grand, & Maurer, 2002). However, the driver of this late maturity was still extended experience. Thus, over the past 35 years, it has been argued that adult-like face recognition does not reach full maturity until adolescence, and that the causal mechanism for this maturity was 10 or more years of practice.

In this review, we argue that modern evidence, and careful attention to methodological issues, supports a very different conclusion. We argue the data no longer support a theory in which the only face representation present at birth is a mere orienting device (Morton & Johnson, 1991), and that good discrimination of individual faces takes many years of practice to achieve. Rather, we argue that adult expertise results from face-specific perceptual mechanisms that require at most 5 or so years of face experience to become fully mature (and possibly less), and that it also has genetic and innate contributions.

Our review begins (see following section: "Children reach adult behavioural performance levels very late in development. Why?") by noting that performance on laboratory tests of face identification improves dramatically throughout childhood and into adolescence, and evaluating two theories of why adult performance is reached so late (*general cognitive development theory* and *face-specific perceptual development theory*). The second section ("A role for nature: Genetic contributions and innateness in face individuation") reviews the evidence of innateness (defined here as "present at birth") and of genetic determinants of face recognition ability. The third section ("What effects of experience are there?") describes situations in which experience does influence face recognition, including other-race effects.

We raise several core methodological and logical errors that frequently limit the conclusions that can be drawn from developmental studies of face recognition. These include a failure to make the logical distinction between laboratory *performance* and actual ability in everyday life (*competence*); the presence of restrictions of range (including floor or ceiling effects) that prevent valid quantitative comparisons across wide age ranges; and a general observation that task difficulty has a substantial impact on the age at which the task purports the ability to be "mature". We also raise a more subtle methodological issue affecting the neuroimaging literature—namely, the potential effects of using adult-sized head coils on children in functional magnetic resonance imaging (fMRI).

We conclude that the role of experience in the development of the mechanisms of face identification has been substantially overestimated. The emerging picture is that mechanisms supporting face recognition are mature early and are also driven to an important extent by our evolutionary history.

CHILDREN REACH ADULT BEHAVIOURAL PERFORMANCE LEVELS VERY LATE IN DEVELOPMENT. WHY?

We first describe, and assess theories of, the basic developmental course of face recognition. Perhaps the most striking aspect of typical development is the late age at which performance on face tasks reaches adult levels. Despite children having many years of social interaction—across infancy with caregivers, across childhood and into adolescence with a wide variety of friends, schoolmates, and teachers—performance on laboratory face recognition tasks does not reach adult levels until adolescence. This late performance maturity occurs on both memory (Carey, Diamond, & Woods, 1980; O'Hearn, Schroer, Minshew, & Luna, 2010) and discrimination tasks usually considered "perceptual" because they minimize memory demands (e.g., same–different decision; Mondloch et al., 2002).

Before we present our review, two general points are worth making. First, although the historical explanation of late performance maturity was that core perceptual processes did not emerge until quite late in development (10 years for "holistic processing"; Carey & Diamond, 1977; Carey et al., 1980), the early behavioural research supporting this idea has been clearly refuted. It is thus unfortunate that even quite recent articles, particularly in the neuroimaging literature, have sometimes emphasized only these few early findings (e.g., Aylward et al., 2005; Golarai et al., 2007; Scherf, Behrmann, Humphreys, & Luna, 2007; Scherf, Luna, Avidan, & Behrmann, 2011).

Second, researchers almost universally refer to developmental improvement in task *performance* as an improvement in children's face recognition "*abilities*". However, it is important to emphasize that these data are all from experimental laboratory tasks. The extent to which the age-related improvement in laboratory task performance reflects improvement in real face recognition abilities, as used in everyday life, is not known. Moreover, this can be very difficult to ascertain (see section entitled "Quantitative maturity: Is there any ongoing development of face perception mechanisms beyond early childhood?").

In the remainder of this section, we describe two theories of late performance development: (a) face-specific processing matures early and ongoing task improvement reflects development of general cognitive factors; and (b) face recognition itself continues to develop late, via development of face-specific perceptual mechanisms observed in adults. We then evaluate these theories with respect to, first, the age at which face mechanisms emerge *qualitatively* (i.e., the youngest age group in which a given mechanism is present) and, second, the age at which they become mature *quantitatively* (i.e., the youngest age at which they operate at adult levels of efficiency).

The explanations

General cognitive development theory

This theory (Carey, 1981; Crookes & McKone, 2009; Gilchrist & McKone, 2003; McKone & Boyer, 2006; Mondloch, Maurer, & Ahola, 2006; Pellicano, Rhodes, & Peters, 2006; Want, Pascalis, Coleman, & Blades, 2003) proposes that perceptual coding of faces is fully mature early in development, and all subsequent development on experimental task performance results from development of other general factors. While the theory does not state an exact age that perceptual face coding reaches maturity, 5 years has been suggested as a maximum. The specific general factors that produce later task improvement are presumed to depend on the task and can include: ability to concentrate on the task and avoid distractions; ability to narrow the focus of visual attention to small stimuli; ability to use deliberate task strategies; metacognition (e.g., ability to know when one has successfully learned); and general perceptual development (e.g., vernier acuity as relevant to judging distances between facial features).

All these abilities develop substantially across childhood, and most improve further into adolescence (Betts, Mckay, Maruff, & Anderson, 2006; Bjorklund & Douglas, 1997; Davidson, Amso, Anderson, & Diamond, 2006; Flavell, 1985; Flavell & Wellman, 1977; Pastò & Burack, 1997; Skoczenski & Norcia, 2002). Further, all have clear potential to contribute to face task performance. To illustrate, children may fail to attend to the task on some trials due to high distractibility, which is difficult to avoid even in the most child-friendly designs. Consequently, children's accuracy will be pushed towards chance, and reaction times will be increased, even if their underlying face recognition skills were equal to those of adults. Thus, the debate between general cognitive development theory and face-specific perceptual development theory (discussed next) is not whether general cognitive development contributes to development in performance on laboratory face tasks but whether, once general cognitive factors are accounted for, there is any development in face perception per se.

Face-specific perceptual development theory

This theory (e.g., Carey & Diamond, 1977; Carey et al., 1980; de Heering, Rossion, & Maurer, 2012; Golarai et al., 2007; Mondloch et al., 2002; Scherf et al., 2011) acknowledges that infants show some early proficiency with faces, but argues that face task performance reaches adult levels late because (a) face perception mechanisms themselves continue to develop into late childhood and adolescence, and (b) the cause of this development is ongoing experience with faces. These ongoing improvements in face processing are presumed to contribute directly to improvements on face perception tasks (e.g., sequential face discrimination) and also to affect face memory (e.g., by allowing more robust encoding of novel faces, or more precise comparisons to distractors at retrieval). Researchers have raised four specific proposals about exactly what perceptual mechanisms might be developing. These are: ability to perceptually encode novel faces; holistic/configural processing; face-space coding; and specialized neural mechanisms for faces as seen in adults. We describe each of these ideas in more detail in the following review of the development of these mechanisms.

Predictions of the general and face-specific explanations

The general cognitive development theory predicts that all key aspects of face recognition should be both qualitatively present and quantitatively mature early in childhood. In contrast, the face-specific perceptual development theory would be supported if either qualitative or quantitative development of face mechanisms was observed. We begin by considering qualitative development.

Qualitative maturity: Presence of key face-coding mechanisms early in development

In strong contrast to the early (1970s to mid-1990s) view that children under age 10 did not possess basic face mechanisms, more than 25 years of research has now tested essentially every key property of adult face recognition and has established that each is present at the youngest age tested, including even infants where investigated. Where early studies did not show an effect in a particular age group, subsequent studies have established that the failure to detect the effect resulted from methodological problems, the most common being floor effects in young children (e.g., for holistic processing assessed via the inversion effect, see Carey et al., 1980 vs. Carey, 1981; or for distinctiveness effects in face-space, see R. A. Johnston & Ellis, 1995 vs. Gilchrist & McKone, 2003). Table 1 summarizes the key findings (references follow in the review). Infant findings come from looking-time measures. Results for children 3 years and older come from studies testing children on the same tasks as adults, sometimes adapted slightly to reduce overall difficulty and avoid floor effects in the youngest age groups (e.g., children learn faces in smaller sets).

Table 1. *Core face recognition effects qualitatively present early in development*

	Newborns	Later infancy	3 years	4 years	5 years	6 years	7 years	8 years	9 years +
Basics - encoding of novel faces									
Discrimination of individual faces	☺	☺	☺	☺	☺	☺	☺	☺	☺
Recognition across view change	☺	☺				☺		☺	☺
Recognition despite paraphernalia (hats, etc)			?				☺		☺
Holistic/configural properties									
Inversion effect on discrimination	☺	☺	☺	☺	☺	☺	☺	☺	☺
Disproportionate inversion effect (faces > objects)			☺	☺	☺		☺		☺
Composite effect	?	☺	☺	☺	☺	☺		☺	☺
Composite effect faces not objects			☺	☺	☺				
Composite effect, upright not inverted		☺				☺			☺
Part-whole effect, upright not inverted				☺	☺	☺	☺	☺	☺
Part-in-spacing-altered-whole effect, upright not inverted				☺	☺				
Sensitivity to spacing changes		☺	☺	☺	☺	☺	☺	☺	☺
Inversion effect on spacing sensitivity		☺		☺	☺	☺	☺	☺	☺
Thatcher illusion, upright not inverted	☺					☺	☺	☺	☺
Perceptual bias to upright in superimposed faces						☺	☺	☺	☺
Internal-over-external features advantage in familiar faces				☺	☺	☺	☺	☺	☺
Face-space properties									
Distinctiveness effects		☺		☺	☺	☺	☺	☺	☺
Atypicality bias			☺	☺	☺	☺	☺	☺	☺
Face-space dimensions (e.g., multidimensional scaling)				☺			☺	☺	☺
Adaptation aftereffects (figural)				☺	☺	☺	☺	☺	☺
Adaptation aftereffects (identity)					☺	☺	☺	☺	☺
Norm-based adaptation aftereffects				☺	☺		☺	☺	☺
Attractiveness effects	☺	☺	☺	☺	☺	☺	☺	☺	☺
Other race effects		☺	☺	☺	☺	☺	☺	☺	☺
Neural Properties									
Fusiform Face Area				☺	☺	☺	☺	☺	☺
N170 (or precursor in infants)		☺		☺	☺	☺	☺	☺	☺
Right hemisphere advantage		☺		☺	☺	☺	☺	☺	☺
Inversion modulates neural response		☺			☺	☺	☺	☺	☺
Face-selective cells, macaques		☺							

Note: A very wide range of core face recognition effects are present early in development. ☺ =phenomenon tested and found to be present; grey cell=not yet tested in children or babies this young; white cell=not specifically tested at this age but can be assumed to be present given presence at younger age; ?=a study has tested this, but results unclear as to whether phenomenon is present or not. Note that we have not included viewpoint tuning, which appears to undergo qualitative change in infancy at approximately 7 months (see section entitled "Coding of profile views"). The section, "Qualitative maturity: Presence of key face-coding mechanisms early in development" gives references for each result and description of tasks. "Later infancy" generally means 3 to 12 months; exact ages given in the first section.

Basic ability to encode novel faces

As a source of face-specific perceptual development, late development in ability to encode novel faces was proposed by Carey (1992, p. 95): "young children do not form representations of newly encountered faces as efficiently as do adults". A more modern variant is that children may have specific difficulty in encoding faces in a manner that allows generalization of recognition across viewpoint change (Mondloch, Geldart, Maurer, & Le Grand, 2003).

The evidence clearly indicates that the ability to encode novel faces is present very early in life, including cross-view recognition. Key findings are:

Discrimination of individual faces. Ability to discriminate similar faces (same age, sex, race, either without hair[1] or all with similar hair) above chance has been demonstrated using habituation-then-novelty-preference paradigms in newborns (Pascalis & de Schonen, 1994; Turati, Bulf, & Simion, 2008; Turati, Macchi Cassia, Simion, & Leo, 2006) and in older infants (e.g., 3, 6, 9 m.o.,[2] Kelly et al., 2009; Kelly et al., 2007; Pascalis, de Haan, Nelson, & de Schonen, 1998). In children, face discrimination has been demonstrated following a single learning trial in sequential matching (e.g., 3 y.o., Sangrigoli & de Schonen, 2004a), memory (e.g., 4 y.o., Carey, 1981), and implicit memory (repetition priming, 5–6 y.o., Crookes & McKone, 2009).

Recognition across view change. Recognition of a face learned in a single image generalizes to another view in newborns (between front and three-quarter, although not three-quarter and profile; Turati et al., 2008) and in older infants (3, 6, 9 m.o., Kelly et al., 2009; Kelly et al., 2007; 4 m.o., Turati, Sangrigoli, Ruel, & de Schonen, 2004; 3, 6 m.o., Pascalis et al., 1998). In children, above-chance cross-view recognition occurs in simultaneous and sequential matching (6, 8, 10 y.o., Mondloch et al., 2003; 7, 8–12, 12–15 y.o., P. J. Johnston et al., 2011), and memory (9–12 y.o., O'Hearn et al., 2010).

Recognition despite paraphernalia. Early claims suggested that children could not recognize face identity in the presence of distracting paraphernalia (hats, etc.; Carey & Diamond, 1977). However, simply making the faces larger revealed this ability (7, 10 y.o., Lundy, Jackson, & Haaf, 2001; plus similar nonsignificant trend in 3 y.o., marked as "?" in Table 1).

Holistic processing

Development in holistic/configural processing (henceforth referred to as holistic processing) has been heavily investigated as a potential source of face-specific perceptual development. In adults, the exact nature of holistic processing is not fully understood, but it is widely agreed (e.g., Maurer Le Grand, Mondloch, 2002; McKone & Yovel, 2009; Rossion, 2008) to (a) include strong perceptual integration of information across the whole face, (b) include processing of the "second-order" ways in which a face deviates from the basic shared first-order configuration found in all faces (i.e., two eyes, above nose, above mouth), and (c) be strongly sensitive to face orientation, with holistic processing present for upright faces but largely absent for inverted faces. One theory proposes that the key aspect of "second-order" information is exact spacing between face features (e.g., nose–mouth distance) and that spacing coding is a separate subcomponent from perceptual integration (Maurer et al., 2002); another proposes a single holistic representation of all facial information including both spacing information and second-order information about exact shape of local features (e.g., eye shape, nose size, etc.; McKone & Yovel, 2009; Tanaka & Farah, 1993; Yovel & Duchaine, 2006).

The classic theory that holistic processing did not emerge until age 10 (Carey et al., 1980) has been rejected by the evidence. There is no support for the old view that children use a feature-based method for recognizing faces. Rather, there is substantial evidence of early presence of all aspects of holistic coding (including second-order relations). Moreover, like adults', children's holistic processing disappears with face inversion. Findings are:

Inversion effect on discrimination. In adults, ability to discriminate similar faces is reduced when they are turned upside down (e.g., Yin, 1969). Although inversion effects on face recognition are not directly

[1] Many studies exclude hair because it is a simple cue that can be used to recognize photographs without requiring face processing (e.g., prosopagnosics use hair cues in experiments even when they cannot recognize people in real life; Duchaine & Nakayama, 2006).

[2] Where a study tested separate age groups and found a clear effect present in each, we list all ages separately (e.g., "3, 6, 9" m.o.); where a study showed an effect in a combined age group but did not split by exact age, we indicate the age range of the group (e.g., "3–6" y.o.). Note, m.o. = month old; y.o. = year old.

diagnostic of holistic processing (because processing style is not directly measured in either orientation), a lack of inversion effect in development could reasonably be taken as evidence of a lack of holistic processing. However, orientation sensitivity is present throughout development. Babies discriminate faces upright but fail to discriminate the same stimuli inverted (newborns, Turati et al., 2006; 5–6 m.o., Fagan, 1972; across view change, 4 m.o., Turati et al., 2004). In children, discrimination is better upright than inverted in both short- and long-term memory tasks (3 y.o., Sangrigoli & de Schonen, 2004a; 3 y.o., Macchi Cassia, Kuefner, Picozzi, & Vescovo, 2009; 4, 5, 6, 10 y.o., Carey, 1981; 5–6 y.o., Brace et al., 2001; 7 y.o., Flin, 1985; 7 y.o., Crookes & McKone, 2009).

Disporportionate inversion effect (faces > objects). In adults, the inversion effect for faces is usually substantially larger than that for within-class discrimination of objects (for review, see McKone et al., 2007). In children, this pattern occurs in sequential discrimination (shoes, 3–4 and 5 y.o., cars, 3–4 y.o. in males only and in all 5 y.o., Picozzi, Macchi Cassia, Turati, & Vescovo, 2009; shoes 9–10 y.o., Teunisse & de Gelder, 2003) and long-term memory (labradors, 7 y.o., Crookes & McKone, 2009; houses, 10 y.o., Carey & Diamond, 1977).

The composite effect. We now turn to more direct measures of holistic processing, specifically the "perceptual integration" aspect for those favouring a subcomponents view. In adults, combining the top half of one individual (e.g., Barack Obama) with the bottom half of another (e.g., Will Smith) creates the percept of a new person. For famous faces, this results in longer naming times for a target half (e.g., top) when the halves are aligned than in a control misaligned condition (e.g., Young, Hellawell, & Hay, 1987). For novel faces, the composite effect is demonstrated by reduced accuracy in perceiving that two identical top halves, combined with different bottom halves, are the *same* when aligned as when misaligned (e.g., Le Grand, Mondloch, Maurer, & Brent, 2004).

In children, the composite effect occurs on both the naming and the same–different versions (unfamiliar faces 4, 5, 6 y.o., de Heering, Houthuys, & Rossion, 2007; 6 y.o., Mondloch, Pathman, Maurer, Le Grand, & de Schonen, 2007; 8–13 y.o., Susilo, Crookes, McKone, & Turner, 2009; and familiar faces 6, 10 y.o, Carey & Diamond, 1994), as well as in a variant using a two-alternative forced-choice (2AFC) response (3, 4, 5 y.o., Macchi Cassia, Picozzi, Kuefner, Bricolo, & Turati, 2009). Infants also show a composite effect for top–bottom combinations (3 m.o., Turati, Di Giorgio, Bardi, & Simion, 2010; newborn results were ambiguous, hence the "?" in Table 1) and for inner–outer feature combinations (inner features of one old face combined with outer features of another old face is treated as a novel individual, 6–8 m.o., Cohen & Cashon, 2001).

Composite effect for faces not objects. In adults, the composite effect is present for faces but not other objects (e.g., dogs, Robbins & McKone, 2007). Children show this adult-like pattern (effect for faces but not cars: 3, 4, 5 y.o., Macchi Cassia, Picozzi, et al., 2009).

Composite effect, upright but not inverted. In adults, the composite effect is found for upright faces but is absent or greatly reduced for inverted faces (e.g., Robbins & McKone, 2003; Young et al., 1987). This same pattern is found in children (6, 10 y.o., Carey & Diamond, 1994), and infants (6–8 m.o., Cohen & Cashon, 2001; Ferguson, Kulkofsky, Cashon, & Casasola, 2009).

Part–whole effect, upright not inverted. The part–whole effect is also commonly taken as a reasonably direct measure of holistic integration. In the part–whole effect, memory for a face part (e.g., Bill's nose) is poorer in isolation (Bill's nose versus John's nose) than in the context of the original whole face (Bill's nose in Bill's face versus John's nose in Bill's face). Children show the adult-like pattern (Tanaka & Farah, 1993) of a whole-over-part advantage for upright but not inverted faces (4, 5 y.o., Pellicano & Rhodes, 2003; 6, 8, 10 y.o., Tanaka, Kay, Grinnell, Stansfield, & Szechter, 1998).

Part-in-spacing-altered-whole effect, upright not inverted. In this variant, memory for a face part (Bill's nose) is poorer in a spacing-altered version of the face (Bill's nose in Bill's face with the eyes shifted further apart) than in the original unaltered face. Like adults (Tanaka & Sengco, 1997), children show this effect for upright but not inverted faces (4, 5 y.o., Pellicano et al., 2006).

Sensitivity to spacing changes and inversion effect on spacing sensitivity. Changes in spacing between facial features are detected by children (3, 4 y.o., Macchi Cassia, Turati, & Schwarzer, 2011; 4 y.o., McKone & Boyer, 2006; 4, 5 y.o., Pellicano et al., 2006; 4 y.o., Mondloch & Thomson, 2008; 6, 8, 10 y.o., Mondloch et al., 2002; 6–7 y.o., Gilchrist & McKone, 2003; 8 y.o., Mondloch et al., 2006; 6–8, 8–10, 10–12 y.o., Baudouin, Gallay, Durand, & Robichon, 2010) and by infants (5 m.o., Hayden, Bhatt, Reed, Corbly, & Joseph, 2007). Inversion disrupts this performance (most of the same studies, youngest ages: 4, 5 y.o., Pellicano et al., 2006; and 5 m.o., Hayden et al., 2007).

Thatcher illusion, upright not inverted. In adults, flipping the orientation of eyes and mouth relative to the rest of the face leads to a percept of a bizarre face upright but not inverted (P. Thompson, 1980), an illusion taken as evidence of holistic processing. The illusion, and its orientation sensitivity, is found in children (6–10 y.o., Lewis 2003; 6, 7, 8, 10 y.o., Donnelly & Hadwin, 2003) and newborns (Leo & Simion, 2009).

Perceptual bias to upright in superimposed faces. Like adults (Martini, McKone, & Nakayama, 2006), children perceive an upright face more strongly than an inverted face when the two are overlaid in transparency (6–10 y.o., Donnelly, Hadwin, Cave, & Stevenage, 2003).

Internal-over-external features advantage in familiar faces. Adults' memory for familiar faces relies more on internal features than on external features such as hairstyle (Ellis, Shepherd, & Davies, 1979), a result sometimes attributed to holistic processing. This same pattern occurs in children (4, 8, 14 y.o., Ge et al., 2008; 5–6, 7–8, 10–11 y.o., Wilson, Blades, & Pascalis, 2007).

Face-space coding

Given the clear evidence of early presence of holistic processing, recent interest has increased in *face-space* coding as a possible source of face-specific perceptual development. Face-space is a multidimensional perceptual space with the following properties: Dimensions code physical attributes that are useful in differentiating faces; each individual face is a point; the centre is the average face; and distinctive faces lie further away from the centre, while typical faces lie closer to the average (e.g., Valentine, 1991). The face-space concept has been valuable in explaining a range of phenomena (see below) not accounted for by holistic processing. Regarding development, a key assumption of standard face-space theories is that the dimensions of face-space arise through experience and that tuning continues throughout life (e.g., Goldstein & Chance, 1980; R. A. Johnston & Ellis, 1995; Valentine, 1991). Theoretically, it has been proposed that children's face-space could use fewer dimensions than that of adults, or the same dimensions but differently weighted, or could use exemplar-based coding (absolute values on dimensions) rather than norm-based coding (deviation vector from average), or could have weaker ability to update the norm of face-space based on recent experience, or could code discriminations along each dimension less finely; finally, it has been proposed that occupation of children's face-space by fewer exemplars might functionally affect face perception (Chung & Thomson, 1995; Hills, Holland, & Lewis, 2010; Humphreys & Johnson, 2007; Jeffery et al., 2011; R. A. Johnston & Ellis, 1995; Nishimura, Maurer, Jeffery, Pellicano, & Rhodes, 2008).

Again, the evidence regarding face-space coding does not indicate any qualitative development with age. That is, results show the presence of all adult phenomena at the youngest age tested. Findings are:

Distinctiveness effects. Face-space coding predicts better memory for distinctive than typical faces (due to lower exemplar density further from the average and thus fewer confusable neighbours), but faster classification as a face for typical faces (due to closeness to average). Children show both these effects: memory advantage for distinctive faces (6–7 years, Gilchrist & McKone, 2003; 9, 11, 13 y.o., R. A. Johnston & Ellis, 1995); face classification advantage for typical faces (5, 7, 9, 11, 13 y.o., R. A. Johnston & Ellis, 1995). Children also appear to perceive distinctiveness in a similar way to adults: They can, above chance, choose the more distinctive face in a pair defined by *adult* distinctiveness ratings (4 y.o., McKone & Boyer, 2006). Distinctiveness can also be varied by *caricaturing* a face (exaggerating the way it deviates from the average, i.e., increasing the "identity strength") and anticaricaturing (reducing identity strength by morphing the face towards the average). Children judge caricatures as more distinctive than anticaricatures (6, 8, 10 y.o., Chang, Levine, & Benson, 2002). Children, like adults, are also quicker to name caricatured versions of previously learned faces than the original face or anticaricatured versions (6, 8, 10, y.o., Chang et al., 2002). Infants also distinguish caricatures and anticaricatures, with longer longest looks to the former (6 m.o., Rhodes, Geddes, Jeffery, Dziurawiec, & Clark, 2002), and distinguish average from nonaverage face length (with average preferred; 6–7 m.o., L. A. Thompson, Madrid, Westbrook, & Johnston, 2001).

Atypicality bias. Like adults, children perceive a 50/50 morph between a typical and a distinctive face as more strongly resembling the distinctive (atypical) "parent" (3–4, 5–6, 7–8, 9–10, 11–12 y.o., Tanaka, Meixner, & Kantner, 2011).

Face-space dimensions (e.g., multidimensional scaling, MDS). Multidimensional scaling on similarity ratings can be used to calculate the structure of the underlying perceptual face-space. MDS reveals a face-space in children similar to that of adults: Typical faces fall closer to the centre than more distinctive faces; the number of dimensions in the solutions is the same; and dimensions code similar facial attributes (e.g., nose–mouth distance, face width; 7–8, 9–10, 11–13 y.o., Pedelty, Levine, & Shevell, 1985; 8 y.o., Nishimura, Maurer, & Gao, 2009). Consistent with use of adult-like dimensions, children, like adults, choose the most distinctive of two faces when these differ only in spacing between features, or only in local features (4 y.o., McKone & Boyer, 2006).

Adaptation after-effects (figural). Face after-effects are typically explained as a shift in the perceived average of face-space to reflect the types of faces to which one has been exposed. In adults, "figural" after-effects occur with adaptation to consistent distortions of face structure: Adapting to a face with high eyes makes eyes appear low in a normal face (Robbins, McKone, & Edwards, 2007), or adapting to a centre-contracted face makes a normal face appear expanded (Rhodes, Jeffery, Watson, Clifford, & Nakayama, 2003). Such after-effects occur in children (expansion, 4–6 y.o., and eye height, 4–5 y.o., Jeffery et al., 2010; expansion, 5, 8 y.o., Short, Hatry, & Mondloch, 2011; expansion, 8 y.o, Anzures, Mondloch, & Lackner, 2009; eye height, 6–12 y.o., Hills et al., 2010). As in adults, the after-effects survive change in stimulus size between adaptor and test, discounting a low-level vision explanation (4–5 y.o., Jeffery et al., 2010).

Adaptation after-effects (identity). In the identity after-effect, adaptation to one individual (e.g., Dan) makes the average face appear like its opposite in face-space (i.e., "anti-Dan", an individual with all facial attributes opposite to those of Dan), while adaptation to another individual (e.g., Jim) shifts the perceived average towards that face's opposite (anti-Jim). Like adults (Leopold, O'Toole, Vetter, & Blanz, 2001), children demonstrate identity after-effects (5, 6, 7, 8–9 y.o., Jeffery et al., 2011; 8 y.o., Nishimura et al., 2008; 8 y.o., Pimperton, Pellicano, Jeffery, & Rhodes, 2009; 8–14 y.o., Pellicano, Jeffery, Burr, & Rhodes, 2007), including with size-changes (8 y.o., Pimperton et al., 2009; 7 y.o., Jeffery et al., 2011).

Norm-based adaptation after-effects. In adults, two after-effect patterns have been used to argue that face-space uses norm-based coding (each individual coded as a deviation from the average) rather than exemplar-based coding (each individual coded via their absolute value on each face dimension without reference to an average; Rhodes & Jeffery, 2006; Robbins, McKone, & Edwards, 2007). Both norm-based patterns are shown by children. After-effects are larger from adaptors far from the average than from adaptors closer to the average (eye height, 4–5 y.o, Jeffery et al., 2010; identity, 7 y.o., Jeffery et al., 2011). And, after-effects are larger from adaptors falling along the face-space trajectory running from the target through the centre ("opposites", e.g., anti-Dan for Dan) than from adaptors lying off this trajectory ("nonopposites", e.g., anti-Jim for Dan; 8 y.o., Nishimura et al., 2008).[3]

Attractiveness effects. Like adults, children rate faces closer to the average (centre of face-space) as more attractive than faces further from the average (11, 14 y.o., Saxton, Debruine, Jones, Little, & Roberts, 2009). Like adults (Rhodes, Jeffery, Watson, Clifford, & Nakayama, 2003), in adaptation studies children rate an unaltered face structure as most attractive prior to adaptation, and the most attractive stimulus shifts towards the new perceived average after adaptation (8 y.o., Anzures et al., 2009; 5, 8 y.o., Short et al., 2011). Individuals of all ages also prefer, or rate as most attractive, faces with the height of the internal feature block experienced most often by their age group (i.e., high for infants, low for young children, normal from puberty when children's faces take on adult proportions; 5 m.o., Geldart, Maurer, & Henderson, 1999; 3, 4, 9, 12 y.o., Cooper, Geldart, Mondloch, & Maurer, 2006), again suggesting ability to update a face-space average that in turn drives perceived attractiveness.

In other attractiveness effects, newborns show attractiveness preference in natural faces, driven by internal features of the face, and occurring for upright not inverted faces (Slater, Bremner, et al., 2000; Slater, Quinn, Hayes, & Brown, 2000).

Other-race effect (ORE). Adults discriminate other-race faces more poorly than own-race faces, a result often explained as tight clustering of other-race faces in face-space (Valentine, 1991). This ORE is present in children (3, 4, & 5 y.o., Sangrigoli & de Schonen, 2004a; 5–6 & 8–9 y.o., Pezdek, Blandon-Gitlin, & Moore, 2003; 6–14 y.o., de Heering, de Liedekerke, Deboni, & Rossion, 2010) and in infants aged 6 months and older (Kelly et al., 2009; Kelly et al., 2007). It has been reported in 3 m.o. but at this age was abolished with a small amount of exposure to other-race faces (Sangrigoli & de Schonen, 2004b). Adults also show *race-contingent after-effects*: Adaptation can cause observers to simultaneously perceive normal Caucasian faces as expanded and normal Asian faces as contracted (Jaquet, Rhodes, & Hayward, 2007). This indicates partially distinct neural coding of different race faces. The same effect occurs in children (5, 8 y.o., Short et al., 2011).[4]

Specialized neural mechanisms for faces

So far, we have demonstrated early qualitative presence of three key face attributes: ability to encode novel faces, holistic processing, and face-space. The fourth possible source of face-specific perceptual development is the face-selective neural mechanisms found in adults. Note that our interest here is in cortical-level mechanisms because the topic of our review is children's face individuation skills (for review of subcortical mechanisms proposed to support orientation to faces in early infancy, see Johnson, 2005). Results for children and babies support early qualitative presence of adult-like neural mechanisms.

The fusiform face area (FFA). In adults, the FFA in the midfusiform gyrus responds 2–3 times more strongly to faces than to within-class

[3] This result holds when the opposite and nonopposite adaptors are equally dissimilar from the target and when the test trajectory for nonopposite adaptors is between nonopposite-and-target rather than opposite-and-target (8–9 y.o., Jeffery et al., 2011).

[4] Although note that contingency in 5-year-olds was driven by adaptation only to one of the races.

discrimination of objects (houses, hands, flowers, cars, birds; e.g., Grill-Spector, Knouf, & Kanwisher, 2004; Kanwisher, McDermott, & Chun, 1997). It has been the primary focus in child fMRI research because it is reliably identified in almost all adults.

Results for ages 10 and up are clear-cut. Like adults, both adolescents and preadolescents show an FFA (8–11 y.o., Passarotti, Smith, DeLano, & Huang, 2007; 9.8–12 y.o., Joseph, Gathers, & Bhatt, 2011; 10–12 y.o., Passarotti et al., 2003; 11–14 y.o., Scherf et al., 2007; 11–14 y.o., Scherf et al., 2011; 12–14 y.o., Aylward et al., 2005; 12–16 y.o., Golarai et al., 2007; 7–17 y.o., Peelen, Glaser, Vuilleumier, & Eliez, 2009). This is found even with quite small sample sizes (e.g., 10 in three of the eight cited studies) and with group-defined FFAs (Aylward et al., 2005; Joseph et al., 2011; Passarotti et al., 2003; Passarotti et al., 2007), which are less sensitive than individual-defined regions of interest (ROIs; because a region can be missed when averaging over individuals with different exact anatomical locations).

Results in younger children vary, but overall make a strong case for presence of an FFA at the earliest ages tested when the more powerful designs are used. Using group-defined ROIs and only small sample sizes, the first studies did not report an FFA (8–10 y.o. with 8, Aylward et al., 2005; 5–8 y.o. with 10, Scherf et al., 2007). However, with power improved by using either individually defined ROIs or group designs with larger sample size (thereby making group analyses less affected by individual differences in anatomical location), all recent studies have identified an FFA in mid childhood (7–11 y.o. 20, Golarai et al., 2007; 7–11 y.o. 22, Pelphrey, Lopez, & Morris, 2009; 5–9.7 y.o. 23, Joseph et al., 2011) and even earlier where tested (4–5.8 y.o. 15, Cantlon, Pinel, Dehaene, & Pelphrey, 2011; 5–8 y.o. 10, individual ROI, Scherf et al., 2007).

The N170. The adult N170 is a face-selective event-related potential (ERP) peak over occipito-temporal sensors, usually maximal on channels T5 (left hemisphere) and T6 (right hemisphere). The peak is larger for faces than for within-class discrimination of objects. Its neural source probably includes the FFA, but also area STS (superior temporal sulcus), thought to be involved in processing the dynamic aspects of faces (e.g., gaze, expression) rather than identity (Dalrymple et al., 2011; Itier & Taylor, 2004; Sadeh, Podlipsky, Zhdanov, & Yovel, 2010).

The N170 occurs in children (4 to 14 y.o., Taylor, McCarthy, Saliba, & Degiovanni, 1999, 1999; 4 to 15 y.o., Taylor, Edmonds, McCarthy, & Allison, 2001; 4 to 10 y.o., Henderson, McCulloch, & Herbert, 2003), even when the N170 is identified in individual participants to avoid conflating it with the later N250 component (4–6 y.o., 6–8 y.o., 8–10 y.o., and older age groups, Kuefner, de Heering, Jacques, Palmero-Soler, & Rossion, 2010). In infants, N170 precursors (N290 and P400) are present and are stronger for human than for monkey faces (3 m.o., Halit, de Haan, & Johnson, 2003; 6 m.o., de Haan, Johnson, & Halit, 2003).

Right hemisphere advantage. In adults, right-handers' recognition of facial identity is more accurate following brief presentation to the left visual field, LVF (right hemisphere) than to the right visual field, RVF (left hemisphere; e.g., Ellis & Shepherd, 1975), the FFA is usually larger in the right hemisphere (rFFA) than the left (lFFA; e.g., Kanwisher et al., 1997), and the face-selective N170 is also strongest over the right hemisphere (e.g., Bentin, Allison, Puce, Perez, & McCarthy, 1996).

The same right hemisphere dominance is found in development. A LVF advantage occurs for face identification in children (5, 7, 11 y.o., Young & Ellis, 1976; 7–9 y.o, Marcel & Rajan, 1975; 7, 10, 13 y.o., Young & Bion, 1980; all participants right-handed) and infants (4–10 m.o., de Schonen & Mathivet, 1990), and also for perceiving the Thatcher illusion (right-handed, 8–10 & 11–13 y.o., Anes & Short, 2009). In fMRI, right hemisphere dominance is also observed (i.e., rFFA larger than lFFA; 7–11 y.o., Pelphrey et al., 2009; 10–12 y.o., Passarotti et al., 2003; 11–14 y.o., Scherf et al., 2007; note, we evaluated only studies that reported at least 90% right-handers). In ERP, right hemisphere dominance for the face-selective N170 is present from early childhood (all age groups 4 y.o. and up, 92% right-handed, Kuefner et al., 2010), and the infant precursor N290 shows a different magnitude to human and monkey faces only in the right hemisphere (3 m.o., Halit et al., 2003). In infant near-infrared spectroscopy (NIRS), response is stronger for upright faces than for control objects (vegetables) in the right hemisphere, but not in the left (5–8 m.o., Otsuka et al., 2007).

Inversion modulates neural response. Differential neural response to upright and inverted faces occurs in adults. It also occurs in development, although the direction of the effect does not always remain stable across age. In fMRI, the adult pattern is a higher response to upright than to inverted faces in the FFA (Yovel & Kanwisher, 2005; but see Haxby et al., 1999), but the opposite direction has been found in children (8–11 y.o., Passarotti et al., 2007). In ERPs, the adult pattern is a larger N170 for inverted than for upright faces (e.g., Bentin et al., 1996): The infant precursor N290 shows this direction (3 m.o., Johnson et al., 2005; see also Halit et al., 2003), but children aged 4–9 years show the other direction (larger N170 upright than inverted, Taylor, Batty, & Itier, 2004). In babies, the face-selective NIRS response (faces > objects) is significantly larger for upright than for inverted faces (5–8 m.o., Otsuka et al., 2007).

Face-selective cells in monkeys. Adult macaques show strong face-selective responses from temporal lobe neurons ("face cells"), which cluster into face-selective patches visible with fMRI (Tsao et al., 2006). In infant macaques, face selectivity of single units is present at the youngest ages tested (<2 m.o., Rodman, Scalaidhe, & Gross, 1993).

Individuation in fMRI. One study has tested whether children's FFA, like adults', shows discrimination of individual faces. Scherf et al. (2011) used fMR-adaptation, looking for greater blood-oxygen-level-dependent (BOLD) contrast to blocks of different-identity faces than to blocks of the same repeated face image. Results showed discrimination in the FFA in adolescents (11–14 y.o.; specifically lFFA, but note that handedness was not reported). This was not found in 6–10 y.o., but this conclusion is questionable for reasons outlined later (see section "Evidence arguing fMRI conclusions in children younger than 10 years can sometimes be wrong, even when studies meet current 'best practice'").

Coding of profile views

We have separated out profile face views because this is the only situation where converging evidence indicates a qualitative change with age. This occurs during infancy (not childhood). Adults can recognize faces in any viewpoint, although they are slower for profiles than for front or three-quarter view (McKone, 2008). In human babies, coding of profiles has not been observed in early to mid infancy. Young babies discriminate identity in front- and three-quarter-view faces (e.g., newborns, Turati et al., 2006; 3 m.o., Kelly et al., 2009) but do not discriminate profiles (5 m.o., Fagan, 1979). Older babies do discriminate profiles (7 m.o., Fagan, 1976, Fagan, 1979). In converging evidence, face-selective neural response with NIRS (face > objects) is found for front-view faces but not profiles at 5 m.o., while older babies do show face-selective response for profiles (8 m.o., Nakato et al., 2009). Regarding generalization across views, recognition of faces in profile that were previously learned in front or three-quarter view is not found in newborns (Turati et al., 2008), it is established in 12 m.o. (Rose, Jankowski, & Feldman, 2002), and there is contradictory evidence regarding 7 m.o. (present, Fagan 1976; absent, Rose et al., 2002). Overall, these results argue for: a lack of profile coding at 5 months; followed by coding sufficient to support within-profile discrimination by 7–8 months; and extension to support generalization across views by 12 months, or perhaps earlier.

Summary of qualitative presence

In summary, there is broad agreement across studies that adult mechanisms of face perception are qualitatively present early in development (Table 1). In behavioural studies, this includes phenomena associated with all aspects of holistic processing (including sensitivity to "second-order relations" defined as spacing between face features), all aspects of basic individuation (for front and three-quarter views), and all aspects of face-space coding. Indeed, research over the last 20 years has gradually pushed back the age at which all these phenomena have been observed and has now reached children of 3–4 years, in most cases, and infancy where tested. In neural studies, results are slightly more variable but are overall consistent with the conclusion: The FFA and N170 are present early; a right hemisphere advantage is present early; face-selective cells are present early; and the only partially discrepant result is that neural inversion effects, while present early, sometimes appear in the opposite direction from those in adults. The only replicated qualitative change that our review revealed is a lack of coding of faces in profile view in early infancy that emerges in later infancy.

The conclusion supported by the modern evidence is strikingly different from the early ideas of Carey et al. (1980) that basic mechanisms of face perception, such as holistic processing, were not present at all below 10 years and thus required a decade of experience to emerge. The results we have reviewed argue that much less experience is required to develop core face mechanisms. Indeed, it may be that no experience at all is required for some (e.g., holistic processing has now been demonstrated even in newborns; Thatcher illusion in Leo & Simion, 2009; also see the section entitled "A role for nature: Genetic contributions and innateness in face individuation").

Quantitative maturity: Is there any ongoing development of face perception mechanisms beyond early childhood?

To return to what explains the late age at which laboratory task performance reaches adult levels, our review so far indicates no *qualitative* development of face-specific perceptual mechanisms in the early childhood to adult range. However, to fully discriminate the general cognitive development and face-specific perceptual theories, we need to address the rather trickier question of whether there is *quantitative* development in face-specific mechanisms. For example, the question now is not merely is there an FFA in 6–10-year-olds, but is it as large as that in adults, or not is there a composite effect in 5-year-olds, but is it as strong as that in adults?

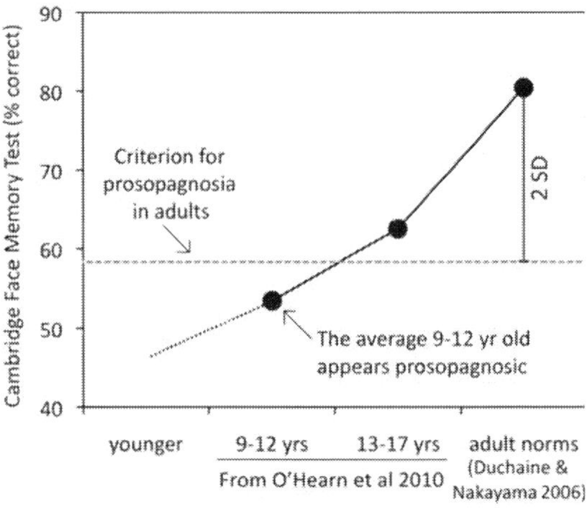

Figure 1. *Are all young children prosopagnosic? The plot illustrates that, if we were to believe that all (or even a substantial proportion of) age-related improvement on face tasks reflects improvements in face recognition, then the average child would be so poor they would be classified as prosopagnosic even at age 9–12. Note that younger children would perform more poorly again. Data are from typical developing children in O'Hearn et al. (2010), with adult norms from the larger-*N *control sample in Duchaine and Nakayama (2006). We use standard conservative criterion for prosopagnosia—that is, poorest 2% of population (score poorer than 2* SDs *below the mean). Note: Cambridge Face Memory Test (Duchaine & Nakayama, 2006) chance score = 33%.*

To address quantitative change, this section first notes that "children are not prosopagnosic". Then, for behavioural, N170, and fMRI studies in turn, we summarize previous findings, describe methodological issues that invalidate the usual interpretation of many of these findings as evidence for quantitative development (although note that many studies still remain valid and useful regarding qualitative presence), and discuss the results of the studies that we argue best overcome these methodological difficulties.

Children are not prosopagnosic: Laboratory tasks dramatically underestimate children's real-world face recognition abilities

Previously, we made the point that general cognitive skills contribute to performance on laboratory face tasks and improve with age. But, how great is this contribution? Recent results from the

Cambridge Face Memory Test (CFMT)—the most valid (and reliable) method of measuring real-world face recognition ability in adults (Bowles et al., 2009; Duchaine & Nakayama, 2006; McKone et al., 2011; Wilmer et al., 2010)—argue that it is actually substantial, and that laboratory tasks dramatically underestimate children's real world face recognition abilities. Figure 1 plots results from typically developing pre-adolescents (9–12 y.o.) and adolescents (13–17 y.o., O'Hearn et al., 2010) on the adult CFMT (i.e., comparing performance of adults and children on exactly the same task, as is typical of the developmental face recognition literature). If cognitive development makes only a minor contribution to task performance, then children might perform more poorly than adults—due either to the lack of cognitive maturity or to immature face perception systems—but we would expect this disadvantage to be relatively small. This is because typical 9–12-year-olds, in everyday life, do not have significant trouble learning and remembering faces, unlike adults with prosopagnosia who have significant real-world difficulties recognizing faces of even very familiar individuals. In contrast, Figure 1 shows that, relative to adult performance, the CFMT would diagnose children's face recognition as being so poor that the average 9–12-year-old would qualify as prosopagnosic (i.e., > 2 standard deviations below the adult mean). Further, the level of apparent "disability" would be even worse in younger children (who also have no trouble learning their schoolmates).

These results argue it is not just a small amount of the age-related development on laboratory tasks like the CFMT that reflects general cognitive development, but a large amount.

Age of quantitative maturity in behavioural studies: Avoiding restriction of range shows maturity by early childhood

We now review previous quantitative findings, beginning with behavioural tasks. Almost all studies reporting behavioural measures have included statistical tests for quantitative comparison across age and have interpreted the results as theoretically meaningful: For example, if there is a significant Age × Inversion interaction, then the authors conclude that the size of the face inversion effect increases with age, and thus holistic processing improves. There are dozens of studies including this type of analysis (a few recent references are de Heering et al., 2012; Macchi Cassia et al., 2011; Meinhardt-Injac et al., 2011). The conclusion drawn in the vast majority was that the face mechanism under investigation improved with age. Unfortunately, this conclusion is often invalid, due to a basic methodological issue.

This issue we refer to as the *restriction of range problem* (as raised by Carey, 1981; Chung & Thomson, 1995; Crookes & McKone, 2009). When attempting to cover a large age range (e.g., 5 y.o. to adults), it is rare to be able to design a task that is neither too difficult for the youngest children nor too easy for the adults. In the extreme case, of course, this can lead to complete floor or ceiling effects, where there is no potential to see any difference between conditions because performance is at chance, or perfect, in both conditions. Disturbingly, even some recent studies published in good journals have included quantitative comparisons made across groups in the presence of clear floor effects in the youngest children or ceiling effects in the adults (e.g., Macchi Cassia, Picozzi et al., 2009; Meinhardt-Injac et al., 2011); in our view, it should be automatic on the part of authors (and reviewers and readers) to avoid drawing any conclusions from the affected age groups.

Equally important, but more subtle, is that even without a complete floor or ceiling effect, there can still exist the possibility of a restriction of range problem (Figure 2). This is relevant because many of the key perceptual components of face recognition are demonstrated using differences between conditions (e.g., inversion effects, composite effects).

In Figure 2A, let's assume we have conducted a study on the size of the inversion effect on recognition memory for faces. In adults, a typical size of this inversion effect is 20% (e.g., upright = 85% correct, inverted = 65% correct). This means there is restricted range to see an adult-sized inversion effect as soon as children's upright performance

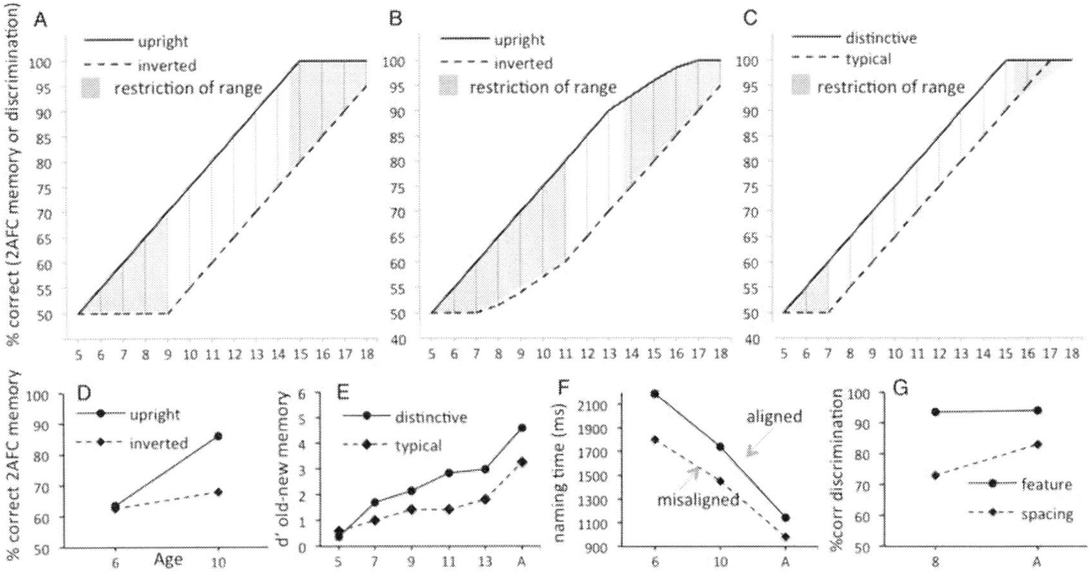

Figure 2. *The methodological issue of restriction of range in behavioural studies. (A) Assuming the underlying inversion effect on face memory (difference between upright and inverted) were a 20% reduction in accuracy, then setting the task difficulty to suit the 9–14-year-old age range leads to restriction of range to show this size of inversion effect in 5–8-year-olds and in 15–18-year-olds. This plot assumes that range becomes restricted only when one condition fully reaches chance (50% correct) or scale maximum (100%). (B) On the alternative assumption that there is some flattening out of measured values before 50% or 100% are reached, then the restriction of range problem affects even more ages (5–10-year-olds and 14–18-year-olds). (C) If the underlying difference between conditions is smaller, as is usually the case in adult studies for the distinctiveness effect (i.e., difference in memory for distinctive faces and typical faces), then the restriction of range problem affects fewer ages (5–6-year-olds and 16–18-year-olds). (D & E) Examples of real data where there is evidence of restriction of range in younger age groups that could potentially account for the Age × Condition interaction without needing to propose that the effect of interest genuinely increases in size with age. (D) In Carey et al. (1980) the inversion effect is 17.5% in the 10-year-olds. To be able to measure a difference of this size in the 6-year-olds would have required being able to measure inverted accuracy below chance. (E) A similar example for the distinctiveness effect from R. A. Johnston and Ellis (1995). The measure was* d′ *rather than percentage correct, so chance is 0. (F) Although we have illustrated the issue using accuracy, restriction of range also affects reaction time: Generally, two conditions will show a smaller difference between them when the overall reaction times are faster. In developmental studies, this often leads to effects appearing to be smaller in adults than in children, as illustrated for the composite effect (difference in naming times for aligned and misaligned composites) from Carey and Diamond (1994). (G) Studies arguing that one condition (e.g., detection of changes to spacing-between-features) matures later than another (detection of changes to local features) are also prone to drawing this conclusion falsely from restriction of range where the two conditions are not matched for difficulty (data from Mondloch et al., 2004).* Notes: *We have illustrated these issues for faces, and comparing two conditions in typically developing children, but they potentially apply widely in developmental psychology (e.g., for comparison of two types of verbal stimuli; for comparison of typically developing and atypically developing groups). A = adult; all other* x*-axis values are age in years. 2AFC = two-alternative forced-choice. To view a colour version of this figure, please see the online issue of the Journal.*

drops below 70% (assuming chance is 50%; i.e., upright performance of 69% in children would mean that to demonstrate an inversion drop of 20% would require being able to measure performance below chance).[5] This problem, widely ignored in the developmental face literature, means that the difference between two conditions in one age group may falsely appear to be larger or smaller than in another simply because overall performance on the task changes with age, and so one end of the age

[5] Thus, even showing that conditions are significantly greater than chance in the youngest group does not ensure that restriction of range has been avoided.

range or the other has a problem with restriction of range.

Unfortunately, as illustrated in Figures 2A–2C, there is no obvious way of determining when range restriction has occurred. This is partly because the exact way in which restriction might affect the functions for the two conditions being compared is unknown: For example, functions might be shaped like those in Figure 2A (straight lines until one hits chance or 100%) or like those in Figure 2B (the two functions begin to curve towards one another some distance prior to hitting chance or 100%). It is also partly because the mean accuracy level at which range restriction starts to occur will probably vary depending on the specific conditions compared: As illustrated in Figure 2C, if the memory difference between two conditions (e.g., distinctive and typical faces) is smaller, then restriction of range may not occur until more extreme age groups (cf. Figure 2A). Together, this means it is impossible to set out a rule for avoiding restriction of range; for example, it could not be said that "restriction is avoided if the mean of Condition A and Condition B is not greater than 90%, or less than 60% (in a 2AFC test)" or similar.

Turning to empirical findings, Figures 2D–2F illustrate three examples where restriction of range almost certainly occurred. Our observation is that the literature contains many cases like D and E, where there is potential restriction of range in the young age groups. Such studies typically find a larger difference between the conditions at older ages (e.g., Carey et al., 1980; de Heering et al., 2012; R. A. Johnston & Ellis, 1995). However, interpreting these studies as good evidence that the effect of interest genuinely increases with age implies that one would also need to accept as equally valid the conclusion of the (fewer) studies that have potential restriction of range present in the older age groups. As illustrated by one example in Figure 2F (Carey & Diamond, 1994; also see Ellis, Ellis, & Hosie, 1993; de Heering et al., 2007; Macchi Cassia, Picozzi et al., 2009), such studies typically find that the difference between the conditions of interest gets smaller with age; if this result were to be taken as valid in the way that the patterns in D and E have automatically been assumed to be valid, then the conclusion would be that face perception mechanisms (e.g., holistic processing) weaken with age. Most researchers have been rightly hesitant to draw this conclusion.

Another case where restriction of range is a potential issue is where the interest is not in comparing the difference between two conditions at each age, but instead in asking which of two conditions develops faster or matures (reaches adult levels) first. Example questions have been whether there is "special" development for faces, compared to nonface objects, and whether children have late maturity of discriminating "second-order relations" in faces (spacing between features, as opposed to local feature shape). Here, restriction of range can become a problem where the two conditions being compared are not matched in difficulty at one end of the age range,[6] because results are open to the interpretation that it is simply the easier condition which reaches adult level first because this condition approaches ceiling performance at an earlier age (e.g., Golarai et al., 2007; Mondloch, Dobson, Parsons, & Maurer, 2004; Mondloch et al., 2002).

Because a very high proportion of the literature is affected by one or more of these methodological problems, we argue that most studies do not, in fact, address the question of whether face-specific mechanisms develop quantitatively with age.

So, what happens when these problems are avoided? We plot results of studies that have done so in Figures 3–5. These studies avoided potential problems associated with restriction of range via various methods. Some (indicated with green dot; Figures 3A & 3B) compare rate of development for faces versus objects where stimulus sets are matched for difficulty (e.g., by matching performance in the youngest age groups).

[6] Matched accuracy requires that two conditions have equivalent means *and* that these means are not approaching ceiling or floor. It is not sufficient to show that two conditions have near-perfect accuracy in adults (e.g., 97% versus 99%): The "matching" (unless also present on reaction times) could reflect simply a ceiling effect.

Others (red dot; Figures 3C, 3D, 3F, 3M & 4B) experimentally matched performance across ages in a "baseline" condition (e.g., upright faces, for an inversion study), for example by using longer presentation times, or smaller learning set sizes, for the younger age groups. Others used exactly the same procedure across the adults and children, and the conditions of interest just happened to produce no sign of restriction of range across the ages tested (blue dot ; Figures 3E, 3G-I, 3K & 4A), or show some suggestion of possible restriction of range but had no significant Age × Condition interaction (pink dot ; Figures 3J & 3L). Others (yellow dot; Figures 4C-L) used methods not prone to restriction of range because the measure is not accuracy (where children's poorer concentration can push scores artificially towards chance); rather, there is no "right answer", and participants choose the face or identity that best matches their perception (atypicality bias; and shifts in face perceived as most normal in adaptation after-effects).

Inspection of Figures 3–5 indicates a remarkable convergence of results. In contrast to the classic interpretation of the literature, findings suggest that face perception mechanisms are not only qualitatively present in early childhood, but also quantitatively mature at an early age. This includes *ability to perceptually encode a novel face*, where Figures 3A–3B do not support the face-specific perceptual development theory prediction that performance should improve more steeply with age for faces than for a comparison object class (Crookes & McKone, 2009; P. J. Johnston et al., 2011),[7] and Figure 3C shows no change in the amount of implicit memory (repetition priming benefit) for novel faces between 5–6 years and adult (Crookes & McKone, 2009). It also includes all aspects of *holistic/configural processing*. Beyond the earliest age tested (generally 4–7 years), results show: no increase with age in the *inversion effect* for faces (Figures 3D–3E); no increase with age in the *disproportionate inversion effect* for faces versus objects (Figures 3F–3G); no increase with age in the *composite effect* (Figure 3H; there is no floor effect because chance is not 50%); no significant increase with age in the *part–whole effect* (Figures 3I–3J); no increase with age in the *inner face advantage* in identifying personally familiar faces (Figure 3K); and no increase with age in *sensitivity to spacing* between features (Figures 3L–3M).

Results also imply no quantitative change in *face-space*. This includes the ORE (Figure 4A; Pezdek et al., 2003; also Sporer, Trinkl, & Guberova, 2007) and memory enhancement arising from increased *distinctiveness* (spacing distinctiveness, Figure 3M; local feature distinctiveness such as making eyebrows bushier, Figure 4B). From 5–6 years, the *atypicality bias* (extent to which a 50% morph looks more like the distinctive rather than the typical parent) does not increase (Figure 4C; bias was weaker in 3–4-year-olds); this argues that exemplar density varies with distance-from-centre to the same degree in children and adults. In adaptation after-effect experiments comparing children and adults on exactly the same tasks (Figures 4D–4L), children's ability to update face norms based

[7] We review studies where the object class is theoretically similar to faces (animate objects with exemplars sharing a first-order configuration). Interestingly, however, face memory might develop faster than memory for houses or scenes (which activate different brain areas from discrete objects, i.e., the parahippocampal place area). In two studies, accuracy was similar for faces and houses/scenes in the youngest age group (and above floor), making comparison of developmental trends valid. Both these studies found stronger development for faces than houses (across 6 to 10 years, Carey & Diamond, 1977) and scenes (across 7–11 to 12–16 years, Golarai et al., 2007). Our conclusion that there is no development of face-specific mechanisms is based on the presumption that discrete objects form a better control class for faces than do houses/scenes. The results reviewed do not rule out the possibility that mechanisms common to both faces and objects might develop at a different rate than those used to code houses and scenes.

[8] Children do show a larger after-effect than adults for an asymmetric manipulation of eye height that breaks the first-order face configuration (Hills et al., 2010). This could suggest greater flexibility in the range of faces that can be coded (see "Effects of age and early experience on the flexibility of tuning to different face subtypes"), but it could arise from mid-level-vision responses to the vernier offset of the eyes: vernier offset is less precisely coded in children than in adults (Skoczenski & Norcia, 2002) and could plausibly produce after-effects.

on recent exposure is as strong as adults': After-effects are no weaker in children (eyes up–down symmetrically, Figures 4D and 4L, Hills et al., 2010; Jeffery et al., 2010; expanded Figure 4E, Jeffery et al., 2010; Dan–anti-Dan, Figures 4F–4K, Jeffery et al., 2011; Nishimura et al., 2008; Nishimura, Robertson, & Maurer, 2011; Pimperton et al., 2009). The only possible age effect in Figure 4 is a slightly larger identity after-effect in 5–7-year-olds than in 8-year-olds and adults (Jeffery et al., 2011; note that figural after-effects are not larger in 4–6 y.o. than in adults, Jeffery et al., 2010).[8] Further, the amount by which identity after-effects are larger for far-from-average adaptors than for close-to-average adaptors is equal in 7-year-olds and adults (Figure 4J, Jeffery et al., 2011), indicating equal reliance on norm-based rather than exemplar-based coding, plus equal sensitivity to differences in distinctiveness (80% vs. 40% identity strength adaptor). The amount by which after-effects increase as presentation time of the adaptor is increased is equal in 8-year-olds and adults (Figure 4K, Nishimura et al., 2011), indicating equal sensitivity to build-up of adaptation and arguing that children can update face norms as rapidly as adults. And the amount by which the figural after-effect (eyes up–down) generalizes across identity change in the face (i.e., reduction when adaptor and test differ in identity compared to when they are the same in identity) is equal for 6–12-year-olds and adults (Figure 4L, Hills et al., 2010), arguing that the overlap in neurons coding two different face identities is the same in children as in adults.

Finally, we consider whether detection of *spacing changes* matures later than that of *feature changes* (Mondloch et al., 2002). Post 8 years of age, it is now widely agreed that improved spacing sensitivity is not specific to faces nor based on face experience: it occurs at the same rate for houses and (nonexperienced) monkey faces as for human faces (Figure 5, Mondloch et al., 2006; Robbins, Shergill, Maurer, & Lewis, 2011). Younger than 8 years, there is still controversy: McKone and Boyer (2006) found 4-year-olds were equally sensitive to spacing and feature changes; Mondloch and Thomson (2008) argued that the lack of delay for spacing could have been because the spacing changes were, according to their physical measurements, outside the normal range in natural faces; however, in response, we note that Mondloch and Thomson did not compare the *feature* changes to physical norms, and McKone and Boyer equated *perceived* spacing and feature changes, so both were comparably normal.

In summary, across all these studies comprising 26 separate findings from multiple different laboratories there is now strong evidence arguing that the core behavioural mechanisms of face perception reach early quantitative maturity.[9] Regarding the exact age, 4–5 years seems a reasonable upper age limit from the figures (although note that some phenomena have not been tested below 6–8 years).

[9] In conflict, a recent adult study appears to suggest very late quantitative maturity: Germine et al. (2011) reported face memory peaks at 32 y.o. Because general cognitive function should not change over 20–32 years, this appears to imply that the amount of lifetime experience with faces is a key driver of face recognition ability. However, the "age" effect could reflect a confound with the ORE. Data were internet-collected via the http://www.testmybrain.org site. Face stimuli were Caucasian. Participants' race or country of origin were not recorded, and they could have participated from anywhere in the world. More recent data from testmybrain (2011 sample, four years later than the original; L. T. Germine, personal communication, August 26, 2011) reported the country in which participants grew up. Grouping participants into majority-Caucasian countries (US, Europe, etc.) or other countries (Asia, Africa, etc.), results showed noticeable variation across age in proportion from majority-Caucasian countries. In some age ranges, this could not explain face recognition performance (e.g., recognition declined across 34–65 years despite proportion-Caucasian increasing). However, across the crucial 20–32-year-old range, proportion-Caucasian increased significantly with age (from approximately .71 at 20 years to .81 at 32 years, $r = .61$, $p = .027$). If this confound was present in the original sample, then the improvement in face recognition between 20 and 32 could have reflected reduction in the ORE (noting that this would also predict the observed changes for upright and not inverted) rather than an age/experience effect.

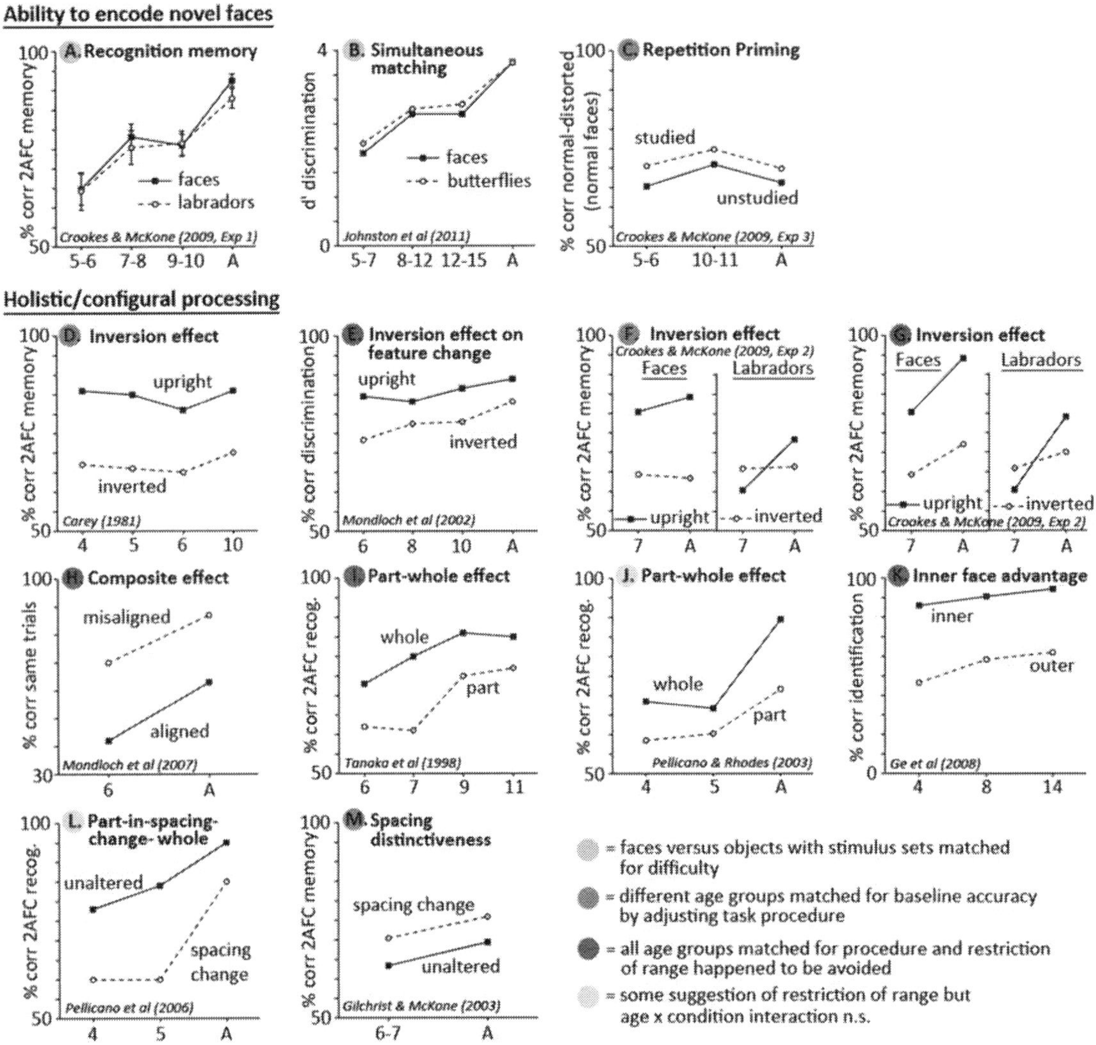

Figure 3. *Results of behavioural studies avoiding restriction of range problems for novel face encoding and holistic processing. Results imply early quantitative maturity of face-specific perceptual mechanisms. (A–C) For novel face encoding: Discrimination increases with age at the same rate for faces and difficulty-matched object classes, and repetition priming does not change across age. (D–M) For holistic/configural processing, all standard effects are as large in young children as in older groups. (See the section entitled "Age of quantitative maturity in behavioural studies: Avoiding restriction of range shows maturity by early childhood" for details of studies.) Coloured dots indicate the method used to avoid restriction of range issues: (A & B) faces versus objects with stimulus sets matched for difficulty; (C, D, F, M) different age groups matched for baseline accuracy by adjusting task procedure; (E, G, H, I, K) all age groups matched for procedure and restriction of range happened to be avoided; (J & L) some suggestion of restriction of range but age x condition interaction n.s. All plots show age in years on the x-axis; A = adult. 2AFC = two-alternative forced-choice. To view a colour version of this figure, please see the online issue of the Journal.*

Age of quantitative maturity in neural mechanisms

This leaves us only with the neural underpinnings of face recognition to consider as possible sources of face-specific development. In our previous reviews (Crookes & McKone, 2009; McKone, Crookes, & Kanwisher, 2009), we noted an apparent difference between the developmental literature on behaviour, suggesting early quantitative

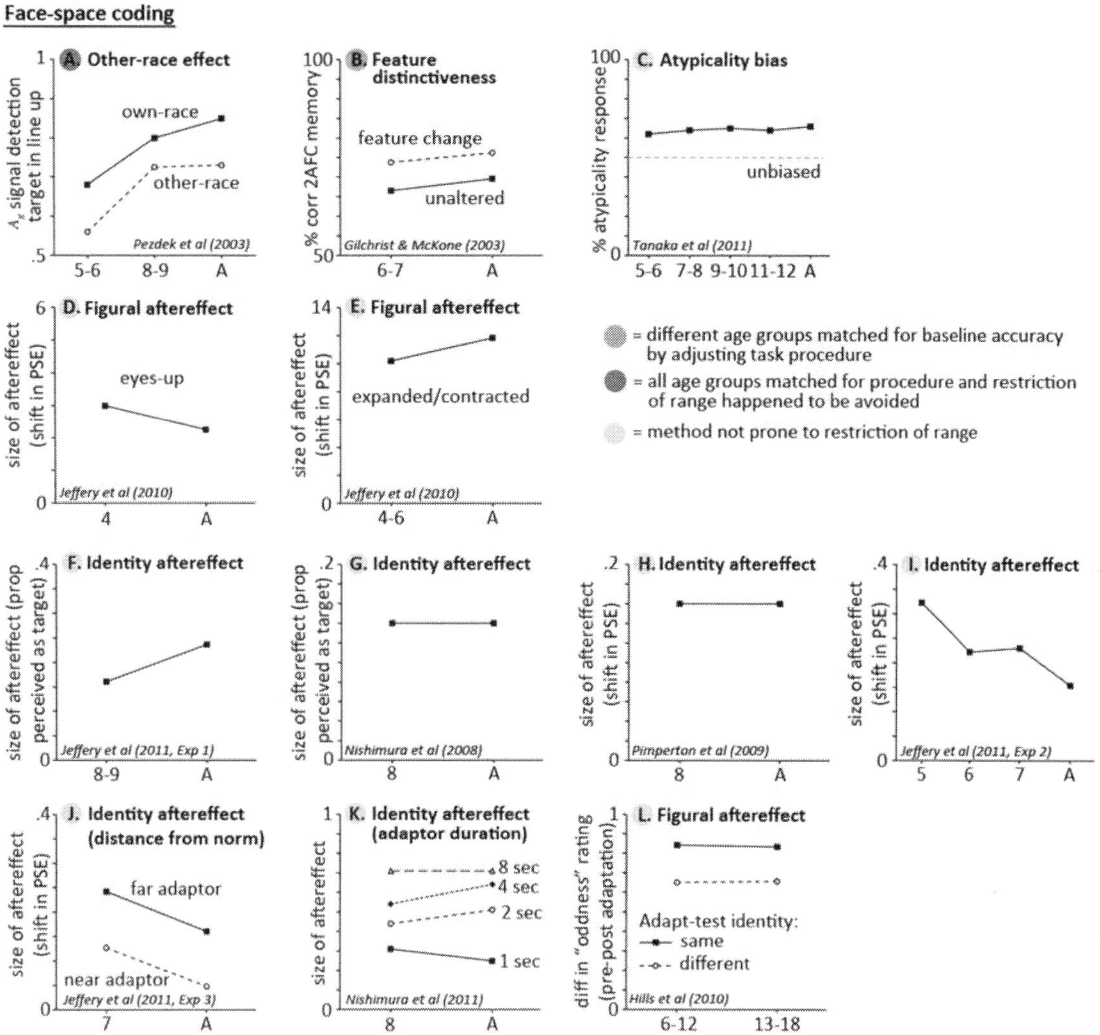

Figure 4. *Results of behavioural studies avoiding restriction of range problems for face-space coding. Results again imply early quantitative maturity of face mechanisms. Across all plots, the only significant changes with age were in identity after-effect studies testing children 7 years and younger; these ages demonstrated larger identity after-effects than adults, not smaller. Coloured dots indicate the method used to avoid restriction of range issues: (B) different age groups matched for baseline accuracy by adjusting task procedure; (A) all age groups matched for procedure and restriction of range happened to be avoided; (C-L) method not prone to restriction of range. (See the section entitled "Age of quantitative maturity in behavioural studies: Avoiding restriction of range shows maturity by early childhood" for details.) All plots show age in years on the* x-*axis; A = adult. 2AFC = two-alternative forced-choice. PSE = point of subjective equality. To view a colour version of this figure, please see the online issue of the Journal.*

maturity, and the results for neural mechanisms, which suggested late maturity. Recent evidence has largely resolved this discrepancy for the N170, but not fMRI.

N170 studies. Prior to 2010, studies of the N170 all indicated quantitative change across early childhood to late adolescence, with good agreement regarding its form: N170 *latency* decreased by

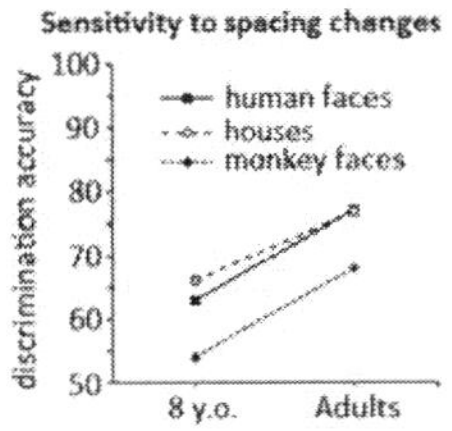

Figure 5. *Age-related changes in sensitivity to spacing between parts (e.g., distance between eyes or between two windows) are not face-specific or driven by face experience after 8 years of age. Rate of improvement with age is the same for experienced face type (human), nonexperienced face type (monkey), and nonface objects (houses). Plot combines data from Mondloch, Maurer, and Ahola (2006; human and monkey faces, using sequential same–different task) and Robbins et al. (2011; houses, using delayed match-to-sample task).*

~100 ms between 4–5 years and adulthood, with the steepest decrease before 10 years of age; *amplitude* had a "U" shaped developmental trajectory, smallest for children 10–11 years of age, and larger both younger and older; and *topography* was marked by a dominant posterior positivity rather than negativity in children, becoming adult-like in the midteenage years (4 to 14 y.o., Taylor et al., 1999; 4 to 15 y.o., Taylor et al., 2001; 4 to 10 y.o., Henderson et al., 2003). The N170 also sometimes appeared double-peaked in young children, having both an early (N170a) and a later (n170b) peak (Taylor et al., 2004), in contrast to adults' single N170 peak.

However, Kuefner et al. (2010) pointed out that ERP latency, amplitude, and topography can change due to age-related changes in any number of general factors unrelated to perceptual processes or even brain function (e.g., skin conductivity; skull thickness; head size; electroencephalography signal-to-noise ratio; attention). They used a higher density of channels than previously to improve signal-to-noise in young children, controlled for age-related variations in the P1, avoided grand averaging to isolate the N170 response from that of the preceding P1 and the later N250 (peak confound can occur when there is large interindividual and intertrial variance, and young children's data are grand-averaged), and examined face-specificity by testing car stimuli. Results showed that none of the previously reported age-dependent changes in latency, amplitude, or topography of the N170 were specific to faces. The effect of age on the N170 for faces was the same as that for cars, on both latency (Figure 6A) and amplitude. Results also implied that the previously reported "N170b" was in fact the N250, and that this confound accounted for the apparent large (100-ms) decrease in "N170"

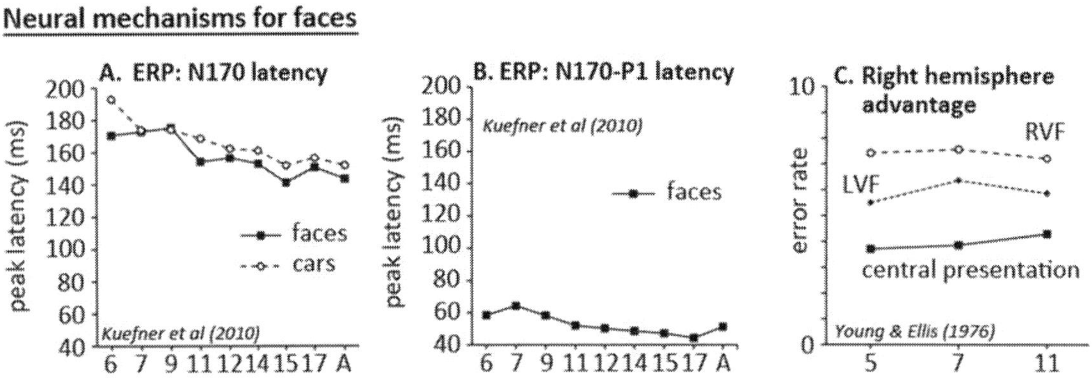

Figure 6. *Results of neural studies avoiding methodological problems that support early quantitative maturity of face-specific mechanisms. (A) Latency of the N170 peak over right occipitotemporal areas (electrode P08). (B) Results of subtracting out age differences in latency of P1 (i.e., N170 latency minus P1 latency). (C) Right hemisphere advantage in visual field (left visual field, LVF; right visual field, RVF) study that avoided restriction of range by equating baseline accuracy for central presentation. (See the section entitled "Age of quantitative maturity in neural mechanisms" for details.) All plots show age in years on the* x-*axis; A = adult. ERP = event-related potential.*

latency with age in previous studies: Latency reduction with age was much smaller for the true N170 (Figure 6A), and indeed when further isolated from age-related changes in P1 the face N170 latency was found to decrease by only 10–15 ms between 4 and 9 years (and no more after that; Figure 6B). Finally, the latency advantage for faces compared to cars did not change with age (Figure 6A). Overall, Kuefner and colleagues found that the electrophysiological markers of face-sensitive perceptual processes do not change throughout development, from 4 years to adulthood.

Right hemisphere bias. Also consistent with early neural maturity, the degree of right hemisphere bias for face recognition does not increase quantitatively after early childhood. Considering studies that reported at least 90% right-handers: Kuefner et al. (2010) found that the amount by which N170 amplitude was larger over the right hemisphere than the left hemisphere showed no systematic developmental trend from age 6; a visual field study equating baseline accuracy (longer presentation times for younger children) found no change in degree of LVF advantage over 5 to 11 years (Figure 6C, Young & Ellis, 1976); and fMRI studies found that, if anything, the strength of the right hemisphere bias decreased with age (Scherf et al., 2007; only rFFA and not lFFA observed in 7–11 y.o., Pelphrey et al., 2009).

fMRI studies of the FFA. Both size and selectivity of the FFA have been of interest: *size* because increases are predicted by gradual construction of functionally specific regions of cortex (constructivist view, Quartz, 1999); and *selectivity* (i.e., amount by which response is higher to faces than control objects) because increases are predicted by the theoretical perspective that redundant and irrelevant neuronal connections exist from birth and are gradually eliminated on the basis of experience (Changeux & Danchin, 1976). All fMRI studies to date have reported an increase in FFA size with age (Aylward, et al., 2005; Golarai, et al., 2007; Golarai, Liberman, Yoon, & Grill-Spector, 2010; Joseph, et al., 2011; Passarotti, et al., 2003; Passarotti, et al., 2007; Peelen, et al., 2009; Pelphrey, et al., 2009; Scherf, et al., 2007; Scherf, et al., 2011)—up to three-fold larger in adults than children—that extends into adolescence (e.g., smaller even in 13–16 y.o. than in adults, Golarai et al., 2007). One study also found that rFFA size was correlated with behavioural face recognition memory performance (and not with place or object memory), separately in children and adolescents although not in adults (Golarai et al., 2007). Several studies have reported increased selectivity of the FFA, sometimes revealed as increased magnitude of FFA response to faces without change in its response to objects (Golarai, et al., 2007; Golarai, et al., 2010; Joseph, et al., 2011; Peelen, et al., 2009; Scherf, et al., 2007) and in one study revealed as decreased response of the FFA to nonface stimuli (Cantlon et al., 2011).

While these findings appear to support face-specific perceptual development, there are potentially serious methodological issues. As we noted earlier, many studies (Aylward et al., 2005; Joseph et al., 2011; Passarotti et al., 2003; Pelphrey et al., 2009) rely exclusively or primarily on group analyses, rather than individual-subject analyses. Group analyses are problematic because an apparent difference in FFA volume between children and adults could result from a difference in variability of anatomical location, even if the volumes of FFA measured individually were identical between children and adults (for direct evidence that group analyses can underestimate volume or selectivity of functional regions, see Saxe, Brett, & Kanwisher, 2006; Scherf et al., 2007).

Another issue, potentially affecting even the individual-subject analyses, is that signal-to-noise ratio is likely to be lower in young children. This is partly because children might move their heads more, but also due to a previously unnoted problem—namely, the use of adult-sized head coils to collect fMRI data on child-sized heads. Of the 10 previous studies, 3 explicitly report using an adult head coil (Golarai et al., 2007, 2010; Pelphrey et al., 2009), and we presume the remaining studies also did so because, to the best of our knowledge, these groups do not possess a paediatric coil. It has recently been shown that, because children's heads are smaller (and hence farther from the coil) than adults' heads, adult coils have low signal-to-noise ratio over time (tSNR) for scanning children (Keil et al., 2011). tSNR is the most important metric for sensitivity in a given fMRI acquisition protocol (e.g., Triantafyllou, Polimeni, & Wald, 2011); it measures fluctuations from thermal and physiological noise sources and is defined as mean intensity of an ROI or pixel in a resting functional time-series divided by its standard deviation across time. The fact that tSNR in an adult head coil increases with head size (and thus age) of the participant raises the possibility that even individual-analysis studies, with good control for head movement, may have underestimated the volume (and perhaps selectivity) of the children's FFA.

Importantly, some studies have reported control areas to argue that low tSNR in children was not the source of the increase in FFA size. Considering individual-subject analyses, results are mixed regarding the parahippocampal place area (PPA) with some studies finding increased size with age (Scherf et al., 2011; lPPA in Golarai et al., 2007) and some not (Scherf et al., 2007; rPPA in Golarai et al., 2007). Regarding areas that code discrete objects rather than places or scenes, Peelen et al. (2009) found the fusiform body area (FBA) did not increase in size, and object-area lateral occipital complex (LOC) is also developmentally stable (Golarai et al., 2007, 2010; Scherf et al., 2007). Demonstrating age stability of a control area nicely rules out many potential confounds (e.g., head movement) as the origin of the smaller FFAs in children observed in these studies. However, it does not necessarily rule out lower tSNR in children arising from head coil size. This is particularly the case for the LOC. For a given head coil size, tSNR is lower for brain regions further from the coil than for those closer to the coil (Keil et al., 2011). This could mean that the effect of adult head coil size on children's small heads could be more severe for medial regions (e.g., FFA, FBA) than for lateral regions (e.g., LOC). Potentially, this could explain why the FFA appears to increase with age while the LOC remains stable; that is, there is little negative effect of using an adult head coil on the LOC because it is sufficiently close to the coil regardless of head size.

Overall, from this discussion, we would not like to conclude that there is not a genuine change in the size and/or selectivity of the FFA with age; this remains a possibility from the presently available evidence. But on the other hand, given the methodological issues, we would not like to conclude there *is* genuine change in the FFA with age. This is particularly the case because, as we next discuss, there is evidence arguing that fMRI in young children can sometimes produce nonsensical conclusions due to lack of sensitivity.

Evidence arguing that fMRI conclusions in children younger than 10 years can sometimes be wrong, even when studies meet current "best practice"

Scherf et al. (2011) examined whether the FFA was capable of making individual-level discriminations between faces, using fMR-adaptation (difference between different-face and same-face blocks). Importantly, the study made strong efforts to collect good fMRI data in children, including individual-subject analyses, independently defined ROIs, matching children and adults for head motion, and good alignment between anatomical and functional scans.

Results showed no face individuation in children aged 6–10 years in the FFA. Critically, however, a whole-brain analysis was also included, and no fMR-adaptation was revealed anywhere in the entire brain (see Figure 7). This contradicts known evidence that the brains of 6–10-year-olds *can* adapt to individual faces: Both repetition priming and adaptation after-effects are found, at adult strength, in this age range (Figure 3C, Figures 4D–4L; also note that fMR-adaptation can be observed, for other stimuli, in 4-year-olds, Cantlon, Brannon, Carter, & Pelphrey, 2006). Interpreting Scherf et al.'s (2011) lack of fMRI discrimination as genuinely reflecting the ability of children's brains to discriminate faces would also

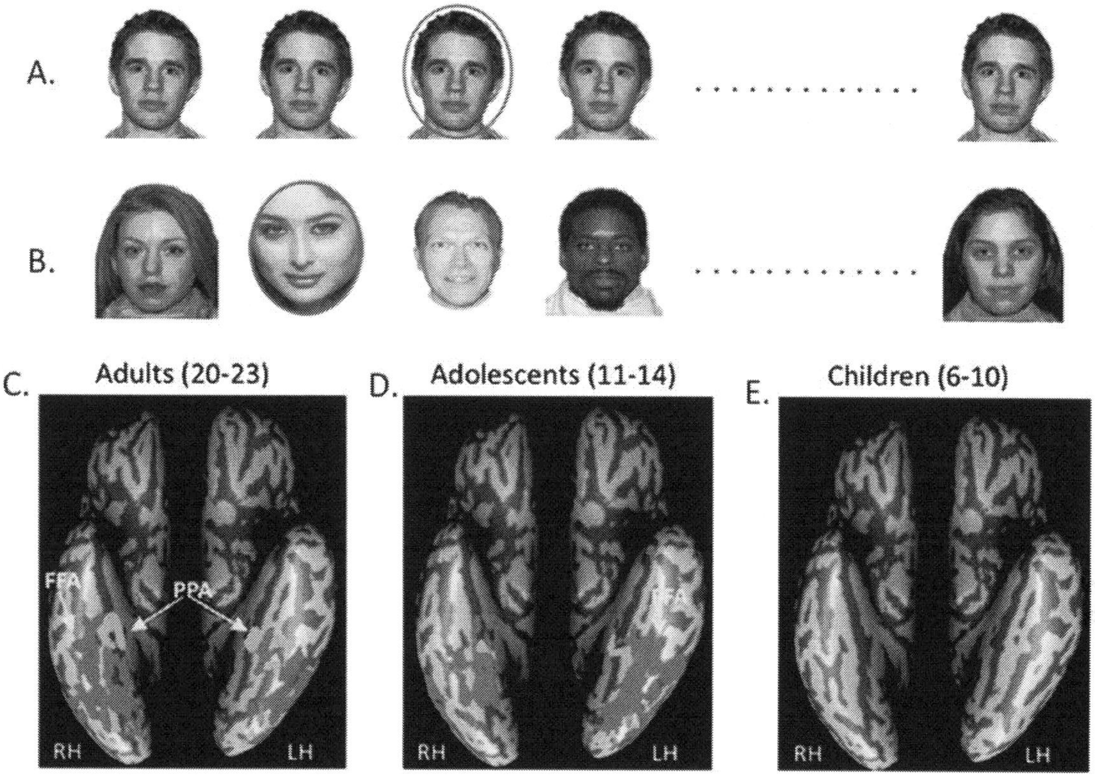

Figure 7. *Evidence that even a well-controlled functional magnetic resonance imaging (fMRI) study can fail to reveal an effect that other evidence suggests must be present in children. Stimuli and results from Scherf et al. (2011). (A, B) Face stimuli used to examine individual-level face discrimination via fMRI-adaptation. In separate blocks, participants viewed consecutive images of (A) identical faces or (B) different faces, pressing a button when a circle surrounded the stimulus. (C–E) Results of whole brain voxelwise analysis evaluating individual-level adaptation effects within each age group in the adaptation task. Individual-level adaptation was computed as different > identical for faces (red) and houses (green) in separate contrasts (*p $> .025$*, corrected). Scherf and colleagues report that adults and adolescents (left fusiform face area, FFA, only for adolescents) exhibited selective individual-level adaptation for faces in the fusiform gyrus, which was centred on the classic FFA region. Children failed to exhibit individual-level adaptation in any region, inconsistent with behavioural adaptation and excellent behavioural ability to discriminate faces at this age and the expectation that even primary visual cortex should be able to discriminate the faces in (B).* To *view a colour version of this figure, please see the online issue of the Journal. From "'What' Precedes 'Which': Developmental Neural Tuning in Face- and Place-Related Cortex", by K. S. Scherf, B. Luna, G. Avidan, and M. Behrmann, 2011,* Cerebral Cortex, 21, *pp. 1963–1980. Copyright 2011 by Oxford University Press. Adapted with permission.*

appear to make the absurd prediction that children aged 6–10 go about their daily lives unable to tell apart even dramatically different faces (variation in sex, race, expression, presence or absence of hair; Figure 7B). However, contrary to Scherf et al.'s (2011) suggestion that their result "converges with several behavioral studies" (p. 1975), the lack of neural discrimination disagrees strongly with behavioural discrimination. Mondloch et al. (2002) found that 6–10-year-olds averaged 87% correct for discriminating successive static images even of very similar faces (all Caucasian women, all the same age, all wearing a shower cap) presented for only 200 ms (cf. 800 ms per face in Scherf et al.).

We thus suggest the Scherf et al. (2011) study provides evidence that fMRI data in young children can fail to detect effects that should be present. This cannot be due merely to the sample size (Scherf et al. used the same N in older groups, in which fMRI adaptation was clearly found; Figure 7) and so demonstrates a lack of sensitivity, perhaps due to low tSNR in children. The fact that even a decently controlled experimental design leads to conclusions that are probably incorrect leads one to have serious doubts about the interpretation of other fMRI face results in children under 10 years (i.e., a region is absent, smaller, or less selective than in adults) as reflecting immature neural processing of faces.

Summary of quantitative maturity

We have argued the results of behavioural, N170, and hemispheric difference measures support the general cognitive development theory of late task improvements, with no change in face-specific perceptual processing beyond the age of perhaps 4–6 years. The number of behavioural studies avoiding the problem of restriction of range has increased substantially in the last 2–3 years (see Figures 3 and 4). The new findings of these studies, together with better controlled N170 data, support early maturity of face-specific mechanisms including ability to perceptually encode a novel face, holistic processing (including spacing sensitivity), face-space coding, and rapid face processing. Overall, these findings make a strong case that the ability to recognize faces quickly and accurately does not depend on extended experience over many years, as proposed by Carey et al. (1980; although note that we do not rule out some important effects of experience, e.g., during infancy; see the sections entitled "Coding of profile views", "Innateness: Critical period", "Innateness: Perceptual narrowing", "Effects of experience during infancy").

At present, fMRI results appear discrepant with those of the other techniques. Some or all of this discrepancy may be due to methodological issues—such as scanning children in an adult-size head coil—which mean that fMRI studies to date may have underestimated the size or selectivity of the FFA in children. However, the discrepancy could also reflect a genuine difference. If so, one possible explanation is that an increasing FFA size reflects the number of individuals with whom a participant is familiar, and that average FFA size increases across development simply because adults have met, and stored the faces of, more people than children have. Under this interpretation, storing more faces in the FFA would require more neurons, and these might be taken over for this purpose from surrounding areas of body or object-general cortex. Another idea is that measured FFA size might be determined by top-down processing as well as bottom-up face perception, and that children engage in this top-down processing less readily. Both of these ideas are empirically testable: for example by comparing same-age participants with low versus high number of known individuals (e.g., from small country-towns versus large cities), or on tasks with low versus high top-down demands (e.g., passive viewing versus 3-back matching) to see whether these variables affect measured FFA size.

A ROLE FOR NATURE: GENETIC CONTRIBUTIONS AND INNATENESS IN FACE INDIVIDUATION

The review so far indicates that experience with faces plays a weaker role in our ability to recognize faces than traditionally believed. Complementing this finding, there is now clear evidence of a role for "nature" in face individuation. This includes both *genetic* contributions and *innate* contributions (in the sense of being present at birth). Note that genetics and innateness are independent issues because genetically influenced processes can occur late in development (e.g., onset of puberty; onset of dyslexia when children learn to read) rather than necessarily at birth. The evidence comes from studies of twins, families, neonates, visually deprived monkeys, critical periods, and perceptual narrowing.

Genetic contribution to individual differences in ability: Twin and family studies

Twin studies demonstrate that individual differences in face recognition have a heritable genetic component. Twin studies use the logic that differences in a cognitive ability are heritable if the correlation is higher for monozygotic twins (identical twins, who share 100% of their genes) than for dizygotic twins (fraternal twins, who share an average of 50%). Results show heritability of face individuation, for fMRI activation pattern across the ventral visual stream (Polk, Park, Smith, & Park, 2007) and for behavioural discrimination (Wilmer et al., 2010; Zhu et al., 2010). Results also indicate face-specific heritability: There is heritability for holistic processing (face inversion and composite effects, Zhu et al., 2010), no heritability for recognition of houses or inverted faces (Zhu et al., 2010), and no heritability of ventral stream activation patterns for stimuli unlikely to have any special evolutionary status (written words and chairs, Polk et al., 2007). Independence of the face heritability from the heritability of general cognitive abilities (i.e., intelligence, or "*g*") is also indicated: Singleton studies show very low correlation between face memory and verbal memory or IQ (Bowles et al., 2009; Wilmer et al., 2010; Zhu et al., 2010). The twin studies also show that the heritable contribution to face recognition is large (specifically, 100% of familial resemblance is genetic, i.e., monozygotic correlation equal to twice or more times the dizygotic correlation; Wilmer et al., 2010; Zhu et al., 2010). The contribution of nonfamilial environment was significant but modest in both studies (see McKone & Palermo, 2010).

Also consistent with heritability is the fact that developmental prosopagnosia—a lifetime inability to recognize faces without any known brain injury—can run in families across generations (Grueter et al., 2007; Kennerknecht, Pluempe, & Welling, 2008; Schmalzl, Palermo, & Coltheart, 2008). Again arguing for face-specificity, this can occur independent of intelligence (Dobel, Bölte, Aicher, & Schweinberger, 2007; Duchaine, Germine, & Nakayama, 2007) and sometimes coexists with normal within-class discrimination of objects (Lee, Duchaine, Wilson, & Nakayama, 2010).

These results argue that face-specific individuation plus the component mechanism of holistic processing both have a component derived from genetic differences between individual people, heritable across generations.

Innateness: Neonates and visually deprived monkeys

Visual abilities present immediately after birth, or in monkeys deprived of all face input, cannot be derived from experience and so reveal *genetic influences* (on average face recognition ability, not individual differences) in isolation from any visual learning. Table 1 shows that human newborns individuate and holistically process faces. Babies in these studies were 1–3 days old, giving a maximum of perhaps 12 hours of visual experience of any kind (newborns sleep 16 hours per day plus have their eyes shut during breastfeeding and crying). It seems unlikely that the small amount of face experience would be sufficient for a purely learning-based system to support the level of fine discrimination ability observed.

Sugita (2008) raised macaques with no exposure to faces (human caregivers wore full face masks), but otherwise normal visual experience in a complex environment. On their first experience with faces, at age 6–24 months, the monkeys could discriminate very subtle differences between individual faces (both spacing and feature changes).

Together, these results strongly imply that face individuation and holistic processing abilities are present at birth, without experience.

Innateness: Critical period

Another source of evidence for neural systems being present at birth can be a *critical* (or *sensitive*) *period* (Sengpiel, 2007), in which environmental input of the appropriate stimulus type is required within a specified period after birth to avoid the system being taken over for other purposes. In the textbook example, cats are born with cells tuned to all line orientations, but if raised in an environment containing only vertical lines, they lose neural and behavioural sensitivity to horizontal lines.

For faces, patients born with dense cataracts disrupting all pattern vision (and subsequently removed) show, later in life, normal recognition of same-image faces (Ostrovsky, Andalman, & Sinha, 2006; Putzar, Hötting, & Röder, 2010). However, despite many years of post-cataract-removal exposure to faces, they show impaired performance on cross-view recognition (Geldart, Mondloch, Maurer, de Schonen, & Brent, 2002; Putzar et al., 2010) and no face composite effect (Le Grand et al., 2004). Further, patients with left-eye-only or bilateral cataracts—which produce a deficit of early input to the right hemisphere due to the wiring of the infant visual system—show a deficit in processing spacing information in faces, while patients who had had right-eye-only cataracts do not (Le Grand, Mondloch, Maurer, & Brent, 2003), a pattern predicted by the normal role of the right hemisphere in holistic processing.

Taken together, the results indicate some form of critical period in infancy for individuation of faces across views, and for holistic processing.

Innateness: Perceptual narrowing

A final phenomenon associated with innate abilities is perceptual narrowing across infancy, in which an ability present in younger babies disappears in older babies. Perceptual narrowing is best known in language (e.g., Kuhl, Tsao, & Liu, 2003): Infants are born able to discriminate phoneme boundaries from all languages in the world (e.g., English and Mandarin), but from age 6–12 months lose this ability for nonexperienced languages (English for a child from a monolingual Mandarin-speaking family). This type of result is used to argue that a representational capacity (e.g., for faces) is present at birth, that this can initially be applied to a wide range of stimuli from the class (e.g., a wide range of face subtypes), and that its range gets restricted during the first several months of life to include only the kinds (i.e., face species, or races) seen in this period.

Perceptual narrowing occurs for faces. Infants younger than approximately 6 months can individuate faces of races (Asian, Caucasian, African)—and, indeed, species (monkey and sheep faces)—that they have never experienced: Nonexperienced types are then gradually "tuned out", with this process complete at 9 months (Kelly et al., 2009; Kelly et al., 2007; Pascalis, de Haan, & Nelson, 2002; Scott & Monesson, 2009; Simpson, Varga, Frick, & Fragaszy, 2011). Sugita's (2008) monkeys also showed perceptual narrowing, with initial ability to individuate human faces disappearing after a month of exposure to only macaque faces.

Holistic processing also undergoes perceptual narrowing. Using the Cohen and Cashon (2001) version of the composite effect, holistic processing occurs for both own and other-race faces in young infants (4 m.o. Caucasian babies looking at Caucasian and African faces) but only for own-race faces in older infants (8 m.o., Ferguson et al., 2009).

Together, these results argue that babies are born with a broadly tuned ability to represent individual faces, and holistically code them, without experience. The fact that young human babies can individuate nonhuman primate and indeed sheep faces suggests that the underlying representation is rather old in evolutionary terms and might, for example, include all mammal faces.

Summary of genetics and innateness

Overall, these results provide a compelling array of evidence that there are both genetic and innate contributions to face recognition. Importantly, evidence from all techniques—heritability, newborns, critical periods, and perceptual narrowing—now supports such contributions for face individuation, and also for one of the key supporting mechanisms long presumed to be "special" to faces—namely, holistic processing. Regarding the breadth of the innate representation, the individuation for monkey and sheep faces in humans, and of human faces in monkeys, argues that this ability emerged quite some time ago in evolution and is possibly part of a general conspecific recognition mechanism available to all mammals.

It is interesting to note that, to date, possible genetic or innate contributions to face-space coding have received essentially no investigation. Attractiveness effects have been reported in newborns (Slater, Bremner, et al., 2000; Slater, Quinn, et al., 2000) but stimuli were natural faces that did not vary specifically in terms of distance from the average face, making it difficult to tie the result specifically to face-space. Theoretically, it has been almost universal in the literature to assume that face-space develops entirely from lifetime exposure. In fact, however, no studies have tested this assumption (i.e., there are no twin studies, no perceptual narrowing studies, etc.). We suggest that it remains plausible that face-space may have genetic contributions or be present in some form at birth. It would be valuable for researchers to test this hypothesis in future.

WHAT EFFECTS OF EXPERIENCE ARE THERE?

So far we have emphasized situations in which ongoing lifetime experience with faces does not influence face recognition. We now briefly summarize situations in which experience does have an effect. We do not, of course, propose that infants are born with a fully operational face recognition system that requires no experience at all to mature. Instead, we argue that current results leave it open that quantitative and indeed qualitative change in core face coding could take place across infancy and/or into the uninvestigated preschool years; and also that later experience can fine-tune adult face recognition for particular individual faces, or particular subsets of faces.

Effects of experience during infancy

One effect of experience across infancy is a *qualitative change in viewpoint effects*, with identity information coded in front- and three-quarter-view faces from birth, but coding of profile views emerging only after mid infancy (section entitled "Coding of profile views"). This raises an intriguing idea. Adult macaques have face-selective cells organized in a three-stage process of increasing view-invariance across three posterior-to-anterior face patches (Freiwald & Tsao, 2010). If, of view-specific cells, fewer are selective for profiles than for other views, then the baby findings might reflect a gradual development of a similar pathway, ultimately achieving view-invariance of neural coding.

Second, *perceptual narrowing* occurs across infancy (section entitled "Innateness: Perceptual narrowing"). The perceptual narrowing described so far represents a *loss* of ability with experience; that is, younger babies can do something (individuate faces of nonexperienced races and species) that is lost in older babies as a consequence of experience in the first months of life. In language, the likely functional reason for the loss of discriminability in nonexperienced categories is to fine-tune the system towards experienced categories and thus improve discrimination within the native language (Kuhl et al., 2006). Perceptual narrowing for faces might similarly enhance ability to discriminate commonly experienced face subtypes—that is, discrimination of own-species own-race faces might be initially crude and subsequently improve concurrent with the loss of ability to discriminate other-species and other-race faces. Potentially consistent with this prediction, Humphreys and Johnson (2007) found that the physical difference between faces required to produce novelty preference was smaller in 7-month-olds than in 4-month-olds. Unfortunately, however, there was no control stimulus (e.g., inverted faces), so it is unclear whether this reflects improvement in tuning of face mechanisms across infancy, or general improvement in vision or memory.

Finally, the type of perceptual discriminations an infant is required to make affects whether or not a face subtype is spared from perceptual narrowing. Perceptual narrowing is prevented for experienced face classes only where the experience involves individual-level categorization (e.g., monkeys are individually named) and not basic-level categorization (monkeys are experienced but are all labelled "monkey"; Pascalis et al., 2005; Scott & Monesson, 2009). This implies that the reason babies remain able to individuate human faces across infancy in everyday life is that they have regularly experienced people being identified at the individual level.

Effects of experience 12 months to 3 years

Although we have argued that the current literature implies full quantitative maturity of face recognition by 4–5 years of age (at least in behaviour and ERP), we emphasize that there is nothing to rule out important quantitative improvements occurring between infancy and 4 years. It is generally not possible to quantitatively compare children aged 0–3 years to adults on the same tasks. Indeed, there are almost no data at all on face recognition between 12 and 36 months (note the jump from later infancy straight to 3 years in Table 1), because this intermediate age range is notoriously difficult to test.

In language—the other key ability supporting crucial social interaction in children—there is dramatic change in ability over the first 36 months of life. Potentially, the same could be true of face recognition. This means that an important task for developmental researchers is to develop face tasks suitable for assessing face-coding mechanisms in the 12–36-month age range.

Effects of age and early experience on the flexibility of tuning to different face subtypes

Clearly, experience can influence the relative ability to code different subtypes of faces, as demonstrated in the other-race effect. We emphasize, however, that the early quantitative maturity of face-specific mechanisms that we have argued for (see Figures 3–5) refers to *own*-race face recognition ability. Thus, we do not see any evidence that the good discrimination for own-race faces is a result of experience with own-race faces after 4–5 years of age. However, it seems plausible that the adult ORE is a result of the lack of experience with other-race faces prior to 4–5 years. Experience with other-race faces during adulthood may then become important and improve other-race performance, but, importantly, this does not indicate late experience-related changes in ability to code faces per se, but instead in ability to apply established mechanisms to a different subset of faces.

It is also possible that the degree to which experience with other-race faces may facilitate discrimination might change across development. At 3 months, the decrement for other-race faces observed in one study was rapidly overcome by just a few trials of experience (Sangrigoli & de Schonen, 2004b). There is also evidence of flexibility into middle childhood: Korean children adopted to Caucasian countries at 3–9 years of age, and expected to have a deficit for Caucasian faces at adoption, show good memory for Caucasian faces when tested several years post adoption (de Heering et al., 2010; Sangrigoli, Pallier, Argenti, Ventureyra, & de Schonen, 2005; although see Sugita, 2008, for a potentially contradictory finding in macaques). And, in language, flexibility to "relearn" a language tuned out in infancy appears higher in children than in adults; for example an English-speaking 5-year-old relocated to France will become a fluent speaker with perfect grammar and accent, but even extensive exposure as an adult to a non-native language is usually insufficient to attain native-speaker levels of proficiency. Therefore, flexibility of the face system may be higher earlier in development than later.

Interestingly, in adulthood the degree to which experience can improve discrimination of certain face types might rely on reactivating latent effects of exposure from early childhood. Macchi Cassia, Kuefner et al. (2009) found that adults with recent experience of infants (first-time mothers) showed inversion effects for infant faces, but only if they also had had younger siblings when they were children (i.e., both early childhood and adult experience with infant faces). Further, women who had had younger siblings, but were not mothers (i.e., early childhood experience only) did not show inversion effects for infant faces. This study argues that experience with a face subtype in early childhood can lie dormant until reactivated by further experience in adulthood. An analogy from language would be that an English speaker who has lived for a while in France as a child can subsequently forget most of their French but still relearn it as an adult with good accent and grammar, whereas an English speaker who has had adult-only experience of French does not achieve the same outcome.

Age-independent effects of experience

Finally, some effects of experience can occur at any age and are thus unrelated to any particular developmental stage. In *familiarity effects*, adults continue to learn new faces throughout life. This improves perceptual discrimination: Matching the correct face photograph to a low-resolution video image is more accurate for familiar than for unfamiliar faces (Bruce, Henderson, Newman, & Burton, 2001; Burton, Wilson, Cowan, & Bruce, 1999). *Adaptation after-effects* (section entitled "Face-space coding") also indicate purely experience-based changes in the responses of perceptual representations of faces, as do *training effects* on ability to discriminate trained and novel faces (e.g., in an adult prosopagnosic, DeGutis, Bentin, Robertson, & D'Esposito, 2007). Crucially, however, there is no evidence that these types of experience alone produce any fundamental qualitative change in face processing either neurally or cognitively: Holistic processing, face-space effects, and FFA activation all occur strongly for both familiar and unfamiliar faces (Carbon et al., 2007; Kanwisher et al., 1997; Le Grand et al., 2004; Webster & MacLin, 1999; Young et al., 1987).

Summary of effects of experience

The important conclusions regarding the effects of experience are that (a) there are some, (b) it seems likely that these might be stronger earlier in development than later, although learning of faces continues throughout life, (c) after 4–5 years they affect recognition ability for certain subtypes of faces rather than improving overall face recognition ability per se (which is already mature for own-race faces), and (d) we currently have no information at all as to at what age face perception reaches maturity in the 0 to 4 years age range.

CONCLUSION AND FUTURE DIRECTIONS

Conventional wisdom has long held that face recognition develops slowly, with experience as its primary engine. The modern findings support almost a complete reversal of this view. The data no longer support a theory in which the only face representation present at birth is a mere orienting device, and good individual-level face discrimination takes many years of practice to achieve. Rather, infants are born with a rich capacity to represent the structure of upright faces, and this supports face individuation, and holistic processing, rather than merely drawing attention to faces. Inherited genetic influence is also indicated, from twin studies, on both behaviour (individuation ability and holistic processing) and the pattern of ventral stream responses to faces. Qualitatively, findings indicate that all adult-like face recognition processes are present at the earliest ages tested (typically 3–4 years and in many cases infancy); the striking breadth of this evidence is summarized in Table 1. Further, face processes appear quantitatively fully mature early, by perhaps 5 years, as indicated by evidence from a now substantial set of behavioural and ERP studies that have avoided methodological problems common in previous literature (Figures 3–5). Regarding experience, there are substantial effects during infancy, including perceptual narrowing and a critical period for holistic processing and cross-view recognition. Post infancy, it seems plausible that there are ongoing effects of experience on quantitative performance in children younger than 4 years, although direct investigation is lacking. However, continuing experience beyond this age does not produce continuing improvements in face recognition at least for our most frequently experienced face types (i.e., own-race, own-species faces).

Our conclusions may depart dramatically from the traditional view of protracted development of face individuation skills but they are entirely consistent with children's real-world need for face recognition. Crucially, the demands placed on children's face individuation skills do not differ substantially from those placed on adults' skills. Children would struggle socially if they could not distinguish numerous individuals from early in childhood. These social demands are particularly important as children enter school where they need to quickly learn many new faces. Children's laboratory test scores at this age suggest that, like adult prosopagnosics, they would struggle to learn these new people. Yet they do not. Further, it makes evolutionary sense to have a face system capable of rapid, accurate face recognition from an early age to support social development and, ultimately, survival.

Our review has also highlighted a number of areas for future research. First, behaviourally, it is imperative to develop face tasks suitable for the notoriously difficult 12-to-36-month age range. To be of theoretical value, these tasks need to allow valid quantitative comparison of face effects to be made with older children, rather than merely qualitative demonstration of effects known to exist in infants. Second, concerning behavioural studies in children four years and over, it would be valuable to investigate whether the developing cognitive mechanisms that we have argued drive improvement in laboratory face tasks contribute at all to face recognition performance in naturalistic settings (i.e., where social interest would be expected to drive attention to faces, concentration, etc.). Third, the current conflict between behaviour and fMRI regarding the age of quantitative maturity of face perception mechanisms needs to be resolved. Importantly, this is no longer a conflict between behaviour and brain (N170 results have now been shown to be consistent with our behavioural conclusions), but instead fMRI results conflict with those from behavioural, ERP, and right hemisphere advantage studies. We have suggested at least two possible approaches: Test children in child-sized head coils to match tSNR across age groups and see whether the age-related changes in the FFA disappear or hold up; and test the hypothesis that FFA size is related to the number of faces known to the observer (e.g., compare children from small country-town schools and large city schools). Finally, in terms of innate and genetic contributions to face recognition, there has been no investigation of face-space coding. Data about this domain would be valuable in clarifying whether the effects of human's evolutionary history are apparent not only on face individuation ability, holistic processing, and ventral stream response to faces, but indeed to all aspects of face recognition.

REFERENCES

Anes, M. D., & Short, L. A. (2009). Adult-like competence in perceptual encoding of facial configuration by the right hemisphere emerges after 10 years of age. *Perception*, *38*(3), 333–342.

Anzures, G., Mondloch, C. J., & Lackner, C. (2009). Face adaptation and attractiveness aftereffects in 8-year-olds and adults. *Child Development*, *80*(1), 178–191. doi:10.1111/j.1467-8624.2008.01253.x

Aylward, E. H., Park, J. E., Field, K. M., Parsons, A. C., Richards, T. L., Cramer, S. C., et al. (2005). Brain activation during face perception: Evidence of a developmental change. *Journal of Cognitive Neuroscience*, *17*(2), 308–319.

Baudouin, J.-Y., Gallay, M., Durand, K., & Robichon, F. (2010). The development of perceptual sensitivity to second-order facial relations in children. *Journal of Experimental Child Psychology*, *107*, 195–206.

Bentin, S., Allison, T., Puce, A., Perez, E., & McCarthy, G. (1996). Electrophysiological studies of face perception in humans. *Journal of Cognitive Neuroscience*, *8*(6), 551–565.

Betts, J., Mckay, J., Maruff, P., & Anderson, V. (2006). The development of sustained attention in children: The effect of age and task load. *Child Neuropsychology*, *12*, 205–221.

Bjorklund, D. F., & Douglas, R. N. (1997). The development of memory strategies. In N. Cowan (Ed.), *The development of memory in childhood* (pp. 201–246). Hove, UK: Psychology Press.

Bowles, D. C., McKone, E., Dawel, A., Duchaine, B. C., Palermo, R., Schmalzl, L., et al. (2009). Diagnosing prosopagnosia: Effects of ageing, sex, and participant-stimulus ethnic match on the Cambridge Face Memory Test and Cambridge Face Perception Test. *Cognitive Neuropsychology*, *25*(5), 423–455.

Brace, N. A., Hole, G. J., Kemp, R. I., Pike, G. E., Van Duuren, M., & Norgate, L. (2001). Developmental changes in the effect of inversion: Using a picture book to investigate face recognition. *Perception, 30,* 85–94.

Brants, M., Wagemans, J., & Op de Beeck, H. P. (2011). Activation of fusiform face area by greebles is related to face similarity but not expertise. *Journal of Cognitive Neuroscience, 23*(12), 3949–3958.

Bruce, V., Henderson, Z., Newman, C., & Burton, M. A. (2001). Matching identities of familiar and unfamiliar faces caught on CCTV images. *Journal of Experimental Psychology: Applied, 7*(3), 207–218.

Burton, A. M., Wilson, S., Cowan, M., & Bruce, V. (1999). Face recognition in poor-quality video: Evidence from security surveillance. *Psychological Science, 10*(3), 243–248.

Cantlon, J. F., Brannon, E. M., Carter, E. J., & Pelphrey, K. A. (2006). Functional imaging of numerical processing in adults and 4-y-old children. *PLoS Biology, 4*(5), e125.

Cantlon, J. F., Pinel, P., Dehaene, S., & Pelphrey, K. A. (2011). Cortical representations of symbols, objects, and faces are pruned back during early childhood. *Cerebral Cortex, 21*(1), 191–199.

Carbon, C. C., Strobach, T., Langton, S., Harsányi, G., Leder, H., & Kovács, G. (2007). Adaptation effects of highly familiar faces: Immediate and long lasting. *Memory and Cognition, 35*(8), 1966–1976.

Carey, S. (1981). The development of face perception. In G. Davies, H. D. Ellis, & J. Shepherd (Eds.), *Perceiving and remembering faces* (pp. 9–38). New York, NY: Academic Press.

Carey, S. (1992). Becoming a face expert. *Philosophical Transactions of the Royal Society of London: B, 335,* 95–103.

Carey, S., & Diamond, R. (1977). From piecemeal to configurational representation of faces. *Science, 195,* 312–314.

Carey, S., & Diamond, R. (1994). Are faces perceived as configurations more by adults than by children? *Visual Cognition, 1*(2/3), 253–274.

Carey, S., Diamond, R., & Woods, B. (1980). Development of face recognition—A maturational component? *Developmental Psychology, 16*(4), 257–269.

Chang, P. P. W., Levine, S. C., & Benson, P. J. (2002). Children's recognition of caricatures. *Developmental Psychology, 38*(6), 1038–1051.

Changeux, J. P., & Danchin, A. (1976). Selective stabilisation of developing synapses as a mechanism for the specification of neuronal networks. *Nature, 264,* 705–712.

Chung, M.-S., & Thomson, D. M. (1995). Development of face recognition. *British Journal of Psychology, 86*(1), 55–87.

Cohen, L. B., & Cashon, C. H. (2001). Do 7-month-old infants process independent features of facial configurations? *Infant and Child Development, 10,* 83–92.

Cooper, P. A., Geldart, S. S., Mondloch, C. J., & Maurer, D. (2006). Developmental changes in perceptions of attractiveness: A role for experience? *Developmental Science, 9*(5), 530–543.

Crookes, K., & McKone, E. (2009). Early maturity of face recognition: No childhood development of holistic processing, novel face encoding, or face-space. *Cognition, 111*(2), 219–247.

Dalrymple, K. A., Oruç, I., Duchaine, B., Pancaroglu, R., Fox, C. J., Iaria, G., et al. (2011). The anatomic basis of the right face-selective N170 in acquired prosopagnosia: A combined ERP/fMRI study. *Neuropsychologia, 49,* 2553–2563.

Davidson, M. C., Amso, D., Anderson, L. C., & Diamond, A. (2006). Development of cognitive control and executive functions from 4 to 13 years: Evidence from manipulations of memory, inhibition, and task switching. *Neuropsychologia, 44*(11), 2037–2078.

DeGutis, J. M., Bentin, S., Robertson, L. C., & D'Esposito, M. (2007). Functional plasticity in ventral temporal cortex following cognitive rehabilitation of a congenital prosopagnosic. *Journal of Cognitive Neuroscience, 19*(11), 1790–1802.

de Haan, M., Johnson, M. H., & Halit, H. (2003). Development of face-sensitive event-related potentials during infancy: A review. *International Journal of Psychophysiology, 51*(1), 45–58.

de Heering, A., de Liedekerke, C., Deboni, M., & Rossion, B. (2010). The role of experience during childhood in shaping the other-race effect. *Developmental Science, 13*(1), 181–187.

de Heering, A., Houthuys, S., & Rossion, B. (2007). Holistic face processing is mature at 4 years of age: Evidence from the composite face effect. *Journal of Experimental Child Psychology, 96,* 57–70.

de Heering, A., Rossion, B., & Maurer, D. (2012). Developmental changes in face recognition during childhood: Evidence from upright and inverted faces. *Cognitive Development, 27,* 17–27.

de Schonen, S., & Mathivet, E. (1990). Hemispheric asymmetry in a face discrimination task in infants. *Child Development, 61*(4), 1192–1205.

Diamond, R., & Carey, S. (1986). Why faces are and are not special: An effect of expertise. *Journal of Experimental Psychology: General, 115*(2), 107–117.
Dobel, C., Bölte, J., Aicher, M., & Schweinberger, S. R. (2007). Prosopagnosia without apparent cause: Overview and diagnosis of six cases. *Cortex, 43*(6), 718–733.
Donnelly, N., & Hadwin, J. A. (2003). Children's perception of the Thatcher illusion: Evidence for development in configural processing. *Visual Cognition, 10*(8), 1001–1017.
Donnelly, N., Hadwin, J. A., Cave, K., & Stevenage, S. (2003). Perceptual dominance of oriented faces mirrors the distribution of orientation tuning in inferotemporal neurons. *Cognitive Brain Research, 17,* 771–780.
Duchaine, B., Germine, L., & Nakayama, K. (2007). Family resemblance: Ten family members with prosopagnosia and within-class object agnosia. *Cognitive Neuropsychology, 24*(4), 419–430.
Duchaine, B. C., & Nakayama, K. (2006). The Cambridge face memory test: Results for neurologically intact individuals and an investigation of its validity using inverted face stimuli and prosopagnosic participants. *Neuropsychologia, 44,* 576–585.
Ellis, H. D., Ellis, D. M., & Hosie, J. A. (1993). Priming effects in children's face recognition. *British Journal of Psychology, 84,* 101–110.
Ellis, H. D., & Shepherd, J. W. (1975). Recognition of upright and inverted faces presented in the left and right visual fields. *Cortex, 11*(1), 3–7.
Ellis, H. D., Shepherd, J. W., & Davies, G. M. (1979). Identification of familiar and unfamiliar faces from internal and external features: Some implications for theories of face recognition. *Perception, 8*(4), 431–439.
Fagan, J. F. (1972). Infants' recognition memory for faces. *Journal of Experimental Child Psychology, 14*(3), 453–476.
Fagan, J. F. (1976). Infants' recognition of invariant features of faces. *Child Development, 47*(3), 627–638.
Fagan, J. F. (1979). The origins of facial pattern recognition. In M. H. Bornstein & W. Keesan (Eds.), *Psychological development from infancy: Image to intention.* Hillsdale, NJ: Lawrence Erlbaum Associates.
Ferguson, K. T., Kulkofsky, S., Cashon, C. H., & Casasola, M. (2009). The development of specialized processing of own-race faces in infancy. *Infancy, 14*(3), 263–284.
Flavell, J. H. (1985). *Cognitive development* (2nd ed.). Englewood Cliffs, NJ: Prentice-Hall.
Flavell, J. H., & Wellman, H. M. (1977). Metamemory. In R. V. Kail & J. W. Hagen (Eds.), *Perspectives on the development of memory and cognition* (pp. 3–33). Hillsdale, NJ: Lawrence Erlbaum Associates.
Flin, R. H. (1985). Development of face recognition: An encoding switch? *British Journal of Psychology, 76,* 123–134.
Freiwald, W. A., & Tsao, D. Y. (2010). Functional compartmentalization and viewpoint generalization within the macaque face-processing system. *Science, 330,* 845–851.
Ge, L., Anzures, G., Wang, Z., Kelly, D. J., Pascalis, O., Quinn, P. C., et al. (2008). An inner face advantage in children's recognition of familiar peers. *Journal of Experimental Child Psychology, 101,* 124–136.
Geldart, S., Maurer, D., & Henderson, H. (1999). Effects of the height of the internal features of faces on adults' aesthetic ratings and 5-month-olds' looking times. *Perception, 28,* 839–850.
Geldart, S., Mondloch, C. J., Maurer, D., de Schonen, S., & Brent, H. P. (2002). The effect of early visual deprivation on the development of face processing. *Developmental Science, 5*(4), 490–501.
Germine, L. T., Duchaine, B., & Nakayama, K. (2011). Where cognitive development and aging meet: Face learning ability peaks after age 30. *Cognition, 118,* 201–210.
Gilchrist, A., & McKone, E. (2003). Early maturity of face processing in children: Local and relational distinctiveness effects in 7-year-olds. *Visual Cognition, 10*(7), 769–793.
Golarai, G., Ghahemani, D. G., Whitfield-Gabrieli, S., Reiss, A., Eberhardt, J. L., Gabrieli, J. D., et al. (2007). Differential development of high-level visual cortex correlates with category-specific recognition memory. *Nature Neuroscience, 10,* 512–522.
Golarai, G., Liberman, A., Yoon, J. M., & Grill-Spector, K. (2010). Differential development of the ventral visual cortex extends through adolescence. *Frontiers in Human Neuroscience, 3,* 80.
Goldstein, A. G., & Chance, J. E. (1980). Memory for faces and schema theory. *Journal of Psychology, 105*(1), 47–59.
Grill-Spector, K., Knouf, N., & Kanwisher, N. (2004). The fusiform face area subserves face perception, not generic within-category identification. *Nature Neuroscience, 7*(5), 555–562.
Grueter, M., Grueter, T., Bell, V., Horst, J., Laskowski, W., Sperling, K., et al. (2007). Hereditary

prosopagnosia: The first case series. *Cortex*, *43*(6), 734–749.

Halit, H., de Haan, M., & Johnson, M. H. (2003). Cortical specialisation for face processing: Face-sensitive event-related potential components in 3- and 12-month-old infants. *NeuroImage*, *19*(3), 1180–1193.

Harel, A., Gilaie-Dotan, S., Malach, R., & Bentin, S. (2010). Top-down engagement modulates the neural expressions of visual expertise. *Cerebral Cortex*, *20*, 2304–2318.

Haxby, J. V., Ungerleider, L. G., Clark, V. P., Schouten, J. L., Hoffman, E. A., & Martin, A. (1999). The effect of face inversion on activity in human neural systems for face and object perception. *Neuron*, *22*(1), 189–199.

Hayden, A., Bhatt, R. S., Reed, A., Corbly, C. R., & Joseph, J. E. (2007). The development of expert face processing: Are infants sensitive to normal differences in second-order relational information? *Journal of Experimental Child Psychology*, *97*, 85–98.

Henderson, R. M., McCulloch, D. L., & Herbert, A. M. (2003). Event-related potentials (ERPs) to schematic faces in adults and children. *International Journal of Psychophysiology*, *51*(1), 59–67.

Hills, P. J., Holland, A. M., & Lewis, M. B. (2010). Aftereffects for face attributes with different natural variability: Children are more adaptable than adolescents. *Cognitive Development*, *25*(3), 278–289.

Humphreys, K., & Johnson, M. H. (2007). The development of "face-space" in infancy. *Visual Cognition*, *15*(5), 578–598.

Itier, R. J., & Taylor, M. J. (2004). Source analysis of the N170 to faces and objects. *Neuroreport*, *15*(8), 1261–1265.

Jaquet, E., Rhodes, G., & Hayward, W. G. (2007). Opposite aftereffects for Chinese and Caucasian faces are selective for social category information and not just physical face differences. *The Quarterly Journal of Experimental Psychology*, *60*(11), 1457–1467. doi:10.1080/17470210701467870

Jeffery, L., McKone, E., Haynes, R., Firth, E., Pellicano, E., & Rhodes, G. (2010). Four-to-six year-old children use norm-based coding in face-space. *Journal of Vision*, *10*(5), 18.

Jeffery, L., Rhodes, G., McKone, E., Pellicano, E., Crookes, K., & Taylor, E. (2011). Distinguishing norm-based from exemplar-based coding of identity in children: Evidence from face identity aftereffects. *Journal of Experimental Psychology: Human Perception and Performance*, *37*(6), 1824–1840.

Johnson, M. H. (2005). Subcortical face processing. *Nature Reviews. Neuroscience.*, *6*, 766–774.

Johnson, M. H., Griffin, R., Csibra, G., Halit, H., Farroni, T., de Haan, M., et al. (2005). The emergence of the social brain network: Evidence from typical and atypical development. *Development and Psychopathology*, *17*(3), 599–619.

Johnston, P. J., Kaufman, J., Bajic, J., Sercombe, A., Michie, P. T., & Karayanidis, F. (2011). Facial emotion and identity processing development in 5- to 15-year-old children. *Frontiers in Psychology*, *2*(26), 1–9.

Johnston, R. A., & Ellis, H. D. (1995). Age effects in the processing of typical and distinctive faces. *The Quarterly Journal of Experimental Psychology*, *48A*(2), 447–465.

Joseph, J. E., Gathers, A. D., & Bhatt, R. S. (2011). Progressive and regressive developmental changes in neural substrates for face processing: Testing specific predictions of the interactive specialization account. *Developmental Science*, *14*(2), 1–15.

Kanwisher, N., Mc Dermott, J., & Chun, M. M. (1997). The fusiform face area: A module in human extrastriate cortex specialized for face perception. *Journal of Neuroscience*, *17*(11), 4302–4311.

Keil, B., Alagappan, V., Mareyam, A., McNab, J., Fujimoto, K., Tountcheva, V., et al. (2011). Size-optimized 32-channel brain arrays for 3T pediatric imaging. *Magnetic Resonance in Medicine*, *66*, 1777–1787.

Kelly, D. J., Liu, S., Lee, K., Quinn, P. C., Pascalis, O., Slater, A. M., et al. (2009). Development of the other-race effect during infancy: Evidence toward universality? *Journal of Experimental Child Psychology*, *104*, 105–114.

Kelly, D. J., Quinn, P. C., Slater, A., Lee, K., Ge, L., & Pascalis, O. (2007). The other-race effect develops during infancy: Evidence of perceptual narrowing. *Psychological Science*, *18*(12), 1084–1089.

Kennerknecht, I., Pluempe, N., & Welling, B. (2008). Congenital prosopagnosia—A common hereditary cognitive dysfunction in humans. *Frontiers in Bioscience*, *1*(13), 3150–3158.

Kuefner, D., de Heering, A., Jacques, C., Palmero-Soler, E., & Rossion, B. (2010). Early visually evoked electrophysiological responses over the human brain (P1, N170) show stable patterns of face-sensitivity from 4 years to adulthood. *Frontiers in Human Neuroscience*, *3*(67), 1–22.

Kuhl, P. K., Stevens, E., Hayashi, A., Deguchi, T., Kiritanim, S., & Iverson, P. (2006). Infants show a facilitation effect for native language phonetic perception between 6 and 12 months. *Developmental Science*, *9*(2), F13–F21.

Kuhl, P. K., Tsao, F.-M., & Liu, H.-M. (2003). Foreign-language experience in infancy: Effects of short-term exposure and social interaction on phonetic learning. *Proceedings of the National Academy of Sciences of the United States of America*, *100*, 9096–9101.

Lee, Y., Duchaine, B., Wilson, H. R., & Nakayama, K. (2010). Three cases of developmental prosopagnosia from one family: Detailed neuropsychological and psychophysical investigation of face processing. *Cortex*, *46*(8), 949–964.

Le Grand, R., Mondloch, C. J., Maurer, D., & Brent, H. P. (2003). Expert face processing requires visual input to the right hemisphere during infancy. *Nature Neuroscience*, *6*(10), 1108–1112.

Le Grand, R., Mondloch, C. J., Maurer, D., & Brent, H. P. (2004). Impairment in holistic face processing following early visual deprivation. *Psychological Science*, *15*(11), 762–768.

Leo, I., & Simion, F. (2009). Face processing at birth: A Thatcher illusion study. *Developmental Science*, *12*(3), 492–498.

Leopold, D. A., O'Toole, A. J., Vetter, T., & Blanz, V. (2001). Prototype-referenced shape encoding revealed by high-level aftereffects. *Nature Neuroscience*, *4*(1), 89–94. doi:10.1038/82947

Lewis, M. B. (2003). Thatcher's children: Development and the Thatcher illusion. *Perception*, *32*, 1415–1421.

Lundy, B. L., Jackson, J. W., & Haaf, R. A. (2001). Stimulus properties, attentional limitations, and young children's face recognition. *Perceptual and Motor Skills*, *92*, 919–929.

Macchi Cassia, V., Kuefner, D., Picozzi, M., & Vescovo, E. (2009). Early experience predicts later plasticity for face processing: Evidence for the reactivation of dormant effects. *Psychological Science*, *20*(7), 853–859.

Macchi Cassia, V., Picozzi, M., Kuefner, D., Bricolo, E., & Turati, C. (2009). Holistic processing for faces and cars in preschool-aged children and adults: Evidence from the composite effect. *Developmental Science*, *12*(2), 236–248.

Macchi Cassia, V., Turati, C., & Schwarzer, G. (2011). Sensitivity to spacing changes in faces and nonface objects in preschool-aged children and adults. *Journal of Experimental Child Psychology*, *109*, 454–467.

Marcel, T., & Rajan, P. (1975). Lateral specialization for recognition of words and faces in good and poor readers. *Neuropsychologia*, *13*(4), 489–497.

Martini, P., McKone, E., & Nakayama, K. (2006). Orientation tuning of human face processing estimated by contrast matching on transparency displays. *Vision Research*, *46*(13), 2102–2109.

Maurer, D., Le Grand, R., & Mondloch, C. J. (2002). The many faces of configural processing. *Trends in Cognitive Sciences*, *6*(6), 255–260.

McKone, E. (2008). Configural processing and face viewpoint. *Journal of Experimental Psychology: Human Perception and Performance*, *34*(2), 310–327.

McKone, E., & Boyer, B. L. (2006). Sensitivity of 4-year-olds to featural and second-order relational changes in face distinctiveness. *Journal of Experimental Child Psychology*, *94*(2), 134–162.

McKone, E., Crookes, K., & Kanwisher, N. (2009). The cognitive and neural development of face recognition in humans. In M.S. Gazzaniga (Ed.), *The cognitive neurosciences* (Vol. IV, pp. 467–482). Cambridge, MA: Bradford Books.

McKone, E., Hall, A., Pidcock, M., Palermo, P., Wilkinson, R. B., Rivolta, D., et al. (2011). Face ethnicity and measurement reliability affect face recognition performance in developmental prosopagnosia: Evidence from the Cambridge Face Memory Test–Australian. *Cognitive Neuropsychology*, *28*(2), 109–146.

McKone, E., Kanwisher, N., & Duchaine, B. C. (2007). Can generic expertise explain special processing for faces? *Trends in Cognitive Sciences*, *11*(1), 8–15.

McKone, E., & Palermo, R. (2010). A strong role for nature in face recognition. *Proceedings of the National Academy of Sciences of the USA*, *107*(11), 4795–4796.

McKone, E., & Yovel, G. (2009). Why does picture-plane inversion sometimes dissociate perception of features and spacing in faces, and sometimes not? Toward a new theory of holistic processing. *Psychonomic Bulletin and Review*, *16*(5), 778–797.

Meinhardt-Injac, B., Zöllig, J., Persike, M., Martin, M., Seiffge-Krenke, I., & Meinhardt, G. (2011). Developmental changes in the microgenesis of face perception revealed by effects of context and inversion. *Vision Research*, *51*(12), 1338–1350.

Mondloch, C. J., Dobson, K. S., Parsons, J., & Maurer, D. (2004). Why 8-year-olds cannot tell the difference between Steve Martin and Paul Newman:

Factors contributing to the slow development of sensitivity to the spacing of facial features. *Journal of Experimental Child Psychology, 89,* 159–181.

Mondloch, C. J., Geldart, S., Maurer, D., & Le Grand, R. (2003). Developmental changes in face processing skills. *Journal of Experimental Child Psychology, 86,* 67–84.

Mondloch, C. J., Le Grand, R., & Maurer, D. (2002). Configural face processing develops more slowly than featural face processing. *Perception, 31,* 553–566.

Mondloch, C. J., Maurer, D., & Ahola, S. (2006). Becoming a face expert. *Psychological Science, 17*(11), 930–934.

Mondloch, C. J., Pathman, T., Maurer, D., Le Grand, R., & de Schonen, S. (2007). The composite face effect in six-year-old children: Evidence of adult-like holistic face processing. *Visual Cognition, 15*(5), 564–577.

Mondloch, C. J., & Thomson, K. (2008). Limitations in four-year-old children's sensitivity to the spacing among facial features. *Child Development, 79*(5), 1513–1523.

Morton, J., & Johnson, M. H. (1991). CONSPEC and CONLERN: A two-process theory of infant face recognition. *Psychological Review, 98*(2), 164–181.

Nakato, E., Otsuka, Y., Kanazawa, S., Yamaguchi, M. K., Watanabe, S., & Kakigi, R. (2009). When do infants differentiate profile face from frontal face? A near-infrared spectroscopic study. *Human Brain Mapping, 30,* 462–472.

Nishimura, M., Maurer, D., & Gao, X. (2009). Exploring children's face-space: A multidimensional scaling analysis of the mental representation of facial identity. *Journal of Experimental Child Psychology, 103*(3), 355–375. doi:10.1016/j.jecp.2009.02.005

Nishimura, M., Maurer, D., Jeffery, L., Pellicano, E., & Rhodes, G. (2008). Fitting the child's mind to the world: Adaptive norm-based coding of facial identity in 8-year-olds. *Developmental Science, 11*(4), 620–627. doi:10.1111/j.1467-7687.2008.00706.x

Nishimura, M., Robertson, C., & Maurer, D. (2011). Effect of adaptor duration on 8-year-olds' facial identity aftereffects suggests adult-like plasticity of the face norm. *Vision Research, 51*(11), 1216–1222. doi:10.1016/j.visres.2011.03.013

O'Hearn, K., Schroer, E., Minshew, N., & Luna, B. (2010). Lack of developmental improvement on a face memory task during adolescence in autism. *Neuropsychologia, 48,* 3955–3960.

Ostrovsky, Y., Andalman, A., & Sinha, P. (2006). Vision following extended congenital blindness. *Psychological Science, 17*(12), 1009–1014.

Otsuka, Y., Nakato, E., Kanazawa, S., Yamaguchi, M. K., Watanabe, S., & Kakigi, R. (2007). Neural activation to upright and inverted faces in infants measured by near infrared spectroscopy. *NeuroImage, 34,* 399–406.

Pascalis, O., de Haan, M., & Nelson, C. A. (2002). Is face processing species-specific during the first year of life? *Science, 296,* 1321–1323.

Pascalis, O., de Haan, M., Nelson, C. A., & de Schonen, S. (1998). Long-term recognition memory for faces assessed by visual paired comparison in 3- and 6-month-old infants. *Journal of Experimental Psychology: Learning, Memory & Cognition, 24*(1), 249–260.

Pascalis, O., & de Schonen, S. (1994). Recognition memory in 3- to 4-day-old human neonates. *Neuroreport, 5,* 1721–1724.

Pascalis, O., Scott, L. S., Kelly, D. J., Shannon, R. W., Nicholson, E., Coleman, M., et al. (2005). Plasticity of face processing in infancy. *Proceedings of the National Academy of Sciences of the United States of America, 102*(14), 5297–5300.

Passarotti, A. M., Paul, B. M., Bussiere, J. R., Buxton, R. B., Wong, E. C., & Stiles, J. (2003). The development of face and location processing: An fMRI study. *Developmental Science, 6*(1), 100–117.

Passarotti, A. M., Smith, J., DeLano, M., & Huang, J. (2007). Developmental differences in the neural bases of the face inversion effect show progressive tuning of face-selective regions to the upright orientation. *NeuroImage, 34*(4), 1708–1722.

Pastò, L., & Burack, J. A. (1997). A developmental study of visual attention: Issues of filtering efficiency and focus. *Cognitive Development, 12,* 523–535.

Pedelty, L., Levine, S. C., & Shevell, S. K. (1985). Developmental changes in face processing: Results from multidimensional scaling. *Journal of Experimental Child Psychology, 39*(3), 421–436, doi:10.1016/0022-0965(85)90050-5.

Peelen, M. V., Glaser, B., Vuilleumier, P., & Eliez, S. (2009). Differential development of selectivity for faces and bodies in the fusiform gyrus. *Developmental Science, 12*(6), F16–F25.

Pellicano, E., Jeffery, L., Burr, D., & Rhodes, G. (2007). Abnormal adaptive face-coding mechanisms in children with autism spectrum disorder. *Current Biology, 17*(17), 1508–1542.

Pellicano, E., & Rhodes, G. (2003). Holistic processing of faces in preschool children and adults. *Psychological Science, 14*(6), 618–622.

Pellicano, E., Rhodes, G., & Peters, M. (2006). Are preschoolers sensitive to configural information in faces? *Developmental Science, 9*(3), 270–277.

Pelphrey, K. A., Lopez, J., & Morris, J. P. (2009). Developmental continuity and change in responses to social and nonsocial categories in human extrastriate visual cortex. *Frontiers in Human Neuroscience, 3,* 25.

Pezdek, K., Blandon-Gitlin, I., & Moore, C. (2003). Children's face recognition memory: More evidence for the cross-race effect. *Journal of Applied Psychology, 88*(4), 760–763.

Picozzi, M., Macchi Cassia, V., Turati, C., & Vescovo, E. (2009). The effect of inversion on 3- to 5-year-olds' recognition of face and nonface visual objects. *Journal of Experimental Child Psychology, 102,* 487–502.

Pimperton, H., Pellicano, E., Jeffery, L., & Rhodes, G. (2009). The role of higher level adaptive coding mechanisms in the development of face recognition. *Journal of Experimental Child Psychology, 104*(2), 229–238.

Polk, T. A., Park, J., Smith, M. R., & Park, D. C. (2007). Nature versus nurture in ventral visual cortex: A functional magnetic resonance imaging study of twins. *Journal of Neuroscience, 27*(51), 13921–13925.

Putzar, L., Hötting, K., & Röder, B. (2010). Early visual deprivation affects the development of face recognition and of audio-visual speech perception. *Restorative Neurology and Neuroscience, 28,* 251–257.

Quartz, S. R. (1999). The constructivist brain. *Trends Cognitive Science, 3,* 48–57.

Rhodes, G., Geddes, K., Jeffery, L., Dziurawiec, S., & Clark, A. (2002). Are average and symmetric faces attractive to infants? Discrimination and looking preferences. *Perception, 31*(3), 315–321.

Rhodes, G., & Jeffery, L. (2006). Adaptive norm-based coding of facial identity. *Vision Research, 46*(18), 2977–2987. doi:10.1016/j.visres.2006.03.002

Rhodes, G., Jeffery, L., Watson, T. L., Clifford, C.W. G., & Nakayama, K. (2003). Fitting the mind to the world: Face adaptation and attractiveness aftereffects. *Psychological Science, 14*(6), 558–566, doi:10.1046/j.0956-7976.2003.psci_1465.x.

Robbins, R., & McKone, E. (2003). Can holistic processing be learned for inverted faces? *Cognition, 88,* 79–107.

Robbins, R., & McKone, E. (2007). No face-like processing for objects-of-expertise in three behavioural tasks. *Cognition, 103*(1), 34–79.

Robbins, R., McKone, E., & Edwards, M. (2007). Aftereffects for face attributes with different natural variability: Adapter position effects and neural models. *Journal of Experimental Psychology: Human Perception and Performance, 33*(3), 570–592.

Robbins, R. A., Shergill, Y., Maurer, D., & Lewis, T. L. (2011). Development of sensitivity to spacing versus feature changes in pictures of houses: Evidence for slow development of a general spacing detection mechanism. *Journal of Experimental Child Psychology, 109,* 371–382.

Rodman, H. R., Scalaidhe, S. P., & Gross, C. G. (1993). Response properties of neurons in temporal cortical visual areas of infant monkeys. *Journal of Neurophysiology, 70*(3), 1115–1136.

Rose, S. A., Jankowski, J. J., & Feldman, J. F. (2002). Speed of processing and face recognition at 7 and 12 months. *Infancy, 3,* 435–455.

Rossion, B. (2008). Picture-plane inversion leads to qualitative changes of face perception. *Acta Psychologica, 128,* 274–289.

Sadeh, B., Podlipsky, I., Zhdanov, A., & Yovel, G. (2010). Event-related potential and functional MRI measures of face-selectivity are highly correlated: A simultaneous ERP–fMRI investigation. *Human Brain Mapping, 31,* 1490–1501.

Sangrigoli, S., & de Schonen, S. (2004a). Effect of visual experience on face processing: A developmental study of inversion and non-native effects. *Developmental Science, 7*(1), 74–87.

Sangrigoli, S., & de Schonen, S. (2004b). Recognition of own-race and other-race faces by three-month-old infants. *Journal of Child Psychology and Psychiatry, 45*(7), 1219–1227.

Sangrigoli, S., Pallier, C., Argenti, A. M., Ventureyra, V. A., & de Schonen, S. (2005). Reversibility of the other-race effect in face recognition during childhood. *Psychological Science, 16*(6), 440–444.

Saxe, R., Brett, M., & Kanwisher, N. (2006). Divide and conquer: A defence of functional localizers. *NeuroImage, 30*(4), 1088–1096.

Saxton, T. K., Debruine, L. M., Jones, B. C., Little, A. C., & Roberts, S. C. (2009). Face and voice attractiveness judgments change during adolescence. *Evolution and Human Behavior, 30*(6), 398–408. doi:10.1016/j.evolhumbehav.2009.06.004

Scherf, K. S., Behrmann, M., Humphreys, K., & Luna, B. (2007). Visual category-selectivity for faces, places and objects emerges along different developmental trajectories. *Developmental Science*, *10*(4), F15–F30.

Scherf, K. S., Luna, B., Avidan, G., & Behrmann, M. (2011). "What" precedes "which": Developmental neural tuning in face- and place-related cortex. *Cerebral Cortex*, *21*(9), 1963–1980.

Schmalzl, L., Palermo, R., & Coltheart, M. (2008). Cognitive heterogeneity in genetically-based prosopagnosia: A family study. *Journal of Neuropsychology*, *2*, 99–117.

Schultz, R. T. (2005). Developmental deficits in social perception in autism: The role of the amygdala and fusiform face area. *International Journal of Developmental Neuroscience*, *23*, 125–141.

Scott, L. S., & Monesson, A. (2009). The origin of biases in face perception. *Psychological Science*, *20*(6), 676–680.

Sengpiel, F. (2007). The critical period. *Current Biology*, *17*, R742–R743.

Short, L. A., Hatry, A. J., & Mondloch, C. J. (2011). The development of norm-based coding and race-specific face prototypes: An examination of 5- and 8-year-olds' face space. *Journal of Experimental Child Psychology*, *108*(2), 338–357, doi:10.1016/j.jecp.2010.07.007.

Simpson, E. A., Varga, K., Frick, J. E., & Fragaszy, D. (2011). Infants experience perceptual narrowing for nonprimate faces. *Infancy*, *16*(3), 318–328.

Skoczenski, A. M., & Norcia, A. M. (2002). Late maturation of visual hyperacuity. *Psychological Science*, *13*(6), 537–541.

Slater, A., Bremner, G., Johnson, S. P., Sherwood, P., Hayes, R., & Brown, E. (2000). Newborn infants' preference for attractive faces: The role of internal and external facial features. *Infancy*, *1*(2), 265–274.

Slater, A., Quinn, P. C., Hayes, R., & Brown, E. (2000). The role of facial orientation in newborn infants' preference for attractive faces. *Developmental Science*, *3*(2), 181–185.

Sporer, S. L., Trinkl, B., & Guberova, E. (2007). Matching faces: Differences in processing speed of out-group faces by different ethnic groups. *Journal of Cross-Cultural Psychology*, *38*(4), 398–412, doi:10.1177/0022022107302310.

Sugita, Y. (2008). Face perception in monkeys reared with no exposure to faces. *Proceedings of the National Academy of Sciences of the United States of America*, *105*(1), 394–398.

Susilo, T., Crookes, K., McKone, E., & Turner, H. (2009). The composite task reveals stronger holistic processing in children than adults for child faces. *PLoS One*, *4*(7), e6460.

Tanaka, J. W., & Farah, M. (1993). Parts and wholes in face recognition. *The Quarterly Journal of Experimental Psychology*, *46A*(2), 225–245.

Tanaka, J. W., Kay, J. B., Grinnell, E., Stansfield, B., & Szechter, L. (1998). Face recognition in young children: When the whole is greater than the sum of its parts. *Visual Cognition*, *5*, 479–496.

Tanaka, J. W., Meixner, T. L., & Kantner, J. (2011). Exploring the perceptual spaces of faces, cars and birds in children and adults. *Developmental Science*, *14*(4), 762–768.

Tanaka, J. W., & Sengco, J. A. (1997). Features and their configuration in face recognition. *Memory and Cognition*, *25*(5), 583–592.

Taylor, M. J., Batty, M., & Itier, R. J. (2004). The faces of development: A review of early face processing over childhood. *Journal of Cognitive Neuroscience*, *16*(8), 1426–1442.

Taylor, M. J., Edmonds, G. E., McCarthy, G., & Allison, T. (2001). Eyes first! Eye processing develops before face processing in children. *Neuroreport*, *12*(8), 1671–1676.

Taylor, M. J., McCarthy, G., Saliba, E., & Degiovanni, E. (1999). ERP evidence of developmental changes in processing of faces. *Clinical Neurophysiology*, *110*(5), 910–915.

Teunisse, J. P., & de Gelder, B. (2003). Face processing in adolescents with autistic disorder: The inversion and composite effects. *Brain and Cognition*, *52*(3), 285–294.

Thompson, L. A., Madrid, V., Westbrook, S., & Johnston, V. (2001). Infants attend to second-order relational properties of faces. *Psychonomic Bulletin and Review*, *8*(4), 769–777.

Thompson, P. (1980). Margaret Thatcher: A new illusion. *Perception*, *9*(4), 483–484.

Triantafyllou, C., Polimeni, J. R., & Wald, L. L. (2011). Physiological noise and signal-to-noise ratio in fMRI using multi-channel array coils. *NeuroImage*, *55*(1), 597–606.

Tsao, D. Y., Freiwald, W. A., Tootell, R.B. H., & Livingstone, M. S. (2006). A cortical region consisting entirely of face-selective cells. *Science*, *311*, 670–674.

Turati, C., Bulf, H., & Simion, F. (2008). Newborns' face recognition over changes in viewpoint. *Cognition*, *106*, 1300–1321.

Turati, C., Di Giorgio, E., Bardi, L., & Simion, F. (2010). Holistic face processing in newborns, 3-month-old infants, and adults: Evidence from the composite face effect. *Child Development*, *81*(6), 1894–1905.

Turati, C., Macchi Cassia, V., Simion, F., & Leo, I. (2006). Newborns' face recognition: Role of inner and outer facial features. *Child Development*, *77*(2), 297–311.

Turati, C., Sangrigoli, S., Ruel, J., & de Schonen, S. (2004). Evidence of the face inversion effect in 4-month-old infants. *Infancy*, *6*(2), 275–297.

Valentine, T. (1991). A unified account of the effects of distinctiveness, inversion, and race in face recognition. *The Quarterly Journal of Experimental Psychology*, *43A*(2), 161–204.

Want, S. C., Pascalis, O., Coleman, M., & Blades, M. (2003). Face facts: Is the development of face recognition in early and middle childhood really so special? In O. Pascalis & A. Slater (Eds.), *The development of face processing in infancy and early childhood* (pp. 207–221). New York, NY: Nova Science Publishers.

Webster, M. A., & MacLin, O. H. (1999). Figural aftereffects in the perception of faces. *Psychonomic Bulletin and Review*, *6*(4), 647–653.

Wilmer, J. B., Germine, L., Chabris, C. F., Chatterjee, G., Williams, M., Loken, E., et al. (2010). Human face recognition ability is specific and highly heritable. *Proceedings of the National Academy of Sciences*, *107*(11), 5238–5241.

Wilson, R. R., Blades, M., & Pascalis, O. (2007). What do children look at in an adult face with which they are personally familiar? *British Journal of Development Psychology*, *25*, 375–382.

Yardley, L., McDermott, L., Pisarski, S., Duchaine, B. C., & Nakayama, K. (2008). Psychosocial consequences of developmental prosopagnosia: A problem of recognition. *Journal of Psychosomatic Research*, *65*(5), 445–451.

Yin, R. K. (1969). Looking at upside-down faces. *Journal of Experimental Psychology*, *81*(1), 141–145.

Young, A. W., & Bion, P. J. (1980). Absence of any developmental trend in right hemisphere superiority for face recognition. *Cortex*, *16*(2), 213–221.

Young, A. W., & Ellis, H. D. (1976). An experimental investigation of developmental differences in ability to recognise faces presented to the left and right cerebral hemispheres. *Neuropsychologia*, *14*, 495–498.

Young, A. W., Hellawell, D., & Hay, D. C. (1987). Configurational information in face perception. *Perception*, *16*, 747–759.

Yovel, G., & Duchaine, B. (2006). Specialized face perception mechanisms extract both part and spacing information: Evidence from developmental prosopagnosia. *Journal of Cognitive Neuroscience*, *18*(4), 580–593.

Yovel, G., & Kanwisher, N. (2005). The neural basis of the behavioral face-inversion effect. *Current Biology*, *15*(24), 2256–2262.

Zhu, Q., Song, Y., Hu, S., Li, X., Tian, M., Zhen, Z., et al. (2010). Heritability of the specific cognitive ability of face perception. *Current Biology*, *20*(2), 137–142.

Core knowledge of object, number, and geometry: A comparative and neural approach

Giorgio Vallortigara

Center for Mind/Brain Sciences, University of Trento, Rovereto, Italy

Studies on the ontogenetic origins of human knowledge provide evidence for a small set of separable systems of core knowledge dealing with the representation of inanimate and animate objects, number, and geometry. Because core knowledge systems are evolutionarily ancient, they can be investigated from a comparative perspective, making use of various animal models. In this review, I discuss evidence showing precocious abilities in nonhuman species to represent (a) objects that move partly or fully out of view and their basic mechanical properties such as solidity, (b) the cardinal and ordinal/sequential aspects of numerical cognition and rudimentary arithmetic with small numerosities, and (c) the geometrical relationships among extended surfaces in the surrounding layout. Controlled rearing studies suggest that the abilities associated with core knowledge systems of objects, number, and geometry are observed in animals in the absence (or with very reduced) experience, supporting a nativistic foundation of such cognitive mechanisms. Animal models also promise a fresh approach to the issue of the neurobiological and genetic mechanisms underlying the expression of core knowledge systems.

Keywords: Core knowledge; Space; Geometry; Number; Objects; Intuitive physics; Animacy; Chicks.

According to a prominent hypothesis (Carey, 2009; Spelke, 2000), human cognition is composed of a set of core systems for representing significant aspects of the environment—namely, objects, persons, spatial relationships, and number. The hypothesis maintains that core knowledge systems are shared by other animals and are in place at birth. Studies on object, number, and space representation (e.g., Beran, Decker, Schwartz, & Schultz, 2011; Brannon, 2006; Cantlon & Brannon, 2006; Tommasi, Chiandetti, Pecchia, Sovrano, & Vallortigara, 2012; van Marle, Aw, McCrink, & Santos, 2006) in a variety of species provide evidence for the generality of the core knowledge systems in other animals. The hypothesis that core knowledge systems are available at birth is difficult to test in human infants, because of the unavoidable limitations on the control of early experience. It is important to note, however, that similar limitations are also apparent with other altricial species, whose young are born in a relatively immature state. Consider as an example

Correspondence should be addressed to Giorgio Vallortigara, Center for Mind/Brain Sciences, University of Trento, Corso Bettini 31, Rovereto, 38068 Italy. (E-mail: giorgio.vallortigara@unitn.it).

This work has been prepared thanks to the support from the Provincia Autonoma di Trento and the Fondazione Cassa di Risparmio di Trento e Rovereto. Thanks also to Dr Sang Ah Lee for commenting on a previous version of this paper.

http://www.psypress.com/cogneuropsychology http://dx.doi.org/10.1080/02643294.2012.654772

the issue of preferential orientation of neonates to human faces. A complete absence of face stimulation could not be feasible even in neonates studied a few hours after birth. However, similar limitations arise in animal work. Sugita (2008) reported that infant Japanese monkeys reared with no exposure to any faces for 6–24 months showed nevertheless a preference for human and monkey faces. However, monkeys were separated from their mother within a few hours after birth (Sugita, 2008, p.1), making possible, in principle, very fast learning of face characteristics. Besides, it could be argued that monkeys (or other altricial animals) maintained for several months without exposure to faces might show an abnormal pattern of psychological development. On the other hand, testing monkeys soon after birth even in simple behavioural tasks would prove impractical because of their motoric immaturity.

Luckily enough, nature seems to have provided biologists with appropriate model organisms for investigation of every sort of scientific problem—"*God's organisms*", in the words of neuroscientist Steven Rose (2000). There are species that are extremely precocial with regard to their pattern of motor development, making possible quite sophisticated behavioural analyses at an early age (i.e., soon after birth or hatching) combined with a very precise control on the effects of past (even in utero or in ovo) sensory experiences, including a complete lack of some of them. Here I champion the use of the young domestic chick as a "God's organism" for investigation of the origin of knowledge.

Criticisms concerning whether evidence for cognitive abilities available at birth indicate innateness stress that one cannot exclude a role of experience and learning in utero or in ovo (this was one of the arguments of Lehrman, 1953, in his debate with Lorenz, 1965, about so-called "instinctive behaviour"). Actually, control of stimulation in embryo would be possible to some degree using animal models. But there are reasons to doubt that evidence for a role of stimulation in embryo could produce prima facie evidence against innateness. An example comes from some work carried out recently in my lab. We took advantage of the phenomenon of filial imprinting, the process by which animals like young chicks and ducks develop a strong social attachment to the first conspicuous visual object they are exposed to soon after hatching (see Natural-born physicists section). We found that newly hatched chicks show a spontaneous preference for consonant over dissonant intervals when coupled with a visual imprinting object to approach (Chiandetti & Vallortigara, 2011a). Chicks in these experiments were incubated and hatched in soundproof environments, but of course they could hear the sounds produced by themselves as embryos. However, chick vocalizations in embryo are produced spontaneously, and therefore their structure (consonant or dissonant) cannot be learned. Thus, if one assumes that the preference for consonance in newly hatched chicks cannot be said to be innately predisposed because it might actually arise from sensory stimulation in embryo, then it remains to be explained why the motor system of these embryos should be predisposed to produce consonant (rather than dissonant) intervals. The innateness that has been expunged from the sensorial side reappears in the motoric side.

I believe that we must be careful to keep separate the issue of the *origin* of information an organism appears to possess from the way in which information is actually encoded in the brain and exhibited in behaviour. We know very well that the road from genes to behaviour is a complex one and that development always implies a mixture of genetic, epigenetic, and experience factors (Bateson & Gluckman, 2011; Marcus, 2004). Nonetheless, the issue of the origin of information is different from that of the development of behaviour, because it should take into account the adaptiveness exhibited by organisms in behaviour. Consider the classical reply provided by Lorenz (1965) to Lehrman's criticisms. Let's assume, said Lorenz, that the aggressive behaviour exhibited by the famous three-spined stickleback fish to objects that are red on their belly is not innately predisposed but it is in some way learned in embryo as the empiricists would argue. Now, the issue is: How do the stickleback fish know that attacking things that are red in their bellies is good for them? In fact the behaviour of attacking things that are red in their bellies is adaptive to the fish because it happens that things with red bellies are, in their natural environment, their male conspecifics. But what is the origin of *this* information that fish seem to possess? How do they possibly learn, in embryo, that they are going to meet male conspecifics with red bellies in their environment? Clearly, this cannot be learned during ontogeny. And, if we do not believe that there is some sort of preestablished harmony in the world that could account for biological adaptations, then this is knowledge that is part of their phylogenetic memory—knowledge that has been shaped by natural selection over the course of natural history and that resides in the animals' genome (Lorenz, 1965).

Similarly, in the case of the preferences of newly hatched chicks for consonance, the point is not *whether* some role of experience could be associated with exposure in embryo to consonant or dissonant stimuli but rather *why* it should be good for chicks to approach stimuli emitting consonant rather than dissonant sound intervals after hatching. My guess is that since harmonic spectra are prominent features of sounds in a natural environment, they could serve, as do certain visual cues (e.g., biological motion, self-propelled motion, to be discussed in the Natural-born "Life detectors" section), as a guide to newly hatched chicks to imprint preferentially on to animate rather than inanimate objects. (Recently, Johnson-Laird, Kang, & Leong, in press, argued that what determines the dissonance of chords—with harmonic partials—for human listeners is a combination of some basic principles of tonal music with "roughness", which occurs with sounds with harmonic partials and sounds with nonharmonic partials; the latter may be more frequent in the natural world: Philip Johnson-Laird, personal communication, 11 October 2011). And, again, *this* knowledge (that it is good for a newly hatched chick to approach animate rather than inanimate objects and to imprint on them) cannot have been acquired by learning during ontogeny; it is the result of a "learning" that has occurred during phylogeny and has been incorporated into the genome.

In this review, I discuss evidence showing precocious abilities in very young chicks to represent basic mechanical properties of physical objects such as solidity, basic properties such as self-propelled motion that are used to identify certain objects as animate, cardinal, and ordinal/sequential aspects of numerical cognition and rudimentary arithmetic with small numerousness of discrete objects, and finally the geometrical relationships among these objects in the surrounding layout. Controlled rearing studies will provide evidence that these abilities are observed in chicks in the absence (or with very reduced) experience. I argue by comparison with the data available for the newborns of our own species that, overall, the empirical evidence supports a nativistic foundation of core knowledge cognitive mechanisms.

Natural-born physicists

When considering what aspects of knowledge are apparent in biological organisms prior to their first contacts with the objects of their experience and what then emerges thanks to the effects of experience with these objects, different theories seem to have been more or less successful in different domains. Historically, nativist theories have generally found greater favour in the domain of sensory development (e.g., Blakemore & Van Sluyters, 1975; Held & Hein, 1963; Walk, Gibson, & Tighe, 1957). Nativist and empiricist theories have generated acrimonious debates—and have found mostly equal favour until recently—in the domains of abstract concepts like number and geometry (see for the history of the debate reviews in Carey & Spelke, 1996; Platt & Spelke, 2009; Spelke, 1998). Empiricism has, however, always held major consideration in the domain of object mechanics (e.g., Mandler, 1988). For it seemed quite obvious that our knowledge of how objects behave comes from observing their behaviour, acting upon them, or both.

Consider a basic concept of object mechanics—the fact that a solid object cannot occupy the same space as another solid object. In seminal experiments (Baillargeon, 1995; Baillargeon, Spelke, & Wasserman, 1985), it was shown that three-and-a-half-month-old infants form representations of hidden objects and make the inference that a solid object cannot move through the space occupied by another solid object. Evidence has since been collected that nonhuman animals also represent physical objects and reason about the motion of physical objects in accordance with the basic constraint of solidity of material bodies (Call, 2007; Kundey, De Los Reyes, Taglang, Baruch, & German, 2009; Pattison, Miller, Rayburn-Reeves, & Zentall, 2010). Nevertheless, the fact that human infants exhibit evidence for object permanence and inference about the physical properties of objects starting from three and a half months of age is compatible with both a nativist and an empiricist view, the former arguing for maturation and the latter for learning. Controlled-rearing studies of animals could help to disentangle the different views.

We recently investigated naïve physics conceptions in newborn chicks (Chiandetti & Vallortigara, 2011b). The domestic chick is a precocial species that has been largely used as a model system in ethology and neurobiology for the study of early learning (Andrew, 1991; Rogers, 1996), and recently it has become a focus of interest and insight with respect to several classical issues in developmental psychology, taking advantage in particular of the behavioural techniques made available by filial imprinting (for reviews see Vallortigara, 2004, 2006, 2009b; Vallortigara, Regolin, Chiandetti, & Rugani, 2010). Imprinting is the learning process by which the young of some animals learn the characteristics of an object—usually a social partner—by simply being exposed to it soon after hatching (Bateson, 2000; Horn, 2004). As in other forms of learning, there are biological predispositions that act to guide and facilitate imprinting in young chicks. We made use of both imprinting and its associated predispositions as a tool for investigation of the topic of the origins of knowledge.

In our experiments on intuitive physics, separate groups of chicks were imprinted on objects of different size (see e.g., Figure 1 top). At test, chicks were placed (singly) in a transparent holding box and were able to see the imprinting object moving along a straight midline towards two identical screens (Figure 1 middle left). Their view was then obscured by an opaque partition, and the imprinting object was removed. The screens were replaced with two other screens that were no longer identical. For example, the height (middle right) or width (bottom left) or slant (bottom right) of the two screens was changed so that only one screen but not the other was large/tall/slanted enough (in different experiments) for the imprinting object to be hidden behind or beneath it. The partition was then removed, and the chicks were allowed to search for the object. Chicks typically choose to search only behind the screen that could hide the object.

We wondered whether the possibility of pecking at the imprinting object during rearing was instrumental to the chicks' intuition of impenetrability of the object. However, when a transparent polyester substrate screen prevented chicks from touching and pecking the object during exposure, the animals showed at test the same preference as chicks reared in direct contact with the imprinting object. Thus, apparently, chicks had very sophisticated abilities concerning physical objects and the properties of occlusion in the absence of specific experience. They seemed to be born with a sort of intuitive physics (and see also Regolin, Rugani, Stancher, & Vallortigara, in press).

I can anticipate an objection: The domestic chick and the human newborn are only remotely related from a phylogenetic point of view, and one could doubt whether these data have any relevance to the origins of human cognition. I return to discuss this issue in greater depth later on. But it should be stressed at this point that the choice of a successful animal system model in biology is not based on phylogenetic relatedness, but on the nature of the problem under investigation (otherwise fruit fly genetics would be totally irrelevant to human genetics). Thus, let us consider some other example of how fruitful the use of the

Figure 1. *Top: Examples of the imprinting objects that chicks were reared with. Middle and bottom: Photographs of the experiments (see text for details). To view a colour version of this figure, please see the online issue of the Journal.*

domestic chick as a system model for investigation of core knowledge mechanisms could be.

Natural-born "life detectors"

Physical objects comprise a category of entities that have special properties for biological organisms—namely, other living things. Converging evidence from neuropsychology (Caramazza & Shelton, 1998) and developmental psychology (S. C. Johnson, 2000) suggests that humans are equipped with mechanisms for attending to and recognizing living things, in particular other animals. An example comes from a study by New, Cosmides, and Tooby (2007) showing that human observers are faster and more accurate at detecting change in animals than they are at detecting change in a variety of inanimate objects, ranging from vehicles to buildings and tools. However, we know little as to the extent to which these mechanisms are in place at birth and about the possible role of experience in shaping them. Even more importantly, we largely ignore the specific underlying neural mechanisms (Mormann et al., 2011). As in other fields of biological sciences, animal models may be instrumental in providing clues to the nature and origin of internal mechanisms.

In 1988, Gabriel Horn and Mark Johnson carried out some groundbreaking studies showing that, contrary to widely held beliefs, filial imprinting seems to consist of two separate processes: an inborn predisposition of the young bird to attend to visual stimuli that resemble a broody hen, and a learning mechanism (which would be guided and supported by the innate predisposition) to learn by exposition about the specific, unique characteristic of a particular mother hen (M. H. Johnson & Horn, 1988). Subsequently, Johnson moved to studies on human infant face preferences and together with John Morton published a series of seminal papers (see for a review, M. H. Johnson & Morton, 1991) arguing that a similar two-mechanism device would be available to human neonates for face recognition. According to their model, infants are born with some information about the structure of faces. This structural information, termed Conspec, guides the preference for face-like patterns found in newborn infants. Conspec is contrasted with a device termed Conlern, which is responsible for learning about the visual characteristics of conspecifics.

Subsequent work, however, has cast some doubt as to the precise nature of the Conspec mechanism. In particular, it has been argued that contrary to Johnson and Morton's (1991) theory, newborn infants' preferences for faces would be a secondary effect determined by nonspecific biases due to constraints imposed by the immature visual system of the child. Turati, Simion, Milani, and Umilta (2002) provided evidence that the preference for face-like stimuli would be determined by an "up–down bias" that would direct baby's attention toward any configuration presenting more elements in the upper part (a "top-heavy configuration").

However, as noted above, human newborns cannot be completely prevented from being exposed to faces. Thus, it is unclear as to whether part of the controversy depends on an effect of early learning or on transient effects related to the maturation of the visual system. In fact a recent study failed to show any top-heavy bias in 3- to 5.5-month-old infants (Chien, 2011). Carefully controlled studies with animals could help to resolve this issue.

Surprisingly, no further work after M. H. Johnson and Horn's (1988) paper had been done on newly hatched chicks to investigate what specific features of the head region stimulate Conspec. We have recently undertaken such a research, and our results suggest that chicks have indeed an inborn preference to approach face-like stimuli, resembling their head region. Completely naïve, newly hatched chicks prefer face-like stimuli to features-on-top stimuli (e.g., they preferred the stimulus on the left in the pairs of figures shown in Figure 2; Rosa-Salva, Regolin, & Vallortigara, 2010). Note that in this case, the preference is not the outcome of exposure learning—that is, of filial imprinting—for chicks exhibit the preference to approach face-like stimuli without any previous experience. The preference, however, does affect the imprinting process by guiding and canalizing the range of objects the chicks are more likely to imprint to.

We also tested the prediction that both newly hatched chicks and human newborns will demonstrate similar preferences for face stimuli over spatial-frequency-matched structured noise (see, for example, Figure 3). This prediction was confirmed, providing strong converging evidence that many vertebrates have a domain-relevant bias toward faces shortly after hatching or birth

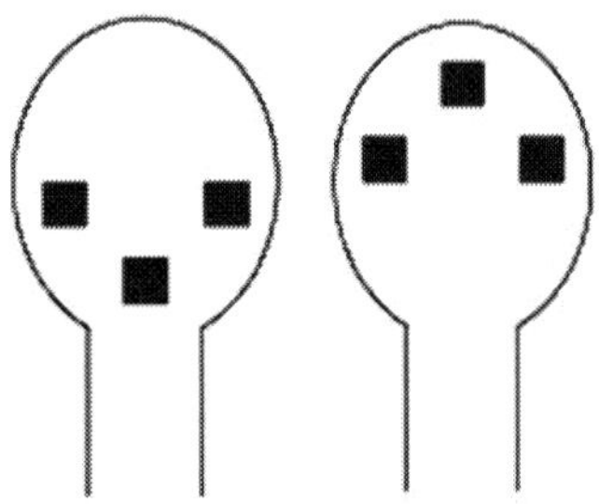

Figure 2. *Examples of the stimuli used by Rosa Salva et al. (2010) for testing newborn chicks' preferences for face-like stimuli.*

Figure 3. *Example of stimuli (images of a face and of the scrambled noise control) used in the newborns' and chicks' study by Rosa Salva et al. (2011). To view a colour version of this figure, please see the online issue of the Journal.*

(Rosa Salva, Farroni, Regolin, Vallortigara, & Johnson, 2011; and see also McKone et al., 2012 this issue, for a nativist position on face perception).

A second line of research involves work that was instead initiated in my own lab, concerning inborn preferences for biological motion. Even in this case, a route from initial research on the chick to subsequent research on the human newborn can be traced back. But first I shall consider some historical roots of my research.

If you look at ethology textbooks, you will find the general assertion that object motion facilitates imprinting. Curiously enough, however, no one has checked whether all types of motion are identically effective or if animals are especially sensitive to particular types of motion. In order to disentangle the stationary visual characteristics of the mother hen (its shape) from the dynamic aspects of it (its motion), we used point-light displays. It is well known that when a small number of points of light are attached to the torso and limbs of a moving organism, and only such points of light are visible, the animation can correctly convey information as to the animal's activity (Johansson, 1973). We tested naïve, newly hatched chicks, lacking any previous visual experience, to investigate whether they showed a spontaneous preference to approach stimuli depicting biological rather than

Figure 4. *Example of the point-light display stimuli used in the Vallortigara et al. (2005) study on predisposition for biological motion in chicks. To view a colour version of this figure, please see the online issue of the Journal.*

nonbiological motion (Vallortigara, Regolin, & Marconato, 2005). One point-light sequence (see, e.g., Figure 4) represented a "walking hen" (13 points of light located on the digitalization of the video-recording of a real animal). Three other sequences were used as "foil sequences". These were: "rigid motion" sequence (a single frame from the walking hen animation sequence was randomly selected and was moved rigidly about its vertical axis so as to produce the motion of a rotating rigid hen-like object); "random motion" sequence (the same set of points of light moved in arbitrary directions); and "scrambled hen" sequence (the same set of points of light as those employed for producing the walking hen and in the same set of frames as those used for the walking hen were used, only now the original position of each point was spatially displaced by a fixed amount consistently throughout the animation. Every single point of light, although displaced as compared with its position in the walking hen animation, moved identically in this sequence as it did in the walking hen. As a result, this last display no longer conveyed perception of a hen to human observers, though it retained the appearance of the biological motion of some kind of unidentified creature).

The results showed that naive chicks exhibit clear and consistent preferences in approaching certain types of movements. Intriguingly, however, chicks' choices seemed to reflect a generic preference for the patterns of biological motion rather than a specific preference for the typical form of the motion of a hen. The walking hen was chosen as much as the scrambled hen, though both the walking hen and the scrambled hen were preferred to the rigid and random motion. This finding suggests that chicks preferentially approach semirigid motion, the type of motion that is exhibited by vertebrate animals. In semirigid motion, some points maintain a fixed distance from each other (e.g., two points placed close on the same limb), but can nonetheless vary their distance with respect to other points (e.g., with respect to points located on the torso). Such a pattern of semirigid motion is shared by the walking and the scrambled hen, even though the latter does not match any existing biological creature. As a control for this hypothesis, we used the motion of a point-light cat, a species that can predate on young chicks. As predicted, chicks did not exhibit any preference between the walking hen and a walking cat point-light sequence, though they did prefer the walking cat to the random and to the rigid motion.

The predisposition found for certain kinds of motion shares characteristics in common with those earlier demonstrated for the head and neck region of a hen to artificial objects (M. H. Johnson & Horn, 1988). Similarly to this preference for form, the preference for movement is not species-specific. When considered together, these findings seem to fit a general scheme for cognitive development of recognition of other animals based on the interaction between two separate and independent systems. The first of these systems directs the attention of the young animal toward the appropriate class of objects to learn about, in the absence of any prior specific experience (e.g., in the case of motion, those objects that move semirigidly). The second system is concerned with learning about the peculiar characteristics of the objects to which attention has been directed by the first system. Given that in a natural environment it is more likely that the newly hatched chick would encounter a mother hen rather than a cat, a developing predisposition to pay attention to objects showing the characteristic motion of vertebrates would assure the highest probability to learn (by way of the imprinting mechanism) about the specific pattern of motion of the mother hen. Could these findings be generalized to the human species? As in the case of face-like preferences, the answer seems to be positive.

An inborn predisposition to attend to biological motion has long been theorized for the human species, but had so far not been demonstrated. In particular, no preference for biological motion was reported for human infants of less than 3 months of age (Fox & McDaniel, 1982). Recently, however, Simion, Regolin, and Bulf (2008) tested 2-day-old babies' discrimination after familiarization and their spontaneous preferences for biological versus nonbiological point-light animations, using the same type of stimuli (i.e., walking hens) as that used in our research with newly hatched chicks. Newborns were shown to be able to discriminate between the two different patterns of motion and, when first exposed to them, selectively preferred to look at the biological motion display. This preference was also orientation dependent: Newborns looked longer at upright displays than at upside-down displays (and the same result was previously reported for newly hatched visually naïve chicks; Vallortigara & Regolin, 2006). Overall, these parallel results in the two species strikingly support the hypothesis that detection of biological motion is an intrinsic capacity of the vertebrate visual system, which is presumably part of an evolutionarily ancient and non-species-specific system predisposing animals to preferentially attend to other animals (see J. Brown, Kaplan, Rogers, & Vallortigara, 2010, for evidence in other species, and Kaiser et al., 2010 for clinical implications for the study of autism).

Recent research on human infants has provided important evidence for early sensitivity to causal agency (animacy) and intention (for a review, see Biro et al., 2007, and see the seminal work by Leslie, 1982, 1984). We thus decided to investigate whether evidence for an inborn preference for objects conveying an impression of causal agency or intention can be observed in newly hatched visually inexperienced chicks (Mascalzoni, Regolin, & Vallortigara, 2010).

Chicks were presented with a video showing two objects, of different colours, on a stage, initially shown at rest. Then one object was shown to move slowly until contact with the other object, thus producing (to a human observer at least) the classical Michotte's (1963) launching effect (see O'Connell & Dunbar, 2005, for evidence that animals are sensitive to Michotte's perceived causality). The second object thus moved along a straight trajectory for the same length as the previous one, stopping before exiting from the stage. After this exposure phase, chicks were tested in a free-choice task for spontaneous preference for the two different objects. Complete balancing for use of different colours and left–right direction of movement was ensured during exposure and at test. If chicks do attribute a notion of animacy to the object that starts moving and contacts the other object, then a preference for such an object would be evinced in free-choice preference tests, irrespective of its colour and direction of movement. This is precisely what we found. The results of other experiments showed that only when one of the two objects appeared as being self-propelled and the other not self-propelled did a preference emerge, as a choice for the self-propelled stimulus. Physical contact without physical causation (e.g., when both objects appeared as being self-propelled), or physical causation without any cues about the nature of the motion of "the causal object" (i.e., whether it is self-propelled or not), abolished any preference, showing that physical contact in itself was not capable of producing causal inference (Mascalzoni et al., 2010).

Chicks came from a dark incubator and hatchery; hence, they had not had any chance to be exposed visually to the motion of animate objects, apart for the controlled imprinting–exposure phase. Thus, the preference for the self-propelled object cannot be accounted for in terms of any specific learning. The minimal interpretation of our finding is that chicks are innately sensitive to self-propulsion as a crucial cue to animacy (or mechanical agency in the sense of having internal cause of action, see Leslie & Keeble, 1987).

The idea that sensitivity to self-produced motion could lie at the foundations of the clear-cut divide that the brain operates between the two basic domains of physical (inanimate) and intentional (animate) objects is not new—it dates back at least to Aristotle (*Physics*, translated by P.H. Wickstead and F.M. Cornford, Harvard University Press, Cambridge, 1980). The sensitivity to self-produced motion may be sufficient to adaptively constrain the early commitment of a highly precocial animal as to what to imprint on. It remains of course to be determined whether chicks are also innately endowed with a sensitivity to other movement properties, such as efficiency of goal approach (as humans and adult primates seem to be, e.g., Rochat, Serra, Fadiga, & Gallese, 2008), which serve as cues to intentional agency. In any case, our findings are compatible with the idea that many vertebrate species, including humans, have primitive neural pathways that ensure a bias to attend to, or preferentially process, sensory information about other living entities.

The great advantage of an animal model such as the chick lies in the possibility of using invasive neurobiological techniques to investigate neural mechanisms in combination with the behavioural techniques described above. In nonhuman primates, a number of studies have reported neurons sensitive to occlusion and context in several brain areas (e.g., superior temporal sulcus, posterior parietal cortex, inferotemporal cortex; Assad & Maunsell, 1995; Duncan, Albright, & Stoner, 2000; Kovacs, Vogels, & Orban, 1995). For example, Baker, Keysers, Jellema, Wicker, and Perrett (2001) reported that neurons of the anterior superior temporal sulcus in the rhesus monkey show activity correlated to occlusion of objects. These responses could be hypothesized to contribute to the ability for object permanence and aspects of intuitive physics. However, it is difficult in primates to investigate these neural mechanisms in very young animals with precise control of past sensory experience. We are now trying to unveil these mechanisms in the chick. The first step involves the use of immediate early genes expression (such as *c-fos*) to identify target regions in the brain that appear to be stimulated by stimuli associated with specific predispositions. Our preliminary results suggest an involvement of the optic tectum. Interestingly, among the areas that have been hypothesized to be part of the human subcortical face-detection route (see M. H. Johnson, 2005), the superior colliculus, pulvinar, and amygdala all have homologues within the avian brain (respectively, optic tectum, nucleus rotundus, and amygdala).

Natural-born mathematicians

Number is another core domain of knowledge that might be encoded precociously in the vertebrate brain. Again, we took advantage of filial imprinting for studying it in newborn chicks. Because of protection to predators and avoiding heat dissipation, young chicks tend to prefer to approach larger numbers of social partners. Thus, by exposing chicks to different numbers of artificial imprinting objects and then observing the animals in free-choice tests with sets of different number of objects, we could explore their numerical abilities. In a series of experiments (Rugani, Kelly, Szelest, Regolin, & Vallortigara, 2010), we imprinted separate groups of chicks on three or one imprinting objects and then tested chicks' choice between three and one objects. When chicks were reared with three objects, they preferred three objects at test; when they were reared with one object, they still preferred three objects at test. Apparently they went for more. When tested with two versus three, a more difficult task, the results were similar: Reared with three, they preferred three; reared with two, they preferred three again. Choice in a group of chicks tested without any imprinting did not yield any preference for the larger number of objects, thus showing that preference for the large number was clearly related to imprinting. However, it could be that chicks were not using number in this task but were simply estimating the overall volume or area or something like that. This has been shown to occur in human infants in some circumstances. For instance, when objects have similar properties or are from a domain in which physical extent can be particularly important (e.g., food, see Feigenson, Carey, & Hauser, 2002), infants seem to favour extent over number. When, however, a task requires reaching for individual objects (e.g., Feigenson & Carey, 2005) or objects contrasting in colour, pattern, or texture (Feigenson, 2005), then infants seem to respond to number and not to extent. Something similar seems to occur in chicks when they were imprinted on objects of different shape, colour, area, and volume and were then tested for choice with completely different novel objects (in size, colour, and shape with respect to the exposure imprinting phase). These novel objects were controlled in their continuous extent (volume or surface area) such that they were the same in the three-element and in the two-element stimulus display. This time, when reared with three objects, chicks chose at test three objects; when reared with two objects, they chose two objects, showing their capacity to use number when continuous extent was equated (Rugani, Regolin, & Vallortigara, 2010).

Early availability of small numerosity discrimination by chicks strongly suggests that these abilities are in place at birth. Even basic arithmetic seems available at birth in chicks. In some experiments (Rugani, Fontanari, Simoni, Regolin, & Vallortigara, 2009), we reared chicks with five identical imprinting objects. At test, each chick was confined to a holding pen, behind a transparent partition, from where it could see two identical opaque screens. The chick saw two sets of imprinting objects—a set of 3 objects and a set of 2 objects; each set disappeared (either simultaneously or one by one) behind one of the two screens. Immediately after the disappearance of both sets, the transparent partition was removed, and the chick was left free to move around and search within the arena. Chicks spontaneously inspected the screen occluding the larger set of 3 (and did so even when continuous physical variables were controlled for). In further experiments, after an initial disappearance of two sets (i.e., 4 objects disappeared behind a screen and 1 behind the other), some of the objects were visibly transferred, one by one, from one screen to the other before the chick was released into the arena. Even in this case, chicks spontaneously chose the screen hiding the larger number of elements, and they did so irrespective of the directional cues provided by the initial and final displacements. Thus, chicks could compute, at their very first experience, a series of subsequent additions or subtractions of objects that appeared and disappeared over time, suggestive of early proto-arithmetic capacities. Intriguingly, whereas evidence using conditioning procedures in this species suggest a set size effect for small numerosities at about 3 items (Rugani, Regolin, & Vallortigara, 2008), in the imprinting experiments by Rugani et al. (2009), computation is done for larger sets (up to 5 items).

Currently nothing is known about the neural mechanisms underlying these abilities (and others, e.g., Pepperberg, 1994, 2006a, 2006b) in the avian brain, and it would certainly be interesting to investigate the existence of nerve cells tuned to number, as those described in the monkeys brains in parietal and frontal cortex (Nieder, Freedman, & Miller, 2002; Nieder & Miller, 2004). Candidate areas in the avian brain include the mesopallium and nidopallium caudolaterale (e.g., Butler & Cotterill, 2006). However, suggestive evidence of basic mechanisms shared and possibly homologous in the vertebrate brain comes from studies involving the ordinal/sequential aspects of numerical cognition.

Like other animal species (e.g., Chittka & Geiger, 1995; Dacke & Srinivasan, 2008; Davis & Bradford, 1986), chicks have been shown to possess the ability to identify an object on the exclusive basis of its position in a series of identical objects. When trained to peck at, for example, the 3rd, 4th, or 6th position in a series of 10 identically spaced locations, chicks learned accurately to identify the correct position (Rugani, Regolin, & Vallortigara, 2007). Control experiments ruled out the possibility they were using distances as a cue. For instance, when chicks were trained to peck at the fourth position and were then tested with a new sequence in which the distance from the starting point to each position was manipulated in such a way that ordinal position and distance from the starting point were different from those during initial training, chicks correctly pecked at the fourth serial position, even if that position was now located much farther away than before.

Interestingly, a bias for the left hemispace was found in these experiments. Chicks were trained to peck a selected position in a sagittally oriented series of identical elements. During test, the array was rotated by 90 degrees and oriented in a fronto-parallel fashion with respect to the chick's starting point, such that the correct position could not be located on the basis of absolute distances from the starting point. Chicks selected only the fourth position from the left end, and not the fourth from the right end, which was chosen at chance level. In subsequent work, adult nutcrackers (*Nucifraga columbiana*) and newborn domestic chicks were compared in a similar task in which they were trained to peck at either the 4th or the 6th element in a series of 16 identical and aligned positions. Again, when the array was rotated 90 degrees, both species showed a bias for the correct position from the left but not from the right end (Rugani, Kelly, et al., 2010).

The birds' bias is reminiscent of the human mental number line phenomenon. As early as 1880, Galton (Galton, 1880) showed that humans describe and think of numbers as being represented on a mental number line, which is usually oriented from left to right (see also Dehaene, 1997). It is typically maintained that the spatial orientation of the human mental number line is linked to writing and reading habits. We wondered, however, if it may depend, at least in part, on biologically specific biases in the allocation of attention in extracorporeal space. A preference for targets located on the left hemispace may be due to a bias in the allocation of attention, somewhat similar to that shown by humans and dubbed as "pseudoneglect" (e.g., Jewell & McCourt, 2000). In fact, "pseudoneglect" phenomena have been described in birds with selective allocation of attention to the left hemifield during free foraging (Chiandetti, 2011; Diekamp, Regolin, Gunturkun, & Vallortigara, 2005). Somewhat similar phenomena of pseudoneglect favouring the left hemifield have been described also for amphibians (Vallortigara, Rogers, Bisazza, Lippolis, & Robins, 1998; and see for general reviews, MacNeilage, Rogers, & Vallortigara, 2009; Vallortigara, 2000; Vallortigara & Rogers, 2005).

We thus embarked on a series of systematic studies in order to better understand the nature of the bias shown by the chicks in the ordinal number task (Rugani, Vallortigara, Vallini, & Regolin, 2011). We found that when accustomed to systematic changes in interelement distances during training or when faced with similar spatial changes at test, chicks identify as correct the target positions from both the left and the right end. Experiments also showed, however, that ordinal position was spontaneously encoded even when interelement distances were kept fixed during training (in spite of the fact that distances between elements sufficed for target identification without any numerical computation).

We thus believe that asymmetries in these serial ordering tests can be accounted for with a simple model that assumes differential encoding and coupling in the two hemispheres for spatial and numerical information. The finding that, even after training with fixed interelement distances, chicks encoded serial ordering and not just distances between the elements suggests that two separate representations are formed during training. The first representation concerns serial ordering as such—that is, without any association with magnitude of distances on a spatial scale. Such a representation would encode something like: The target is in the 4th position—that is, after the 3rd container and before the 5th container—without any specification of the distances between the ordinal positions of the containers. The second representation, on the other hand, would be of a spatial nature, encoding magnitude of distances between containers in a relational fashion. Association of the purely ordinal and the purely spatial representation would provide the animal with a mental line of number.

The purely ordinal representation would be bilaterally represented in the left and right cerebral hemispheres, and activation of this representation would not produce any imbalance in the activity of the two hemispheres. As a result, allocation of attention would be identically directed towards both the left and the right visual hemifields. This is supported by the fact that when following fronto-parallel presentation of the line of elements, distances are changed at test, chicks could choose the correct target from both the left and the right ends. In contrast, the purely spatial representation would be unilaterally represented in the right hemisphere. This is supported by independent evidence provided by both behavioural (Tommasi & Vallortigara, 2001; Vallortigara, Pagni, & Sovrano, 2004) and lesion (Tommasi, Gagliardo, Andrew, & Vallortigara, 2003) studies showing that spatial information is encoded selectively into the right hemisphere in the chick forebrain (review in Vallortigara, 2009a, and see also next section). As a result, when at test chicks are faced with a fronto-parallel line of elements whose relational spatial encoding matches the serial ordering, extra activation of the right hemisphere would occur, favouring allocation of attention to the left hemispace and thus producing a bias to "count" selectively from left to right. When, however, because of a change in the spatial arrangement of the distances, chicks are faced with a line of elements in which spatial properties do not match those acquired during training, the chicks rely on serial ordering alone. The outcome in this case is the bilateral activation of both cerebral hemispheres and the unbiased allocation of attention along both hemifields, resulting in chicks showing identical propensity "to count" from left to right and from right to left. Possible implications of these findings from animal models to human asymmetries in spatial attention deserve scrutiny (see, e.g., Loetscher, Schwarz, Schubiger, & Brugger, 2008; Siman-Tov et al., 2009).

Natural-born geometers

Animals show very sophisticated knowledge of their spatial layout, with some rudimentary understanding of geometric properties (Vallortigara, 2009a). This has been originally shown in seminal studies by Cheng (1986) with rats and by Spelke (Hermer & Spelke, 1994, 1996) with children. A simple example is shown in Figure 5. Imagine you are located in an empty rectangular room, with identically coloured walls and no external cues. In a corner there is a visible goal. Then you are displaced from the room and, with your eyes covered, turned around passively a few times. Finally, you are reintroduced into the room. The goal object is no longer visible. Your task is to figure out the corner where the goal object was previously located. Apparently, all corners look identical, and perhaps you would search at random among the four corners. However, if you ponder a little bit on the problem you could realize that there is a partial—though not complete—solution to the disambiguation of the corners. This is because you can make use of the geometry of the enclosure—its rectangular shape. For instance, when you are facing the corner indicated by the small blue square on top (see Figure 5), there will be on your right side a short wall and on your left side a long wall. Only another location will stand in the same geometric relationships with respect to the shape of the room—namely, the rotationally equivalent corner located on the opposite side along the diagonal (indicated by the small blue square on the bottom of Figure 5). These two corners cannot be distinguished from each other as they are geometrically equivalent, but they can be distinguished from the remaining two other

Figure 5. *Schematic representation of the rectangular enclosure task to study use of geometry in spatial reorientation in animals and children (image courtesy of Cinzia Chiandetti). To view a colour version of this figure, please see the online issue of the Journal.*

Figure 6. *Schematic representations of the arrangements of the accessible openings on pipes (correct cylinders: darker arrows; incorrect cylinders: lighter arrows) during training in the fixed access and in the variable access condition. To view a colour version of this figure, please see the online issue of the Journal.*

corners. In order to solve the task, therefore, two very simple forms of geometric knowledge are needed: the ability to discriminate *metric properties* of surfaces as surfaces (short wall vs. long wall) and the ability to discriminate what is called *sense* in geometry (left vs. right).

Several species have been proved able to solve this geometrical task. For instance, we demonstrated this in domestic chicks (Vallortigara, Zanforlin, & Pasti, 1990), in fish (redtail splitfins, *Xenotoca eiseni*; Sovrano, Bisazza, & Vallortigara, 2002, 2003), and, very recently, in bumblebees (Sovrano, Rigosi, & Vallortigara, 2011).

Competing theories have been formulated as to how organisms reorient themselves in these circumstances (see Spelke, 2011). One key finding has been that whereas computation of geometric properties is commonly observed with extended surfaces (such as enclosures similar to that of Figure 5), using freestanding objects arranged in the shape of rectangular arrays results are more variable (see Pecchia & Vallortigara, 2010a). Recently we provided evidence that a key determinant of animals' abilities to compute geometrical properties to reorient is not whether the landmarks are discrete objects or environment boundaries, but whether the animals are exposed to the same view while retrieving the goal or not (Pecchia, Gagliardo, & Vallortigara, 2011; Pecchia & Vallortigara, 2010b, in press). Usually retrieving a goal at an enclosure corner constrains the animal's viewpoint (promoting viewpoint-dependent learning), whereas retrieving it at a free-standing object usually does not. To allow comparison of similar versus different viewpoints while retrieving goals at otherwise identical locations, we used a task in which the goal (food) was hidden in cylinders, each with four openings on different sides, only one of which was accessible (see Figure 6). The spatial location—cylinder—was then dissociated from the viewpoint experienced while retrieving food from it, which was determined by the side of the opening that was accessible. Chicks that saw fixed views during training (i.e., had the same perspective on the layout when retrieving food) could recall locations using either boundaries or discrete objects, whereas chicks that saw variable views could not succeed even with both cues available at the time. This provides evidence for view-based reorientation to either boundaries or configurations of objects, at least in chicks.

According to this theoretical approach, movements in space are deduced by comparing specific contents of panoramic views (visual snapshots) at the target and at the current location, following a minimal mismatch criterion (Cartwright & Collett, 1982, 1983). The hypothesis of a view-based strategy for spatial reorientation does not make any assumption of separate computation processes between information provided by extended surfaces and those provided by freestanding objects in an array. However, it remains to be seen whether this also hold true for humans (and children). An important limitation to the generality of these findings concerns the methods used. Typically in animal studies a "reference memory" paradigm is used in which subjects learn over reinforced training to navigate to a goal location, such as a food source (as in the studies with the cylinders described above). In other studies, especially in those of human navigation, a spontaneous "working memory" procedure is used in which subjects are shown, without repeated reinforcement training, the goal at a particular location and then are observed after some time has passed, from a different viewpoint, or after they have been inertially disoriented. Using working memory tasks, evidence against purely image-matching theories has been obtained. For instance, in contrast to the prediction based on global matching, it has been shown that children fail to reorient by sharp contrast borders produced by a two-dimensional rectangle flashed against the floor of a circular-shaped room (Lee & Spelke, 2011). Children also fail to reorient by geometry in an array of freestanding objects (Lee, Shusterman, & Spelke, 2006; Lee & Spelke, 2008, 2010) even when the objects are connected together by a thin cord (Lee & Spelke, 2011). Similar results have been obtained in chicks in a working memory task (Lee, Spelke, & Vallortigara, 2012). Thus, it could be that a panoramic view (snapshot) approach to spatial reorientation only holds for those circumstances in which repeated trials and learning allow organisms to form such snapshot memories.

As in the case of intuition of physical properties of objects and of number, we found that little, if any, experience is needed to young chicks to deal with geometry (Chiandetti & Vallortigara, 2008). We tested the navigational abilities of newborn chicks reared in enclosures of different shapes and metrical properties (Figure 7). Rectangular enclosures provided metrically distinct surfaces connected at right angles and two principal axes of symmetry (Figure 7, left). Geometric information was not available, in contrast, in circular enclosure (Figure 7, right), in which there was also an infinite number of principal axes. In C-shaped enclosures (Figure 7, middle), neither right angles nor differences in wall length were available, although the first principal axis was available to encode shape. Chicks proved to be equally capable of learning and performing navigational tasks based on geometric information irrespective of rearing in different environments

In a particularly revealing experiment, chicks were trained in a rectangular-shaped enclosure with panels at the corners providing salient featural cues (as shown in Figure 8a). Rectangular-reared and circular-reared chicks proved equally able to learn the task. Nonetheless, one could have expected that encoding of purely geometric information was stronger in animals reared in a

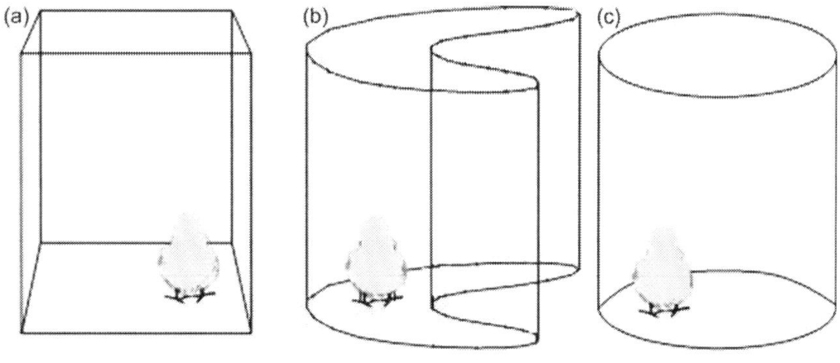

Figure 7. *An illustrative representation of the rearing condition used to raise single chicks in controlled rearing experiments of geometry; (a) rectangular, (b) C-shaped, and (c) circular home cages. To view a colour version of this figure, please see the online issue of the Journal.*

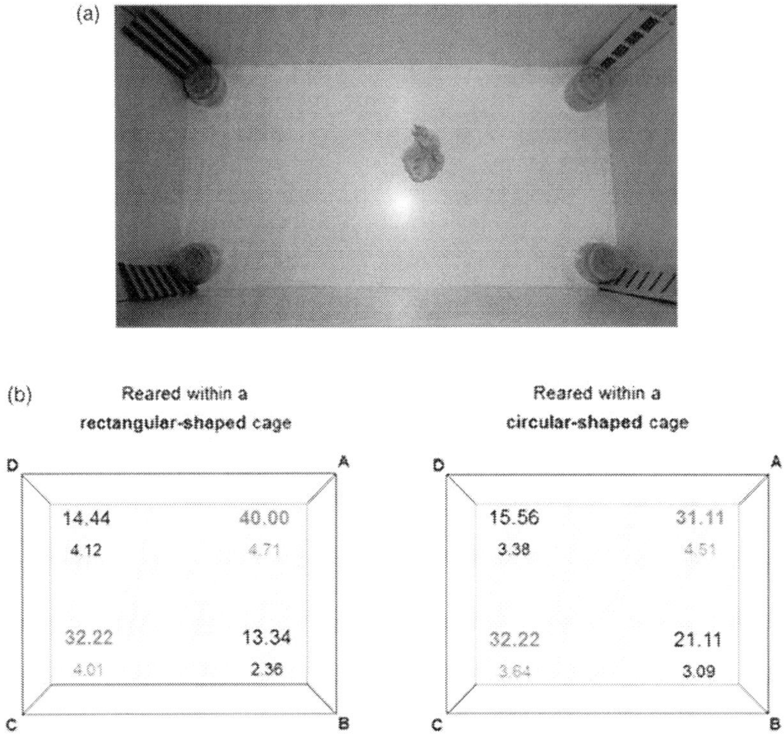

Figure 8. *Set-up for training chicks with panels at the corners. (a) Panels were removed at test, revealing similar choice for the two geometrically correct corners in chicks reared in a rectangular or in a circular enclosure. (b) Numbers indicate means of choices with standard errors below. To view a colour version of this figure, please see the online issue of the Journal.*

rectangular environment. In contrast, when tested after removal of the panels, both rectangular- and circular-reared chicks showed similar evidence that they had spontaneously encoded geometric information, choosing the two geometrically correct corners (Figure 8b). These results strongly suggest that effective use of geometric information for spatial reorientation does not require experience in environments with right angles and metrically distinct surfaces.

Similar results have been obtained in fish. A. A. Brown, Spetch, and Hurd (2007) reared fish (*Archocentrus nigrofasciatus*) in rectangular or circular tanks and then tested their reorientation abilities in a rectangular tank without any featural cues. Similarly to chicks, results revealed no differences in learning abilities between circular- and rectangular-reared fish. When trained with featural information present, fish proved able to learn both types of information. However, when these cues were in conflict, fish raised in a circular tank showed greater reliance on featural information than fish raised in a rectangular tank. This would suggest that rearing experience, though not affecting the ability to encode geometry, might affect the relative dominance in the use of geometric and nongeometric cues when animals are facing conflicting information. Intriguingly, such an effect was not observed in chicks (Chiandetti & Vallortigara, 2010). Perhaps this discrepancy between the species could be accounted for in terms of distinction between altricial and precocial organisms (Vallortigara, Sovrano, & Chiandetti, 2009). The species of fish used by A. A. Brown et al. (2007) shows biparental, prolonged care, whereas domestic chicks are immediately largely independent from parental care. Altricial species may therefore be more sensitive to external stimulation (or to be open to such stimulation for a more extended period of time); hence, fish may be affected by rearing experience concerning nongeometric cues.

Overall our findings suggest that the foundation of natural geometry, at least in its most basic aspects, is far removed from any strictly linguistic and cultural constraint (see also Dehaene, Izard, Pica, & Spelke, 2006; Izard, Pica, Spelke, & Dehaene, 2011; Spelke, Lee, & Izard, 2010) and is deeply rooted in phylogenetic history. Education certainly determines our refinement in geometric skills—namely, our engaging in symbolic, exact manipulation of geometric concepts and measurements. However, *basic* metric and geometry emerge from nonsymbolic abilities that are widespread across different species and developmental levels (Spelke & Kinzler, 2009) and that are not experience dependent. Further support to this view comes from evidence that when such a core knowledge system is not working in the proper way, the use of geometry alone may be severely compromised. This is the case of Williams syndrome (WS), a genetic disorder in which patients exhibit impaired spatial abilities with relatively preserved language abilities (Landau, 2011). Lakusta et al. (2010) recently found that adults with WS searched at random in the standard task of the rectangular enclosure (with the walls uniformly coloured) though they were able to use featural information (with one wall of a different colour) to reorient themselves.

The use of simple animal models, which allow scientists to perform controlled-rearing studies, may open the door to research linking specific genes (Osborne, 2006) and elderly related spatial detriments (Fellini, Schachner, & Morellini, 2006) to reorientation impairment.

Comparative research investigating the role of hippocampus as a crucial area for representing space is long dated (O'Keefe & Nadel, 1978); however, the hippocampal involvement in the geometric module task is controversial (Bingman, Erichsen, Anderson, Good, & Pearce, 2006; Burgess, 2008; Vargas, Bingman, Portavella, & Lopez, 2006; Vargas, Petruso, & Bingman, 2004). In the chick brain, we found evidence for a role of the hippocampal formation in place-finding tasks in which birds were required to find the centre of an enclosure (Tommasi et al., 2003). Whether this could be generalized to the rectangular geometry task is unclear, because place-finding tasks lack the essential component of the spatial disorientation of the animals. Evidence is clear, on the other hand, for a predominant role of the right hemisphere in using geometry in the rectangular reorientation task in experiments with monocularly tested chicks, which took advantage of complete decussation at optic chiasma and limited interhemispheric communication in the chicken's brain (Vallortigara et al., 2004). Interestingly, a lateralization favouring the right hippocampus was also reported in place finding tasks involving estimation of distances between the walls and the centre of a square-shaped enclosure (Tommasi et al., 2003).

Different families of cells strictly related to specific spatial demands have been discovered in the parahippocampal circuit (place cells: O'Keefe & Dostrovsky, 1971; head direction cells: Taube, Muller, & Ranck, 1990; grid cells: Fyhn, Molden, Witter, Moser, & Moser, 2004; border cells: Barry et al., 2006; Solstad, Boccara, Kropff, Moser, & Moser, 2008). Single cell recording when rat pups explore an open environment outside the nest for the first time showed that head-direction cells show adult-like properties from the beginning; place and grid cells are also present from the beginning but their selectivity is refined gradually (Langston et al., 2010; Wills, Cacucci, Burgess, & O'Keefe, 2010). Thus, electrophysiological data clearly support evidence from controlled rearing studies.

Conclusion

Chicks show sophisticated core knowledge mechanisms at a very precocial age, when the chances that they have acquired them by exposure to objects and events properties, if any, are extremely reduced. Of course it is impossible to prevent an organism from having sensory and motor experience of some sort. One could argue that our chicks at least should have had the experience of pecking (which is a behaviour occurring also in ovo in order to hatch). However, it should be stressed that any empiricist interpretation should be specific about the type of experience that is needed in order to account for evidence of early core knowledge mechanisms (see also Spelke, Breinlinger, Macomber, & Jacobson, 1992). Consider the case of intuitive physics described in the Natural-born physicists section. Generic experience of pecking in itself cannot explain our findings: Chicks could encounter different types of physical materials: some soft, some liquid, and some offering resistance to pecking in their environment. Thus, one must argue that it is the specific experience of touching and pecking the solid imprinting object that is crucial. However, even when chicks were prevented from any direct physical contact with the imprinting object, they chose the screen with the proper physical features (note also that the imprinting object that was visually available to the chicks was never observed to contact other objects, thus ruling out the possibility that chicks learned about object solidity by observing the ways in which moving objects interact with each other).

It seems to me that a reasonable account of these findings is to argue that, although animals can certainly learn a lot about the physical properties of objects, they seem to do so precisely because they possess inborn core knowledge mechanisms that guide and constraint their intuitive inferences concerning material object properties such as solidity. Similar Kantian arguments can be put forward for the evidence I described concerning number and space cognition.

One could argue that the pattern of development of precocial species may be peculiar and that it does not generalize to humans. However, the evidence I discussed constitutes a sort of "proof of existence". The findings provide evidence that a certain capacity can fully develop in the absence of a *specific* experience contribution. One could argue of course that humans are different, and that although it is possible, in principle, for natural selection to shape creatures that are able to deal with basic object, number, and space knowledge without resorting to specific experiences with objects and events in the environment, a different path was followed with our species; I doubt this should be so, however. Certainly our species depends on learning and experience to a degree that is incommensurable in comparison to other species, especially in the form of language and cultural transmission. But exactly because we are so dependent on learning we need some "necessary knowledge" that is inborn and that could operate as a guide for learning by experience (see Natural-born "life detectors" section on how biological predispositions guide exposure learning about animate objects).

Chicks and human newborns are different in the pattern of development. Humans are the most altricial of the species. However, it should be considered that some differences between altricial and precocial species may turn out to be the by-product of maturation rather than learning. For instance, the ability to mentally complete partly occluded objects (*amodal completion*) is apparent in chicks soon after hatching (Lea, Slater, & Ryan, 1996; Regolin & Vallortigara, 1995) whereas in human infants it is only from about 4 months of age (Kellman & Arterberry, 1998). One could argue that perhaps chicks are equipped from the start with the mechanisms for completing partly occluded objects, whereas humans would learn about it in a period of about 4 months, taking advantage of experience with occluding events in the world. Recently, however, it has been shown that when stroboscopic motion is used instead of continuous motion (the former being processed early in development by subcortical structures), neonates of only a few hours of life show evidence of amodal completion similarly to chicks (Valenza & Herman, 2011; Valenza, Leo, Gava, & Simion, 2006). Thus, maturation of certain other areas of the brain seems to be necessary in altricial species in order to exhibit in behaviour mental competencies that are actually already available from the start—that is, competencies that are predisposed in the brain at birth.

All this is not to detract from human uniqueness. Clearly, human language and other types of experience may influence the development of uniquely human forms of physical, numerical, and spatial knowledge (Landau & Lakusta, 2009; Spelke, 2003; Spelke et al., 2010). But they can operate that way because of inbuilt necessary knowledge largely shared by all vertebrate brains.

REFERENCES

Andrew, R. J. (Ed.). (1991). *Neural and behavioural plasticity: The use of the chick as a model.* Oxford, UK: Oxford University Press.

Assad, J. A., & Maunsell, J. H. (1995). Neuronal correlates of inferred motion in primate posterior parietal cortex. *Nature, 373,* 518–521.

Baillargeon, R. (1995). Physical reasoning in infancy. In M.S. Gazzaniga (Ed.), *The cognitive neurosciences* (pp. 181–204). Cambridge, MA: MIT Press.

Baillargeon, R., Spelke, E. S., & Wasserman, S. (1985). Object permanence in five-month-old infants. *Cognition, 20,* 191–208.

Baker, C. I., Keysers, C., Jellema, T., Wicker, B., & Perrett, D. I. (2001). Neuronal representation of disappearing and hidden objects in temporal cortex of the macaque. *Experimental Brain Research, 140,* 375–381.

Barry, C., Lever, C., Hayman, R., Hartley, T., Burton, S., O'Keefe, J., et al. (2006). The boundary vector cell model of place cell firing and spatial memory. *Reviews in the Neurosciences, 17,* 71–97.

Bateson, P. (2000). What must be known in order to understand imprinting? In C. Heyes & L. Huber (Eds.), *The Evolution of Cognition* (pp. 85–102). Cambridge, MA: The MIT Press.

Bateson, P., & Gluckman, P. (2011). *Plasticity, robustness, development and evolution.* New York, NY: Cambridge University Press.

Beran, M. J., Decker, S., Schwartz, A., & Schultz, N. (2011). Monkeys (*Macaca mulatta* and *Cebus apella*) and human adults and children (*Homo sapiens*) enumerate and compare subsets of moving stimuli based on numerosity. *Frontiers in Comparative Psychology, 2,* Article 61.

Bingman, V. P., Erichsen, J. T., Anderson, J. D., Good, M. A., & Pearce, J. M. (2006). Spared feature-structure discrimination but diminished salience of environmental geometry in hippocampal-lesioned homing pigeons (*Columba livia*). *Behavioral Neuroscience, 120,* 835–841.

Biro, S., Csibra, G., & Gergely, G. (2007). The role of behavioral cues in understanding animacy, agency and goal-directed actions in infancy. In C. von Hofsten & K. Rosander (Eds.), *Progress in brain research: From action to cognition* (p. 303). Elsevier.

Blakemore, C., & Van Sluyters, E. C. (1975). Innate and environmental factors in the development of the kitten's visual cortex. *Journal of Physiology, 248,* 663–716.

Brannon, E. M. (2006). The representation of numerical magnitude. *Current Opinion in Neurobiology, 16,* 222–229.

Brown, A. A., Spetch, M. L., & Hurd, P. L. (2007). Growing in circles: Rearing environment alters spatial navigation in fish. *Psychological Science, 18,* 569–573.

Brown, J., Kaplan, G., Rogers, L. J., & Vallortigara, G. (2010). Perception of biological motion in common marmosets (*Callithrix jacchus*): By females only. *Animal Cognition, 13,* 555–564.

Burgess, N. (2008). Spatial cognition and the brain. *Annals of the New York Academy of Sciences, 1124,* 77–97.

Butler, A.B., & Cotterill, R. M. J. (2006). Mammalian and avian neuroanatomy and the question of consciousness in birds. *Biological Bulletin, 211,* 106–127.

Call, J. (2007). Apes know that hidden objects can affect the orientation of other objects. *Cognition, 105,* 1–25.

Cantlon, J., & Brannon, E. M. (2006). Shared system for ordering small and large numbers in monkeys and humans. *Psychological Science, 17,* 401–406.

Caramazza, A., & Shelton, J. R. (1998). Domain-specific knowledge systems in the brain: The animate–inanimate distinction. *Journal of Cognitive Neuroscience, 10,* 1–34.

Carey, S. (2009). *The origin of concepts.* New York, NY: Oxford University Press.

Carey, S., & Spelke, E. S. (1996). Science and core knowledge. *Philosophy of Science, 63,* 515–533.

Cartwright, B. A., & Collett, T. S. (1982). How honey bees use landmarks to guide their return to a food source. *Nature, 295,* 560–564.

Cartwright, B. A., & Collett, T. S. (1983). Landmark learning in bees—Experiments and models. *Journal of Comparative Physiology, 151,* 521–543.

Cheng, K. (1986). A purely geometric module in the rat's spatial representation. *Cognition, 23,* 149–178.

Chiandetti, C. (2011). Pseudoneglect and embryonic light stimulation in the avian bra. *Behavioral Neuroscience, 125*(5), 775–782. doi:10.1037/a0024721

Chiandetti, C., & Vallortigara, G. (2008). Is there an innate geometric module? Effects of experience with angular geometric cues on spatial reorientation based on the shape of the environment. *Animal Cognition, 11,* 139–146.

Chiandetti, C., & Vallortigara, G. (2010). Experience and geometry: Controlled-rearing studies with chicks. *Animal Cognition, 13,* 463–470.

Chiandetti, C., & Vallortigara, G. (2011a). Chicks like consonant music. *Psychological Science, 22,* 1270–1273.

Chiandetti, C., & Vallortigara, G. (2011b). Intuitive physical reasoning about occluded objects by inexperienced chicks. *Proceedings of the Royal Society of London, B, 278,* 2621–2627.

Chien, S. H.-L. (2011). No more top-heavy bias: Infants and adults prefer upright faces but not top-heavy geometric or face-like patterns. *Journal of Vision, 11*(6), 1–14.

Chittka, L., & Geiger, K. (1995). Can honey bees count landmarks? *Animal Behaviour, 49,* 159–164.

Dacke, M., & Srinivasan, M. V. (2008). Evidence for counting in insects. *Animal Cognition, 11,* 683–689.

Davis, H., & Bradford, S. A. (1986). Counting behavior by rats in a simulated natural environment. *Ethology, 73,* 265–280.

Dehaene, S. (1997). *The number sense.* New York, NY: Oxford University Press.

Dehaene, S., Izard, V., Pica, P., & Spelke, E. S. (2006). Core knowledge of geometry in an Amazonian indigene group. *Science, 311,* 381–384.

Diekamp, B., Regolin, L., Gunturkun, O., & Vallortigara, G. (2005). A left-sided visuospatial bias in birds. *Current Biology, 15,* R372–R373.

Duncan, R. O., Albright, T. D., & Stoner, G. R. (2000). Occlusion and the interpretation of visual motion: Perceptual and neuronal effects of context. *Journal of Neuroscience, 20,* 5885–5897.

Feigenson, L. (2005). A double dissociation in infants' representation of object arrays. *Cognition, 95,* B37–B48.

Feigenson, L., & Carey, S. (2005). On the limits of infants' quantification of small object arrays. *Cognition, 97,* 295–313.

Feigenson, L., Carey, S., & Hauser, M. (2002). The representations underlying infants' choice of more: Object files vs. analog magnitudes. *Psychological Science, 13*(2), 150–156.

Fellini, L., Schachner, M., & Morellini, F. (2006). Adult but not aged C57BL/6 male mice are capable of using geometry for orientation. *Learning and Memory, 13,* 473–481.

Fox, R., & McDaniel, C. (1982). The perception of biological motion by human infants. *Science, 218,* 486–487.

Fyhn, M., Molden, S., Witter, M. P., Moser, E. I., & Moser, M. B. (2004). Spatial representation in the entorhinal cortex. *Science, 305,* 258–264.

Galton, F. (1880). Visualised numerals. *Nature, 21,* 252–256. doi:10.1038/021252a0

Held, R., & Hein, A. (1963). Movement-produced stimulation in the development of visually guided behavior. *Journal of Comparative and Physiological Psychology, 56,* 872–876.

Hermer, L., & Spelke, E. S. (1994). A geometric process for spatial reorientation in young children. *Nature, 370,* 57–59.

Hermer, L., & Spelke, E. S. (1996). Modularity and development: The case of spatial reorientation. *Cognition, 61,* 195–232.

Horn, G. (2004). Pathways of the past: The imprint of memory. *Nature Reviews Neuroscience, 5,* 108–120.

Izard, V., Pica, P., Spelke, E. S., & Dehaene, S. (2011). Flexible intuitions of Euclidean geometry in an Amazonian indigene group. *Proceedings of the National Academy of Sciences, 108,* 9782–9787.

Jewell, G., & McCourt, M. E. (2000). Pseudoneglect: A review and meta-analysis of performance factors in line bisections tasks. *Neuropsychologia, 38,* 93–110.

Johansson, G. (1973). Visual perception of biological motion and a model for its analysis. *Perception and Psychophysics, 14,* 201–211.

Johnson, M. H. (2005). Subcortical face processing. *Nature Reviews Neuroscience, 6,* 766–774.

Johnson, M. H., & Horn, G. (1988). Development of filial preferences in dark reared chicks. *Animal Behaviour, 36,* 675–683.

Johnson, M. H., & Morton, J. (1991). *Biology and cognitive development: The case of face recognition.* Oxford, UK: Basil Blackwell.

Johnson, S. C. (2000). The recognition of mentalistic agents in infancy. *Trends in Cognitive Sciences, 4,* 22–28.

Johnson-Laird, P. N., Kang, O. E., & Leong, Y. C. (in press). On musical dissonance. *Music Perception.*

Kaiser, M. D., Hudac, C. M., Shultz, S., Lee, S. M., Cheung, C., Berken, A. M., et al. (2010). Neural signatures of autism. *Proceedings of the National Academy of Sciences USA, 107,* 21223–21228.

Kellman, P. J., & Arterberry, M. E. (1998). *The cradle of knowledge.* Cambridge, MA: MIT Press.

Kovacs, G., Vogels, R., & Orban, G. A. (1995). Selectivity of macaque inferior temporal neurons for partially occluded shapes. *Journal of Neuroscience, 15,* 1984–1997.

Kundey, S. M. A., De Los Reyes, A., Taglang, C., Baruch, A., & German, R. (2009). Domesticated dogs' (*Canis familiaris*) use of the solidity principle. *Animal Cognition, 13,* 497–505. doi:10.1007/s10071-009-0300-6

Lakusta, L., Dessalegn, B., & Landau, B. (2010). Impaired geometric reorientation caused by genetic defect. *Proceedings of the National Academy of Sciences, 107*(7), 2813–2817.

Landau, B. (2011). The organization and development of spatial cognition: Insights from Williams syndrome. In J. Burack, R. M. Hodapp, G. Iarocci, & E. Zigler (Eds.), *Handbook of intellectual disabilities and development* (2nd ed.). New York, NY: Oxford University Press.

Landau, B., & Lakusta, L. (2009). Spatial representation across species: Geometry, language, and maps. *Current Opinion in Neurobiology, 19*(1), 12–19.

Langston, R. F., Ainge, J. A., Couey, J. J., Canto, C. B., Bjerknes, T. L., Witter, M. P., et al. (2010). Development of the spatial representation system in the rat. *Science, 328,* 1576–1580.

Lea, S. E. G., Slater, A. M., & Ryan, C. M. E. (1996). Perception of object unity in chicks: A comparison with the human infant. *Infant Behavior and Development, 19,* 501–504.

Lee, S. A., Shusterman, A., & Spelke, E. S. (2006). Reorientation and landmark-guided search by young children: Evidence for two systems. *Psychological Science, 17,* 577–582.

Lee, S. A., & Spelke, E. S. (2008). Children's use of geometry for reorientation. *Developmental Science, 11,* 743–749.

Lee, S. A., & Spelke, E. S. (2010). A modular geometric mechanism for reorientation in children. *Cognitive Psychology, 61,* 152–176.

Lee, S. A., & Spelke, E. S. (2011). Young children reorient by computing layout geometry, not by matching images of the environment. *Psychological Bulletin and Review, 18,* 192–198.

Lee, S. A., Spelke, E. S., & Vallortigara, G. (2012). *Spontaneous reorientation behavior in chicks: Evidence for evolutionary continuity across distantly related species.* Manuscript in preparation.

Lehrman, D. S. (1953). Critique of Konrad Lorenz's theory of instinctive behavior. *Quarterly Review of Biology, 28,* 337–363.

Leslie, A. M. (1982). The perception of causality in infants. *Perception, 11,* 173–186.

Leslie, A. M. (1984). Spatiotemporal continuity and the perception of causality in infants. *Perception, 13,* 287–305.

Leslie, A. M., & Keeble, S. (1987). Do six-month-old infants perceive causality? *Cognition, 25,* 265–288.

Loetscher, T., Schwarz, U., Schubiger, M., & Brugger, P. (2008). Head turns bias the brain's internal random generator. *Current Biology, 18,* R60–R62.

Lorenz, K. (1965). *Evolution and the modification of behaviour.* Chicago, IL: University of Chicago Press.

MacNeilage, P. F., Rogers, L. J., & Vallortigara, G. (2009). Origins of the left and right brain. *Scientific American, 301,* 60–67.

Mandler, J. M. (1988). How to build a baby: On the development of an accessible representational system. *Cognitive Development, 3,* 113–136.

Marcus, G. F. (2004). *The birth of the mind: How a tiny number of genes creates the complexities of human thought.* New York, NY: Basic Books.

Mascalzoni, E., Regolin, L., & Vallortigara, G. (2010). Innate sensitivity for self-propelled causal agency in newly hatched chicks. *Proceedings of the National Academy of Sciences, 107,* 4483–4485.

McKone, E., Crookes, K., Jeffery, L., & Dilks, D. D. (2012 this issue). A critical review of the development of face recognition: Experience is less important than previously believed. *Cognitive Neuropsychology, 29,* 174–212.

Michotte, A. (1963). *The perception of causality.* New York, NY: Basic Books.

Mormann, F., Dubois, J., Kornblith, S., Milosavljevic, M., Cerf, M., Ison, M., et al. (2011). A category-specific response to animals in the right human amygdala. *Nature Neuroscience, 14,* 1247–1249.

New, J., Cosmides, L., & Tooby, J. (2007). Category-specific attention for animals reflects ancestral priorities, not expertise. *Proceedings of the National Academy of Sciences USA, 104,* 16598–16603.

Nieder, A., Freedman, D. J., & Miller, E. K. (2002). Representation of the quantity of visual items in the primate prefrontal cortex. *Science, 297,* 1708–1711.

Nieder, A., & Miller, E. K. (2004). A parieto-frontal network for visual numerical information in the monkey. *Proceedings of the National Academy of Sciences USA, 101,* 7457–7462.

O'Connell, S., & Dunbar, R.I. M. (2005). The perception of causality in chimpanzees (*Pan* spp.). *Animal Cognition, 8,* 60–66.

O'Keefe, J., & Dostrovsky, J. (1971). The hippocampus as a spatial map. Preliminary evidence from unit activity in the freely-moving rat. *Brain Research, 34,* 171–175.

O'Keefe, J., & Nadel, L. (1978). *The hippocampus as a cognitive map*. Oxford, UK: Oxford University Press.

Osborne, L. R. (2006). Molecular basis of a multisystem disorder. In C. A. Morris, H. M. Lenhoff, & P. P. Wang (Eds.), *Williams–Beuren syndrome: Research, evaluation, and treatment* (pp. 18–58). New York, NY: JHU Press.

Pattison, K. F., Miller, H. C., Rayburn-Reeves, R., & Zentall, T. (2010). The case of the disappearing bone: Dogs' understanding of the physical properties of objects. *Behavioural Processes, 85,* 278–282.

Pecchia, T., Gagliardo, A., & Vallortigara, G. (2011). Stable panoramic views facilitate snap-shot like memories for spatial reorientation in homing pigeons. *PLoS ONE, 6*(7), e22657. doi:10.1371/journal.pone.0022657

Pecchia, T., & Vallortigara, G. (2010a). Re-orienting strategies in a rectangular array of landmarks by domestic chicks (*Gallus gallus*). *Journal of Comparative Psychology, 124,* 147–158.

Pecchia, T., & Vallortigara, G. (2010b). View-based strategy for reorientation by geometry. *Journal of Experimental Biology, 213,* 2987–2996.

Pecchia, T., & Vallortigara, G. (in press). Spatial reorientation by geometry with freestanding objects and extended surfaces: A unifying view. *Proceedings of the Royal Society of London B.* doi:10.1098/rspb.2011.2522

Pepperberg, I. M. (1994). Evidence for numerical competence in an African Grey parrot (*Psittacus erithacus*). *Journal of Comparative Psychology, 108,* 36–44.

Pepperberg, I. M. (2006a). Gray parrot numerical competence: A review. *Animal Cognition, 9,* 377–391.

Pepperberg, I. M. (2006b). Grey parrot (*Psittacus erithacus*) numerical abilities: Addition and further experiments on a zero-like concept. *Journal of Comparative Psychology, 120,* 1–11.

Platt, M. L., & Spelke, E. S. (2009). What can developmental and comparative cognitive neuroscience tell us about the adult human brain? *Current Opinion in Neurobiology, 19,* 1–5.

Regolin, L., Rugani, R., Stancher, G., & Vallortigara, G. (in press). Spontaneous discrimination of possible and impossible objects by newly hatched chicks. *Biology Letters.* Advance online publication. doi:10.1098/rsbl.2011.0051.

Regolin, L., & Vallortigara, G. (1995). Perception of partly occluded objects by young chicks. *Perception and Psychophysics, 57,* 971–976.

Rochat, M.-J., Serra, E., Fadiga, L., & Gallese, V. (2008). The evolution of social cognition: Goal familiarity shapes monkeys' action understanding. *Current Biology, 18,* 227–232.

Rogers, L. J. (1996). Behavioral, structural and neurochemical asymmetries in the avian brain: A model system for studying visual development and processing. *Neuroscience Biobehavioral Reviews, 20,* 487–503.

Rosa-Salva, O., Farroni, T., Regolin, L., Vallortigara, G., & Johnson, M. H. (2011). The Evolution of social orienting: Evidence from chicks (Gallus gallus) and human newborns. *PLoS ONE, 6*(4), e18802.

Rosa-Salva, O., Regolin, L., & Vallortigara, G. (2010). Faces are special for newly hatched chicks: Evidence for inborn domain-specific mechanisms underlying spontaneous preferences for face-like stimuli. *Developmental Sci*ence, *13,* 565–577.

Rose, S. (2000). God's organism? The chick as a model system for memory studies. *Learning & Memory, 7,* 1–17.

Rugani, R., Fontanari, L., Simoni, E., Regolin, L., & Vallortigara, G. (2009). Arithmetic in newborn chicks. *Proceedings of the Royal Society B, 276,* 2451–2460.

Rugani, R., Kelly, D. M., Szelest, I., Regolin, L., & Vallortigara, G. (2010). Is it only humans that count from left to right? *Biology Letters, 6,* 290–292.

Rugani, R., Regolin, L., & Vallortigara, G. (2007). Rudimental numerical competence in 5-day-old domestic chicks: Identification of ordinal position. *Journal of Experimental Psychology: Animal Behavior Processes, 33,* 21–31.

Rugani, R., Regolin, L., & Vallortigara, G. (2008). Discrimination of small numerosities in young chicks. *Journal of Experimental Psychology: Animal Behavior Processes, 34,* 388–399.

Rugani, R., Regolin, L., & Vallortigara, G. (2010). Imprinted numbers: Newborn chicks' sensitivity to number vs. continuous extent of objects they have been reared with. *Developmental Science, 13,* 790–797.

Rugani, R., Vallortigara, G., Vallini, B., & Regolin, L. (2011). Asymmetrical number-space mapping in the avian brain. *Neurobiology of Learning and Memory, 95,* 231–238.

Siman-Tov, T., Papo, D., Gadoth, N., Schonberg, T., Mendelsohn, A., Perry, D., et al. (2009). Mind your left: Spatial bias in subcortical fear processing. *Journal of Cognitive Neuroscience, 21,* 1782–1789.

Simion, F., Regolin, L., & Bulf, H. (2008). A predisposition for biological motion in the newborn baby. *Proceedings of the National Academy of Sciences USA, 105,* 809–813.

Solstad, T., Boccara, C. N., Kropff, E., Moser, M. B., & Moser, E. I. (2008). Representation of geometric borders in the entorhinal cortex. *Science, 322,* 865–868.

Sovrano, V. A., Bisazza, A., & Vallortigara, G. (2002). Modularity and spatial reorientation in a simple mind: Encoding of geometric and nongeometric properties of a spatial environment by fish. *Cognition, 85,* B51–B59.

Sovrano, V. A., Bisazza, A., & Vallortigara, G. (2003). Modularity as a fish views it: Conjoining geometric and nongeometric information for spatial reorientation. *Journal of Experimental Psychology: Animal Behavior Processes, 29,* 199–210.

Sovrano, V. A., Rigosi, E., & Vallortigara, G. (2011). *Spatial reorientation by geometry in bumblebees.* Manuscript submitted for publication.

Spelke, E. S. (1998). Nativism, empiricism, and the origin of knowledge. *Infant Behavior and Development, 21,* 181–200.

Spelke, E. S. (2000). Core knowledge. *The American Psychologist, 55,* 1233–1243.

Spelke, E. S. (2003). What makes us smart? Core knowledge and natural language. In D. Gentner & S. Goldin-Meadow (Eds.), *Language in mind: Advances in the investigation of language and thought.* Cambridge, MA: MIT Press.

Spelke, E. S. (2011). Natural number and natural geometry. In E. Brannon & S. Dehaene (Eds.), *Space, Time and Number in the Brain: Searching for the Foundations of Mathematical Thought* (pp. 287–317). Attention & Performance XXIV, Oxford University Press.

Spelke, E. S., Breinlinger, K., Macomber, J., & Jacobson, K. (1992). Origins of knowledge. *Psychological Review, 99,* 605–632.

Spelke, E. S., & Kinzler, K. D. (2009). Innateness, learning, and rationality. *Child Development Perspectives, 3,* 96–98.

Spelke, E. S., Lee, S. A., & Izard, V. (2010). Beyond core knowledge: Natural geometry. *Cognitive Science, 34,* 863–884.

Sugita, Y. (2008). Face perception in monkeys reared with no exposure to faces. *Proceedings of the National Academy of Sciences USA, 105,* 394–398.

Taube, J. S., Muller, R. U., & Ranck, J. B. (1990). Head-direction cells recorded from the post-subiculum in freely moving rats. I. Description and quantitative analysis. *Journal of Neuroscience, 2,* 420–435.

Tommasi, L., Gagliardo, A., Andrew, R. J., & Vallortigara, G. (2003). Separate processing mechanisms for encoding geometric and landmark information in the avian hippocampus. *European Journal of Neuroscience, 17,* 1695–1702.

Tommasi, L., Chiandetti, C., Pecchia, T., Sovrano, V. A., & Vallortigara, G. (2012). From natural geometry to spatial cognition. *Biobehavioral and Neuroscience Reviews, 36*(2), 799–824.

Tommasi, L., & Vallortigara, G. (2001). Encoding of geometric and landmark information in the left and right hemispheres of the avian brain. *Behavioral Neuroscience, 115,* 602–613.

Turati, C., Simion, F., Milani, I., & Umilta, C. (2002). Newborns' preference for faces: What is crucial? *Developmental Psychology, 38,* 875–882.

Valenza, E., & Herman, B. (2011). Early development of object unity: Evidence for perceptual completion in newborns. *Developmental Science, 14,* 799–808.

Valenza, E., Leo, I., Gava, L., & Simion, F. (2006). Perceptual completion in newborn human infants. *Child Development, 77,* 1810–1821.

Vallortigara, G. (2000). Comparative neuropsychology of the dual brain: A stroll through left and right animals' perceptual worlds. *Brain and Language, 73,* 189–219.

Vallortigara, G. (2004). Visual cognition and representation in birds and primates. In L. J. Rogers & G. Kaplan (Eds.), *Vertebrate comparative cognition: Are primates superior to non-primates?* (pp. 57–94). New York, NY: Kluwer Academic/Plenum Publishers.

Vallortigara, G. (2006). The cognitive chicken: Visual and spatial cognition in a non-mammalian bra. In E. A. Wasserman & T. R. Zentall (Eds.), *Comparative cognition: Experimental explorations of animal intelligence* (pp. 41–58). Oxford, UK: Oxford University Press.

Vallortigara, G. (2009a). Animals as natural geometers. In L. Tommasi, M. Peterson, & L. Nadel (Eds.), *The biology of cognition*. Cambridge, MA: MIT Press.

Vallortigara, G. (2009b). Original knowledge and the two cultures. In E. Carafoli, G. A. Danieli, & G. O. Longo (Eds.), *The two cultures: Shared problems* (pp. 125–145). New York, NY: Springer Verlag.

Vallortigara, G., Pagni, P., & Sovrano, V. A. (2004). Separate geometric and non-geometric modules for spatial reorientation: Evidence from a lopsided animal brain. *Journal of Cognitive Neuroscience, 16,* 390–400.

Vallortigara, G., & Regolin, L. (2006). Gravity bias in the interpretation of biological motion by inexperienced chicks. *Current Biology, 16,* R279–R280.

Vallortigara, G., Regolin, L., Chiandetti, C., & Rugani, R. (2010). Rudiments of mind: Insights through the chick model on number and space cognition in animals. *Comparative Cognition and Behavior Reviews, 5,* 78–99.

Vallortigara, G., Regolin, L., & Marconato, F. (2005). Visually inexperienced chicks exhibit spontaneous preference for biological motion patterns. *PloS Biology, 3,* 1312–1316.

Vallortigara, G., & Rogers, L. J. (2005). Survival with an asymmetrical brain: Advantages and disadvantages of cerebral lateralization. *Behavioral and Brain Sciences, 28,* 575–589.

Vallortigara, G., Rogers, L. J., Bisazza, A., Lippolis, G., & Robins, A. (1998). Complementary right and left hemifield use for predatory and agonistic behaviour in toads. *Neuroreport, 9,* 3341–3344.

Vallortigara, G., Sovrano, V. A., & Chiandetti, C. (2009). Doing Socrates experiment right: Controlled rearing studies of geometrical knowledge in animals. *Current Opinion in Neurobiology, 19,* 20–26.

Vallortigara, G., Zanforlin, M., & Pasti, G. (1990). Geometric modules in animal's spatial representation: A test with chicks. *Journal of Comparative Psychology, 104,* 248–254.

van Marle, K., Aw, J., McCrink, K., & Santos, L. R. (2006). How monkeys (Cebus apella) enumerate objects and substances. *Journal of Comparative Psychology, 120,* 416–426.

Vargas, J. P., Bingman, V. P., Portavella, M., & Lopez, J. C. (2006). Telencephalon and geometric space in goldfish. *European Journal of Neuroscience, 24,* 2870–2878.

Vargas, J. P., Petruso, E. J., & Bingman, V. P. (2004). Hippocampal formation is required for geometric navigation in pigeons. *European Journal of Neuroscience, 20,* 1937–1944.

Walk, R. D., Gibson, E. J., & Tighe, T. J. (1957). Behavior of light- and dark-reared rats on a visual cliff. *Science, 126,* 80–81.

Wills, T. J., Cacucci, F., Burgess, N., & O'Keefe, J. (2010). Development of the hippocampal cognitive map in preweanling rats. *Science, 328,* 1573–1576.

Index

Page numbers in *italic* type refer to tables

Kolibri 360 GmbH
Ferdinand-Jühlke-Straße 7
99095 Erfurt, Deutschland
produktsicherheit@kolibri360.de